MIMESIS
INTERNATIONAL

PHILOSOPHY

n. 11

GENEVIEVE VAUGHAN

THE GIFT
IN THE HEART
OF LANGUAGE

The Maternal Source of Meaning

TABLE OF CONTENTS

I dedicate this book to my children and grandchildren and to all the people who want to live in a gift economy, whether they know it or not.

FOREWORD

Susan Petrilli

The title and subtitle "The Gift in the Heart of Language. The Maternal Source of Meaning" capture the sense of the content and intent of this book. The key words: "gift" and "language" are associated with "heart", and in the subtitle with "meaning" and "maternal source"; here "meaning" resounds not only in a nudely semantic sense, but is also open to meaning in the sense of "significance", "import", "value".

A book on language? No doubt, but in relation to the *maternal* and to the *gift*; therefore, *homo loquens-donans* with all the immediate, even evident implications this expression involves. However, these implications which are of the existential and vital order, including the "economic", are also deliberately underestimated, unacknowledged, hidden.

"Gift or exchange": this is a central theme in the book. It introduces us to the identification of two logics: *quid pro quo* and unilateral gift (section 2.0).

A book on semiotics? Yes, this too. The problem of communication runs throughout the whole book like a filigree. A paragraph – from the very title – significantly indicating the sense in which problems of communication, sign and meaning are considered, reads as "Semiotics, mother sense and material communication" (section 3.6).

While the first part places a hypothesis "The Gift Hypothesis", the second part proceeds from this hypothesis – amply developed throughout the first part of the book – to "The Enigmas of Language and Exchange". It deals with what emerges as a double fetishism in today's world: that of commodities and that of language, both faces of the same reality: a reality that denies the gift, removes it and with it the maternal at its foundation.

The question of value – linguistic value and economic value – calls for reconsideration in the "light of the gift". On the one hand, this leads to 1) a "revisitation" of the (mechanistic) dichotomy between "structure and superstructure" (section 6.6) and to understanding that in Marx, in spite of his critique of "abstract labor", abstract labor remains: that is, labor "abstracted from gift giving", precisely (as explicitly anticipated in the title itself of section 8.6); and on the other, to 2) reconsideration of the relation identified by Ferdinand de Saussure between linguistic value and economic value with a ground-breaking discussion of the foundations of linguistics in general, including generative-transformational linguistics in Noam Chomsky's conception.

Consequently this book, proceeding in terms that are always finely argued and closely documented, develops "the Gift hypothesis" in terms of the question of "Generalizing the Gift" (Ch. 10).

A feminist book? Formations, identifications and standpoints (characteristic of feminist movements) aside, a great merit of this book is that is delineates in the light of its particular approach and of the situation today, with its specific problems, "Some consequences for feminism" (section 10.10).

At this point, let me add that what I have particularly at heart in this book on *The Gift in the Heart of Language* and consider as one of its most fascinating aspects is what it succeeds in putting forward beyond mere *alternatives*: because alternatives as such remain trapped in the same logic subtending the system they aim to replace.

The discussion is not at all about mere *alternatives*; instead, it is about something that is radically *other*. This is a book, precisely, that has *something else altogether other* to say and propose: *other* with respect to a world founded on communication sadly incapable of taking it's distances and differentiating itself from exchange as practiced in terms of *quid pro quo logic,* giving for the sake of returns (*do ut des*). Nor is it hard to see, in fact, that the exchange of commodities characteristic of patriarchal capitalist society is – by now globally – assumed as a model and paradigm for linguistic communication and linguistic value.

Therefore, the book's invitation to the reader: consider the possibility of renewal that the maternal source of meaning and value can gift.

INTRODUCTION

In this book I won't spend much time trying to prove whether unilateral giving is possible or impossible. That attempt has been made many times over. Instead I want to show how things can be if we radically accept that unilateral giving is not only possible but commonplace, as I believe it is. If we take the hypothesis seriously, we can see that it explains a lot. I try to bring unilateral gifting forward in the analysis of language and the economy, but it can be found everywhere. Then of course what needs to be explained is why we are *not* doing much more of it, at least not consciously. That is part of this book as well.

Philosophical inquiry into epistemology has usually left out the fundamental mother-child experience, looking for the origin of thought in individual development or in adult experience, perhaps with a dim memory of the personal childhoods of the philosophers. The experience of being a mother puts the adult in contact with a mind that is both similar to and very different from her own. Although it may not be possible to recapture one's own childhood or infancy, it is possible to understand something of the origin of thought through caring for and attending to the minds and bodies of very young children. This is a 'refresher course' in practical epistemology which most male philosophers have not had, at least until very recently under the influence of feminism. That is one reason mothering/being mothered, this fundamental experience, has been left out of philosophy. Another reason is the sexism of capitalism and the exclusion of gift economy structures from its exchange-based episteme. Men as well as women who are not mothers, nevertheless have all had mothers or care givers of some kind. The model of the maternal gift economy has been available to everyone in early childhood because it is necessary for survival.

Patriarchal capitalism and its ideology have eliminated mothering and the gift economy from a world view that validates the market. This view is partial; it cancels an important part of human life and therefore its products are questionable. Indeed in practice it seems that this worldview and its accompanying motivations are leading us to planetary death. The denial of the importance of the mothering economy is made necessary because the market and gift giving are configured in a structural relation of 'parasite' and 'host' that organizes society at many levels. It permeates daily life as well as race, class, national and international relations. If the parasitic relation were visible the 'host' would struggle to be free, so it is kept hidden as such to the people involved. What we do see of it is the suffering of women and female children world wide, which we consider in terms of intersectional oppressions, injustice, underdevelopment, second class citizenship, but which is actually the condition of being, along with their impoverished fathers, sons and brothers, the hosts, the matter from which the mechanism of capitalism draws its sustenance on a daily basis. Of course it befits the mechanism to cover its tracks, discount the sources of its success and maintain its own supremacy and self-made sembiance.

I do not use this description for name-calling, but will try to make the way the mechanism functions quite explicit in the book. Attempts to view the gift economy as a radical alternative to the market have been hampered because they have not shown how the two economies of gift and exchange are interconnected; they have not shown that the profits of the few are actually composed of the gifts of the many. These gifts have to come from somewhere. Integrating gifting into the market in one place means exploiting more gifts elsewhere.

In fact, it is not easy to look at this situation head-on because most of us are either its victims or its beneficiaries. Those who are its victims are usually so overburdened by work for survival that they have little time to think and organize, though some do, and more do all the time. Those who are its beneficiaries easily fall prey to denial and to all the fail-safes the system has put in place for keeping them ignorant of the truth of their own parasitical function.

The worldwide women's movement needs to join with the indigenous people's movement, the movements against racism and war and especially with the movements for an alternative economy and for the environment. Each of these movements needs to recognize its place within the gift paradigm and acknowledge the gifts of social change it is trying to give, coordinating with the others to create deep and lasting alternative ways of living. Although gift initiatives inside the system may help to mitigate and diversify it internally, it is not by becoming efficient actors in capitalist patriarchy[1] that women (or men) in these movements can

---

1   Initiatives for a 'caring economy' (Folbre 2001, Eisler 2007) and for a philosophy of care (among many Gilligan 1982, Noddings 1983, Ruddick 1995, Held 2007)

create a better global future. We have to change the big picture in order to change the small one and vice-versa, so we cannot just succeed individually in a parasitic and self-and-other destructive system. We need to take a perspective outside of – or at least beyond and before - the system. That perspective is provided by the maternal gift economy.

It is also an aspect of the system that it puts us in competition and conflict with each other in an either-your-life-or-mine way. However, cooperation is as important for us humans as was the cooperation among bacteria that created the first nucleated and multicelled organisms. It is cooperation within our species that gave us the competitive edge among species (Margulis 1981, Sahtouris 1999). In order to cooperate ... we have to be able to give to and receive from each other.

We cannot survive or evolve as a species by competing internally, but our competitive socioeconomic system has now placed us on this tragic brink. Part of the destruction of cooperation has been the erasure of the maternal model of free giving and receiving. For those living inside the system, not knowing or consciously embracing that model is just part of the way things are. Even mothers themselves may not give value to it.

Although the erasure is systemic, one might consider it a generalized 'hermeneutical' or 'testimonial' injustice (Fricker 2009) for which the remedy is not 'individual epistemic virtue but ... a conceptual revolution' Langton (2010). Or, in the shorter term it might be seen as due to neo-liberal (feminist) 'post-maternal thinking', which Stephens (2011) attributes to a kind of cultural forgetting. However, it is more accurate to think of it as a paralysis in the host induced by the parasite, both symbionts formed of one and the same species[2] and both embedded in a context of acute cognitive dissonance caused by a conflict between the logics of gift and of exchange. The discounting of the host practiced by the parasite is rewarded by the validation of the system and the profits of those who succeed in it.

This book is an attempt to restore what has been individually and socially erased; it is, after all, a secret that on some level everybody already knows. Reading our problems, successes and failures through the lens of market exchange does not allow us to understand the secret because the lens factors out gift-giving. However, it is only in contrast to the unilateral gift economy that we can critique many of the negative complexities of market exchange and that we can see the solutions that the unilateral

---

    do not envision care as a systemic alternative to capitalism.
2   They also coexist often in the same person.

gift already provides. The reemergence of the gift economy also allows us to accept its explanatory power in the many other areas of life from which it has been excluded.

Recasting speaking and listening as giving and receiving and language itself as a collection of word-gifts and possible gift-based constructions allows us to draw radically different conclusions about communication, with many ripple effects into other areas of inquiry. It also allows us to look at the market as a *distortion* of maternal gift communication and its logic. In this vein, 'sexual difference' or at least 'maternal difference' can be cast as economic: the necessary practice of a unilateral gift economy 'in the belly of the beast'. Thus the 'war between the sexes' becomes a kind of Cold War between the two economies.[3]

Once we have a viewpoint radically different from that of the market we can see such terms as 'symbolic exchange' (Baudrillard 2001 [1988]) as misleading, since words, signs and symbols themselves have to do with gifting prior to exchange. We can take heart from this and realize that, as I hope to show, the alternative to the market logic is already both inside and outside of language and is also a basic factor, commonplace in maternal practice. Like the market economy as such, the political economy of the sign leaves out the maternal gift. Restoring it changes the whole picture.

In the 1970s, the French feminists Luce Irigaray (1974, 1977), Helene Cixous (1975) and Julia Kristeva (1969) engaged with mothering, gifting and language using a psychoanalytic frame, so that the questions they addressed and the ways they addressed them are somewhat different from mine, which are influenced by cognitive psychology and new research on infants. They thought about language itself and about the Symbolic Order within a framework based on the work of Marx, Saussure, Freud, and Lacan. Looking at language as gifting, on the other hand, restores the maternal practice to language and to the Symbolic Order.[4] The primacy of the maternal gift outside or beyond exchange is the key.

Irigaray critiques the market and elucidates its masculine bias while calling upon the gift economy as the alternative. Kristeva presents the *cho-*

---

3   I intend 'economy' in the sense of (mainly) material provisioning of goods to needs, rather than in the French sense where 'économie is more happily used in a metaphorical sense, to refer to the way in which something is organized, than it is in English' (Still 1997: 150). I believe we begin in childhood with the material maternal economy and proceed to linguistic and symbolic levels.

4   See Luisa Muraro *L'Ordine Simbolico della Madre* (1991) where the mother teaches language to the child, who participates in her order but is then absorbed into the Symbolic Order of the father.

ra, the semiotic Pre-Oedipal period as fundamental. Cixous is the radical groundbreaker, whose feminine economy is an opening into the maternal gift paradigm. However she proposes *écriture féminine* while I am proposing not writing but language itself as maternal. I want to challenge the symbolic order from within by changing our conception of it, that is, by reconceiving language and communication as unilateral gifting, modeled on provisioning, on the maternal gift economy.

The consequences of this approach are many, and I will discuss them throughout the book. To give a few examples: on the basis of this kind of analysis, verbal violence and sexist terminology (which have long been under the scrutiny of feminists) can be seen as distortions and contradictions of the maternal gift structure. As we shall see, even physical hitting can be understood as a derivation of the gift gesture (see below, 1.16). In a more practical political vein, it becomes contradictory to say that the appeal to free speech justifies pornography and the buying of votes by corporations if speech itself is based on free gifting beyond the market, rather than on exchange. In fact we could say that being free (gratis) is not free (liberated)... except to be commercialized.

In recent years, inspired by the gift economy of the internet and quickened by the urgency of financial crises, many practical gift economy experiments have sprung up and many new books have been written about it with increasing popular followings (see, for example, Charles Eisenstein's *Sacred Economics*, 2011). However, these initiatives have not borne out the promise of the French feminist work. Even the important French *Revue du MAUSS*, which has been promoting the gift economy since 1981, does not address mothering and rarely addresses women in general.[5] Their first and so far only issue on women and gifting *Que donnent les Femmes?* was published in 2012. Perhaps the insistence of Marcel Mauss (1990 |1923|) on the three-step process of 'gift exchange' (giving, receiving and giving back) obscures the original two-step process of giving and receiving. His followers have not gone beyond that mode.

At present mothering seems to have nothing to do with the gift economy or with the practical alternative economic experiments. Perhaps this is also due to the contradictions within the feminist movement itself and the accusations of 'essentialism' that feminists have raised against the French women philosophers and others, discrediting mothering as an appropriate

---

5   Both Lewis Hyde (2007 |1979|) and Jacques Godbout (1998) have briefly mentioned women and gift giving in their work but they have not elaborated upon it much, as well they might not, leaving it to women to elucidate further.

feminist argument. I address this issue in various ways in this book because
I believe it is an impediment to social change.

Organization of the book

The organization of this book has been difficult because each part needed
to come before the others. In order to talk about the gift in language I had
to discuss what the gift is. In order to do that I had to say why we have not
recognized its importance before, and since I believe this is due to patriarchy and the exchange economy I had to explain their negative influence.
On the other hand, a critique of the exchange economy requires a description of the gift economy, which is its deep alternative and the beginning of
the thread in which exchange is a knot. I believe exchange is a linguistic
device and therefore I had to discuss language before I discussed exchange.
This tangle of issues is perhaps one reason they have not been approached
in quite this way before. I have tried to solve the organizational problem by
introducing all the themes together, but have concentrated more attention
on them individually in the different chapters.

Thus Part One of the book contains a discussion of the gift economy
and mothering together with a presentation of the image schema of the
gift and the way it alters mainstream ideas about language and linguistics.
In Part Two I introduce what I am calling 'the image schema of virtualization' and the way it is used in categorization and exchange, resulting
in giftless thinking. This discussion is the basis for a re-characterization
of money as an incarnated or embodied, 'devirtualized' word (which has
now been revirtualized by the new computer technology). In this regard I
discuss Marx's General Equivalent and the one-to-many 'classical' concept form. I address several philosophical issues such as Russell's regress
and the type-token distinction, which might otherwise cloud the picture
I am presenting of the market where money functions as an exosomatic
concept form that feeds back into our thinking and emphasizes patriarchal structures. Finally I consider value, meaning and identity in the light
of the previous discussions.

I have several purposes in writing this book. I want to present an alternative view of language and economics, but I also want to show how this
view could change the common conception of many aspects of the ways
we think. It is as if, by starting from gift-giving instead of exchange, we
could peel off a layer of thinking that has been attached to our worldview
for centuries. I try to do this in a number of ways.

My view of capitalist patriarchy makes me irreverent regarding the patterns that have led us to this end of the world scenario. We are like fish who are draining all the gift water out of their pond and are left gasping and flopping on the rapidly drying mud flat of the market. Radical change is necessary and I hope this book will show directions in which it can happen. The paradigm shift I propose is relatively simple. It requires us to develop a functional concept of mothering-being mothered, generalize it, and use it as an interpretative key. The gift economy is one of the generalizations/extensions of mothering-being mothered. Communication is another. Language is still another. The beginning of knowledge in the relation between children and their caregivers must be given an important place in epistemology. This can provide an altered self-concept of the human being that can encourage our species not to self-destruct through exacerbated individualism.

My strategy in the first part of this book is simply to make the hypothesis of the gift and follow it as best I can through various aspects of economics, philosophy and linguistics. It is just a matter of giving the hypothesis to you, hoping that you will provide it some hospitality, entertaining it at least for a moment. I am trying to give giving to you. See how versatile it is? See how easily the gift goes up to a meta-level as soon as it gets its foot in the door?

The second half of the book is an analysis of exchange, money and the market that requires the hypothesis of the gift in language to be presented first, as I have done in the first half of the book. At the same time, the presentation and validation of the gift hypothesis also requires the analysis and criticism of the exchange economy and a description of the negative ways the two interact. Each must be seen against the background and in the context of the other. Once that has been done, the two approaches can be used together to explore the reasons for the apocalyptic socio-economic and environmental conditions we are now experiencing.

After a characterization of the gift hypothesis I begin the book with a discussion of the projection of the giving-receiving dyad onto nature as a basic cognitive process. The dyadic process is formed in the mother child interaction as described by the new current of infant research represented by Colwyn Trevarthen (1979), Stein Bråten (1991), [6] Andrew Meltzoff (1977) and many others. While the psychoanalytic approach includes the mother as an important factor in the etiology of psychological disease and some researchers like Winnicott (1990) and Stern (1998, 2000) have given

---

6   See also Bråten's edited volumes 1998 and 2007.

appreciative attention to the mother-child dyad, the importance of mothering/being mothered as a *model* for cognitive processes and language has not been widely investigated even by infancy researchers. Nor has the research on mirror neurons by Gallese, Fogassi, Fadiga, Rizzolati (1996) and their collaborators and followers given enough attention to the fact that what the child's and the mother's mirror neurons are registering must be experiences of nurturing/being nurtured.

In the second half of the book I sketch a theory of exchange and money as distortions of material and linguistic gifting and I try to show that they form a configuration of extended mind which is the embodiment of a concept-forming process. This distortion and its feedback into the mind are responsible for many of our problems and the negative effects of monetized exchange on us.

I try to show that humans are elaborating the relevance of the world for each other all the time with the result that we have many kinds of relevance, which we call moral, aesthetic, linguistic, and economic 'values', the common origin of which is not recognized in mothering-gifting. The relevance of different parts of the world – *world*-gifts – stimulates us to pass them on to others through *word*-gifts, conferring gift value on the receivers as we do so. Meaning is made through a multilevel construction of gifts of which the self as giver-and-receiver is also part.

I believe that problem-solving is also gift-giving to satisfy needs. This lets me include as gifts all the innumerable initiatives for social change that people are doing, trying to solve the problems created by the patriarchal capitalist system. Many people are thinking about what can be done to create alternatives to the system. The movements for the commons, for degrowth, for subsistence economies, for peer to peer relations, for eco-villages, for workers' cooperatives like Monfalcon in Spain and movements like the Zapatistas in Mexico and the Landless Workers' Movement in Brazil, the alternative currencies and the de-monetization movements, as well as the growing gift economy movement itself are made up of people who are theoretically and practically experimenting with new economic configurations (a number of individuals are also voluntarily living without money![7]). I think it is very positive that there is such collective ferment because the eventual economies that will result will be collective products, tested and refined by the many. I hope, though, that they can be informed by indigenous theory and practice and

7   Heidemarie Schwermer in Germany www.livingwithoutmoney.org and Mark
      Boyle www.themoneylessmanifesto.org in Ireland, for example.

by matriarchal studies and maternalist gift economy studies. I want this book to be a step in that direction. It does not provide recipes for creating a functioning gift economy, but is an attempt to give mothering an important place in informing whatever economic alternatives the collective mind chooses. The gift economy is the beginning but it is also the final goal towards which many social experiments are moving and it should be kept as the goal, so that they will keep tending towards a deep alternative.

Astronomy has given us a perspective that shows how small the Earth is among the stars and geology has shown how brief our human time has been in planet Earth's history. According to archeological studies, patriarchy's time has also been limited to about 5000 years (Gimbutas 1989) and history tells us that capitalism's time has been very brief indeed. Although patriarchal capitalism now seems to have spread successfully over the globe, it also appears to be threatening the existence of life. This is the context in which we all now speak and write. But patriarchal capitalism/capitalist patriarchy is not permanent, it is only a brief flash, a millisecond in universal and planetary time. We should keep in mind these dimensions of the problems we are facing.

Disclosure

I speak as one of those who have been privileged by this patriarchal capitalist economy, but I am a woman and a mother and perhaps for this reason, I have embraced the task of trying to find out what is wrong in order to change it. I have had the time and the resources and the good luck to work on it for a lifetime. Many or most women in my position have not addressed social change theoretically and therefore theirs/ours has been a voice that has not been heard. It is ironic and tragic that the women who are motivated to want radical change are usually those who do not have the resources, time and energy to theorize it. Those who do have the resources are often just as disempowered by lack of faith in their own capacities. I went through several bouts of mental illness, years of psychoanalysis and many changes in order to arrive at this point. I realize that among other advantages such as being white and relatively well educated, I have had the possibility of being an independent researcher mainly outside of academia. If I had been in the academic world I would have had to follow its currents and would not have been able to stick to my intuitions long enough to work through and justify them. In fact, they were very different from the accepted canon.

I want to introduce myself briefly, because I think it is important to disclose where I am 'coming from'. I was born in 1939 in Corpus Christi, Texas. My father was a lawyer and my mother was a beautiful and intelligent woman with a college education. Her father was also a lawyer and he made money in the oil business. After my grandfather died my father took care of all the family business. After my father died in 1983, my brother took up the business. Early on, I realized that most people had considerable economic problems that we did not have and when I grew older I realized that we were in the exploiter, not the exploited, camp. Since then I have been working to understand why this situation exists and trying to change it. It has become clear to me that whatever the individual circumstances are, the problems are systemic.

I married an Italian professor of philosophy, Ferruccio Rossi-Landi in 1963 and moved to Italy, where my political consciousness expanded. In the mid 60s I had the first of my three daughters and I began working on the idea of economics and language because that was an area in which my husband had become involved. In 1972 I translated his book, *Linguistics and Economics* (1975) while he was writing it. Soon after we were married, in 1964 he had been invited by some Italian professors, Gianni Scalia, Pietro Bonfiglioli and Agostino Pirella, to collaborate on a journal. Inspired by the French Journal *Tel Quel* and the work of Georges Bataille, they wanted my husband, who had spent a year at Oxford and a year in US universities (where I met him), to do the Philosophy of Language part of the application of Marx's analysis of the commodity and money to language. Although the journal never happened, Ferruccio took up the challenge and wrote several books on the subject.

Already back then in the 1960s, as our children began coming into our lives, I realized that language could not be based on the market. If there was an economy involved, it had to be of a deeply different kind, more like the nurturing I was doing as I took care of them. I finally wrote some essays in semiotics in 1980 and 1981, where I distinguished communication from exchange – as I continue to try to do in this book.

In 1979 we got a divorce and I joined a feminist consciousness-raising group. I learned about the economic importance of women's free work in the home and soon began to see it as gift work which was also a kind of communication. I also began to connect gift-giving with the non-market gift economies of many indigenous peoples.

In 1983 I went back to the USA where I created a grants program and an all-women multicultural feminist foundation for social change called The Foundation for a Compassionate Society. We did a number of concrete projects for social change locally and internationally. They were inspired by the gift economy as an expression of what at the time I called 'women's values' and now would call 'maternal' or 'mothering values'. Those who read this book will understand that I believe that everyone has these values because everyone has had to be mothered in order to survive. The maternal model has to be there. Its processes are covered with a layer of market thinking and justification, but they are there. I show that they are also present in language and communication.

The last events put on by the foundation were the conference on the gift economy held in Las Vegas in 2004 and a second congress of Matriarchal studies (following the first congress held by German philosopher Heide Goettner-Abendroth in Luxembourg in 2003). We organized the conference under the direction of Goettner-Abendroth in Texas in 2005.

After this final event, I closed the foundation and devoted myself to writing about the theory that had informed my own practice for so many years. I had published a book in 1997, *For-Giving, a Feminist Criticism of Exchange*, and had also presented the theory in numerous articles and conference papers. I edited two books, one of essays, *Il Dono/The Gift: a Feminist Perspective* (Rome, Meltemi Editore, 2004) and another, a book coming from our conference: *Women and the the Gift Economy, a Radically Different Worldview is Possible* (Toronto, Inanna Press, 2007). I also published a book on my website, *Homo Donans*, in 2007, which is now available online in digital version in English and Italian with VandA publishing. *For-Giving* has been translated into several languages: Italian, German, Spanish, Turkish, and Albanian and is available with VandA as well. Many of the issues I address in this book are already broached in that one and may further inform the reader if she or he wishes.

I have continued to work on the theory of the gift economy because after years of trying to practice it in the foundation I realized that the theory of a maternal economy is missing in society as a whole. As much as we may practice gift-giving unconsciously or consciously, or try to bring forth social change based on it, if we do not understand what we are doing and why, if we do not know the structural and systemic reasons for the dire situation we are in and the reasons for our commitment to the gift, we will never make the necessary far-reaching radical changes. The point is to generalize gift-giving, to generalize the model of mothering in abundance, to understand the impediments to this generalization and dismantle them.

The privileged few, individuals and corporations, control most of the academic world through funding (a manipulative use of gifting). They influence research to feed back to them ideas that help them make more money and maintain their positions. I want to challenge their beliefs as well as the beliefs of the many who have been influenced by education. This book is addressed to everyone, at all levels of society. Even those who now have money and power had mothers and caregivers. Even they can make a paradigm shift. And they must if the future is to be saved.

I remember when I was young, listening to and eventually participating in many discussions. Personal opinions were very important in my parents' milieu, under a kind of general rubric of patriotism and EuroAmerican and family exceptionalism. Recently I went back to my home town and participated in a dinner table conversation that was much the same as many I had listened to as a child. We argued politely until the *pater familias* imposed his point of view. I realize that to change that point of view and similar ones, which together create a great hinterland of the conserative decision making in the US, a radically different approach is necessary. It is difficult to give a radically different approach at the dinner table. Perhaps this book can help others who want to make inroads in the hinterland by changing the conversation.

There is now widespread unhappiness in the USA and around the globe: poverty, racism, economic violence, mass murders, sexual violence, police brutality, gang brutality, fear, disillusionment, objectification through consumerism and advertising. Porn takes the place of love and even of personal erotic dreams. Trafficking in children, women, men, organs and arms are some of the new permutations of exchange and force. Wars are fought on pretexts, but they actually serve the 'economy' of arms industries and oil companies. Water, seeds, forests, species, knowledges are privatized and made scarce.

Maternal gifts bring trust, while exchange breeds suspicion but detours around it through an equation of value. State terrorism is the paranoid mode of attack and reprisal corresponding to advanced (sic!) corporate capitalism worldwide. Instead of our neighbors spying on us and reporting to the government, as happened during Stalinism, the government does it directly. The great gift potential of the free internet has become the means of access of the government and of commerce into our lives and minds.

As situations worsen, learned powerlessness takes the place of creative initiatives for change. Those who do take truthful initiatives become pariahs, subject to government attack. Witness Chelsea Manning, Julian Assange, Edward Snowden. The prison industrial complex allies with the military industrial complex and the food and agriculture industrial complex to control and exploit us. The appeal to 'free speech' allows the media to engage in deep propaganda and manipulation by misinformation, advertising even to babies and young children (Klein 2000) so that their gift economy years are polluted by the market. Education is seen as a solution to poverty but is counted as successful when the educated are integrated in the system that creates the poverty, when they understand and believe its principles and operate in it with profit. Students are encouraged to study 'stem' (science, technology, engineering and mathematics) subjects on the edge of environmental disaster that the stem activities have created. Inventions of war like drones embody the psychotic detached intellect to the extent that people far away can be killed on command by the flick of a finger of an operator following orders at home. Widespread poverty, violence and disease are the fate of the many while the very few are stratospherically rich.

Most of all though, the winds are rising and the earth is shaking. Hurricanes, tornadoes, freak storms, typhoons, tsunamis, earthquakes and upheavals abound, chasms and sink holes are opening. The ice is melting and the sea is dying.

We are all concerned at some level but we are trying to ignore what we have done. Again that forgetting!

I believe that the way out of this disaster is to re-value the mother-child relation, and the paradigm of the generous mother-in-abundance.[8] Presently the system has to create enough scarcity to force people to work for it for money. Mothers are disempowered and made to over-give and self-sacrifice by this scarcity and the accompanying lack of community. Typically the system blames the victim but in this case the mother, liberated from victimization, is actually the solution to overturning the system – and doing so nonviolently.

All of us have been mothered to some extent or we would not have survived, and we have the model of mothering within us for both material and verbal gift-giving.

If the model of mothering structures language, it is our main communicative way of action, our main guide line as we cross the narrow bridge over the abyss.

I hope this book will show how patriarchy and the market have altered our humanity, making us believe that we are part of a nature red in tooth and claw instead of a cooperative and creative nurturing species at home on Mother Earth. Unfortunately, we have fulfilled the old negative prophecy. It is time for a positive new one.

---

8   Pace Bataille! Women, mothers would know what to do with the excess production. Save it for the lean years. Distribute it to friends. Produce less. It is the market economy that is threatened by abundance.

ACKNOWLEDGMENTS

Since part of the economy of giving is receiving I want to express my gratitude for the many gifts that have been given to me by the people I have known throughout these many years.

I want to thank my daughters, Amelia, Beatrice and Emma for their continuing acceptance and love. I am especially grateful to Emma, who has supported me with encouraging words almost every day since I began this work.

I am very grateful to my friend Susan Petrilli who has continued to find good in everything I do and has pushed me to finish this long effort.

I am grateful to my brother for his ongoing support and tolerance of our differences, political and otherwise.

I thank my cousin, Sissy Farenthold for the help she gave me in starting the Foundation for a Compasionate Society.

I thank Liliana Wilson for her help with the illustrations and the cover art, Chiquie Estrada, Sally Jacques, Candace Ross, Mary Nell Mathis, Frieda Werden and all those near and far with whom I have worked for social change over the years including all the women who were part of the Foundation.

I thank the women of the International Feminists for a Gift Economy and everyone on the gift economy e list.

I thank my Italian friends and collaborators especially Francesca Lulli, Francesca Colombini, Laura De Micheli, Daniela Degan, Maria Luisa Gizzio, Franca Clemente and the women of the Casa Internazionale delle Donne.

I thank those who have in one way or another read and commented (positively or negatively) on the various versions of the manuscript: Mary Condren, Veronika Bennholdt-Thompson, Kellia Rameres-Watson, Ann Key, Candace Kant, Paula Bauman, Augusto Ponzio and especially Susan Petrilli to whom I am endlessly grateful for her help and support!

Many thanks also to the people at Mimesis International for their very fast and efficient work.

LIST OF FIGURES

PART ONE

THE GIFT HYPOTHESIS

CHAPTER I

THE MATERNAL GIFT PARADIGM

> *In conversing about what it will take to reclaim our planet we agreed that what Earth needs more than anything is mothering. Earth, Mother Earth, needs mothers, regardless of gender...*
> from Alice Walker "Democratic Motherism" (2013)

1.0 Motherers

The direct maternal satisfaction of needs remains unrecognized because society is organized around exchange: *do ut des*, giving in order to receive an equivalent, using the satisfaction of others' needs for our own benefit. Perhaps because exchange fits with some other aspects of the way we know (which we will explore in chs), we often neglect the process of direct need-satisfaction, which is, after all, more fundamental. Leaving out direct giving-and-receiving and starting investigations of human life with exchange means we do not start with the source but somewhere downstream. Thus, our explanations remain partial and sometimes misleading. Moreover, the view from exchange discounts and discredits the very possibility of unilateral giving, as postmodern philosophers like Derrida (1992), Bourdieu (1977) and Lyotard (1974) show in various ways.[1] Having a starting point that is already located in exchange, they can never return to the mother and the free gift. The absence of the model of mothering from their discussions makes them uninteresting for one who starts where human life starts, with mothers (or other care givers) and children. Many books have been written on gift-giving in recent years, especially after the economic crash of 2008 showed that capitalism is not working. None of them, however, ground gift-giving in mothering and

---

1   An important exception here is Helene Cixous (1997 [1975]). A case in point is Bourdieu's (1977) work on symbolic exchange and honor among men in Kabylia in which he did not notice the rich symbolism of generations and birth present in women's art and crafts, revealed by Kabyl writer Malikam (2007 [1996]).

being mothered. The lack of this fundamental piece alters their analysis and their planning as well as their leadership styles. Gift-giving, like language, is something in which everyone is competent, so all of us feel entitled to explain it. Nevertheless, since we also practice monetized exchange on a daily basis and personally experience the contradictions between gift and exchange, we feel justified in being skeptical. On the other hand, not everyone experiences the intimate and detailed need-satisfying care of mothering.[2] Unfortunately that important voice has been left out of the discourse not only of gift economy theorists but also of Western feminists, who in the last decades have been mainly 'post maternal' (Stephens 2012).

This book refocuses on the direct unilateral satisfaction of needs because the way of exchange – the market and money – have proven enormously destructive, creating many new needs that can never be satisfied, and depleting the nurturing economy as a whole. It is my hope that by showing how the unilateral satisfaction of needs (giving, together with its complement: receiving, and its extension: giving again – passing it on) can be seen as a basic structure of language, so that a new kind of validation for direct need-satisfaction can be derived. Perhaps this can also make giving less vulnerable to exploitation and plunder.

Our socio-economic system, capitalist patriarchy, is responsible for many aspects of this situation.[3] If we were living in a gift economy based on the values of care, a matriarchy,[4] our ways of knowing and interacting would be very different; we would collectively recognize the importance of the direct satisfaction of needs among adults as well as the importance of mothering and being-mothered as children. As it is, we live in a mixed system where a market economy, which is based on exchange, coexists with a hidden nurturing or provisioning gift economy. In this dualistic system, the market economy takes the gifts/provisions, transforming them into profit.

Understanding the importance of the mother-child experience, in which there is an intentional giver as well as a creative or willing receiver, and generalizing it, leads us to map mothering onto our surroundings as the giv-

---

2   But see Sarah Hardy's (2013) evolution through caregiving by 'mothers and others' Dean Falk's (2009) 'putting the baby down' theory of language origins and the 'ancestral parenting practices' with 'multiple caregivers' discussed by Darcia Narvaez (2012).

3   The concentration on exchange instead of needs allows us to carry on as usual despite the needs of billions of people living in poverty and disease.

4   Not a mirror image of patriarchy – see Sanday (2002).

er in a dyad in which the perceiver is the receiver.[5] Restoring the centrality of mothering/being-mothered and projecting this interaction would allow us to complete our epistemological picture in this way. With the judicious use of some of the discoveries of contemporary neuroscience, it could also let us understand care as the interface between ourselves and the world.

I propose that it is necessary to make what I am calling 'the gift hypothesis' in order to find the continuities that link mothering, gender, cognition, economics, language, neuroscience, politics, humans and the rest of life on Earth. According to this hypothesis, the way we know is shaped in childhood by gift-giving and receiving; we continue to function in the same way as adults even when we are investigating what we consider to be objective non-gift processes. Whether these non-gift processes are buried deep in the brain, or are parts of our everyday lives in our particular cultures, or exist among galaxies in outer space, we continue to know them with our gift-based, mother-and-child-based ways of knowing. That is how they become relevant to humans.

Whatever we are thinking about, from the embrace of lovers to the pathways among neurons to the trajectories of light, and from the centrifugal and centripetal spins of galaxies to the interactions of genes, we understand our world in terms of need-satisfying gifts and gift trajectories that we project outward. Gift-giving and receiving form the lens through which the world becomes meaningful to us both individually and collectively. According to the gift hypothesis, the paths of light, the interaction of neurons, and the 'fit' of creatures with each other and with their ecological niches make sense for us when we study them, because giving and receiving constitute the source of many or perhaps even of all of the maps we project upon the world. The peculiarity of humans that children are born undeveloped and incapable of independent survival, requires the motherer to become an intentional environmental niche for the child in the first years. By nurturing or maternal 'gift-giving' I mean the focussed care that is given to children, the direct satisfaction of needs by gifts and services upon which the child's survival depends. The caregiver recognizes the need of the other, whether expressed or not and procures, makes or does something that satisfies that need. This is 'material communication' having to do with the basic life-sustaining transmission and reception of goods.

Again and again, the mother or other caregiver has to recognize the child's needs and satisfy them appropriately. The child has to receive and utilize what is given (and at times elicit the care of the mother). This in-

---

5   Thus, we would have a justification of the idea of Mother Earth or Mother Environment at a very fundamental level.

teractivity forms a simple basic pattern with almost infinite variations, because the gifts and services can be varied endlessly and the pattern can be repeated on many different levels. Thus, the pattern of giving and receiving becomes a projectable 'image schema', which can be recognized in a wide variety of both human and non-human processes in diluted or extended forms. Among these are: transitivity, sending and receiving messages, output and input, agent and patient,[6] cause and effect, the 'donation' of atoms, the leap of the impulse across the synapse, the journey of light across the universe and its reception by the leaf and the retina. And breathing. And communication. And language. In fact, we will see that the 'image schema of the gift' is the (social) source of syntax and finally, of meaning.

What I propose is to phase out the market economy completely. In order to do this we need to find within ourselves something that we did not realize we had, a bedrock that has been invisible, on which to base an alternative construction. To even begin to conceive of doing this, it is necessary to recognize that the logic of exchange does not occupy the whole field of the rational, just as the market does not occupy the whole field of providing for needs. The alternative, gift-giving, has an important and more fundamental logic of its own, a logic of transitivity. The gift logic is simpler than the logic of exchange and also for that reason may be easily 'upstaged' by exchange and made invisible. The consequence of transitive giving-receiving is connection and combination (on conduit metaphor and transitivity, see below 3.7) while the logic of exchange functions according to categorization and identity. Just because exchange is not directly nurturing, it leaves the way open for the transitivity of the gift to be supplanted by the transitivity of force, which results in the prevalence of the active over the passive as exemplified in physical causation (but also in patriarchal violence).

Since in the development of the child, material nurturing, transitive giving-receiving necessarily comes before categorization and before language as well as before the understanding of physical causation, we can say that the transitive logic of nurturing is in evidence before both the logic of identity and the logic of force. It is the logic of transitivity that can serve as the bedrock for an alternative to the market.

Many writers on the gift economy have seen it as an alternative to capitalism even when they have not admitted that gifting may be unilateral. From Marcel Mauss (1990 [1923]) to Lewis Hyde (2007 [1983]) Jacques Derrida (1992) and Caillè and Godbout (2001[1992]), academics have grappled with

---

6   'Agent and patient' are grammatical terms used to refer to the grammatical
     element that initiates the action in a sentence or the one that undergoes it.

the paradoxes of gifting in a society based on the market, and many writers of fiction have explored the same issues (Hoeller 2012). Less common is the connection of gift economy and mothering. Cixous (1997 [1975]) is the forerunner, who proposed the gift economy as gendered[7] and described it also in a poetic sense. More recently, Diprose (2002), and Shaw (2003), and the other authors who do broach the subject, have usually used an ethical approach and a Maussian framework. Perhaps for them, unilateral gift giving seems to come too close to an essentialist interpretation of mothering.

My approach is not based on ethics nor is it essentialist, as I will attempt to demonstrate throughout the book. Rather, I see the difference in the values of gift or exchange as a Marxian superstructure coming from the economic structures (here, the modes of distribution) of gift-giving or of exchange. That is, giving and receiving is a structural economic pattern, both at the individual and at the societal level, and practicing it emphasizes certain values, for example, on the individual level, the values of care and compassion; one large-scale societal example might be the Marshall Plan. (And see Rabbi Michael Lerner's proposal to create similar plans for countries in the Global South (http: //spiritualprogressives.org/newsite/?page_id=114). Market exchange can also be both individual and societal, and practicing it emphasizes other values (individually, there is the exchange of blows in a fist fight; a large scale example might be the wars of 'retaliation' against Afghanistan and Iraq to – presumably – 'pay them back' for the attack on the World Trade Center).[8]

Presently the market creates the context in which most gift-giving has to take place, making it difficult. In fact, unilateral giving does not of itself require sacrifice. Rather, it is the situation of scarcity in which most people are forced to live, artificially created by the market in capitalism that imposes sacrifice. In abundance and community, unilateral giving can take place without interruption as necessary.

At the level of the individual, the maternal need-satisfying gift economy is the source of positive emotions and bonding. Indeed, giving and receiving continue to carry a strong emotional charge throughout life and

---

7   'The (political) economy of the masculine and the feminine is organized by different demands and constraints, which, as they become socialized and metaphorized, produce signs, relations of power, relationships of production and reproduction, a whole huge system of cultural inscription that is legible as masculine or feminine' Cixous (1997[1975]: 152).

8   Hugo Chavez's Bolivarian revolution was an atttempt to redistribute wealth providing free services and land reform. Evo Morales has drawn on his indigenous heritage to create redistributive reforms. Both of these leaders have remained patriarchal while attempting to move towards a gift economy.

they are the basis of both long-term and short-term relationships.[9] Giving and receiving can be elaborated in positive relational gift economies, or distorted and changed by the exchange economy, as we shall see. The criticism of unilateral giving that it creates dependency and disempowers the receiver is only valid in a society based on exchange, where so-called 'independence' actually depends on working for money in the exchange economy. In a gift economy everyone is interdependent and everyone works not for money, but to satisfy needs.

The fact that children are born from the bodies of women and not from the bodies of men has been a major influence on human thinking and social organization since prehistoric times. The magical ability of the mother's womb to conceive, house and produce human life must have seemed overwhelming to our ancient ancestors. Even today it is a source of fear and envy. In fact, patriarchy is, in large part, an attempt by males to dominate and appropriate the life-giving power that produces the material human being (von Werlhof 2011).

However, mothering does not stop at birth. In fact, the body of the child continues to be 'produced' by the daily or even hourly or minute by minute satisfaction of the young child's needs. After giving birth, the mother continues to maintain the child materially by giving her the gifts and services that allow her to live and develop. The child's body is the product of the gift-work of the mother. The mother gives unilaterally and the child receives creatively. Until the child is old enough to survive autonomously, her or his body is the result of mothering and *being* mothered.

The recent importance given to the body in feminist philosophy does not concentrate on the fact that the body is the product of mother care, the gifts and services *beyond* birth. In capitalist patriarchy, an adult woman's body is presently considered her private property and may come under siege by predatory males. She may not consider the importance of its having been given to her not only by birth but by the early gift-work of her mother. In fact, feminist philosophers may consider the body as an embodiment of self, an identity or a performance of gender but not as the receiver and giver of gifts, the locus and product of an alternative economy, which is in opposition to the market and patriarchal capitalism.

For anyone who reaches even relative autonomy, there has to have been a long term complex transfer of matter from one or many persons to her or him, fashioned in appropriate ways and according to proper

9   In this regard see also Jean Baker Miller (1976) and the work of the relational-cultural Jean Baker Miller Training Institute at Wellesley Centers for Women.

timing and rhythms, with psychological and emotional sensitivities and understandings that allow the transfer to be successful and the child to receive and assimilate the goods. I call this transfer 'material communication'. Our bodies are its products and our minds in large part as well. In patriarchal capitalism, this job of material communication is mainly assigned to birthmothers but it can be done by others – fathers, members of the extended family, paid childcare workers. In other cultures, whole villages raise the children.

By understanding the body as the product of gift-work and gift-work as material communication, the gap between material and semiotic processes is bridged from the beginning.[10] The body is the product of material communication and language is the transposition of material communication onto a virtual verbal plane. That is, language is verbal mothering. The so called 'symbolic order of the father' (Lacan 2002) is only an order imposed *post hoc*, strongly influenced not only by patriarchy but also by monetized exchange, which is *altered* or *backwards* material communication.

When we communicate linguistically we are nurturing each other, whatever our gender may be. All positively-abled humans can speak and thus do mothering at least on this virtual plane. They do various kinds of material communication as well. Thus, mothering, both material and virtual, is a capacity typical of the species, not of only one gender. For this reason, in the discussion we are about to undertake, I use the term 'motherer' as including all sexes and genders and focusing on behavior rather than on biology.[11]

Although men can do mothering of young children, women have been assigned this responsibility because of the social interpretation of the biological facts that they give birth to children and have the milk to nurture them. 'Mother, the verb', 'Mother, the job' say the proponents of the new motherhood movement that is now spreading worldwide.[12] By using the word 'motherer' I affirm this anti-essentialist approach regarding a kind of work that ensures the survival of infants and young children by satisfying their needs unilaterally. By 'unilateral', I mean that the motherer provides the life sustenance for the child, but the child does not provide the life sustenance for the motherer. The job of mothering requires detailed atten-

---

10 See Kristeva (1986) on the body and the semiotic and the symbolic processes. Kristeva was using the Freudian-Lacanian characterization of the passive child and narcissistic mother, which has been overturned by recent infancy research. Her language if not her intent also remained inside the exchange paradigm.

11 We might look at this in terms of Kristeva's 'mother-father conglomerate' (1986).

12 See the work of Andrea O'Reilly and MIRCI http: //www.motherhoodinitiative. org/ http: //www.internationalmothersandmotheringnetwork.org/

tion to the child's needs and the provision of goods and services to satisfy them. Successful giving requires an active or even a creative receiver who is able to use the gift that has been given. For this reason when I speak of mothering throughout the book, I am including the receiver and the complementary role of 'being mothered'.

Despite my sincere intention to be inclusive, and my belief that men should mother and embrace their human maternal identities, I realize that birthmothers have been the ones who have done most of this work of mothering in most cultures throughout the centuries and I believe their immense contribution should be recognized. This should not be done by imposing a debt upon the receivers, but should be a part of bringing the gift-giving aspect of our species to the fore. The original model of the motherer is still female. In patriarchy, gift-giving is seen primarily as the gift of women. I am trying to extend it to everyone and thus to undermine patriarchy. In fact, we are all already doing gift-giving in various ways, but males are usually in denial of it so we call it something else ... 'moral behavior' or perhaps 'responsibility', 'kindness', or 'love'.

I also want to give you a typological gift. I believe that solving problems is a kind of gift-giving. The typological problem I want to solve is the one having to do with gender inclusiveness that is addressed in English at present by adding a slash to the gender pronouns he and she, as in s/he. I believe this is a disturbing slash, perhaps phallic and even violent. Including it in the feminine pronoun seems to include these masculinist characteristics in the female. Instead, I propose using ': ' as a sign of nipples which both women and men have, but which directly recall the mother, as in s:he. With this I hope to show that both women and men can follow the maternal model, the model of the gift economy.

Much of the work feminist philosophers have done regarding language has focused on sexist terminology. There have been some triumphs in changing terms to permit women's abilities in all fields to be respected.

My work is more about the nature of language itself. The terms I question are also those having to do with the market. I oppose 'marketism' not just 'sexism' and since I believe capitalism is patriarchal, I believe marketism includes a portion of sexism. Thus, using the word 'exchange' when what is being described is gift giving and turn taking is 'marketism'. However, 'exchange' also contains an aspect of sexism because it hides and denies a common maternal practice, the gifting performed by motherers who are usually women.

I would like to counter a common psychological approach that considers the mother as typically having power over the child and the child as reacting negatively as a victim of this imbalance. The studies of protoconversation in early childhood show that the parent and child make themselves equal to each other, 'matching' gestures, tempos and attitudes. At least in early childhood, they are constructing their similarity rather than their difference. In fact, the power differential is so great that it has to be overcome by the mother's bringing the child 'up', 'raising' h:er. Violent parenting may indeed impose a power relation but so does violence in any aspect of life (in a fight, violence is first matched against violence and then one overcomes and dominates the other).

If mothering in abundance can be identified as the individual level source of the gift economy, and the gift economy is the alternative to capitalism, mothering in abundance is the source of the alternative to capitalism. Presently the domestic sphere is the outpost of the gift economy within the fractured community and the scarcity for the many created by capitalism. Like 'surplus labor', 'reproductive labor' can be understood as gift labor that is seized through the market and transformed into profit and capital. Thus it would be the revolutionary role of feminism to liberate the gift economy and the women, children (and men) who practice it *from* capitalism, not *into* capitalism. Communicating this is an important part of the purpose of this book.

Another part of the book's purpose is to propose the idea that language is based on gifting/mothering/being mothered. I want to show that language *is* the giving and receiving of verbal gifts in abundance. If this is the case, gifting would constitute being human and would establish human relations in two fundamental ways: directly, through other-oriented material need-satisfying behavior, and indirectly, through *virtual* other-oriented need-satisfying behavior in language (and with other signs). This understanding of life and language would change our conception of the human. We would be revealed (to ourselves) as a particularly nurturing species because we give to and receive from each other not only materially but also verbally. Much of our psychological make-up depends on our ability to give and receive at both levels. Both levels profoundly influence our cultures. In fact, what we need now is to liberate gift-based language from the market, not into it, just as we need to liberate gift labor from the market and not into it.

Unfortunately most of the work that (even feminist) philosophers, psychologists and linguists do on early language and even on early childhood, generally, omits the important distinction between gift and exchange. Moreover, the embracing of an objective neurological or sociological approach does not encourage the problematization of the market for linguists and philosophers. For example, in his extensive investigation of

the word 'give', linguist John Newman (1996) does not distinguish between giving money and giving need-satisfying goods (even when he is
using as examples the languages of indigenous groups for whom money
is new and problematic). Philosopher of language John Searle also discusses money and exchange as a social institution with a complete lack
of criticism (1995). The same can be said even for Mark Johnson (1993),
whose work on the metaphors of commerce brings forward the extent to
which the market permeates our discourse.[13] Unfortunately, Johnson also
makes no attempt to criticize the economic status quo and accepts these
metaphors and their 'source area' as givens.

Johnson tells us that the metaphor of commodity transaction for relationships is widespread. He finds the same also in moral thinking. I do not
have space here to list the many convincing metaphors that he proposes
but will mention just one.

The 'causation is a commercial transaction metaphor creates a realm of
exchange, debt, credit and balance within our physical and social interactions. Any event that increases your well being is understood metaphorically as one that gives you money (as in "He profited from his experience,"
or "She was enriched by the relationship"). Suffering a decrease in your
well being is understood as losing money ("He paid for his mistake with
his life" or "Her improprieties cost her her job"). The result of this is a sort
of "social accounting in which one's actions earn credits or create debts to
others…" (Johnson 1993: 41-2).

Johnson says that the commercial transaction metaphor is an imaginative structure coming from our cultural tradition. Undoubtedly it is that,
but it is also a way the market unduly influences our beliefs, creating
a screen that filters free giving out of our minds while validating and
normalizing exchange.

Matriarchal 'pre-market' cultures such as the Iroquois were/are based
on maternal gifting (Mann 2000) that is generalized into the whole society
rather than concentrated only in one gender and focused mainly in the domestic sphere. Such non-market societies demonstrate that it is possible
to generalize gifting; they try to maintain their alternative values even
long after they have been invaded by market colonialism (Armstrong
2007). Sometimes they maintain their values by continuing spiritual practices that honor Mother Earth and nature spirits, with whom they give
and receive. That is, with whom they communicate and form community.
Mother Nature is not, in the case of indigenous cultures, an essentialist

---

13   See also Lakoff's (1987: 293) 'moral accounting schemes'.

designation, because they do not accept as valid the perspective of market exchange that is now subjugating Nature (and mothers) and plundering gifts. In a functioning gift economy, abundant material communication, language structure and linguistic and other forms of sign communication are aligned and they can be used to communicate with a Nature that is also understood as abundant and free, not exploited.

Mother Nature is made up of the aspects of our environmental niche that humans have evolved to receive as given. (Light is not a gift unless there is an eye to receive and use it.) When we criticize the idea of Mother Nature, we still have the perspective of the sun rising instead of the Earth turning. S:he is Mother Nature because we turn to her as mothered children, and, as we learned to do from our own mothers, we put forward our hands and our tools to receive h:er gifts, s:he nurtures us. It is in part our capacity to receive that makes h:er a giver to us. Yet h:er immense variety and creativity of niches for other humans, creatures and plants allow us to adapt to h:er in many different ways, co-adapting, and co-creating with h:er (Thompson 1982).

For our patriarchal capitalist society, Nature and mothers both give without exchange so they are indeed 'closer' to each other, more similar than they are to those men who force gifts (making others give in or give up!) and impose market exchange. Indeed, Nature is exploited and devastated, just as mothering and gift-giving are exploited and devastated because both are aspects of a gift economy located within a context of exchange and patriarchal domination.

It is crucial to understand the reasons why an integrated gift approach has not been widespread before now in the West; these have to do with the hegemony of patriarchy and the market. As we will see in the second half of the book, the market makes use of some other aspects of language and through abstraction, *replays the logic of gift-giving in reverse*. The superstructure and view of the world coming from the market hide gift-giving/ mothering, contradict it and, meshed with patriarchy, further plunder it. Since in the West, success in the market is required for survival, most people are deeply influenced by market ideology. The market and money function as conceptual mechanisms that distort and denature gift-giving.

Even the science that has grown up in the shadow of the market eliminates gift-giving from its explanations. The exciting neuroscientific research, which is now providing new explanations for many of our capacities, nevertheless takes place beyond the mother. It accesses the body's gifts without reference to the very nurturing that allows the body to exist (and it therefore has a politically 'apolitical' position). It is this nurturing/being nurtured that I am saying is an epistemological key that must be recognized even by neuroscience.[14] I do not mean with this to say that those explanations are not correct, but that they are not complete. There is another register of social interaction based in mothering that provides the structure of cognition and language without which brain activity would be meaningless.[15]

Subtracting the gift economy from our picture of the world, while at the same time exploiting it creates a mindset that is impervious to really radical change because it eliminates a deep alternative that is readily available everywhere. This mindset is the product of centuries of Western matriphobic (mis)understanding of the world.

1.1 Infancy research

> 'There has been a revolution in our understanding of intersubjectivity', '… within our lifetimes we have witnessed the overturning of one of the most pervasive myths of social science – the myth of the asocial infant'.
> *(*Meltzoff and Brooks 2007: 149*)*

In recent years, researchers into infancy have discovered that very young children are not cut off from others, solipsistic or egocentric as Freud,[16] Piaget and Skinner believed. Rather they are highly social from a very early age (Meltzoff and Brooks 2007: 149). This new approach, which places infants at the center of attention, also takes a few steps towards reclaiming the centrality of mothering.

Colwyn Trevarthen says, 'Indeed it seems that cultural intelligence itself is motivated at every stage by the kind of powers of innate intersubjective sympathy that an alert infant can show shortly after birth. We are born to

---

14 An illuminating example is the study of grasping by the neuroscientists dealing with mirror neurons. They do not locate grasping as part of giving and receiving (see Gallese and Lakoff 2005). See also 10.4 below.

15 It is not just that brain research lends itself to 'neurosexism' (Fine 2010) and gender stereotyping, but it leaves out the important practical nurturing interaction that is necessary for the brain functions to develop *and* as a model for human sociality to develop.

16 Although Freud did consider the mother-child relations in terms of the child's needs/drives for food and sex, they were seen as aspects of the etiology of the individual personality and its disturbances rather than as structural aspects of communication and epistemology. John Bowlby (1999), on the other hand, proposed attachment in a psychological and ethological sense, beyond the satisfaction of needs (as between goslings and their human mother figure).

generate shifting states of self-awareness, to show them to other persons, and to provoke interest and affectionate responses from them. Thus starts a new psychology of the creativity and cooperative knowing and meaning in human communities' (Trevarthen 2010).[17] Mothering such a being is very different from mothering a dependent solipsist!

When the relationship is free of stress, it has great potential for emotional and intellectual enjoyment. By h:er very 'intersubjective sympathy', the child elicits gifts; the mother gives unilaterally to h:er to satisfy h:er needs and the child creatively receives them. As s:he grows the developing child reacts to unilateral care by imitating it. This is not an exchange but a response that is mainly a repetition of unilaterality. Moreover, when the child cries, s:he is asking for unilateral care. When s:he laughs and coos s:he is giving unilaterally and even h:er bodily functions are unilateral.[18]

The reception of care is creative, not passive.[19] Children must use the nourishment at least physiologically, and they respond socially, interactively to the care they have been given. Once we stop considering receiving as passive, we can also look at children's active exploration of the environment as the development of their creative receiving capacities in that they put themselves in a position to receive the perceptual gifts of their surroundings, for example, by moving towards something, grasping it and putting it in their mouths.

Nor is nurturing a kind of manipulation practiced upon a passive object but need-satisfying engagement with someone who is in h:er turn not only, an explorer and a philosopher (Gopknik 2010) but h:erself a (small) nurturer. If communication is based on nurturing, this view of the interactive infant also changes our view of the character of the motherer, making her someone who is engaged in intense social/material communication with

---

17   This is a novel solution to the nature-nurture question in that the child is born – nature – with the kind of abilities that assure that he or she will be nurtured socially. The patterns deriving from these intersubjective interactions become the basis of gifting at different levels. Is the child's innate 'intersubjective sympathy' then essentialist?

18   One thinks of the distinction between the semiotic and the symbolic made by Julia Kristeva. The gift interaction takes place in the semiotic period. As we shall see, it is not so much the symbolic order of the father that intervenes, but the logic of exchange and the market: capitalist patriarchy. The gift-giving that we are trying to reveal in life and in language restores the conception of transitivity in language to the mother (and in so doing potentially all of language). The very use of the term 'exchange' assimilates the maternal semiotic to the market logic and cancels it.

19   The idea of receiving as passive perhaps derives from the patriarchal view of women as passive receivers.

another human being. Under the right conditions, her care of the child is no more *self*less than any other communicative activity, though it does have the potential for being particularly life-enhancing if it is not burdened by hardship, scarcity and solitude. The interpersonal transitivity experienced by linguistically communicating adults is here available to the mother in a material, prelinguistic form, since the infant does not yet speak.

Infancy researchers are now saying what most mothers must have already realized for centuries: humans are interactive, and jointly creative from the beginning. Stein Bråten calls infants 'altercentric' (1998). Their attention is centered on the (m)other (which mothers must have realized as well).

In proposing mothering as the basis of language, I am not talking about language teaching, language *transmission* per se, but about material nurturing – giving and receiving – as the original model for language. As the child grows older, s:he is able to transfer this interactive material nurturing model onto a virtual plane made of sound, a plane of verbal nurturing, which has already been formed in this way by many generations before h:er. S:he also experiences the verbal sound plane very early in ontogenesis even if s:he does not understand the words. For the child, vocal giving/receiving communication accompanies material communication and is bound up with emotions from the very beginning, even if s:he does not yet understand it. S:he hears the speech of h:er caregivers from birth and already in the womb reacts to the voice of h:er mother.[20]

Even children who are in institutions, and those who are inadequately mothered, have to receive material communication or they do not survive. Their later difficulty with language and social skills is usually due to lack of exposure to language and vocal play as well as to scarce and inadequate nurturing, which also produces an inadequate model of intimate gifting and the consequent lack of development of emotionally rich and jointly creative relationships with others.[21]

---

20 I am also not talking about 'motherese', (or 'baby talk') which has been in the spotlight recently, and is the adult's expression of what s:he imagines the child's language to be. The motherer also often asks the baby many questions: are you hungry? Does anything hurt? Want to take a bath? Want ducky? S:he is letting the child know that what s:he is going to do is a response to that question (that verbal interrogation of the child's need) and s:he is casting about for what may be making the child cry or nervous, what the need may be. S:he gives a voice to h:er attempted 'mind-reading' activity (see note below).

21 Language as the product of generations of collective adult mothering provides a gifting template and thus perhaps teaches itself to some extent. Individual children who are poorly mothered in institutions may be able to learn both language and giving from adult and peer language even if at a later date.

1.2 Language is verbal mothering

If it is the case that language is turn-taking verbal giving/receiving, and mothering/being mothered, it follows then that the nurturing interaction does not disappear in maturity (when we continue to use language), but continues in another register as part of this species-specific[22] verbal gifting, influencing everything we are as humans. What I am talking about here is not any particular language but the language capacity itself, of which the 6900 extant languages – *mother tongues* – are expressions. The phrase 'mother tongue', which is usually used to refer to the language of one's mother or country, has a more general meaning in that language itself *is* verbal mothering. The kind of guesswork and attention to others' communicative needs[23] that is important for the success of early childcare continues, to some extent, in linguistic communication, even among adults who are not doing it on the material plane in that way any longer. For example, 'mind reading' others' needs is necessary for mothering but also for speaking, in that the speaker has to know which word-gifts to give the listener in order to put h:er in a three-part relation with h:erself to some other part of the world.

S:he considers the context and guesses what the other knows and what s:he needs in order to form a relation with the speaker regarding something, and h:er guesses are usually pretty accurate because the same words are used by others to satisfy h:er own cognitive and communicative needs. S:he uses the word 'horse' to talk about horses because that is the word-gift that has been given to her by other speakers and that probably satisfies the listener's cognitive and communicative need regarding horses. In writing and reading, the writer creates the context linguistically from which the readers' new cognitive and communicative needs will arise, and continues to mind-read the reader's needs, although s:he probably does not know h:er personally and therefore must rely on shared standards and knowledge of h:er probable experience.

Because of the way our society functions, as adults we all employ combinations of gift and exchange. Mothering requires more direct gift

---

22 Some other species may have language, but it is certainly central as a defining characteristic of our own species.

23 'Mind-reading' is a technical term from child development studies that refers to the human ability to guess what others are thinking. This guesswork might be seen as a kind of abductive or retroductive reasoning, as theorized by Peirce and Welby (Petrilli 2009: 154). Another technical term, 'joint attention', refers to the ability of children to call the attention of another to some aspect of the world so that both perceive it together.

giving than many other activities, because children need it for survival. However, people who are not mothers often practice gift-giving in various ways. They mind read others' needs and satisfy them at many levels. Although the market has its own impersonal requirements, much conversation goes on about exchanges and many exchanges are directed towards satisfying needs in a second moment, when the product is no longer seen as an exchange value but as a use value. The two logics of gift and of exchange are woven together in life and in our psychological make up. For various reasons, this has had the effect of making unilateral gift-giving invisible or secondary, while exchange is the norm. Nevertheless, we are all capable of both.

Much discussion has taken place among linguists, psychologists and philosophers about the role of language in thinking and in the formation of concepts. From Sapir and Whorf to Wittgenstein, Piaget and Vygotsky and to more recent researchers like Quine, Fodor, Kripke, Rosch and Carey, the spectrum of possible influences between language and concepts has been delved into. Whatever the outcome of these discussions, it is evident that mothering must have an important influence on both pre-linguistic and linguistically-mediated concept formation as well as on thinking itself. In this light, thinking and concept formation are not just abstract rational processes best suited to male brains but are in important ways developments, even derivatives, of mother-child interactivity.

At another level of complication, as we will see in Part 2, looking at language as gift-giving, and as an important element in concept formation, allows us to trace the influence of some aspects of language structure on socio-economic processes (Vaughan 1980, 1997). That is, we can actually recognize a process like monetized exchange, for example, as an embodiment and distortion, not only of material mothering but of cognitive linguistic and (more broadly) semiotic processes.

Even though language has long been considered a key to human epistemology, not only has the maternal aspect of the language capacity not been recognized despite much research into children's cognitive development, but as I have been saying, the importance of the mother-child model for epistemology has been obscure. Nor have we recognized the importance of this model for economics or for human life in general. The feminist rejection of masculine bias – sexism – in the academic world is not only justified but it needs to be even more radical. In fact, the feminist movement in patriarchal capitalism is still far from reaching its fundamental revolutionary potential.

Restoring the mother-child model is a key for re-conceiving the world through a different paradigm and creating deep and far-reaching social change. The perspective we achieve in this way can eventually give us guidelines as to what we should and should not do in constructing alternative economies and social organizations. These are new guidelines, not deriving from a moral or even a practical sense,[24] but from an understanding of the contradictory collective (cognitive, linguistic and economic) processes that are continually alienating us from workable patterns of behavior. With this understanding, the overcoming of these processes can take place not through negative judgment and punishment of individuals or groups, but as a kind of collective healing. In fact, even guilt and vengeance, and crime and punishment, follow the logic of exchange, of paying for crime. What we need is a paradigm that includes mothering/being mothered. This book attempts to provide a rationale for a shift in social focus away from money and the market and towards a gift economy.

1.3 The motherworld or the marketworld?

> As I understand it from my Okanagan ancestors, language was given to us by the land we live within…. All my elders say that it is land that holds all knowledge of life and death and is a constant teacher. It is said in Okanagan that the land constantly speaks. It is constantly communicating. Not to learn its language is to die. We survived and thrived by listening intently to its teachings — to its language — and then inventing human words to retell its stories to our succeeding generations. It is the land that speaks N'silxchn, the old land/mother spirit of the Okanagan People, which surrounds me in its primal, wordless state.
> (Jeannette Armstrong, 'Land' 1997: 175-6)

Motherers themselves are the original environment for their childen[25] and they are part of a co-creative, not a slavish or passive, social and natural world. Although the evolutionary adaptation of humans to our environmental niches has determined our capacities, it appears to us that many aspects of the world are fine-tuned to meet our needs. The pleasures of sensory experience come from a world that is 'just right'. The reason for

---

24   Or even a sociobiological sense. Instead, we may have evolved to be mothered in community (Narvaez et al ed. 2014).

25   In fact, Winnicott talked about mothercare as the environment of the child. He considered the unit to be not the individual but the 'nursing couple', the 'environment-individual set up' (1965).

this rightness is that we have adapted to the natural environment both physically and socially. At the same time, we have also adapted it to us; we have co-evolved, constructing, and being constructed by, our niches. The process is similar to the mother-child relation, which we experience in many ways; indeed, the child adapts to the mother's gifts and increasingly to h:er needs while the motherer adapts to the child's needs and increasingly to h:er gifts. (For the co-creative evolution of creature and niche, see Odling-Smee and Laland 2003).[26] This similarity is a key to the informative character of the gift pattern, which occurs in many different contexts and can be recognized through traces of bodily sensations and emotional responses connected with giving and receiving. The transposition of the pattern onto many levels, its repetition and variation, give it a mobility and versatility that the patterns of other animals' less complex nurturing do not have.

Throughout the book I will be talking about 'world-gifts'[27] and 'word-gifts'. This utilizes, but also transcends, the idealist idea that 'it is the viewpoint adopted which creates the object' (Saussure 1998). Something becomes a gift from the viewpoint of the receiver and passer-on of gifts, and the infant learns that viewpoint in early childhood by being nurtured.

The individual and social perception and reception of the world as giving and gifted spans the distance between subject and object from the beginning of life. It is the viewpoint adopted that creates the object as a world-gift but that viewpoint is social from the beginning because we are all mothered children and as such we receive the nurturing motherworld's and each others' gifts, which have been received by still others individually and collectively through time.

By extending the mothering environment from human mothercare to the rest of our surroundings, which do actualy satisfy most of our material, perceptual and conceptual needs, we relate to them as receivers

---

26 'Organisms choose habitats and resources, construct aspects of their environments such as nests, holes, burrows, webs, pupal cases, and a chemical milieu, and frequently choose, protect, and provision nursery environments for their offspring'. (2003: 1). Human mothering provides such a behavioral and material nursery environment. This involves a co-adaptation. In fact, there is a kind of 'niche construction' in which the baby determines the ways in which the mother will satisfy her needs and vice-versa. The mother is the child's environmental niche.

27 It is as if the language we use already gives us a clue. Think of 'givens', 'sense data'. We should also think of the German philosophers' use of the term 'Es gibt' or italian 'si dà', an impersonal donation of being as theorized by Heidegger in the idea that Being gives itself.

of their gifts which we can pass on to others through language. Seeing ourselves as co-creative receivers allows us to attribute enough of mothering to the world around us to understand it as the motherworld and construct a dyadic relation to it that is animated and recalls the mother-child dyad. World-gifts are thus things, events, actions that are relevant in some way, that nurture our senses, minds and bodies and that we as receivers address as gifts. Not recognizing the importance of the mother-child relation, we cannot recognize the active side that we unconsciously attribute to the world around us.

For children, it is a short step from Winnicott's mother as environment to the environment as mother. This solves a number of philosophical problems that arise about the relation between the mind and the world because it allows the world to be active in providing our perceptions and conceptions. If we think we only apply our words and our thoughts to an epistemologically passive external world, we can never reconnect to it as motherer-giver. Similarly, mothers and women in general have been considered passive, sexually and otherwise, while their unpaid need-satisfying work was considered nothing. Thus our image of knowledge as penetration and as grasping rather than receiving.

The interactive, interpersonal mother-child relation, enhanced by its projections into language and onto the world, forms a lens through which the processes of nature and culture can be recognized, and through which they have meaning and value. In our society, the market and patriarchy have confounded the waters and have cracked the lens while, at the same time, exceptionalizing, discrediting and exploiting mothering-and-being-mothered, focusing it inside the nuclear family with a single female motherer.

I feel justified in presenting and describing 'the motherworld' as the projected[28] gifting aspects of our niche construction, which make our material environmental and cultural surroundings maternal. This maternal character of the world is the necessary complement of the idea of knowing as receiving perceptual and conceptual gifts and it is enhanced by the possibility humans have of passing them on linguistically to others. I characterize speech and writing as well as other forms of sign behavior as gifting. However, I will concentrate on speech and writing. They are the ways we pass on to others perceptual and conceptual

---

28   I believe it is unconsciously projected but as part of our co-creation of and with our ecological niches it is real as well. As the song says, we fly 'Nel blu dipinto di blu' (In the blue, painted blue).

motherworld-gifts using virtual, verbal (vocal or graphic) gifts, which function by being given for them.[29]

Indigenous practices of gifting to nature in gratitude constitute social responses to nature as nurture, which are appropriate to a way of knowing and to a theory of knowledge based on giving and receiving. With their gifts, they include Mother Nature in the community of material communicators and in doing so they are able to attune themselves to Her communicative initiatives as well as to those of the human community.

On the other hand, I will argue that the *theories* of knowledge that we have in patriarchal capitalism are based on the logic of exchange, even though knowledge itself, and the lenses through which we know, are still largely based on giving and receiving. This contradictory situation causes many philosophical problems as well as much bigger problems on the plane of reality.

1.4 Turning the motherworld into mere matter

The view of the world as mere matter is a historical product, as Carolyn Merchant showed. In fact, the shift from *mater* to matter was deeply influenced by patriarchy and capitalism, which, during its development, was abolishing the gift economy by genocide of the indigenous peoples in the Americas, killing witches and healers and oppressing women, mothers and poor people in Europe, and at the same time, eliminating the gift projections onto nature. The cruelty of the economy that destroys, denies, and exploits gifts also alienates its participants from nature and makes them want to assert their dominance over 'it'. Still, in any society, children continue to be born and cared for and this process determines how they know, even if it is later distorted by the adult economy and culture. An epistemology based on mothering/being mothered can be elaborated by turning the child-half of the nurturing dyad outwards, projecting the (m)other-half onto the world and receiving its/h:er gifts. Words, then, are sound gifts that we give to others, satisfying their cognitive and communicative needs, passing on to others the gifts we have received from the motherworld (mothering others and the environment socially in our turn while s:he/they/it/ also mother us).

---

29   We also use innumerable non-verbal signs for the purpose, which after the learning of language-gifting, are perhaps more maternal than they would have been without it.

Robin Dunbar (1996) has shown the importance of grooming among pre-hominid apes for the development of language. He also says that the grooming among pairs was tracked by other apes to the extent that everyone in the group knew who groomed whom. If instead of regarding it as neutral, we look at grooming as nurturing, a service that is performed by one for the other, we can see that these nurturing relations in a community of apes or pre-hominids would be possible precursors of the much more complex gifting among humans. Dunbar proposes that language is *vocal grooming*. Human maternal nurturing would give rise to the possibility of more general and more complex vocal grooming/nurturing. [30] Dunbar mentions the important pre-hominid capacity to recognize third-party relations among others in the group and track them.[31] Even if the pre-hominids used their knowledge of these relations for 'Machiavellian' purposes, as Dunbar and others contend, they would have had to understand their positive aspects first in order to use them in a manipulative way. The ability to track gift relations among others in the group would be an important precursor to recognizing gift relations in our surroundings and to finding them on other planes of reality, such as the plane of vocal sound, where we track what gives to what. Recognizing the gift relation in the external environment is not so different from tracking who gives what to whom because, indeed, each of us is external regarding all others.

I believe that *quid pro quo* exchange itself is the problem not just capitalism, not just the market or money, though these definitely complicate the situation. In fact, exchange is seen as a completely normal and natural, possibly even species-specific behavior.[32] Instead, I hope to show, especially in the second half of the book, that market exchange itself is an artifact

---

30   '... the most plausible starting point for the evolution of language is as a bonding device based on the exchange of social information concerning relationships within the network' (Dunbar 1998: 99). I am saying that the bonding device is made by giving and receiving word-gifts. The bonding derives from nurturing, from the capacity of mother-child giving and receiving to create bonds.

31   'Given that primate social life is characterized by the ability of the animals to recognize relationships between third parties – Jim's relationship with John as well as John's relationship with me – there is a real sense in which the social complexity of a group rises exponentially as its physical size increases' (Dunbar 1996: 63) The tremendous increase in third party relationships that individuals needed to keep track of influenced the increase in brain size among our ancestors and it had 'something to do with the need to weld large groups together' (64). That is, bonding appears to be a result of the relationships and of tracking them.

32   Many experiments test whether chimpanzees and other animals practice 'tit-for-tat' contingent reciprocity, for example Melis, Hare and Tomasello 2007.

of language, of representation and of the otherwise positive creation of a verbal gift plane, which on occasion substitutes for and supplements material gifting. Exchange among humans can probably coexist with unilateral gifting when it involves only symbolic or occasional trades, but when it becomes the social nexus, exchange overtakes, exploits and devalues gift giving. At the same time, the exchange paradigm eliminates the gift paradigm in the explanation of the world. One symptom of this is that we use the word 'exchange' too broadly to cover what is actually turn-taking in unilateral giving.[33] This is a usage that could be relatively easy to correct and correcting it would have far-reaching consequences. Such problems of naming are quite common in academia (see, for example, Fox Keller 2010). Since 'gift' and 'exchange' are terms in common language, the challenge to distinguish them from each other is even more important.

Nevertheless, unilateral giving to satisfy others' needs has a very different relational logic from giving in order to cause the receiver to satisfy one's own need in return. Unilateral giving is transitive and other-oriented, implying the value of the other, while bilateral, contingent giving – *exchange* – is intransitive and ego-oriented, more 'Machiavellian'.[34] Even though objects pass from hand to hand in exchange, they are not gifts: they cancel each other out. Using the word 'exchange' to describe turn-taking, or alternated and repeated gifting, hides the specific logic and implications of the unilateral gift.

Over the last decades, much has been written about gift-giving, mainly following Marcel Mauss's three-step logic of giving, receiving and giving back. In fact, Mauss sees the obligation to give back as the basic social bond. I say instead that giving and receiving, without the obligation to give back, are at the basis of human relations. Unilateral giving to satisfy a need of the other is the basis, the first move, the opening gambit of communication, which can be elaborated socially in many ways, only one of which is the obligatory return gift. Unilateral giving/receiving can be repeated by the same person again and again, as does happen in mother-child nurturing. It can also be repeated using many different kinds of gifts and services: the mother gives food but also cleans, bathes and clothes the child, puts h:er to bed, holds h:er when she cries, shows h:er the birdy at the window, etc. All this is direct gifting care. Within

---

33   As we shall see, considering dialogue as an exchange hides its character as turn-taking verbal gifting (for one example see the otherwise very interesting Lyra 2012).

34   See ch. 2 for a discussion of whether exchange is transitive.

this 'envelope' there is much mutual contingent responsiveness, which, however, is not *quid pro quo* exchange. Even very young children respond to their caregivers and vice-versa their caregivers respond to them. This mutual responsiveness is not an exchange of equivalents and we will not use the word 'exchange' to describe it. Rather it is turn-taking, i.e. alternately giving and receiving.

A new term has arisen among researchers regarding protoconversational interactions between mothers and babies: 'serve and return', taken evidently from the game of tennis (Harvard Center on the Developing Child 2009: 1). The mother 'serves' and the child 'returns the serve', and vice-versa. The repetition or imitation of unilateral giving by both sides is suggested by these terms (and occurs in these games), but it is significant that the idea of nurturing has been eliminated, as it is in the other examples listed above: input and output, agent and patient, etc. Even though the term 'service' is used, the gift initiative is removed from its need-satisfying sense, and placed in the more neutral game context.[35] However, it is worth noting that at least these researchers have avoided the market-based term 'exchange'. In fact, economic exchange only begins to be understood by children at around three to four years of age (Berti and Bombi 1988), while full understanding of commercial practice may not develop until adolescence.

The relations of solidarity that arise through unilateral giving and receiving make it more likely that the receivers will want the needs of the givers to be satisfied as well, so everyone takes gift initiatives and both (or all) givers and receivers find themselves together 'passing the gifts on' in a gifting community.[36] Now in capitalist patriarchy, we are often

---

35 'Growth-promoting relationships are based on the child's continuous give-and-take ("serve and return" interaction) with a human partner who provides what nothing else in the world can offer – experiences that are individualized to the child's unique personality style; that build on his or her own interests, capabilities, and initiative; that shape the child's self-awareness; and that stimulate the growth of his or her heart and mind' (Harvard University, Center on the Developing Child Working Paper 1). Young children develop in an environment of relationships (2009).

36 Darcia Narvaez tells us of the multiple caregivers in hunter-gatherer communities in which the social brain developed. 'Ancestral childrearing practices include extensive, on-demand breastfeeding, constant touch, responsiveness to needs of the child, natural childbirth, and multiple adult caregivers ... When any of these are missing, child outcomes may be negatively affected ... The characteristic of multiple caregivers may be the most fundamental component because it supports the mother in carrying out all the rest of the practices'. (2012: 197). This kind of parenting ensures that 'mammalian emotion systems are properly "wired" and integrated for social relationships' (*ibid.* 201).

nostalgic as adults for childhood, perhaps for a childhood with multiple caregivers that only 'might have been', and that would have stimulated the more complete development of our neuronal pathways and brain architecture (Narvaez 2012).[37]

Because of repeated economic crises and other proofs of dysfunction, there are now many initiatives and theories proposing changes to capitalism and the market. Although I agree that transitions are necessary and gentle transitions are advisable, I believe that exchange itself is the problem, greatly magnified by the market and money. The solution cannot be an improved market or a kinder or more spiritual capitalism as some suggest.[38]

The ultimate goal of economic social change needs to be a moneyless, marketless society with mothering and language, i.e. material and linguistic communication, *not* exchange, as its cornerstones.[39] This is the goal that can inform radical successive approximations of alternatives to capitalism. Thus, for example, if alternative currencies or even time banks have as a final goal the creation of a mothering economy beyond the market, they can be seen as deep alternatives; if not, they remain within the paradigm of exchange, capitalism, and patriarchy because they still embrace and affirm the exchange logic.

Many postmodern thinkers, following Derrida, claim that unilateral giving is impossible. Others, like David Graeber (2011)[40] consider it

---

37 '... Ancestral parenting practices" mentioned previously build a brain that is fully prepared for deep sociality, garnering great pleasure from social relationships. In contrast, when a child is raised with greater isolation from others as in modern Western childrearing (e.g. not physically in contact with others throughout the first years of life, not breastfed for years), the brain is not wired up as well for social relationships and must learn to find pleasure in ways outside of deep social relationships' (Ibid.).

38 Among others see Luigino Bruni (2012), who makes a case for gift-giving as a supplement to the market and Riane Eisler's (2007) caring economy, which emphasizes the importance of carework within the framework of the exchange economy.

39 If language, which is at least as widespread as mothering, *is* based on giving and receiving, it would have a similarly strong influence on human behavior even if we didn't realize it.

40 Here the unilateral 'mothering/being-mothered' piece of the puzzle is missing. Not acknowledging it leaves the field open for the easy installation of debt and obligation as primary. Graeber quotes Satapatha Brahmana 1.7.12, 1-6 'In being born every being born is born as debt owed to the gods, the saints, the Fathers and to men'. The authors of this ancient text also ignored the motherer. Was s:he ignored just *because* no debt was owed to h:er? Graeber contrasts monetized exchange with barter, which he says did not exist. I contrast it not with barter but

peripheral while debt is central. I believe this is because most philosophers until now have not been mothers and have not given the importance to mothering that a practitioner would give. Indeed, they have rejected mothering for their own identities (see 1.15 below on masculation). They have questioned, problematized and denied the possibility of the unilateral gift,[41] thus effectively eliminating its use as a fundamental factor for a theory of knowledge. They are victims of what I believe is the major defect of Western exchange-based philosophy, the attempt to think through the world without including the creative structural importance of mothering and being mothered.

This is an important lacuna because the concept and the logic of unilateral maternal giving and receiving can be seen as the answer to many of the problems that have plagued Western philosophy, including the philosophy of language. Taking the commonplace unilateral maternal gift into account changes everything and puts the mother-child experience back into philosophy and epistemology, from which it has been removed for centuries. This change at the level of ideology will allow us to become conscious of the vast social need that the gift economy can satisfy and it is is crucial in paving the way for urgent practical changes.

The new infant psychology is important in breaking through the patriarchal barrier to knowledge, but it has not yet linked the gift economy to mothering and to language, which is what I am trying to do here.

Many people realize our society needs to change course but many also believe that there is no real alternative to the market, because they think the market is a product of human nature. I want to tell a different new/old story by showing that language is modeled on maternal gift-giving, while market exchange is a distortion of gift-giving *and* of language with money functioning as a material 'word'. Both language and the market would therefore be social products but the market exists as a kind of distorted language or backwards communication. This makes it necessary to understand first what undistorted language and functioning communication may be and then how their distortion in the market affects us all.

Having clarified these themes, I propose that the many oppressions that

---

with gift giving, which has to exist necessarily in all societies at least in mothering, and I am saying, in the structure and practice of language as well.

41   The French school of the gift economy centered on the *MAUSS Revue* does not accept the unilateral maternal gift as primary. Alain Caillè, Jacques Godbout, Serge Latouche, Marcel Henaff and many others are part of this movement. Although many writers mention it, unilateral giving is not considered structural to the gift economy. Lewis Hyde (2007|1983|) is a partial exception.

permeate our world can be understood in terms of the oppression of gift-giving by exchange. In fact, there is an ancient and ongoing struggle between the gift economy and the exchange economy, which until now the exchange economy has won. Some of its weapons have been: discrediting and dismissing the gift economy, making it invisible while taking from it, creating scarcity where abundance should have been, forcing some groups to give while others take, hiding the nefarious taking while enhancing and over-valuing the successful takers, etc.

We have recently seen the cold war between capitalism and communism. Both systems are patriarchal but capitalism, which prevailed, inhabits the field of exchange while communism, at least in theory, espoused a distribution of goods to needs. We have also seen what some call the continuing war between men and women. In fact, the patriarchal construction of gender as the exploitation of women's gifts and services is linked to the same type of exploitation of women (and everyone) by the market. Thus, the oppression of women and mothers is connected to the oppression of the gift economy by the market.[42] We should also mention the 'war within' individuals' hearts and minds, an internal struggle between gift and exchange, which in the West and increasingly globally is being won by exchange as supported by market ideology.

The many movements against the oppressions, of women, children and the elderly, of races, of religions, of workers, of indigenous peoples, of the physically and the mentally ill, of the Global South, of Nature, can unite if the exploitation of the maternal economy of giving by capitalism and patriarchy is recognized as the oppressive process at origin of their diverse problems.

1.5 We need a new definition of the economy

The economy of the economists is a false slice of life, carved out from a wider context that is considered merely 'aneconomic'. By looking at mothering as economic, and 'free' as a mode of distribution of goods to needs (which has lost its mode of production due to coexistence with the market), we not only give value to gift-giving but reframe the exchange economy as well. The market is no longer monolithic but has to divide the field of the creation of value and the distribution of goods with an

---

42   There are also gift economies with 'big men' (Sahlins 1963) that we Westerners
      would consider patriarchal. These have been used to frame the gift economy of the
      internet, particularly the 'hacker' economy.

economy that is even more widespread and is a powerful and intimate part of the everyday life of all. Where there was only one economic logic – *do ut des* – now there are two. The prior logic of unilateral *do ut accipiatis* (I give so that you may receive) as such has been acknowledged. Giving is a transitive process, which gives value to the other,while exchange, i.e. giving in order to receive an equivalent, is intransitive, ego-oriented and gives value not to the other but to the self.

Focusing on the theme of gift-giving/receiving puts economic exchange into a different light, allowing us to see any *do ut des* exchange as a transformation or reversal of gift giving while, as we will see in Part Two, monetized exchange can be viewed as an originally linguistic and conceptual process that has become distorted when placed 'back' on the material plane. Many aspects of our thinking about language and life are deeply influenced by the distorted processes of monetized exchange.

What we need now is a paradigm shift as a way of bringing forward the value and the values of gift-giving and receiving. In this book I try to justify the shift and to sketch what many philosophical (linguistic and epistemological) issues look like from the perspective of the gift paradigm.

These issues have been dealt with by patriarchal academia over many centuries but because the thinkers were rarely, if ever, practicing direct maternal gift-giving themselves, they seem to have missed this fundamental piece of a puzzle, which is not just academic but is the systemic source of the dire problems we have today.

The market requires and creates scarcity for the many. As a way of life it is much less satisfying than gift-giving. It functions according to patriarchal competition for domination and it therefore competes with the maternal gift economy. The gift economy is cooperative, other-oriented and life-enhancing. Unfortunately, the scarcity in which it is presently forced to operate often makes it self-sacrificial. This is not a defect or even a characteristic of gift-giving per se, but a consequence of the depleted context in which it is taking place.[43]

In its struggle to dominate the gift economy and capture its gifts, the market creates the scarcity that in economic textbooks it is said to presuppose. Indeed, it creates the problem to which it pretends to be the solution. By diverting the flow of gifts from the many to the few, the market creates the scarcity that keeps the many subservient, dependent

---

43   The same holds for altruism. In fact, other-centered acts can be free of cost, given an appropriate context. Calculating their importance by how much the giver sacrifices is applying the criteria of exchange to altruism.

for survival on employment in the market system. If too much abundance accrues in the system, it is wasted on trillion dollar (non-nurturing!) wars but also on symbolic excesses, from jewelry and monuments to power to costly political conventions and campaigns.

1.6 The Mauss trap

Unilateral giving sets up the need-satisfying transitivity that is the basis of the gift economy in the sense of material communication or 'provisioning'. Care-giving need-satisfaction, which is a practice that is socially allocated to the (usually female) motherers, is the basis of human life. It may be interpreted as a first step or an opening gambit in 'gift exchange' but this perspective does not acknowledge that the unilateral step is already meaningful on its own. The maternal gift initiative is unilateral.

Even Marcel Mauss mainly omitted unilateral giving from his discussion. He concentrated on the logic of giving, receiving and giving back, which some have playfully called 'the Mauss trap'. However, although he did not elaborate upon it, Mauss did briefly mention 'objects of consumption and common sharing' regarding which he 'found no trace of exchange' (Mauss 1990[1923]:80). However, it is his description of gift economies, as based on the three-step 'trap' logic of giving, receiving and giving back, that has become the standard for Western academic thinking about giving ever since.

Not only is there free 'provisioning' done mostly by women in gift economies as well as in exchange economies, and not only does mothering require much unilateral giving in gift economies as well as in our own market economy, but as we have been saying, the simpler first giving and receiving step of the three-step logic already has a number of implications, without which the 'giving back' aspect would be meaningless.[44]

The initiative to satisfy the need of the other transmits value to the other by implication. In market exchange, giving back an equivalent of what has been given makes the second gift initiative contingent on the first, which alters its character so that the value it transmitted to the receiver by implication is cancelled or changed. In 'symbolic gift exchange', the receiver is obligated to give a return gift, and thus, to give value to the previous giver. The obligation itself diminishes the value that is implied of the receiver

---

44   It would float in the air making necessary the philosophers' (for example Quine's) 'bootstrapping'! (see Carey 2009).

and of the giver, and it is for this reason perhaps that in 'gift exchange' the second giver often adds more onto h:er gift, implying the value of the other by becoming h:erself a 'free' giver.[45]

The logic of exchange, like that of giving, is a relational logic. The relations it mediates may be more negative, because of the constraint to pay back. In the context of the market, the third step, the necessity of giving back an equivalent, makes debt and obligation the basis of the relationship (Douglas 1990: vii; Graeber 2011). The obligation to pay becomes a material, legal and psychological necessity; it can also transform into guilt at not having paid. Both obligation and guilt take the place of a simple response of gratitude as typically happens in the maternal dyad. They also carry with them a necessity of recognition of the giver by the receiver that is not present with the unilateral gift. Moreover, the constraint of giving back can put the giver in a position of power over the receiver. Instead, where giving and receiving is mainly unilateral and egalitarian, the relationship that arises is already positive, one of mutuality, trust and conscious participation, which, as far as children are concerned, we can call reciprocal or shared 'altercentrism' following Stein Bråten. Where everyone does this, mutual multilateral bonding can take place among individuals and on a wide scale.

I believe we are all experts in gauging the relations between gift and exchange in our daily lives without even realizing we are doing it. We know whether others are grateful or resentful, whether they feel obligated towards us or we should feel obligated towards them, whether the seemingly unilateral gift is, in this occasion, a hidden exchange. There is a whole realm of feelings of this sort in capitalist patriarchy of which we are perhaps only semiconscious. Even if they do not always move us directly, these feelings influence us, make us friendly or suspicious, and alter the tenor of our days.

Little children respond to others in creative ways and they also take the initiative in giving to them, instigating mutuality. If we want to get beyond the market filter, we really should not read this as exchange. Instead, it is simply turn-taking: creative reception and response that is imitative in taking the initiative, *prior* to the logic of exchange.

Thus, language itself can be understood as based not on exchange but on taking turns in unilateral creative giving and receiving. Each satisfies the others' cognitive and communicative needs. What appears to anthropologists as the constraint of gift exchange in indigenous cultures might be bet-

---

45   Unfortunately this extra gift has been transformed by capitalism into interest on loans.

ter understood in the light of the giving-receiving frame as an invitation to material dialogue. If we ground our concept of gift-giving in maternal need satisfaction, we can see that symbolic gift exchange is also derived from satisfying needs, albeit symbolic ones.[46] Gift 'exchange' does not stand alone, nor does market exchange.

The use of the term 'exchange' for language is misplaced. One person speaks and the other listens. One person writes and the other reads. In dialogue, the listener also takes the initiative, repeating the process, taking turns in becoming the speaker, giving h:er words *unilaterally* to the listener, who creatively receives them. Similarly if the reader writes a reply in her turn, the fact that there is not a constraint to reply does not mean there is no relation between speaker and listener, writer and reader. The relation is already created by the unilateral satisfaction of the cognitive and communicative needs of one person by the other who is acting in a linguistically nurturing way, using 'word-gifts'. When the receiver does reply, s:he is taking the initiative to give unilaterally again, as a linguistic giver, satisfying the cognitive and communicative needs of the other, who is now a (creative) receiver.[47]

Understanding language as the satisfaction of the needs of the other with word gifts creates a frame that is quite different from language as the communication and understanding of the speaker's 'intention,' which is the common interpretation of psychologists and philosophers. Satisfying others' needs by gifting is other-oriented while expressing an intention, which the other must grasp, focuses on the mental activity of the intender (Grice 1989). Moreover, the understanding of the intention as an attempt to influ-

---

46   In the years that I have worked on this subject it has become clear to me that many aspects of the culture and the economy are also influenced by the existence of gifting at the level of language. For example, 'symbolic gift exchange' can be seen as a custom influenced by dialogic linguistic gifting structures. It is because we are trying to explain human behaviors without the gift in mothering *and* in language that we do not succeed in fully understanding what we are doing.

47   'Growth-promoting relationships are based on the child's continuous give-and-take ("serve and return" interaction) with a human partner who provides what nothing else in the world can offer – experiences that are individualized to the child's unique personality style; that build on his or her own interests, capabilities, and initiative; that shape the child's self-awareness; and that stimulate the growth of his or her heart and mind ... Even the development of a child's brain architecture depends on the establishment of these relationships' (Harvard 1). If it is the case that need-satisfying 'give and take' between motherer and child creates the relationships and the brain architecture, laying down the neural pathways necessary for the child's development, wouldn't giving and receiving word-gifts have a similar effect?

ence the other, to alter h:er beliefs and the content of h:er consciousness frames speech or writing as a cost-benefit and manipulative rather than a nurturing interaction (Sperber and Wilson 1995).

1.7 Paradoxes: Recognition and invisibility

The focus of everyone on exchange and money causes a serious real-life paradox: in order to be recognized, gifts have to be exchanged for money, thus ceasing to be gifts. This is what happens with movements for wages for housework and the integration of care work into the market.[48] Paradoxically, free giving does not seem to exist as a real economic alternative, but only as an adjunct to exchange that has been overlooked, perhaps because it has been mainly women who have been doing it. That is, the devaluing of gift-giving is seen as due to the devaluing of women and not vice-versa. The resolution of the paradox seems to be the monetary recognition of women and their care work, a recognition, which, however, would cancel its gift character. The recognition that is lacking is the social recognition of the positive value of free gifts and at the same time of the function they have in maintaining the whole negative, rapacious system.

We do not realize that by giving to a system of exploitation that takes our gifts and transforms them into profit, we feed and continue to create a parasitic mechanism of which all of us are to some extent the hosts. The parasite denies that the host is the alternative, and makes it appear that the parasite itself is necessary for the host's very existence.

Recent books on gift exchange, like M. Henaff's *The Price of Truth* (2010), consider the motivation for gift 'exchange' to be recognition of the giver. To me, it seems that the individual recognition of gift-givers cannot take place appropriately without the recognition of the place of gift-giving in society at large, beyond individuals, the recognition of the mothering host.

Derrida questioned the very possibility of giving consciously and visibly without the gift's turning into an exchange.[49] Actually, the paradox de-

---

48 I recognize the importance of improving women's lives within the system. However I believe that, without a critical understanding of the paradox, the improvement masks the fundamental systemic gift-taking, which then is also displaced to other arenas of commodification of previously free resources.

49 Perhaps it was Derrida's personal experience with his own mother (complicated by Freudian interpretations) that stood in the way of his recognition of mothering as gift-giving/receiving. In fact, the particular autobiographical experiences of imperfect mothering often stand in the way of the generalization of the prin-

pends on a lack of generalization. Indeed, if everyone were doing gift-giving there would be no particular merit in doing it; no particular ego-reward would accrue, so unilateral gift actions would be understood as such, not as exchanges. But this is, in fact, what happens already in housework and child care. A large number of people, mostly women, are doing unilateral giving and they are unrecognized!

Something similar happens also with language where gift-giving remains invisible though it is fundamental. Neither speaker nor listener, writer nor reader recognizes language as verbal giving (so indeed speakers/writers would qualify as unilateral givers!).

The work of unilateral gift-giving is discounted by patriarchal and exchange-based thinking, explaining away the motivation of giving as 'maternal instinct' or self abnegation. 'Reproductive' work is even ironically negatively 'recognized' by remunerating it, but less than 'productive' work. That is, gifting is treated by the market as worth-less! This is part of a widespread social denigration of mothering and of the possibility of its generalization as matricentrism and, indeed, of matriarchy.[50] Contrary to Derrida, I believe that unilateral gift-giving is very widespread and even commonplace. It is unrecognized as such because we are living in an exchange economy that contradicts and exploits gifts, while validating itself.

In fact, the maternal gift economy may be the 'transcendental signified', which Derrida so influentially refuted. Restoring mothering/being mothered as invisible-in-plain-view, original and necessary unilateral giving and receiving 'outside the text' lets us see that it establishes the first gifting texts and is the material loom on which all their (self-similar!) patterns are woven. Mothering/being mothered forms a primordial structure. It is the communicative, economic and cognitive structure of which all other structures are elaborations.[51] Even Derrida's (1980) appeal to play leads us to protoconversation, not a unified and single center, but an interactive unilateral turn-taking, giving/receiving, delightful process of dialogue[52]

---

ciple for many people. People who have been motherers at least know what they were trying to do and the challenges they faced. Citing Garcia-Marquez's title, we could call it 'mothering in a time of cholera'.

50   Now seen not as mother rule, a mirror image of patriarchy, but as an egalitarian society based on maternal values (Goettner-Abendroth 2013; Sanday 2002).

51   The conception of infants as passive and egocentric masks the true interactive nature of the early gift process.

52   Researchers have found protoconversation among mothers and children in many different parts of the globe (Bråten 1998), so it appears to be a maternal cultural universal.

(dia-logocentrism?), while Phallogocentrism concentrates on the One and is not internally dialogic.

According to Derrida's paradox (that giving cannot be recognized because it thereby becomes exchange), the lack of recognition would seem to 'raise' mothering to the status of a 'pure' gift. However, this gift takes place in a context in which money and exchange value are used in the very process of recognition itself and where they combine with patriarchy to lay down the norm, with the result that unilateral giving becomes invisible, unrecognizable. The hegemony of exchange penalizes the mothering gift economy (making it 'pay'), hiding it and depleting it of the meaning it is repeatedly giving unilaterally.

If everyone were practicing gift-giving wouldn't that imply that the society itself must already be operating in many ways beyond the exchange paradigm? We can indeed give value to that possibility even now, by recognizing maternal gift-giving as an already existing economic alternative to the biopathic market. And suppose we were to find that there are other widespread practices of unilateral giving in society already? This would validate the possibility of generalizing the gift economy in practice.

Characterizing language as gift-giving does just this. Language is a widespread social practice. Recognizing its virtual gift character validates the possibility and importance of a practical material gift economy.

Much of the economic thinking of the feminist movement short-circuits the revolutionary potential of the gift economy by insisting on the integration of women into the market. While laudable in the short term, attempts to give monetary value to the caring economy (Eisler 2007), hide the deep alternative character of the gift economy. We have identified the concept of value with monetary value, but the gift economy has a different kind of value beyond the market (we will be discussing various kinds of value, including gift value in the second half of the book). While it is extremely important to ease the struggle for survival of millions of women (and men) caught in the scarcity created by the market economy, caring economics as envisioned within the market framework would be better formulated as a transitional stage towards a free economy based on caring outside that framework. In the nineteenth century many people wanted to help the slaves have better lives, better food and housing, but there were others, the Abolitionists, who wanted an end to the institution of slavery (Richard Wolf 2013). It is this kind of radical institutional change that needs to be the goal of the feminist movement.

It is important to reconceptualize gift-giving as economic and to discover it in language, because it is the key to understanding our species as *homo donans* but also because the commodification of gift-giving often appears

to be the solution when instead it is the problem. Finding ways to com-
mercialize and take free gifts has been the *modus operandi* of capitalism.
In recent years the privatization and commercialization of the previously
free gifts of water and seeds, and indigenous knowledge and practices,
has diverted the gifts of the South towards Northern corporations, transforming the gifts into profits for Monsanto, Suez, Vivendi, Halliburton,
Merck. Moreover, by moving jobs to the South, the corporations have created hordes of unemployed in the North whose only access to the market is
through drugs, and then in the North we have hunted them down in the war
on drugs and incarcerated them so that they are supported by taxpayers in
the prison-industrial complex. This commodification of the jobless is not
new, it is a variation on the trafficking of poor people for slavery and sex.

There is also the commodification of government, in that the 'democratically elected' representatives are for sale to corporations for considerable sums of money, and after they finish their terms in government,
they go to work for those same corporations.

At a more capillary level, advertising and propaganda have monetarily
recognized many of the gift aspects of housework and childcare, transforming them into commodities by manipulating the consumer choices even of
children. Academia, too, has gotten its pay-offs through teaching market
research and consumer psychology to corporations, turning gifts of language into profit. Like the other previously free gifts of the commons that
have been commodified in the patriarchal capitalist economy, such as water,
land, forests and even air (in debt for nature swaps (Isla 2007), the gifts of
language have been commodified before we even knew they were gifts.

The key of the maternal gift is made invisible and unavailable both by
ignoring it and by privatizing and commercializing it ('giving' it commercial value) and it is still missing as a model though it is everywhere. The
problem is not that the unilateral maternal gift might be the transcendental
signified but that it is overwhelmingly exploited.[53]

The dire poverty created by the market makes the market appear as the
only salvation, the only way to procure the means of giving.

The maternal gift is not even recognized by the movements for alternatives that are now spreading in both the Northern and Southern hemispheres.
The movements for the commons, demonetization, degrowth, wiki and free
knowledge, peer-to-peer are all moving towards an alignment with the ma-

---

53   Derrida's fascination with the (unilateral) gift and his rejection of the tran-
     scendental signified are two poles of the same binary. The solution of the par-
     adox is political.

ternal gift in language and in life. However, neither they nor the gift economy movement, nor the feminist movement itself, recognize the connection of gifting with mothering. In part this is due to the view of men as non-maternal, non-nurturing, and partly it is due to matriphobia and misogyny. Perhaps this book can add some decisive elements to their discussions.

Perhaps it can also add something to the mother movement (motherhood-initiative.org). Even motherers themselves may not recognize their own gift-giving practice as important, not only because society undervalues them but because in capitalism they often live in scarcity and, like everyone else, they focus on market exchange as the way to abundance. Instead, mothering gift-giving should be seen as a life pattern, which is repeated at many levels, a pattern which is largely responsible for the success of the species.

1.8 Host and parasite

In feminism in the West, we criticize the binary oppositions between male and female, mind and body, spirit and matter, but we do not usually even see the divisions we have made between exchange and gift-giving because we do not even recognize that the gift exists. By bringing forward gift-giving as a general principle perhaps we can address the other binaries in new ways, as locations on a spectrum, variations on a theme.

Gift and exchange are not actually binaries. Exchange is an outgrowth of gift-giving, which has become parasitic upon it. On the other hand, because it has been deprived of its mode of production, gift-giving for the time being is dependent on exchange for the goods that are the means of giving. We will be discussing both logics throughout the book and their function in life, in economics, in language, in meaning and in hope for the future.

The question arises: are there more than these two basic economic logics? Certainly, each of the two is elaborated in many ways and their interactions provide many variations. I believe, however, that until the situation of parasitism is recognized and relieved, each of them will be deeply influenced by the presence of the other, impeding the development of independent alternatives. There may be other logics that I have not seen or that have not yet developed. For me, the challenge has been to make the logic of gift-giving visible and to give it value. That is, to reveal the 'host' as an already existing very widespread alternative to exchange, so that exchange, the parasite, cannot occupy the whole relational horizon.

There are several additional reasons for the invisibility of gift-giving that we need to keep in mind. One simple reason I already mentioned is that we use the same word 'exchange' for both giving and exchange. For example, we use 'a communicative exchange' or 'an exchange of words, ideas, opinions', to describe what is really turn-taking in altercentric verbal giving. Or we consider giving as only a failed or partial exchange. Mainly, though, we overextend the term 'exchange' because we do not dignify material gift-giving and receiving by considering it important and communicative in and of itself. We also do this because communication seems to occur only with signs (which do not seem to be given or to have to do with satisfying needs of others).

Instead, the constitution of bodies themselves has to come from the material transmission of primarily non-sign goods, services, 'energies' from bodies, which give and do, to other bodies, which have needs that are before and beyond signs, even though they may be accompanied by signs. This is 'material communication' and it must take place if the child is to survive at all. The parasitism of exchange upon gift-giving consists in the commodification and exploitation of gifts of all kinds: the gifts of nature, culture, labor and love that are taken not only by individuals but are made to nurture the system itself. It has been estimated that women's free labor in the home would add enormously to the GDP of the US, as well as in other countries.[54] This is a measure of the gifts women are giving to the market as a whole, the extent to which housewives nurture the parasite.

1.9 Re-conceiving the child and the motherer

Infant researcher Andrew Meltzoff declares:

> *The recognition of self-other equivalences is the starting point for social cognition, not its culmination.* Given this facile self-other mapping, input from social encounters is more interpretable than supposed by Freud, Skinner, and Piaget. Infants have a storehouse of knowledge on which to draw: they can use the self as a framework for understanding the subjectivity of others. *Homo sapiens* begin the journey of social cognition armed with a common code, a *lingua franca,* that is more fundamental than spoken language. We are not born social isolates. We are fundamentally connected to others right from the start, because they are seen as being 'like me'. This allows rapid and special learning from people (Meltzoff, Kuhl, Movellan, & Sejnowski, 2009). I can learn about myself and potential pow-

---

54 Athough the monetary value of unwaged labor in the home is notoriously difficult to calculate, Marilyn Waring's breakthrough work (1988) made counting women's work an important feminist goal. Recently, Ironmonger and Soupourmas (2012:24), using output rather than input based estimates, proposed that includng the 'Gross Household Product' in the estimate could increase the US GDP by as much as 70% .

ers by watching the consequences of your acts, and can imbue your acts with felt meaning based on my own self-experience. As children's self-experience broadens, their appreciation of others' minds and behavior is enriched and refined. This propels infants beyond what they see or know innately. Social cognition rests on the fact that you are 'like me', differentiable from me, but nonetheless enough like me to become my role model and I your interpreter. (Meltzoff 2013:69)

Although the researchers in this new branch of study have broken through many of the old ways of thinking, they have not recognized the importance of material nurturing/being nurtured as a key for epistemology. However, if we do add nurture to this 'like me' cognition, we can see that the child can understand the interaction of nurturing through the 'like me' bridge. The nurturer is 'like h:er' and s:he is like the nurturer.

The child learns both perspectives of the nurturing interaction: that of the giver and that of the receiver, and both are positively emotionally charged. At the same time, s:he is also registering this experience unconsciously with h:er mirror neurons.

Recent studies on these neurons (Rizzolati and Arbib 1998; Gallese et al 2007) suggest that children as well as adults unconsciously simulate what others are experiencing, so we can infer that infants in some sense *know* what their mothers are experiencing when they are giving to them and vice-versa. Thus, children would know what it is for their motherers to give and the motherer would know what it is for the child to receive. Each would also simulate the response to the other's experience of the other and of knowing/experiencing what each other knows/experiences. That is, the motherer would simulate the child's satisfaction at receiving and the child would simulate the motherer's satisfaction at giving. Moreover, there is kinetic mapping in which the child projects h:er own body map onto the postures, attitudes and muscle tones of the other's body recognizing them there, finding h:erself as 'like h:er' kinetically in the giving and receiving roles. The perspectives of giving and of receiving are available to the child at a very early age. Thus, the material care that children receive and their response to it are an important part of their early sociality and of their knowledge and relations. Material communication – nurturing – is at the same time also interpersonal social communication.

Babies are not born passive but are eminently responsive social creatures. As Colwyn Trevarthen says, 'infant communication, in spite of its cognitive and representational limitations is manifestly inter-mental, inter-subjective or inter-personal' (Trevarthen 1979).

Most studies on mirror neurons do not focus directly on nurturing/receiving nurture, though some do explore eating and drinking or grasping or even giving and taking (Gallese and Lakoff 2005).[55] Perhaps this is due to the fact that experiments with mirror neurons cannot be performed on humans, but even chimpanzee nurturing/receiving nurture would be revealing.

Stein Bråten with characteristic insight, touches briefly on the subject when he comments 'we should expect, for example, that in humans give-mirror neurons should be activated during own giving and while watching the other give and that grasp-mirror neurons be activated during own grasping and while watching the other grasp' (2002: 291).

Exploring the mirror neuron activity of infant and mother during nurturing would let us see the child experiencing the motherer's giving at the same time s:he is receiving and vice-versa. In fact, Bråten proposed to show how 'infants can learn from caregivers and afford care to others in virtue of bodily intersubjective communion enabled by alter-centric participation'.

Much feminist debate has been about whether mothering is biologically or socially motivated, essential instinct or social performance. I will discuss these issues more thoroughly in the next chapter and throughout the book. For now the recent studies of infancy can give us a new view of the mother-child interaction.[56] For the infancy researchers, the solution broached to Nature vs Nurture is that the infant is biologically programmed for sociality. S:he elicits the mother's social responses and learns from 'altercentric participation' (Bråten's term) in h:er interactions with h:er motherer, which, as we have been saying, are most importantly, h:er motherer's caregiving and h:er own receiving and giving. Motherers' and childrens' interactions in rhythmic and emotionally charged protoconversations, games and rituals, establish ongoing narrative structures, contours or 'envelopes' of experience. Since the motherer was once a child, some part of h:er own 'altercentric participatory' childhood learning must feed in to h:er own mothering at least unconsciously, and the same happened with h:er motherer before h:er. S:he learns from h:er child and perhaps can recall at least some of what s:he herself learned as a mothered child (as well as from the mothering s:he has witnessed among others).

---

55 Mirror neurons respond particularly to facial expressions and movements of hands and feet. Hands are also particularly prominent in nurturing, both in giving and in receiving. Although hand gestures, especially 'grasping' have been investigated by mirror neuron researchers (Rizzolati and Arbib 1998, Gallese and Lakoff 2005) , the connection with nurturing has not yet been made.

56 It is significant that women's own perception of their interactions with their infants have not been considered as the valid source of information on the subject. How many mothers must have noticed that their newborns stuck out their tongues in imitation before Meltzoff 'discovered' it? See the books of Demeter Press for women's own voices on mothering.

1.10 Protoconversation

The recent research into newborn and infant sociality has important implications for our concept not only of what childhood is, but also for a concept of non-essentialist but engaged mothering. That is, the motherer is not giving 'selfless' unilateral care to a passive and egocentric 'object'. In fact, s:he is interacting with a highly responsive social being. S:he often has to refresh or relearn altercentric turn-taking giving receiving, beyond exchange[57] from h:er interactions with h:er child. Women's gender role expectations include the capacity for doing this, while patriarchal men's usually do not. Nor do expectations for the buyer and seller roles of the market.

In spite of the important clarification of parts of this early experience by the infancy researchers, I believe that maternal material nurturing still does not receive enough attention. The satisfaction of the child's material needs is itself altercentric gifting interaction. This is what makes it the first human gifting *economic* communication, as well as the link between world and words, the first template of meaning. It is comprised of face-to-face detailed interactive care but also of the motherer's care of the material environment surrounding the child and of h:er procurement and preparation of the gifts to be given: food, clothing etc.

There is a great deal of unilateral care given by the motherer even if some of it is co-creative with the child. The motherer also cares about the child from afar (see Ruddick 1995 for caring about), while doing other domestic work and taking care of other children, or even working in the market to pay the childcare worker. Or s:he plans how to manage her life and daily activities to include the child. The child does not do this in return.

For the child the initiative comes from the outside, from 'reality' (and the motherer knows it because s:he *is* it!). Motherers not only satisfy needs directly, they provide the gift of a home environment for the children and others, maintaining it in a gift state with its provisioning capacities ready, both by 'mind reading' what others will need and by supplying and defining what they are used to, what their habits form around. The home changes according to mode of production or tradition, locality, ethnicity or class. Whether in a village hut or in an apartment in a sky-

---

57   I continue to use the term motherer here and the inclusive 'h:er' even if in Patri-
     archy it has been almost only women who have had and provided this experi-
     ence. This is because Western Patriarchal masculinity is constructed according
     to an anti-maternal ideal.

scraper, wherever it is, unless s:he is born into direst poverty, the child's first environment is full of the gifts of h:er motherers.

1.11 Mothering/being mothered: the process of giving and receiving

When psychologists began to study child development, this context of care and complementarity with the mother was not usually taken into account. For example, Jean Piaget together with Barbel Inhelder and Piaget's wife, Valentine Chatenay, described the early childhoods of their children but proposed a scientific method which, by concentrating on the development of the individual, left out the complementary dyadic unit of mother and child, even though the mother, Chatenay, was herself participating in the investigation.

Recent studies of toddler helpfulness or altruism (Warneken and Tomasello 2006), consider it remarkable that children voluntarily help adults and hypothesize that altruism is an inherited trait. They do not take into account the fact that the toddlers live in a context of maternal care and helpfulness, which for them is costless and 'normal'. For little children, the context of exchange and ego-orientation in which adults live with each other is usually external, somewhere else.[58] Children are creative receivers, and they learn giving as well as receiving by participating in the gift economy with their mothers and imitating them, using their 'like me' bridges. We do not need to look for an altruism gene. A full-immersion early childhood course in giving and receiving teaches helpfulness to children and I believe it teaches them language as well.

The infant research centered around Trevarthen, Stern, Meltzoff, Bråten and others avoids the elimination of the motherer to some extent because s:he is so necessary to the child's survival. Nevertheless, in spite of the revolution in perspective that these studies have provided, giving and receiving as such are not in the foreground.

Even the recent studies dealing with mirror neurons (see Gallese et al. 2007) and young children do not usually take into account that the face and the hands of the motherer are what the child usually sees during the processes of nurturing, and that it is to these that h:er mirror neurons first respond, and vice-versa h:er motherer's mirror neurons respond to the child's face and hands while the child is receiving nurture. That is, giving

---

58   They do not understand exchange until around three or four years of age (Berti and Bombi 1988).

and receiving are aspects of nurturing and are part of a unified interpersonal experience during which the child's and the motherer's neurons mirror each other.[59] In the studies cited above, gestures (Gallese and Lakoff 2005) and specific hand actions like grasping are investigated as intentional rather than as moments of caregiving and receiving in which giver, gift (or service) and receiver are all foregrounded. That is, grasping is often a part of receiving, for example, grasping the cup to drink the milk, or of giving: grasping the cup to bring the milk to the child. The researchers extract the grasping from the context of nurture, even though they say that the mirror neurons register the intention of the grasper (do they just *not see* the intention of nurturing?). They underline the capacity of mirror neurons to distinguish between grasping a cup to drink out of it or grasping it to wash it, but they do not investigate grasping the cup to use it in nurturing.

Allison Gopnik, in her interesting work on the *Philosophical Baby* (2010), sees the child mostly as a statistician calculating probabilities, causes and effects. Similarly, Meltzoff does not emphasize the importance of nurturing, not even for the 'like me' bridge. He considers motor activity as the basis of imitation, without emphasizing that the nurturing interaction is the meaningful behavior of which the motor activity is a part. Also in this vein, Max Planck Institute director Michael Tomasello (2008) is able to write an otherwise very interesting book on communication as cooperation without ever mentioning human mothering. One might think that the attention given to communication among apes by many investigators of human communication takes the place of attention that could otherwise have been given to human mothering.

---

59   It occurred to me that the child who cries closes h:er eyes and cannot see the other's face, so her mirror neurons will not respond to it at the moment. Perhaps this protects the child from experiencing some of the others' negative attitudes towards her.

1.12 Economy, gifts and neuroscience

Figure 1: Mother and child interaction
© Leolintang I Dreamstime.com - Mother And Baby Photo

In this book, I am trying to reveal the mother-child material communication model as one of or the main underlying structures of language.[60] At the same time, it is necessary to show why and how what is actually such an obvious and commonplace explanation has not been taken into account. The story of this model is also the story of its large scale domination and erasure by a different model with a different logic, that of money and economic exchange.

In fact, the neuter and neutral view of objective science leaves the gift aside. In the last decades the rapid development of neuroscience, aided by information theory (transmission of coded information: source-message-receiver) and computer technology, has created new and fascinating descriptions of mental processes that also predictably do not include the nurturing interaction as an explanatory model. My contention instead is that mothering creates or indeed, as we shall see, *is* the lens through which humans, including neuroscientists, actually understand everything. That is, the human '*umwelt*' (von Uexkull 2010) is a '*mutterwelt*', and mothering-being-mothered (with all its permutations) determines the interpersonal significance of experience.

The kinds of explanations given by cognitive science leave out this important piece of the analysis. The omission of the gift hypothesis subtracts the giftless explanations from the fray of politics, economics and morality, though it allows them to return later as an authoritative consolidated

---

60   Dean Falk (2009) suggested that language developed from mothering in prehistory. My idea is not that language is mothering plus vocalizations as Bickerton (2004) says, but that material nurturing itself provides the original communicative pattern that is repeated on the verbal plane.

influence on ideology. These explanations are political because they are apolitical. They are political because they leave out the core maternal interaction and thus it does not acquire any authority, even though men bleeding on battlefields continue to call for their mothers as they die. They are political because they institute a level and a habit of explanation that makes the mother-child altercentric model of interaction insignificant. They are political because they provide a way of understanding society and culture without maternal values, because they take place within the exchange paradigm and supply fodder for new money-making inventions and developments (under cover of objectivity and honest intellectual curiosity), because they are part of hierarchical patriarchal academic structures etc. They are political because they are a development of the capitalist economy that slaughters and exploits indigenous peoples who practiced and still practice (maternal) gift economies.

This is not to say that neurological explanations of language and life are not 'true' but that they leave out the structure of maternal interactive care that makes them (and anything else) meaningful in the first place and that they also detour around the meaning of the neutral needs they are satisfying. It is only the material nurturing that has allowed the development of humans and, therefore, of science at all.

Gift-giving has been ignored as a model or used only metaphorically and its gifts have been packed into the black box of the brain and 'heredity', which is itself material transmission. Now that this black box is being opened and its intricate contents are being studied with new techniques and technologies, it is not surprising that the model, the 'register' of human giving and receiving is still present though invisible. Witness the descriptions of the activity of neurons as 'transmission' and 'reception' of 'action potentials' or 'signals'.

If we can succeed in showing that giving and receiving are a basic model for language (and other sign transmission) we can reconnect the activity of neurons to mothering or at least point out where the metaphor comes from.

In the big picture, what would this imply? That the processes of matter are somehow maternal, nurturing? They do become nurturing when a receiver evolves to receive them, as photosynthesis in plants has evolved to use sunlight or eyes have evolved to see. However, I would look at it another way. When hominid mothering became long-term and intense, varying with all the different aspects of life, it repeated, on the interpersonal plane, processes that were already functioning impersonally among neurons in the brain. The maternal processes were eventually transferred into virtual giving and receiving in language. Looking back at the brain or at sunlight and photosynthesis, we understand them as mothering (or as transposed mothering: the transmission of information, or as communication: sending and receiving 'signals') because as mothered children, we are doing the same thing all the time ourselves[61] even if we don't recognize it as such. Mothering and language let us look back at the non-human processes as 'like me' even if we deny it, refusing to recognize that is what we are doing.

I am not saying that I do not believe the neurological or psychological processes are important on their own, but that mothering and being mothered is not just the trigger but the model and original social process of language and of both pre- and post-linguistic conceptualization, and, therefore, also of thought and of the schemas and metaphors with which we understand thought and its underlying neurological processes. My hypothesis is that language is neither innate nor is it primarily statistical and computational, but, it is learned from the process of being mothered from the beginning.[62] Then mothering and language together create a lens through which we understand the world. Again, a main reason why this has not been recognized is that we live in a gift-denying and mother-denying culture and we function largely according to the logic and mentality of exchange.

Gift-giving is glimpsed but it is pushed back into the womb and beyond the womb, to the genes, as biological 'inheritance', and genetic 'patrimony' as well as into the neural pathways[63] where neurons emit and receive 'impulse-gifts', and 'pass them on'.

On the other hand, monetized market exchange can be seen not only as the contradiction of mothering-gift giving but as a non-nurturing elaboration and embodiment of some other aspects of language in the formation of concepts and the access to the verbal plane. This embodiment has had an enormous and mostly negative influence on human and planetary existence. We will describe this in the second half of the book.

---

61   Semioticians believe everything is a sign or can become one, but they do not acknowledge a maternal core.

62   It is matri-*arke*-al.

63   The very maternal projection that lets us understand the world as giving and receiving is denatured and extended and then 'found' again in our brains, used to cognize neural pathways ('gift trajectories' see 4.9), which are finally used to supplant the maternal model as an explanation.

1.13 No essentialism

The critique of essentialism, which has accompanied the assimilation of women into the market, has been useful in many ways, liberating women from what appeared to be a pre-destined inferior role. However, the critique has also blocked a paradigm shift towards mothering-being mothered – gift-giving – as a general principle in society at large. Not only has the treatment of women and mothers as inferior disqualified gifting and care, but the reaction against that disqualification (and the availability of contraceptives and abortion) have made mothering an individual choice, freeing many women, but particularizing rather than generalizing maternal care, and abandoning the field of the public good to the behavior and values of the market and patriarchy.

An interesting countercurrent has been the Motherhood Movement mobilized by Canadian Andrea O'Reilly, which places mothers and writing by mothers at the center of a movement that now has as many as a million members (www.motherhoodinitiative.org).

My approach to the critique of essentialism has three parts. First, I believe we need to generalize and at the same time desentimentalize (to some extent) mothering and gift-giving and I believe we can do this by considering that they constitute the prototype of transitivity. Second, I propose that we understand gender ideals of masculinity as the problem and that we make them *less* general. In the West, until recently, male children have been taught, as the expectation of their gender role, not to nurture (and see Chodorow 1978). This role, validated by the market, has become the norm for all (see the discussion of 'masculation' below). However, as is clear from the existence of compassionate men and now from the participation of many fathers in childcare, men do not forget or relinquish mothering altogether. (Nor could they ever altogether 'lose' it if language, which they continue to utilize, is based on mothering.) The same applies to women who for whatever reason do not want to nurture or who have patriarchal values. They also participate in generalized mothering in language and cognition and they continue to play a variety of gift-giving and receiving roles in social institutions.

The third part of my approach to the critique of essentialism is based on the investigation of categorization itself. 'Classical' categorization uses the Aristotelian model, which requires necessary and sufficient conditions and a common quality shared by all members of a category. The category 'women' is thus supposed by essentialists to have the common quality of motherhood. Another kind of category, the 'graded category', discovered by Eleanor Rosch in the 1970s, sees members clustered around a prototype, which has somewhat different similarities with different category members, without a common 'essence'.[64] We will be discussing these two kinds of categorization throughout the book and especially in the second half. However, it seems clear that the problem of essentialism arises with the kind of thinking that uses the Aristotelian 'classical' kind of categorization. The problem would thus be an artifact of the way we think about categorization, which itself is a cultural product. Essentialism would not arise with the graded category (which does not have a common quality or essence).

I believe we should also include the perspective of the child, the perspective of *being* mothered, in this discussion. For the child, nuturing, which is necessary for h:er life, comes from the outside. H:er sustenance is not biologically given, as it was in the womb and as it would be for a chick in an egg,[65] but it has to come from the initiative of another. We are looking at gift-giving and receiving not as a biologically imposed predisposition of adult women to nurture, but as an early experience and learned behavior of all children, which is the basis of both material and verbal communication later on. From this perspective, the critique of essentialism as a false generalization of nurturing behavior to women-only can be satisfied, while the mother-child interaction is expanded, generalized and revealed to be a fundamental, pan-human, transitive communicative process. If humans are seen as forming a graded category with a maternal prototype, no essential character is implied. Nevertheless, although there is no common property, there is a common process of giving and receiving both materially and semiotically/linguistically in which all participate, at least to some extent.

---

64   For cognitive psychology, the usual meaning of 'prototype' as 'original model' is left aside, and the prototype is considered in the literature to be statistically extracted from experience as the most typical member of a category. For example, North Americans usually choose the robin as the most typical bird. Various similarities to the prototype determine membership in a graded category. On the other hand, classical categories are based on similarity to an exemplar and all members must have the same necessary and sufficient characteristics. At first, prototypes and exemplars were seen as binarily opposed while now they are beginning to be described as opposite ends of a spectrum (Divjak and Arppe 2013). If children are seen (Gopnik, Meltzoff and Kuhl 1999) as unconscious statisticians, there seems to be no contradiction in the idea that they could extract prototypes as infants by making judgments of typicality. Nevertheless, it seems to me that the word 'prototype' continues to carry with it the idea of 'original model' and that this gives it an important portion of its potency.

65   See Meltzoff's (2011) discussion of Freud's image of the chick in the egg to describe the *psychological* isolation of the infant.

Instead, if we use a classical category of the human with a male exemplar and a common quality – shall we call it 'sapiens'? – there are necessary and sufficient conditions without which some potential members of the category can be excluded (and these have often been the motherers – who seem less rational – and the races and cultures who do not 'know' in the same way that the standard white males know). These two kinds of categorization, and any others that may arise, relativize the problem of essentialism, showing perhaps that it is mainly a product of patriarchy, which is also influenced by the market as we shall see later.

Mothering is learned by being mothered. Nurturing behavior is learned by the child by participating in it with h:er motherer and imitating h:er.[66] Then, when it is necessary to be a motherer as an adult, s:he already, at least unconsciously, knows how.

If Nature is seen as mothering, it is because we use the lens of giving-receiving to see, filter and interpret our surroundings. When we privilege this lens as opposed to that of exchange, we can understand the projection of mothering as informative and indeed epistemologically primary. The problem is not Mother Nature but the privileging of culture as neutral, commercial and male in opposition to nature as mothering. Culture is mothering, too, even if it has been deeply altered by the market and patriarchy.

Nurturing and being nurtured become the prototype (or original model) of interaction. They contain two perspectives, each of which is the reverse of the other, but which each participant can enact, taking turns. Taken together, they, too, are imitated.

At the same time the prototype of the motherer includes the child and vice-versa. The objects, which are used in the nurturing are objects of 'joint attention' even before pointing, beginning with the breast (which points, too, after all).

Young children do not begin to understand exchange and the market until around four or five years of age (Berti and Bombi 1988; Webley 2003; Furnham and Argyle 1998).[67] Infants grow and develop, begin to live, to know and to speak in the maternal gift economy. From the child's point of view, the gifts are free and s:he elicits and also receives without eliciting, unilateral gifts from the motherer at the motherer's own initiative. In h:er turn, the child gives in response to the motherer's requests and initiates

---

66 Through the 'like me' bridge, kinetic recognition, mimesis.
67 'For very young children giving money to a salesperson is a mere ritual. They are not aware of the different values of coins and the purpose of change, let alone the origin of money' (1998: 69).

giving as well in turntaking play. The free character of the gifts is a given for a child who lives beyond exchange.

I am saying that all children must have a minimum of care to survive and this care comes to them early in the gift mode – because they cannot receive it in any other way. It is this unilateral giving and receiving, initiated usually by the motherer but also in turn taking by both sides of the dyad that lays down the social patterns that are later elaborated as gift economy and as language.

Not only male and female roles, but the lack of access to independent sources of gifts of nature and the community also penalize anyone who does not do monetized work and especially those who are responsible for the lives of their children. It is isolation in the context of exchange in scarcity that makes the free labor of motherers difficult, not the maternal economy itself.

Both essentialism and the penalization of mothering are phenomena that emerge from market forces that limit mothering through scarcity while they leverage and plunder the gifts of all for profit.

1.14 'Pre-' capitalist, 'pre-' market values

The encounter between exchange and gift economies within capitalism is similar to the encounter, conquest and encroachment by the European market economy and culture on indigenous peoples wherever they have found them. Indigenous gift economies, many of which existed in the past and still exist in surviving matrilinear, matrilocal, matriarchal societies[68], pose the alternative model that threatens the market. Gift practices have usually been considered barbaric and much has been done by colonizers to eliminate them. The accumulators of capital were shocked at the give-aways of the people of the American Northwest, especially those practicing potlatch (Kuokkannen 2007). Not only was this practice outlawed by the settlers, but there as elsewhere native children were seized, placed in boarding schools and re-educated in the European ways of the market, at the same time depriving them of their languages and enforcing the speaking of English or French. On the other hand, the values of the market also insinuated themselves and transformed the indigenous ways

---

68   See Goettner-Abendroth's *Matriarchal Societies* (2012) for a discussion of a
      number of these societies. Her edited book *Societies of Peace* (2009) brings the
      voices of many indigenous women together. My own edited book *Women and
      the Gift Economy: A Radically Different Worldview is Possible* (2007) is a col-
      lection of essays by indigenous and non-indigenous women.

from within with the help of drugs, alcohol and missionaries. In these and many other ways, the European market culture attacked the native cultures, privatized and enclosed the native lands and forced the gifts of their resources and territories out of their hands and into the grasp of the colonizers. They forced a replacement of maternal or matriarchal gift economies by a patriarchal market economy.

By making the comparison between mothering inside patriarchal capitalism and indigenous gift economies, I do not mean to somehow infantilize the 'pre-' capitalist societies.[69] Rather, I am saying that many of these autonomous pre-colonial indigenous peoples had not broken the continuity with mothering but had developed the logic of direct giving/receiving, elaborating it in non-market nurturing ways, in the direct distribution of goods and services and the creation of culture (gifting in provisioning but also in festivals, spiritual gifts, symbolic gift exchange). But in fact, the market itself is also a way of using gifting – doubling it back and forcing it to be contingent, thereby transforming it into its opposite: giving in order not to give.

In capitalist patriarchy, we consider the market the province of 'adult' behavior. For indigenous gift economies the market – like gender- is not adult but extraneous. Living in an adult gift economy allows for an unbroken continuity with the maternal economy, a continuity that for people in capitalism is broken when we begin to adapt to exchange in late childhood and adolescence. That is, when we enter the so-called 'age of reason' and our gender roles also intensify. Perhaps it was just this break that the settlers intended to cause when they forced the native children into the boarding schools.[70]

I propose that we understand the gift economy as primary and the exchange economy as secondary, a derivative. Isolated in the domestic sphere, ontogenesis is 'pre-' patriarchal even inside of patriarchy and 'pre-' capitalist even inside of capitalism. But patriarchal capitalism is not a more evolved form of society. Rather it is a kind of hybrid. In the patriarchal capitalist, nuclear-family model, the practice of the gift economy becomes

---

69   Nor do I want to romanticize them. I acknowledge the existence of pre-colonial patriarchal societies, but there were/are also those that had viable gift economies: the Iroquois, the Navajo, the Salish, the Hopi 'Gifts are communications in a language of social belonging' (hopifoundation.org).

70   Of course the encounter between the market and Indigenous peoples has also brought about many hybrids. For example there is the market of Juchitàn which is traditionally controlled by women. Gifting continues however through almost daily festivals offered to the community by one woman or another (Bennholdt-Thomsen 1997).

the responsibility of one woman, the mother, while the father is supposed to work in the market economy and provide the means of giving. The village that raised the child has disappeared and so has the extended family. Moreover, as women have joined the paid labor force it is also the mother herself who works in the market economy in order to sustain her own practice of the gift economy with her children.

Capitalist patriarchy controls the means of giving and takes gifts from the maternal gift economy in the same way that, at another level, it takes gifts from 'pre-' capitalist societies and, at still another level, it takes gifts from nature.[71] It creates scarcity and makes autonomous gift-giving almost impossible. Mothering is concentrated mainly in one person per family, and at the same time, it is made gender-specific. Restricting the role of motherer to women only makes it appear that mothering may be women's common essence. The market bleaches mothering out of society at large and paints it into the corner with women, making it appear that only there is it appropriate and 'natural'.

In matriarchal and gender egalitarian societies, there are other arrangements. In some matriarchal societies, the father is nurturing while the mother's brother provides authority (Watson-Franke 2002: 605). In others, the mother's brother provides support for the biological mother in satisfying the physical and psychological needs of the child.[72] In still others, men and women care equally for the children (Du 2003). Males, fathers or uncles – brothers of the mother – also, therefore, do the kinds of detailed nurturing that females, especially biological mothers, are expected to do in patriarchy. Unlike the biological father's relation with the mother, the mother's brother's relation with her is not sexualized, so there is no stimulus for the Oedipus complex in such societies. There is also little or no violence against women.[73] In many societies, there is also collabora-

---

71   Other cultures have other mixtures of exchange and patriarchy and Euro American Capitalist Patriarchy has ways of taking from them as well, creating alliances with the few at the top, using World Bank and IMF loans, corporate economic invasion, etc.

72   The Mosuo in China are a good example. They have 'visiting marriages' and matrilocality (Freeman 2010: passim, Goettner-Abendroth 2012: Ch 5.2, Madiesky 2011).

73   This idea was broached by Malinowsky (1927: ch. 5) and was widely discussed and contested. More recently, Ifi Amadiume (1997: 40) has discussed the lack of Oedipus complex among African groups like the Jeljobe. She says 'The presence of these fundamental matriarchal systems generating love and compassion also means that we cannot take the classical Greek Oedipal principle of violence as a basic paradigm or given in the African context'.

tion among members of the group to do mothering and the child may call 'mother' any number of relatives and friends.

The values of direct need-satisfying gifting are practiced by everyone in matrifocal and matriarchal societies and they permeate the society as a whole. Instead, where men and money are in power and women are made to take on the whole responsibility of gift-giving and care work, the processes and values of the gift economy are not extended to the society as a whole. Rather they are particularized, individualized as personal morality or essentialized as common to one biologically identified gender only. Thus, the basis of essentialism in our culture is the failure of the social generalization of mothering and its compression into the (birth) mother-child relation.

On the other hand, we should mention the 'strategic essentialism' (Spivak) that generalizes the values of non-dominant cultures. In fact, the gift is the non-dominant culture within the economy and culture of dominance.

The caring values, which, calling on Marx's distinction,[74] would be the superstructure of the gift economy, seem to be 'women's values'. Instead they are the birthright of everyone as 'pre-' patriarchal, 'pre-' market values: the superstructure of an economic structure that has been interrupted, splintered into little pieces, allocated to one gender and concentrated inside the isolated home.

In patriarchal capitalist society, the gift economy is gendered female because women do most of the mothering. In indigenous matriarchal societies, this is not necessarily the case because the gift economy and mothering are not restricted to one sex or gender. This ungendered gifting has had the result that indigenous women sometimes do not identify with Euro-American feminism. They find their matriarchal men to be caring and 'maternal'. Euro-American patriarchy *and* the opposition to it are both extraneous to those 'pre-' patriarchal societies. At the same time though, Western patriarchal capitalism plunders indigenous gifts, marginalizes and dominates their communities as it marginalizes, dominates and plunders its own domestic 'pockets' of the gift economy. It dominates also the contexts in which they are/were embedded, the niches made of Mother Nature's now rapidly depleting gifts.

The system of capitalist patriarchy is a gigantic mechanism. In my opinion it is a mistake to target individuals and their greed as the main problem. The mechanism creates the individuals that are functional to it by selecting for them and rewarding both greed for things and greed for power.

---

74 Marx's description of structure and superstructure.

1.15 Sexual difference and masculation

In Italy, where I have lived for much of my life, the feminist philosophy of sexual difference has been particularly important.[75]

My take on it is similar to my approach to the critique of essentialism. The problem lies with the male identity. That is, women are socially assigned the role of motherers because society interprets their biological role as evidence that they should care for their children, and, in that role, they have to practice gift-giving, while men (at least in the West) are 'masculated,' i.e. usually not identified as motherers and they therefore have to search for and find other roles and identities. These roles involve the over-privileging of males, as dominators and exchangers while underprivileging motherers as carers.[76]

The market economy arises as the determined opposite of maternal giving, on the principle of not-giving exchange (and forced giving, leveraged giving, giving to exchange and to those who do not give). If, as is usually the case, we do not consider gift-giving to be 'economic,' we will consider exchange (and the market built on exchange) to be the first, indeed the only economy. Similarly, if we do not recognize women as different from men (at least because they are socially assigned to the gift economy from childhood by the biological fact that they may eventually give birth and give milk), we will consider the male identity to be the first, indeed the only identity.

Instead, the first identity is maternal (Chodorow 1978) for all children brought up by a motherer or motherers, as children must be if they are to survive. The motherer as the first model and this Ideal Cognitive Model

---

75 Luisa Muraro is one of the proponents of this current. She opposed *the symbolic order of the mother* to Lacan's symbolic order of the father. I believe in contrast to Muraro that it is not that mothers' teach language to children (though they sometimes do, especially in Euro America) but that it is the material giving and receiving done by mothers that is the first communication upon which linguistic and other sign communication is modelled and understood. The 'order' that is produced by housework is also a kind of symbolic organization according to Muraro. I agree but I think we also project mothering/giving onto the environment (see Chapter 3).

76 I add the economic aspect of the renunciation of the gift economy to other aspects of 'object relations' discussed by Nancy Chodorow (1978), standpoint theory Nancy Hartsock (1987), etc. In fact the masculine distanced 'cognitive style' is like the capitalist cognitive style that rejects gift-giving in favor of exchange (while continuing to profit from gifts).

(Lakoff 1990) is usually maintained by daughters.[77] In my first book *For-Giving, a Feminist Criticism of Exchange* (1997), I coined the term 'masculation' to name the rejection of gift-giving that is imposed on male children in the social construction of their gender role, the 'manhood script' (Gillmore 1990). This role is invented in opposition to the role of the nurturing mother and thus falsely implies to boys that they should not be maternal. If we understand the maternal role as economic gift-giving we can see that for boys the turn away from the maternal gender identity implies a rejection of the gift economy. Moreover, many boys are encouraged to replace the altercentric identity modeled on the maternal interaction and the 'like me' bridge with an identity modeled on a culturally imposed male ideal that is macho, non-nurturing and dominant, forcing gifts from others rather than just receiving and giving them as happens in the mothering interaction. The imposition of a binary gender identity – either male or female – contradicts the 'like me' bridge that boy children have been constructing with their female motherers and makes them have to construct a bridge with an other who is often distant and disengaged, while the female motherer becomes 'not like me'. This is not the 'fault' of the boys or the parents but is due to a social misperception of what biological sexual differences imply.[78]

Two social options appear to be available for boys to become non-maternal 'real boys'(Pollack 1998) and then 'real men': first, there is the patriarchal orientation towards hitting and domination and second, they may eventually achieve success in the seemingly neuter market, as workers or as professionals in business, the law, academia, etc. Failure in either option appears to feminize them. I believe that the contemporary move towards fathers' nurturing is a very good thing but, unfortunately, changes on the individual level have perhaps only intensified the masculated behaviors on the wider social scale. Nations and corporations continue to practice competition, domination and collective murder even when the individual men, who belong to or work in them, sometimes take the baby out in the pram.

'Male' must thus be understood as the derivative gender identity, which generalizes itself as the first and normal human identity. Then the female

---

77 The Oedipal conflict is thus really an economic gender conflict. Recent studies on concept formation (Voorspoels, Vanpaemel and Storm 2011) show that goal- directed concepts in particlar use Ideal Dimension Models: IDMs. Thus once the girl child has begun to have as her goal to be like the (female) motherer, the mother becomes particularly relevant as her model for her self-concept and vice-versa, for the boy if he has to choose another model, the IDM of the male becomes more relevant.

78 Not all societies have this perception and consequent construction of male gender.

gender is defined in a new binary opposition to this *derivative* male identity, which has been constructed in opposition to the (gift-giving) mother. This new female identity is constructed in binary opposition to the male, whose original identification with the mother, renunciation of that identity and subsequent reconstruction of it in binary opposition to the mother is unrecognized. The female identity becomes that of one who might become a mother and so does not have to or cannot give up the gift economy as males appear to have been privileged to do. Thus, women are considered inferior because they are not men who have had to give up the mothering identity and economy in order to achieve or 'perform' (Butler 1990) their gender role. Women can participate and succeed in the market but they are penalized because they have not given up the role of giving, and so are often forced by the market to give more work for less pay while their 'reproductive' work is made difficult.

Thus 'sexual difference' is an economic/psychological difference caused by the fact that the mother's position as prototype or ideal concept model of the human has been overtaken and eclipsed by a not-giving 'male' model, around which society is organized. Female sexual difference is indeed difference deferred, 'deferance', to use Derrida's term, since it is seen as a difference from the male norm, which itself is actually artificially developed as difference from the mothering norm. The difference of the female child is thus deferred until after the male has been (falsely) established as the norm in contrast to the mother. Then the female is expected to defer (give way) to this male norm.

Under the influence of the artificial identity, masculated men have usurped and distorted all the ideas of what makes us human, how we think, interact, and organize ourselves into social groups. Women have also created their own false identity by preferentially nurturing the men who follow the masculated model and by believing in the superiority of men's culture and interpretations of the world. I want to re-establish the mothering model in all these areas and reclaim it as an interpretative key by showing that yes, mothering is the care of children, but more than that, it is the basic process of language and of the economy of life itself.

Thus adult women and men who are not mothers are nevertheless practicing mothering and being mothered all the time when they speak, when they perform natural functions like breathing and perceiving, and when they give and receive goods to satisfy needs pre- and even post-exchange.

We have to get beyond the ideology of capitalist patriarchy and *homo economicus* to base our concept of the human on giving and receiving. This will give us the radically different concept of ourselves that will allow us to create a peaceful world at last.

The denial of the maternal basis is responsible in large part for the oppression of women who, as potential bearers of children, are also already potential bearers and practicers of the alternative economy. In other words it is not only the psychological conundrum of 'womb envy' that women pose to men, but the threat of a radically different economy that women as mothers pose to capitalism, that causes the violent reactions of patriarchal capitalist men against us. By excising the mother from epistemology, patriarchy has also taken away everyone's reasons for hope and for believing that our species can actually find ways of surviving and living in social and environmental peace.

Perhaps, after all, it is not so negative that the people now proposing the gift economy are mainly relatively young men, like Nipun Mehta of Charity Focus (now Service Space), Alpha Lo of Open Collaboration and 'gift circles', Charles Eisenstein, author of *Sacred Economics* (2011) and Jimmy Wales, founder of Wikipedia: they give no particular importance to mothering. In a way, this protects female motherers from the attack that patriarchy has been practising against their economy for millennia. It also shows that this economy can be espoused and practiced by men. Nevertheless, the fundamental connection of mothering with the gift economy needs to be recognized as a basic structural element of our species. This is very important for understanding what a gift economy is and why and how it can work. It is necessary for the success of the gift economy movement.

The logic of the gift riddles, permeates, gives and gives hope even to a society that is destroying itself through market exchange. The machinations of some and the incompetence of others have caused the disaster in the financial markets and the crash of most of the global economy that has taken place during the eight years I have been writing this book. When I first started working on the idea of the gift economy (though I didn't call it that until the late '70s) some forty-five years ago, Capitalism and Communism were the two opposing economies and it seemed that both were here to stay. In the struggle between the two systems, Soviet Communism eventually 'fell' and Capitalism grew and globalized. It was therefore very important to critique Capitalism from 'within'. Now that the world economy is crashing around us, like the cliffs of polar ice crashing into the warming sea, the defects of capitalism are obvious to all. The financial markets are not the root of the problem however; they are only one more devastating turn of the screw.

The problem starts very simply with the division between the two modes of gift and exchange. This is made more complex because exchange itself is the cancellation of positive gifts, and it coexists with other continuing unilateral giving. The market redirects many gifts towards the exchange process itself, so that they nurture the process and its transformation into a mechanism of self aggrandizement through profit-taking and the unlimited accumulation of money. The patriarchal values aligned with this process drive the financial markets and the desires for infinite power and possession that motivate the 'successful' parts of the system. The 'unsuccessful' parts are forced to live in the scarcity for the many that the above accumulation by the few creates and they are encouraged to blame themselves, bad luck or others' greed (but not the system as such) for their lack of success.

The solution to this paradoxical conundrum is simply to turn back to the female (maternal) model of the human for males as well as for females. I believe that an important step in this direction can be made by discovering mothering in language and, thus, in epistemology.

1.16 Hitting

Unfortunately, giving and receiving also function as the model for harmful 'excessively transitive'(see section 5.1) actions like hitting, hurting, beating, shooting and killing. I believe that masculation alienates little boys and later adult males from recognizing and valuing the giving and receiving they are actually doing, and encourages them to replace it with hitting. Violence becomes the possible content of the empty category that was created when they gave up the mother as the model for their gender (belligerent phrases like 'Take that!', 'You asked for it!', 'It serves you right!' recall gift-giving.) Like giving, hitting touches the other, enters h:er proxemic space and establishes a relationship – though one of dominance and fear rather than one of mutuality and trust. Hitting becomes almost immediately bilateral as retaliation, making the other 'pay', and so enters into the exchange logic rather than the gift logic ('you have to give as good as you get'). Allowing oneself to be hit unilaterally is a source of shame and perhaps of 'feminization' or 'infantilization' for masculated males.

Violence is a deep distortion and negative replay of gift-giving communication.[79] It may even appear to be the basic model of interaction rather than gift-giving and, thus, to justify acts of aggression and war. It may

---

79   'I account for the re-enactment of abuse in terms of the very same life-giving mechanism operating in children's proto-care and in their re-enacting the caregiving they have experienced' (Stein Bråten 2006), OMEP.

appear in a Hobbesean way, to be the basis of human nature and even of reality itself, thus requiring a social contract to offset it.[80]

Violence can also force others into a permanent gift-giving position towards the dominant person, group, nation or race. Hierarchies of power are actually hierarchies of gift-giving 'upwards' held in place by commands and violence 'downwards'. These hierarchies are also used to support and protect the market.

The market serves the artificial masculated gender identity as an equally artificial "environmental niche," an apparently neuter and relatively peaceful but gift-exploiting and gift-denying context in which to exercise the non-giving 'masculine' "ideal concept model's" activities of accumulation (to be bigger) and competition for domination. Women can also give up the free gift-giving maternal model and adapt successfully to this artificial context. However, little girls are not assigned to a gender category that is constructed in binary opposition to the category of their gift-giving motherers, so the are not 'masculated' as boys are. This means that although girls do not have to be motherers to be female, mothering/gift-giving is not excluded *a priori* from their gender concept as usually happens with boys in patriarchy. As adults many women (and many men) practice both economies, the maternal gift economy in their homes and the exchange economy in their jobs, providing the means of giving to their families with their work in the market.

Capitalism itself is 'masculated', i.e. constructed in a way that is similar to artificially non-maternal or anti-maternal masculinity. Capitalism is a mechanism for the denial, redistribution and, indeed, plunder of gifts, channeling them away from the needs of the many and towards the few at the 'top'. This channeling of gifts also has the advantage for the market that it depletes the wider context in which exchanges take place, imposing scarcity on the many and locating power in the hands of the dominant few.

Scarcity makes gift-giving difficult so that the gift economy poses less

---

80   Then gift giving appears to be the mirror image of violence, positive but a fluke. And matriarchy appears to be the mirror image of patriarchy. See Vazquez-Rozas (2007) on high and low prototypical transitivity. She proposes that killing, hitting or breaking are not more transitive than less violent taking, putting, giving or getting.

See also Kristeva (1986: 102) '... the symbol is any joining, any bringing together that is a contract – one that either follows hostilities or presupposes them – and finally any exchange, including an exchange of hostility'. The Freudian 'myth of the asocial child' (Meltzoff and Brooks 2007) makes the idea of contract necessary to provide the social connection. Instead children are altercentric from the beginning. No contract is necessary.

threat to the exchange economy and successful mothering does not threaten the masculated identity. Gift-giving is also discredited because it falsely appears to be the *cause* of the victimization of the individuals who do it, and sometimes even to be the cause of scarcity (because too much has been given). Moreover, gift-giving may be forced upon women against their will in an economy of scarcity, by the social interpretation of their gender role.

Individual nurturing and individual nurturers are held responsible for their own success or failure without considering the system based on market exchange, profit 'making', privatization, exploitation, and the destruction and waste of collective wealth by war, all of which deplete the context in which the nurturing continuation of life has to take place.

Gift-giving appears to be only something tacked onto the market, an exception to the rule, a moral penchant, an altruistic impulse of otherwise egotistical 'man', which should be mistrusted in any case because it contains hidden or delayed exchanges (Bourdieu 1977; Lyotard 1974; Derrida 1992). Or perhaps it seems to come from an inexplicable, 'irrational' and, therefore, instinctual desire to nurture rooted in a female 'nature' that for this reason is not completely 'human'. Or it may be seen as a human weakness used by patriarchy to entrap women. These and many other false views of gift-giving are held by women as well as men, and they help maintain the status quo in which masculated men and the market control everything, even though it is increasingly clear that capitalism and patriarchy simply do not work.[81]

The maternal gift economy is the psychologically original economy because it is necessary for the survival of little children at the beginning of every life.[82] This does not mean it is instinctual or somehow not part of the 'mind'. Rather I would say it is the (minding) basis of mind.

In indigenous societies where the gift economy is practiced in a number of ways in adulthood, there is not such a drastic break between the adult economy and the economy of childhood as there is in capitalism. Thus, there is a continuity of life, which is a factor in the formation of a different kind of individuality and a different configuration of personality. For indigenous peoples, the mother often remains important both in the generalization of mothering and in the recognition of spiritual maternal qualities in Nature as Mother Earth.

I do not think that we Europeans have developed such an uncompas-

---

81   The stereotypical identification of the market logic with reason and reason with men as opposed to 'feminine' emotion is one of the ruses used by the ideology of the market to deny the gift economy.

82   Children who are institutionalized or lack maternal care often have developmental difficulties including language disabilities.

sionate economy because we are greedy, but vice-versa I believe that we are greedy because we have such an uncompassionate and dysfunctional, anti-maternal, economy. The economic structure determines the superstructure, whatever the other feedback loops may also be. To me this means that if we practice the gift economy, we will emphasize those gift-giving characteristics in our behavior and our thinking, and vice-versa, if we practice mainly exchange we will emphasize the negative ego-oriented characteristics of greed and competition for domination. I believe this is the answer to the objection that 'if everybody had the same amount there would always be somebody who would want to have more'. In a maternal gift economy, people want to practice the gift economy.They remain 'altercentric'. In an exchange economy combined with patriarchy, they want to have more.[83] If we continue to identify the male gender with not-giving and make it everyone's goal to be equal to successful males, assimilating everyone into the market mode,[84] we will cancel and further discredit the model of the alternative economy that we have learned from our mothers and still have hidden within us.

The point is to recognize the maternal gift economy and build a new economy on it now, an economy of the 'maternal human' that neither exploits gifts nor discredits them, that cares for the needs of other people and the environment and for their capacity to give and receive and give again. We should encourage men to practice this economy while consciously acknowledging its source in mothering and denouncing patriarchal ways, including the ways hidden by the seeming neutrality and objectivity of the (actually mother-denying and gift-seizing) market. If these men and the women who follow them practice the alternative gift economy and do not acknowledge the maternal basis, they are continuing in patriarchal denial and oppression of mothers and women in general, a kind of transposed hitting, however well-intentioned they may be otherwise.

It is important for us to recognize that we are in a transitional situation now and that unconsciously or consciously, as givers/receivers or exchangers, we are all practicing one economy in the context of the other. If we want to make a radical change, we have to try to make a safe space for a positive transition as much as that is possible in the present situation. This can be aided by the change in perspective that generalizes mothering/gift-

---

83   In fact perhaps the native peoples in the Americas simply did not understand the Europeans' greed.

84   This is the solution proposed for example by micro-credit.

giving and diminishes exchange. I hope this book can provide a rationale for the direction of the change and reveal mothering and indeed language as guides to making it.

CHAPTER II

GIFT OR EXCHANGE

2.0 Two logics: quid pro quo *and unilateral gift*

The 'source areas' of material gift-giving and exchange function according to two opposing but relatively simple interactive relational logics,[1] which we can recognize when they occur both on the level of base or source and on the superstructural or 'target' level. The logic of *quid pro quo* exchange notoriously separates people by putting them in adversarial positions in order to get 'more', while the transitive logic of unilateral gift-giving and receiving unites people, creating bonding, mutuality and community. Exchange typically gives rise to the values of competition for accumulation and domination, which are also identified with patriarchy, while, as I have been saying, the values of care can be considered part of the ideological expression of the gift economy.

The seizure of gifts by the market system is replayed between women and men when men dominate and women, with their gifts to men and to the system, maintain their dominance. Conscious feminists may reject this collusion with their own exploitation but many women continue doing it, because the exchange system creates extreme leverage through scarcity, privileging exchangers over givers, but also because there are logical paradoxes involved. For example, giving to the other gives value to the other, not to the self who is doing the giving. Then the givers themselves sometimes

---

1   I feel justified in calling these interactive patterns 'logics' because they function with premises that consistently imply conclusions and consequences. Direct giving to needs implies the survival of the child and implies h:er value for the giver. Kinetic mapping and mirror neuron simulations result in the 'like me' bridge, the achievement of identification through the giving and receiving process. The receiver also usually gives value to the giver. There is a syllogism – if A gives to B and B gives to C then A gives to C. Exchange is based on an equation between what is given and what is received. The gift is cancelled while the value of the self is implied over the value of the other. Exchange requires quantification and measurement while gift-giving is mainly qualitative.

believe in the superiority of the other and discredit and devalue themselves.

If we give to those who do not give (and thus, who do not pass the gifts on) we will not make a gifting community, so our gifts will not be replenished by other givers and instead giving will deplete us. What is necessary is a community that does not engage in endlessly repeated bilateral exchange but in a multilateral circulation of goods achieved by attention to others' needs and repeated unilateral gifting to satisfy them. The gift economy works well when it is generalized, but those who are practicing it individually in capitalism (for example, as motherers) cannot generalize it because of the context of scarcity. Without a common mode of production for the giving mode of distribution, they are put in the position of having to embrace exchange in order to be able to give.

In a regime where individuals are atomized by widespread exchange, it appears that their economic as well as their moral actions are determined by personal choices. They can choose one product over another; they can choose to be generous or greedy, altruistic or egotistical. These choices,which seem to depend upon the budget or the moral fibre of the individual, can also be seen as one's acting according to the patterns of one logic or another. Good and evil seem to be individual choices and behaviors, while from this perspective, they can be considered economic behaviors stemming from the logics they embody. If this is the case, it is not surprising that in an epoch in which the market dominates almost every aspect of people's lives, gift-giving and its values have appeared exceptional and unrealistic, even 'stupid', or they have been compartmentalized and relegated to the control of patriarchal religions.

The process of the market, based in equations of value, has a self-confirming aspect, which makes it acceptable to many who would otherwise be altercentric or other-oriented. It magnetically draws attention to itself and self-validates, creating the conditions for them to ignore not only the needs of people who are suffering around the corner, but the unfulfilled needs of whole populations, and even to accept that millions of starving children, who should be participating in the maternal gift economy with their parents, are commodified and sold into the sex trade or killed and their organs sold for the pimps' and the killers' profit (http: //www.wearethorn. org/child-trafficking-facts).

The solutions to these terrible and ever-worsening problems are not primarily individual ethical choices but general economic, political and cultural changes in the direction of the gift.

Women (and some men) who do mothering and other free care work are often not conscious that they are practicing a different economy and even a different paradigm from that of masculated men and the market. Instead, they think the differences are due to their personal moral choices or their personal character defects. Yet they sometimes continue to act on the basis of the gift paradigm anyway, even in spite of great difficulty, sometimes in self-sacrificial ways. In conflicts with their male partners, women sometimes continue to propose the maternal model by over-giving and giving way to the man's violence when he 'imitates' (see above) and overpowers the gift model by hitting.

It is as if women were trying to teach gift-giving by doing it. They are right to propose the model but unfortunately men usually respond with even worse violence. These women cannot create the social change individually. They do not realize that the men are acting on the basis of the anti-maternal exchange paradigm, which, combined with patriarchy, continues to be validated socially. The best thing for abused women to do is, as the counsellors say, just get away. In the bigger picture though, the connections between the movement against violence on women and the movement for the gift economy should be made so as to to amplify both.

2.1 Other possible elaborations of the gift

Although patriarchy makes unilateral giving seem unrealistic, sentimental and even saintly, it is actually just the basic transitive interaction in which one person satisfies another's needs. It is the fundamental first step of a transitive logic, which requires a receiver and of which bilateral giving-in-exchange is just one possible elaboration. Other possible elaborations of the gift are: giving unilaterally in turn or at different levels, receiving in turn and at different levels, giving forward, giving unilaterally to many, receiving unilaterally, receiving from many, receiving and passing it on, giving together with others and receiving together with others, giving and receiving different kinds of things in different ways, giving with different rhythms and timing, giving something and taking it back, over- and under-giving, refusing to give, giving manipulatively, giving with force (i.e. pushing, hitting, kicking).[2] In the bilateral giving and receiving, which I call turn taking, each person becomes a unilateral giver in h:er turn. This

2   The question arises as to whether giving to oneself can be considered transitive. I would say yes but only after giving to others has been established and by analogy with other oriented (altercentric) transitivity. Exchange cancels the gift. It is ego-oriented because it is directed towards the ego using the other as a means. It gives value to the ego instead of the other.

develops into reciprocity and there are also many variations on that theme, including what anthropologists call 'generalized reciprocity'. In this kind of economy, where everyone gives to everyone else, relations of mutuality and trust are established throughout the community.

Patriarchy is a negative variation on the gift theme, where as we said, gifts are forced to flow up and down hierarchies, confirming the power of those above and the obedience of those below. Physical violence, shooting, even bombing are negative transpositions of giving and they can be used to maintain the hierarchies.

The logic of the unilateral gift (A gives x to B) is elaborated in many ways while continuing to exist also in its simple form. The logic of exchange is also elaborated and becomes more complex while remaining in its simple form in many transactions. Constructions of exchange can be seen in capitalism, where chains of exchanges for raw materials, machinery and labor channel the gifts of profit through surplus labor towards the top, where they accumulate as capital and are then reinvested in more exchanges. All the complex concatenations of exchange exist alongside the simpler commonplace daily interactions of buying and selling consumer goods.

Projections of exchange into other areas include, as we have noted, the interpretation of communication as exchange but they can also be found under such appellations as the 'marriage market' and 'human capital'. I particularly dislike this term which makes the human being seem to be worth more if s:he is somehow like money.

A kind of 'econo-speak' has become stylish among academics of various kinds. Here it is in philosophy. Susan Carey (2009) uses the idea of buying as a way of expressing that we arrive at a definite conclusion. For example: 'This obvious point does not buy us much' (453) or 'what the theory-theory of conceptual development buys us' (2011: 15); and here in anthropology with Gurven:

> Traditional life-history theory requires that personal energy budgets cover the expenses of growth, maintenance and reproduction, such that body size and resource production are often highly significant predictors of the pace and timing of fundamental life processes ... Social animals, however, can lend and borrow critical resources in ways that inflate budgets and allow investments that otherwise would not be possible given a reliance on one's own efforts. The ability to lend and borrow resources and provide and solicit other forms of aid within and across generations (i.e. intertemporal budgets) can strongly impact selection on age-schedules of mortality and fertility, and prolong lifespan ... (Gurven et al 2012: 807)

Gurven continues with his euphemistic gift-free terminology regarding gifts:

> Resource transfers improve the likelihood that juveniles reach adulthood and reduce adult mortality, thereby extending adult lifespan. Fitness impacts of transfers made by donors of different ages determine the value of being alive at those ages in ways that differ from the standard Hamiltonian formulation of the "force of selection" which includes direct reproduction but ignores transfers ... (*Ibid*)

And from the abstract: 'Our results illustrate the importance of transfers in several key domains and suggest that the absence of transfers would greatly increase human mortality rates throughout the life course' (*Ibid*). 'Resource transfers' are, of course, gifts.

Ideological correspondences of exchange can be seen in 'an eye for an eye', the ancient motivation of revenge against perceived offenders, the modern adversarial legal system, the concept of justice as payment for crime, and the emotion of guilt as the motivation to pay for wrongdoing. A gift approach to these latter issues would be the attempt to know and to satisfy the needs that cause the crimes in the first place.[3]

Telling the truth is consonant with gift giving as the satisfaction of the other's need to know, while lying is consonant with the ego-orientation of exchange. Another effect of the market on our psychology is the duplicity of business and politics. The two levels of equal exchange as expressed by the assertion of equal value on the surface and the plunder of the gifts hidden beneath, habituate us to deception. Both material and linguistic communication become less and less altercentric as more ways are found to use them to deceive.

The other-orientation of gift-givers is a quality required and elicited by the needs of the recipients, while the ego orientation of exchangers is a quality required and elicited by the (meta) needs of market exchange. The gift economy is simply an economy in which the market has not intervened. It has been called 'pre-capitalist' as if capitalism were progress. Instead perhaps we should say gift economies are 'uninfected' by capitalism. Ethics in indigenous gift economies have a lot in common with 'maternal' or 'care' ethics in market-based economies and both are radically differ-

---

3   After the attack on the World Trade Center, Bush both incited the citizenry to go shopping and began a war of punishment aganst Afghanistan with the promise of bringing Bin Laden to justice. There were many people in the US at the time who believed that the attack originated in the needs of people in the poor and exploited countries and that the money spent on the wars should have been used for their benefit.

ent from the cost-benefit ethics of the patriarchal capitalist market. Nevertheless, many Western anthropologists continue to look at gift economies from the perspective of cost-benefit 'rationality'.

In fact, I would prefer to say the values of care should not be categorized as ethics. Rather, they are the consciousness of the world, the superstructure, the episteme, the motivations coming from (and functional to) the economic and cultural practice of gift-giving. In capitalism and patriarchy and even in socialist market-based economies, ethics appears to be a specific realm having to do with individual choice. Altruism appears to be ethical in binary opposition to greed and selfishness as unethical. Instead, altruism or at least orientation towards the other is the necessary and commonplace attitude, which is consonant with the gift economy and with communication.[4] And as we shall see, it is the core process of language. On the other hand, greed and selfishness are functional to the market and to the accumulation of capital.[5]

There is a pernicious tendency to put the cart before the horse. We tend to believe that personal qualities like kindness cause giving and mercy while others like egotism and greed cause domination and excessive accumulation. Of course there are many feedback loops involved but Marx cut through the tangle by identifying the direction of influence as coming first from the economy as cause with the superstructure of ideas and attitudes as effect.

I am trying to suggest that the way this works as it does is that the two contradictory logics of gift and exchange produce different material and ideological effects. Using the intellectual instruments that have been developed in the century after Marx, I also want to suggest that the mechanism of the influence of 'base' on 'superstructure' could now be seen in terms of what cognitive linguistics calls the 'mapping of schemas onto a target area' (Lakoff and Johnson 1980). In the case of the linguists' usage, the source area is the body and the target area is language, while in the case of the economy, the source would be the interpersonal production of life, material communication, according to the mode of gift giving or to the mode of exchange. The first 'target' area in childhood is language construction and a second 'target' area in adulthood is ideology, as made up of values, ideas and beliefs.

---

4   We start life as altercentric towards our nurturers. Again, self-sacrifice is not
     necessary for other-orientation in abundance.
5   However, the two motivations can be combined. One can accumulate capital for
     the security of one's family, for example. This does not make capitalism any
     sweeter though because it is still a zero sum game.

Distinguishing between gift-giving and exchange, and identifying giving/receiving as an important independent source area, which is mapped into language while the child is being intensely nurtured and before s:he learns to exchange, allows us to recognize giving/receiving and give it value as the more fundamental logic. In ontogenesis, transitivity comes even before the recognition of identity. In fact, giving/receiving is a fundamental aspect of children's and motherers' identities. They are similar as players of those roles, and, through the activity of their mirror neurons, they recognize each other as such, at the same time creating positive relationships. The roles are replayed in various ways in adult life and they are probably the basis of the psychological significance of adult gifting – including its potential for manipulation.

With the gift hypothesis we will see giving/receiving as the source area which is mapped into language as syntax and gives rise to meaning. There is also a second mapping coming from gifting[6] that is projected into adult ideology as the values of care and appreciation, altruism and community. On the other hand, the logic of exchange, which is learned after language is 'acquired', is mapped into adult ideology as ego-orientation, desire for accumulation, aggrandizement, and individualism. We will see in Part Two how exchange begins in naming (*iliquid stat pro aliquo*) but comes after it as an economic process.

I will show how the ideology of exchange has taken over the explanation of language while also showing how gift giving and its values can give language a more appropriate explanation. Although this is already an immense challenge I do not consider it an end in itself, but see it as addressing the need for the kind of paradigm shift towards the maternal that is crucial at this dire point in human history. That is, in consonance with the theory, I am trying to 'mind-read' society and satisfy its need for a radically different perspective.

2.2 More about gift versus exchange

Unilateral gift-giving is transitive and other-oriented. The gift or service is given by one person to satisfy the need of the other and this implies the value of the other. (If s:he had not been valuable to the giver, the gift would not have been given).[7] I call this implication 'gift value'. Repeated

---

6   It is influenced in turn by gifting in language as well.
7   The converse relation also holds. If one person does not give to the other, the value of the other is not implied.

gift-giving and receiving confirms the implication and establishes bonds of mutuality and trust between giver and receiver. The giver has to know or accurately guess ('mind-read') the need of the other in order to satisfy it, so the interaction with others has the potential for informing h:er about many different things and people. Vice-versa, the receiver is informed by receiving many different kinds of gifts and services from the motherer and others.

As we just said, there is also a gift syllogism: If A gives to B and B gives to C then A gives to C. Passing gifts on, circulating them, creates relations among many givers and receivers, who thereby form a community. (There is also positive emotion even joy in receiving and passing it on – perhaps a kind of Kristevan *jouissance*?).

Exchange is ego-oriented in that the satisfaction of the need of the other is done to in order to satisfy the need of the 'giver'. Value is given to the self by implication rather than to the other. This is not gift value but its contradiction. It is not direct fruition of use value because it passes through the logic of exchange. In exchange, the satisfaction of the need of the other is a means to the satisfaction of one's own need. The self-nurturing that results is not informed by the autonomy of the fruition of use value nor the life enhancing aspect of receiving gifts, rather the instrumentalization of the other's need creates a power dynamic which has to be offset by an equal instrumentalization of one's own needs by others. Since each is trying to get a free gift of profit the relation is standardized as equally adversarial and possibly deceitful. The kind of value that one gives to oneself through exchange is altered by the power dynamic. It is not gift value, nor is the transaction directly transitive. Rather the short loop back to the self through the exchange process, the cancellation of the gift, the assertion of the exchange value of the commodity, abstract the relation so that the value of the commodity is fetishized, and made more important, taking the place of the value of the people, perhaps even of the self. This makes ownership necessary for self-validation.Though money or a product comes back from the exchange process to the exchanger, there is not the same kind of transitivity that there is in giving-and-receiving or even perhaps in non-market self-nurturing. The implications of value are different and possibly less satisfying, so the exchanger always wants more.

Equal exchange requires quantification, calculation and measurement while gift-giving is mainly qualitative. Thus the kind of investigation into other's needs and into the goods and services that will satisfy them is altered; cost-benefit calculations intervene. While gift-giving takes place not only in response to direct requests but mainly through 'mind-reading'[8] the

---

8   'Mind-reading' is the ability of even very young children to have a 'theory of mind' of others, to know what they are thinking or feeling from their point of view.

needs of the other, exchange is based on 'effective demand'. This is the economists' phrase for the need of the other expressed in terms of money. If the need cannot be expressed in money, it is not recognized and so not satisfied 'economically'.[9] Empathy for the other, which is part of mind-reading, is not considered a factor.

Similarly, in the study of language, recognizing the communicative or cognitive need of the other does not seem to be a factor. Rather, satisfying the other's need only arises as an issue when s:he explicitly asks a question or makes a request. Yet, we do mind-read others all the time and use empathy to select the words they need in order to be able to direct their attention somewhere, and to construct a common ground that will be relevant to them as well as to us.

The necessity for an equal exchange requires establishing an equivalence between two products or between a product and money. This often also requires each exchanger to know what the product is for the other. That is, how much it is worth to h:er. We calculate the damage or advantage to the other of giving up h:er product or getting ours. The attitude towards the other is thus very different from the attitude in gift-giving, where one investigates or guesses the need of the other simply in order to satisfy it (with attention to the well-being and often also to the likes and dislikes of the receiver). The relationship that is established between exchangers is short-term and competitive. It is a relation of mutual exclusion, independence and suspicion rather than mutual inclusion, interdependence and trust (though various kinds of small gifts can "sweeten" it, from a smile to a *lagniappe*).

In exchange, each person's property relation reflects the other's (making them mutually substitutable). The need for each commodity to be equated with the others as calculated in money is widespread and influences us to internalize this process as psychological self- and other-monitoring and evaluation. This attitude is different from the opening or transparency towards the other, which is typical of direct gift-giving and receiving. Philosophically, like the mirroring of the equation of value, the idea of self-reflecting consciousness is now so common it is almost a truism, while the openness towards the other that is necessary for gifting is discredited as 'instinctual' or naive or, on the other hand, is exceptionalized as some kind of moral achievement. Actually, it is just part of the mothering/being mothered job description.

If self-reflecting consciousness, the equation between the self in one moment and some internal self-image or standard, is actually influenced by

9   Social welfare programs may be considered a partial exception here.

monetized exchange, we should ask if it still can be seen as ethical or even as an accurate description of our internal processes. Indeed, self-reflection should be radical and complete enough to include the possibility that its source lies in the market and make us want to change it.

In fact, problems regarding ethics and subjectivities can be clarified by considering them as coming from the conflict between the two economies of gift and exchange. The ethics of care can be seen as the superstructure of the gift economy while the ethics of justice are superstructural to the exchange economy.

2.3 Emotion and reason

I would like to clarify some aspects of my approach. Feminist economist Julie Nelson (2010) calls my work 'feminine' instead of feminist. Nelson says that I 'elevate the right hand column of her Table 1 and completely neglect the left' (p. 242).

"SPLITTING THE WORLD: CONTENT AND MODEL SCHEMAS IN NEOCLASSICAL ORTHODOXY":

Economics	Not economics
Markets	Social life and family
Mental choice	Bodily experience
Individuals	Relationships
Autonomy	Interdependence
Self-interest	Other-interest
Rationality	Emotion
Masculine	Feminine

I take issue with this on several counts, as the reader will probably already understand. First, by re-defining gift-giving as economic, I already challenge the divisions of the two columns. Second, although I certainly recognize their existence, I do believe that markets are pernicious and so do emphasize social life and the family. Third, I do not believe that bodily experience rules out mental choice or any other kind of mental activity. Rather I try to show that not only individual but also interpersonal bodily experience is the basis for much mental activity. Of course, this does not rule out mental activity. On the other hand, I believe that 'mental choice' has been deeply undermined by advertising and other market manipulations such as propaganda (see 'choice' in US elections!). I understand individuals as developing *in* relationships, not independently of them. I think that autonomy as seen by many people in patriarchal capitalism is usually an illusion, a way of ignoring dependence on the gifts of others by calling on the sanitized concepts of 'making' money and 'deserving' profit. I believe that other-interest is a fundamental aspect of our consciousness, which is not recognized as such, and that it is more positive than the kind of self-interest that is promoted by the market. Other-interest in a gift economy does not exclude self-provisioning.

I particularly want to address the issue of rationality and emotion to which Nelson devotes her article. In fact, I believe it is not appropriate to identify the rationality of the market with rationality as such. There is a logic to gift-giving that precedes the logic of the market and lies beneath it. This is the simple but important transitive logic of A gives x to B, which has predictable life consequences. This logic is very flexible in that it can be enacted at different levels and with many different kinds of contents. Giving to satisfy the needs of another gives value to the other by implication, while giving in exchange (to satisfy one's own needs using the other as means) implies only the value of the self. While the logic of the maternal gift is not categorization through equivalence and identity as is the logic of exchange, it does function according to implication and is schematizable and rational. We simply have not viewed it that way and, thus, have been blind to alternatives to exchange and to the market that already exist, in the family, in indigenous matricentric and matriarchal communities and, as I am trying to show, in language.

Throughout history, humans have tried many different kinds of social and economic organization, justified by different kinds of reasoning. The patriarchal capitalist market is only one kind of organization, and a particularly pernicious one. What kind of rationality is it that leads to the destruction of the reasoners themselves and their environment?

Emotions are connected with one's own needs and with recognizing the needs of others. This makes emotions functional for the gift economy, which satisfies needs. The exchange economy instrumentalizes the satisfaction of the needs of others for the satisfaction of one's own need and it is functional in the transaction for the exchangers not to feel very strongly about each other. Thus, it appears that non-mothering men and women who exchange are rational while motherers, especially mothering women, are emotional. Even when women are not motherers they usually do not lose the ability they learned from the interaction with their own motherers to feel emotions and respond to needs. Euroamerican masculated men, on the other hand, have been forced to give up their original identification with their female mothers and seek an identity in opposition to giving, an identity of domination or at least of participation in gift-cancelling exchange. Emotions of grief and fear connected with the early denial of identity with the mother and the transfer of identification to the model of the distant father authority are repressed as are the emotions of empathy that might lead to giving. The market is a safe place for those who want to feel less. Giving, in contrast, seems sticky and full of relational traps. Indeed, gifts can be used for real and emotional bribery and blackmail. That is, they can be used for exchange purposes.[10]

The original identification with the mother is not so much a merging as Freud supposed and as Nelson might think, but an interactive development of selves as the infancy researchers now believe. In this interaction, emotions register and allow us to track all the 'shifting states of self-awareness' (Trevarthen 2010) that arise with their different bodily responses, rhythms and tempos. Antonio Damasio (1994, 1999, 2010) has done extensive research on the neurobiological connections of cognition and reason with emotions. Unfortunately discovering the neurological connections between reason and emotion has also opened up the field of 'neuromarketing'.

I see an important aspect of emotion as allowing oneself to be moved (title of Bråten's edited volume *On Being Moved* [2007]) by needs. The kind of purpose one has in writing books (and reading them) influences the kinds of things one notices. I am not an academic economist, linguist, philosopher or semiotician but just a child – now actually an old woman – of my time. My purpose is to try to understand why we act in such negative ways as a society, so that we can change them. I see a need and am emotionally invested in trying to satisfy it. This is rational.

---

10   The negative side of the gift economy in a closed community is that relations may become obligatory and heavy. A need arises for distance. This might be satisfied in various ways, by widening the community or diminishing obligations, but the appeal to exchange is often seen as the way out, into anonymity. In that sense exchange might be seen paradoxically as a gift satisfying a need caused by excessive gifting. I believe that recognizing the problem would allow the need to be met in other ways inside the gifting community.

2.4 Tracking care and cunning

One more gift process that has been interpreted according to the exchange paradigm while ignoring the gift basis is the individual's understanding of others' giving to others. As I mentioned in the beginning, the tracking of the circulation of gifts among others was discussed by Robin Dunbar (1996), as influential in the origin of language. He believed that complex relations created through grooming among *hominidae* could have been the spark for the brain development of *homo sapiens sapiens*. While this capacity for understanding the relations among others has been used as the basis of the theory of Machiavellian Intelligence, or political cunning, there is a positive bonding and community-forming aspect that must be there before the knowledge of it can be used for individual advantage. In other words, it is only on the basis of the positive social relations created by grooming or by gifting that the cunning manipulation of these relations can take place.

What is important for understanding language as giving and receiving is the idea that not only do individuals themselves interact with each other in dyads or triads or larger multiplicities, but that they can recognize when others are interacting dyadically or triadically or in even more extended ways. That is, they can track 'who gives what to whom'.[11] Turning this ability towards the world around us allows us to track gifts to gifts in the environment. That is, it allows us to understand the color red as having been given to the ball. Moreover, turning this 'tracking' ability towards syntax allows us to see the word 'red' as given to the word 'ball'. This is not Machiavellian in the sense of cunning, rather it is a projection of nurturing onto different players at different levels, recognizing it there and re-enacting it for the purpose of communicative nurturing, using a great variety of word-gifts as means.

In perception, through our continual unconscious or pre-conscious exploration of the world, we find the gifts, the gestalts, the affordances that attract our attention. We explore our surroundings and encounter many gifts, but see them as coming to us, or attracting us to them. We find gifts and we project giving onto the world. Then we give word-gifts, bringing them forward from an internal background to satisfy others' communicative needs and by this nurturing process we bring the world-gifts forward for the attention of listeners/receivers/readers as well. This unconscious

---

11   Among bonobos, groomers and groomees are probably each able to take the perspective of the other in the interaction, since they shift roles often.

maternal two-step in which we all participate[12] lets us create the joint attention and the common topic or focus, which allow us to track gift relations in the world in similar ways. We project gift-giving onto the world and receive our perceptions of it from the world, and we recreate the consequent gift relations by virtualizing/verbalizing and giving the gifts again to others in the form of word-gifts assembled in gift-based grammatical sentences. Like bats doing echolocation, we project nurture onto the world and perceive/receive its gifts and pass them on.[13]

The maternal linguistic commons is the language capacity itself as it is expressed in the thousands of specific mother tongues. Our linguistic competence of a specific language is the collection of the words, the verbal gifts we have to give, together with the ways we have to give them. The gift initiative is the connection between competence and performance: actually giving verbally to satisfy others' communicative and cognitive needs. What we talk about, the focus of our linguistic joint attention, is our momentary common ground, a relevant perceptual/conceptual commons, which we are continually creating and recreating. The idea of a self as 'owner' of knowledge isolates us from the perceptual, conceptual and linguistic commons, and makes consciousness difficult to understand (so we search for it in biology). Instead, if the relation of our selves to our knowledge is having-to-give, it is already more dynamic, fluid and understandable. We receive perceptions and conceptions and ready ourselves to give them again (because we have them to give) using the verbal gifts with which we satisfy the communicative and cognitive needs of others. It is just in its giveability that our knowledge is present to our minds, i.e. conscious.

Recently, biologists have begun exploring the importance of ecological niche construction for evolution (see http: //lalandlab.st-andrews.ac.uk/niche/ and Odling-Smee, Laland and Feldman 2003). The effects a species has on its environmental niche (construction of nests, burrows, creation of waste, food depletion or enhancement, migration), create selective pressures for the further evolution of the species. Odling-Smee and Laland (2009) use niche construction to discuss the evolution of language. I think they are probably right, but certainly the influence does flow in the other direction: language is a means for the social construction of our

---

12   One might think of this process being somatized in an actual basic dance step. Danica Anderson describes the Kolo circle dance with steps transmitted from grandmother to mother to daughter (2012).

13   Thus, though salient perceptions may 'pop out' at us, perhaps they are also 'bouncing back'. Is it too far-fetched to remark that bats nurture their pups intensely as well?

environmental niche as relevant, nurturing and shareable, another possible maternal commons (that begins to be visible when we behave maternally towards each other, even just on the verbal plane). This has allowed the recombination of many of its aspects into a great variety of new niches, which our further evolution has continued to address.

The invention of monetized exchange, in contradiction to gift-giving and language, constructs a niche that selects for anti-nurturing, accumulative, dominant behavior. The market is an artificial environment that pressures humans to evolve in a direction that is in opposition to our maternal language and linguistically mediated, transitive ways of knowing; it turns us away from our highest potential as a species. It moves us in a direction counter to the meaning created by the other-directed relevance of the world, woven through and by linguistic and material gift-giving. It is not surprising that many people now feel that life is meaningless. Recognizing the losses of meaning created by the market is a necessary step in restoring the significance of life and restoring life-enhancing niches for our own and all other species.

CHAPTER III

GIFTING NICHES

3.0 Gifted perceptions

Putting mothering/being mothered back into epistemology also has consequences for our view of perception. The child receives the satisfaction of h:er needs through the initiative of h:er mother or other caregiver(s) and this experience is the most important one for h:er, because h:er survival depends on it. The motherer constitutes an especially proactive environmental niche for the child. Turning this idea around, the environment can be understood as a somewhat less proactive motherer. The child, by creatively receiving her perceptions, projects a proactive gift character onto her surroundings. She generalizes giving to the environment. Everything comes to h:er as a gift or what James Gibson (1979) called an 'affordance' (the ways it can be used)[1] even if s:he actively receives it by reaching for it or crawling to it. S:he lives in a motherworld of gifted perceptions. If s:he is born into an abundant gift economy, s:he can more easily generalize this provisioning character to the world around her, understood as Mother Earth, and this is confirmed by respect for mothers and by maternal goddess images and archetypes in cultures where these exist. S:he can also receive h:er own unconscious selection of attentional focuses as a maternal selection.[2] The capacity for ultra-rapid pre-conscious selection is nature operating in us.

Again, although neuropsychology has made great progress in the study

---

1   According to Gibson, qualities, such as colour, texture, or shape, can be discriminated if we are required to, but what we normally pay attention to is the 'unique combination of qualities that specifies what the object affords us' (Gibson 1977: 75). 'A flat surface, for instance, around the height of the knees, affords sitting-on, while an elongated object of moderate size and weight affords pounding-with' (Susi and Ziemke 2005: 11).

2   There is pre-conscious selection of attentional focuses, which takes place in milliseconds before we are conscious of the focuses (Velmans 1999). Our internalized mother selects what is good or important for us to perceive, just as our mother selected nurturing gifts to give us. This is called pre-conscious or pre-attentive processing.

of perception and childhood development, it has not taken into account the giftedness of life for young children, which is the product and complement of mother work. The study of mirror neurons has revealed the unconscious simulation by the child of others' gestures, particularly of the mouth and the hands. However, although these studies register the importance of the mouth in receiving food and giving language they have neglected the importance of the hands in giving and receiving gifts and performing services. The mirror neuron effects of the mother nurturing the child have only begun to be studied but it is clear that each must unconsciously register and simulate the giving and receiving of the other. Thus, each knows how it feels both to give and to receive. As the saying goes, 'receiving is giving and giving is receiving'.

It turns out we know much more about what others are thinking and feeling than we realized. We not only know at the level of mirror neuron simulation, but we do a lot of putting ourselves in the place of the other, taking h:er perspective and guiding h:er gaze in joint attention by pointing. Children are able to 'mind-read' quite early. They can understand what the other person can perceive from h:er perspective. A number of experiments have been done in this area, which test whether children can distinguish another's perspective from their own. They succeed in the experiments at around four years of age, but they are actually able to share perspectives well before that, in 'joint attention', which I characterize as receiving the same perceptual gift together. (Directing another's gaze towards something, as the child does when pointing, means that the child realizes that the other is not seeing the same thing when her gaze is directed elsewhere!). These capacities develop into the ability to identify others' needs including their needs to know, cognitive needs, which can also be communicative needs: needs for someone else to guide their attention to something and create mutuality (community) between them and towards it.[3] Guiding the other's attention to a perceptual gift is itself a gift (the gift of a gift). Then both inter-actors can receive the perceptual or experiential gift together, that is, they can share it.

We begin life in a world that is given and that can be shared as a knowledge commons (not a world of private property and no trespassing). We develop ways of knowing that are based on being mothered

---

3   Perhaps this seems to be an unjustified extension of the term 'need' in that it is a 'light' necessity. Still without the intervention of the other, one's attention might never be directed towards that particular object. It is the satisfaction of this kind of communicative needs that the gifts of language provide. We shall see the importance of these needs later on.

and on imitating and projecting the model of the motherer, on receiving and giving with h:er, with other people and with our surroundings. Leaving the early mother-child gift experience out of epistemology has made knowledge mysterious by denying its model in ontogeny and then by denying or mystifying gift processes in the rest of life.[4]

3.1 Nature nurtures

Attunement to our environmental niche comes from our human ability to creatively receive its many complex aspects as gifts, collaborating with each other and together projecting the mother, establishing a relation with nature *as if* it were intentionally nurturing us. We do this both individually and together through the joint attention and mind-reading abilities that we learn to use early in the maternal dyad and that accompany us throughout life.

We saw above that children construct a 'like me' bridge with their motherers. They form their identities in recognizing their similarity with h:er and h:ers with them. I propose that once this identity is beginning to form, they can also turn it outwards towards other people and even towards the environment. Thus, joint attention would function as a sort of 'like us' bridge, in that the focus of the joint attention 'comes forward' from a background like a given gift for both attenders, who themselves come forward with gifts in other moments. 'Mother surroundings' is 'like us' and we are also like each other in this triangulated way. These early intersubjective achievements form the structure upon which future communication depends and they continue to be used and developed in an ongoing way. Our material communicative experience, elaborated in this way, allows us to reason from our own cognitive and kinetic responses when we want to know what something is. We can also ask: 'what kind of gift is this for others?', 'How do they feel?'.[5]

---

4   Even if there are no absolute givens – the gift processes themselves are constantly given throughout life and they involve other individuals, the community and the environment.

5   And for ourselves as adults if we attune our responses with theirs and vice-versa? What did or would our 'fluctuating state of consciousness' feel like in this particular case? What would our emotional reactions be, in this case, once aligned with others'? In this way, the experience becomes memorable. Healers tell us that all our experiences are registered somewhere in our bodies. Thus, our bodies are full of reference points, which were, might have been, or could be, registrations or residues of experiences of points of joint attention/reception of perceptual or experiential gifts.

The individual in the intersubjective dyad turns outwards but persists and continues to construct h:er 'like me' and 'like us' identities through material communication and perception. As the child grows up, s:he remains in a dyadic relation with h:er surroundings, by which s:he is nurtured perceptually and is offered affordances and the means of the provision of material needs. However, when s:he is living in a society based on private property and exchange, most of the gifts of the environment – the motherworld – become unavailable to h:er materially, and s:he has to adjust to this contradictory situation.

Nature does not exchange, but 'gives' everything abundantly. The interpretations of Nature as punishing humans or wanting revenge come from the exchange paradigm (and from motherers who embrace it). The interpretation of Nature as nurturing derives from the gift paradigm. Jakob von Uexkull (2010 [1934]) developed the idea of the *umwelt*, now used in ecological semiotics, emphasizing the various pre-established perceptual frameworks that all the various species of animals have for their interactions with their environments. Von Uexkull's prime example was the tick, which only responds to caloric and chemical signals of the presence of mammalian blood. Attached to a branch or a blade of grass it can wait dormant for months until those signals arrive, then in an instant drop to contact with its 'prey' and begin to feed (probably with accompanying sensations). One can imagine the tick's consciousness as blank or dormant, ignorant of everything taking place around it except for the two all-important perceptual sensations. They are what comprise the tick's *Umwelt*. The kind of receiver the tick is, determines the world it can have.

Our *Umwelts* are also determined by the kinds of receivers we are. Dependent but socially alert (Trevarthen 2010) human infants, born with 'active intersubjective minds' are already social receivers. Mothering provides important need-satisfying experiences that have an interpersonal aspect from the beginning. The child's *Umwelt* is already socially selected, made of perceptions provided by the motherer (*gratis*) beginning with the motherer's body, the surroundings, food, living space. The child becomes a receiver who is able to respond to the world, making it relevant by projecting the perspective of the nurturer onto it and receiving nurturing from it.

S:he receives materially and perceptually from the motherer but also receives and perceives together with the motherer in joint attention. S:he actively explores as well in order to receive, to learn what gifts h:er environment provides. In h:er explorations, the gifts s:he finds lead h:er to other gifts. H:er needs become educated by variations in their fulfilment. First, s:he is nurtured only with milk, then water, juice and mashed and then solid food.

In this vein, we can look at Gibson's 'affordances' as gifts we receive from the environment, ways it is relevant to us. The term itself is strange, like the economic term 'effective demand' as if things could pay (or we could pay?) for the experiences they give us. Children discover the 'manipulability', 'chewability', 'throwability' of things (Gibson 2000: 37). Perception is a kind of 'foraging for information' (Gibson 2000: 26). We should think of the foraging as a process of (creative) receiving. The idea of receiving as passive is practically the only thing that keeps us from seeing affordances as gifts. Children actively and with creative receptivity search for affordances and experiment with the world around them. They find out what gifts it gives and creatively receive them. They both construct and are constructed by the environmental and cultural niches in which they fit.

In fact, our sense organs are nature and we use them to find out how other parts of nature nurture us. Many of these parts of nature are now culturally constructed with pre-established affordances, as are for example a rattle or a pacifier. These are given by parents to children, gifts with affordances that are appropriate for the children but not for adults. They are gifts of gifts that satisfy the needs of the receiver. As children's creative receptivity becomes more expert and refined, the affordances in the surroundings seem to become more accurately targeted to the child's needs and abilities, but this is also because the child h:erself is more capable.

In the process of exploration, the surroundings are both made relevant and found to be relevant, full of affordance gifts. Whether they are given by the motherer or by the world, the child is continually in a state of creative receptivity of the gifts and services of her surroundings. S:he also discovers the affordances of giving. S:he learns s:he can also give, imitating the other and that the other can receive from h:er.

For James Gibson, the senses actively select the aspects of the environment that are relevant to the organism's activity. He shows how we continually scan the visual environment. Already Yarbus (1967) had described how we unconsciously pick out the salient aspects of the visual field. Gibson (1977) elaborated upon this.

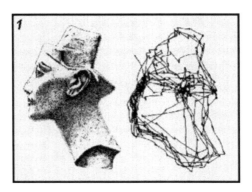

Figure 2: Eye movements pick out salient points
on the bust of Nefertite (Yarbus 1967: 181)

Giving/receiving is fundamental for our lives and the process of our knowledge, and we use it as a lens. Neurological studies in 'salience theory' show that we unconsciously or pre-consciously select pertinent perceptions from a background of many others. This internal filter and guide provides us with perceptual and cognitive gifts in a way that is similar to maternal selections of gifts and services for children. Chiarcos et al. (2011: 15), in their work on salience, tell us that things seem to 'pop out' from a background, calling our attention to them. Adults also do this in the games they play with babies, smiling, putting their faces forward, nodding, saying 'boo', playing peep-eye. They pop out from the background, as gifts coming forward to be perceived as relevant.

Meltzoff says, by 18 months, children react differently to people and to things. They realize that 'human acts are goal-directed but the motions of inanimate objects are not' (Heider 1958, quoted in Meltzoff and Prinz 2002). Thus, children have to supply the intentionality themselves, going towards the objects, fitting them to their needs or exploring them to find out what needs of their own or others they might satisfy. Their own natural curiosity and initiative supply the trajectory of the environmental gift. In the beginning, they have a strong need for oral stimulation and they approach most objects by putting them in their mouths, appreciating and understanding their oral affordances.

Our basic coordinates for understanding the world are established by giving/receiving actions with innumerable variations of content and form. This variety itself to some extent obscures the giving/receiving structure of the basic coordinates. Exchange, which contradicts giving/receiving, confuses the picture even more by instating the opposite pattern.

When the exchange economy is identified as the problem at last, the alignment or meshing of the human maternal gift economy with Mother Nature can be understood as extremely positive, not as evidence of the supposed inferiority of mothering or of women or of nature. This meshing is the basis of epistemology. It gives us the way we know.

If children were not mothered, this physiological or natural interaction would not occur. But then the children would not survive. So they learn from the model of what causes their survival. Its availability for their instruction is guaranteed.

3.2 Motherers' nature

Past and present indigenous (matriarchal) gift economies that function according to the maternal prototype extend the principle of the gift to the community as a whole, which therefore functions according to the generalization of giving and receiving. Both individuals and the community creatively receive from nature and they also form a cultural niche that provides more gifts for community members – a sort of 'second nature' mixed with human mothering/gift-giving. Group giveaways, and individual giving and receiving customs and roles, create the commonality and solidarity that allow the community to thrive.

As a whole, the community is a creative receiver for the gifts of the natural environment, as well as for the gifts of the social environment, and it passes the gifts on among its members and to succeeding generations both materially and linguistically. In fact, language is a way of collectively receiving, thinking about, and transmitting the abundant perceptual and conceptual gifts of the social and natural environment. Passing gifts on to each other is an important factor in establishing and maintaining human society. The verbal plane allows people to be linguistic givers and receivers and to create linguistic community and human gift relations even in cases where the means of material giving and receiving are lacking or privatized.

The fact that humans have language and memory, personal and social histories, makes us into complex givers/receivers and, thus, alters and determines the kinds of gifts our environment gives us by determining our wants and needs and what we can and do receive (and give again). While we have developed as creative receivers, we have also altered (given to) our environmental niches and influenced the kinds of gifts that are given to us by our surroundings. Together these constitute the many and varied gifts to which we give our attention in order to creatively receive them.

The interaction of giving and receiving creates relations among humans of mutuality and trust, rather than reciprocal indifference and autonomy. It originates in the turn-taking giving and receiving of early childhood that creates in everyone a common form of human subjectivity as beings who are givers and receivers both of language and of material goods, services and experiences. There are many individual variations on these basic patterns of communicative identity, according to personal histories, interests, desires, sexual identities and social roles, but without them we do not function as human.

Both as children and as adults, we turn our creative receptivity towards the social and natural environmental niches around us and we receive the gifts of perception, which come forward to us as *gestalts* from the background. These are gifts in that we have a *need* to perceive, which they satisfy. As sensory deprivation experiments have shown, when we are awake, we cannot stay sane very long in a situation in which we perceive nothing. Moreover, as we just saw above, we unconsciously select what we attend to from the perceptual abundance that is given to us.

Our reception of perceptual gifts is 'nature' in that it involves our organisms' constant pre-conscious exploration and scanning of the environment together with a selection of what to attend to, deriving from our unconscious or pre-conscious syntheses of our previous experience (Velmans 2014). We mother ourselves in that we pick out to receive perceptions of things that are relevant for us from the background, just as our motherers picked out need-satisfying gifts for us from the background when we were young. However, we are not conscious of doing this, so it is our own bodies, our biological selves as Motherers Nature that bring forward these gifts to our perception, i.e. that are satisfying our needs to perceive with these gifts. We are mothered children who not only mother others but ourselves and who project mothering onto the world around us and receive from the motherworld, Motherer Nature. This projection is neither fanciful nor far-fetched. It is a true projection and we are, our biological selves, corporeally H:er. We are H:er in our pre-conscious mental functioning and our conscious minds are also H:er because they function according to giving/receiving at other more abstract levels. As I said above, perhaps it is not too far-fetched to think that the connections between our neurons are also established by a kind of giving/receiving of impulses across synapses? In any case, we are able to interpret the connections that way because we have been mothered and unconsciously use that pattern. Our environmental niches 'mother' us because we creatively receive their gifts. We are biologically and perceptually self-motherers. At the same time we are also socially and linguistically self- and other-motherers, receivers of others' gifts and givers of gifts to them.

Our capacity to engage with the environment in this way is also a positive factor for evolution, allowing us from prehistorical times to construct new ways of receiving Motherer Nature's (and Motherer Culture's) gifts and passing them on, like using fire for cooking (mostly by women) (Wrangham 2009), making and using tools for gathering and hunting, and creating traditions of collaboration, all of which have had important effects on our biological as well as our social evolution. Projecting giving/receiving and mothering onto the environment puts us in a relationship with it that is similar to our human relationships.[6] If our concept of mothering is positive, this can also help us bond with the environment and care for it. This bonding could help us in our own evolution as a maternal species. Instead, at the present in the West, we are scientifically and 'objectively' eliminating the projection of gift-giving and mothering and at the same time, tragically, the environment's and our own capacity to give.

Although the eye does not have a beam as was once thought, and is 'receptive' of the light, it explores its surroundings very quickly and, thus, receives visual information from a number of minutely different angles, 'saccadically', perhaps, making up for its lack of 'fingers'. Its proactive receptive capacity is enhanced by being receptive differently , many different times.

Moreover, we travel through our environments creating flows of different perspectives on our surroundings (J. J. Gibson 1979). Our eyes select what to attend to without our being conscious of the selection.[7] One might even say that, perceptually, we are gatherers or even sometimes hunters, but not agriculturalists. We do not plow, sow or reap our perceptions and our reception of them as gifts does not diminish them. Nor do they usually become our private property as such. They form a perceptual commons from which common gifts emerge, passed on among us, given forward by giving verbal gifts to each other for them.

---

6   See the Kungs' relation to the forest as mother for example (Bird-David (1990).

7   Reading is thus a capturing of this movement and focus on a small area, narrowing down the action of the reception, making it more like taking than receiving. We could cite the inventor of the Cherokee alphabet, Sequoyah (1770-1840) who thought 'that if he could make things fast on paper, it would be like catching a wild animal and taming it' (Foreman 1938: 28). Perhaps one could say tha reading is more self-interested than seeing in general, especially reading to 'acquire knowledge'.

3.3 Having (to give) and (having to) give

While women represent *half* the global population and *one-third* of the labor force, they receive only *one-tenth* of the world income and own *less than one percent* of world property. They are also responsible for *two-thirds* of all working hours (Robin Morgan 1984). These statistics have changed very little in the last decades.

Why is it that, in spite of feminism, women still own only a minimal amount of property worldwide even though, in developing countries, they do almost half of the agricultural work (FAO 2015)? The answer is that most of them are motherers who are practicing an alternative economy, the gift economy, which really cannot function well on the basis of private property and scarcity. Women try to provide abundantly. Much of what they have, they have-to-give rather than to keep. That is, it is given freely in a positive sense to husbands, children, other family members, guests and the community at large.

There is also the negative sense that women are forced to give. Those who willingly give unilaterally are vulnerable to those who only take unilaterally and accumulate property without giving and without passing the gifts on. The market mechanism itself takes many free gifts, disguises them by renaming them deserved 'profit', and alters their flow away from the needs of the many. Although gift-giving is often a strategy for survival in scarcity, for the gift economy and the circulation of gifts to function on a wide scale, there needs to be abundance.

Whether in poverty or abundance, motherers make their gifts available to children in a kind of sharing-property relation that is very different from private property. There are gift economies that function on the principle of obligation to give immediately upon request (Bird-David 1990). Although I am not advocating this,[8] there is something like it in mothering, especially regarding children's needs. Private property is very different, based on not-giving (except by force or by trickery, or when leveraged in exchange or moved exceptionally in charity).

It was thought stereotypically for centuries that women, especially mothers, were like Nature and men were the bearers of culture. In a sense this is true bacause Nature is more like mothers in that, like them, it has to

---

8   I think it is important that the giver recognize the need of the other even without h:er asking. A society based on asking could be stressful unless the askers self-regulate by interpreting the needs of the giver, or unless there were enough abundance to make much asking unnecessary. On the other hand, 'mind-reading' leaves the initiative up to the giver, which is more empowering for h:er and, thus, makes it more likely that s:he will give.

give. Men don't have to give as much because in a culture of private property most of the owners have been men and they have not had to give but to possess and to exchange. Does this mean that women should be owners too, as has happened recently? Or does it mean that we should create a general culture of having to give more similar to Nature?

Our experience of our surroundings, like mothering, works according to the principle of having-to-give. Perceptual gifts are 'given' to us unilaterally by our surroundings and we receive them freely, 'pre-consciously choosing' the ones we will attend to and backgrounding or ignoring the others. Similarly, our motherers choose what gifts to give us and what parts of our environment to leave in the background. Sometimes, because of our life circumstances, what is given to us to view may be limited, but our perceptions themselves remain free. That is, except in cases of disabilities, we are always receivers of the gifts of perception, even when we are living in material scarcity and deprivation. Prison is painful to us also because it diminishes the variety of the perceptual gifts we can receive.

The same free perceptual abundance that each of us creatively receives, is available for other people, as well as ourselves, as a relevant perceptual and conceptual commons that is also specified, created and confirmed by language. We can also extend the gift relation to other parts of our environment. That is, using the gift paradigm, looking at the things we perceive through a gift lens rather than a lens of private property we can understand the 'properties' of things as having been given to them. The ball has 'received' the color red and passes the perception on to us when our vision scans and selects it as a focus of our attention. We give a verbal virtual gift for this perceptual gift and say 'red ball', giving 'red' to 'ball' and the gift of both together to the receiver, 'passing it on' in a way that implies our prior reception of the perceptual gift. The listener scans the surroundings as well and turns her attention to the ball to which the color red has been given, which s:he now receives as a perceptual gift jointly with the speaker. The surroundings can also be imaginary, hypothetical, or brought about by literary fabrication, relying on the memory of the listener to supply the details.

When we project the mother and child onto the world, the relation of things to other things and to us becomes understandable in a way that is based on nurturing and grounded in a freely given perceptual commons. Usually this is invisible to us in capitalist patriarchy because we wear the glasses of monetized exchange and private property, which eliminate gift-giving from what we attend to. These glasses bring forward exchange and place gift-giving out of focus in a devalued and seemingly insignificant background. Thus, it is just our market-based economic system that does not allow us to see what we are doing and who we are.

As receivers and givers, our communication with others is, in many cases, part of a relational chain, a proactive passing on of gifts rather than a starting from zero. The virtual verbal gifts of language allow us to pass on to others, at another level, the gifts of perception and experience, which we have received. In so doing, they confirm the gift character of the external originators of the chain: the BALL to which in this case RED has been given, is the (momentary) giver of the perception RED BALL,which we pass on to others with the verbal gifts 'red ball' (according to the gift syllogism). Our natural surroundings nurture us, perceptually and materially in their many parts. But so do our cultural surroundings, the ideas, traditions and interpretations, which have been given to us by others, which we have creatively received and internalized, which we pass on to others and which are also available to our own 'internal scanning'. Thus, even the memory or the imagined experience of a BALL, to which RED has been given, suffices for us to understand that the speaker had that perception to give and that s:he received it from the motherworld, which also had it to give and gave to h:er; s:he then passed it on to us by giving us word-gifts and we can also re-give it by giving word-gifts to others for it.

None of this would be available to us if we had not been nurtured by our motherers, and if we had not grasped the importance of their care-giving behavior, imitating and internalizing it in our turn. But, of course, if we had not received the nurturing, we would not have survived.

Philosophers and psychologists, whether wittingly or unwittingly, use the framework of private property for knowledge. For example, Damasio (2010) talks about knowledge 'belonging' to the self (otherwise, he says, 'how could we know it was ours?'). I would say the kind of belonging appropriate to the self is, rather, having the knowledge available to give, a maternal relation rather than one of private property, the attitude of a potential giver rather than an owner or ego-oriented keeper. (This in spite of the fact that, in the system of private property, we are all seen as mutually exclusive owners). We know it is our knowledge because we have it to give.

We do receive gifts of communication and of perception, which come to us from others or which we access ourselves. But an important aspect of our knowledge consists in our ability to eventually 'pass it on', using the verbal gifts that we have received from the community, the 'commons' of the lexicon, (even if we do not actually say anything at the moment in which we realize we know something). We can continue to bring it up, making it relevant to ourselves, remembering, thinking about it, etc. Except for the case of secrets, the real test of knowledge is the ability to pass it on (which, of course, does not cause us to lose it). We also have to try to give it well, so it will be appropriately received. Understanding our selves in terms of 'possessive individualism' does not lead us to an understanding of language and communication as gift constructions.

Considering nature as a nurturing commons, despite exchange, leads us to call it Motherer Nature because S:he provides the gifts that we have learned to creatively receive and give again.

As I said above, our pre-conscious perceptive capacity selects what to attend to without our being aware of this (maternal) selection This is a capacity that can be influenced by many things outside us: movements, colors, sounds, as well as by our internal purposes and intentions and the syntheses of past experiences. We can also re-combine our experiences in our imaginations. Language acquisition researchers now believe that children (and adults) do statistical sampling and calculation of probabilities (Romberg and Saffran 2010) in order to understand what is happening around them and to find the appropriate words to use. This computational ability of the 'scientists in the crib' (Gopnik, Meltzoff and Kuhl 1999) is also pre-conscious, and its products come to consciousness as gifts.

Though we sometimes have to search for them, words usually arrive in our awareness without effort, ready for our use. At both the conscious and the pre-conscious levels, communicating linguistically implements a collective and individual selection and reception of the abundant perceptual and conceptual gifts of our surroundings. It lets us mother each other on another plane, passing the gifts on to each other verbally, so it is an important factor in the way we establish and maintain individual and social bonds and develop subjectivity. It allows people to be linguistic givers and receivers and to create the linguistic community – the attentional maternal commons and human gift relations – whatever the external context may be.

We do receive perceptions free even if we sometimes 'expend' energy to 'take' them, by going towards their sources, as we move through our environments. The baby crawls towards the brightly colored toy and grasps it; the mountain climber scales the cliff to see the view from the top. The refugee scales the wall or crosses the ocean in a flimsy boat. Hungry children press their faces against the store window. The perceptions they receive are free though the food is not.

Our unconscious selections allow relevant perceptions to come to us by our going to them, given as they are by external and internal Motherer Nature. If necessary, we can also escape from them. We are physiologically prepared to pre-consciously select the things to which we attend. They are gifts from our internal nature and external surroundings that satisfy our needs to perceive and to know.

We realize others also need to know what is happening and we satisfy their needs. That is, we notice what may also be relevant to them. We take the gift initiative to pass the relevant perception, idea or circumstance on to them, thus confirming it as relevant.

'Fire!', 'What a sunset!', 'Look at that dancer's leap!', pass on the perceptual gifts to others, and so do declarative sentences, descriptions, explanations, etc.[9] The interactive process of giving, receiving and passing it on takes place not only among people but between people and the world, the motherworld. Again, knowledge is receiving the gifts of the motherworld and having the ability to pass them on using language, but also using other kinds of perceptual gifts, non-verbal signs we create with our bodies and minds to give to others for them to perceive. We live in and produce intricate gift constructions without seeing or recognizing them as such because we deny the mother and with her the relevance of transitivity. In fact, as I said, from this point of view we can understand knowing itself as transitive: receiving, having, preparing to give again and giving again (without losing).

The market imitates perceptual gifts in another register, manipulating our pre-conscious selection. Products in shop windows or their images on TV and computer screens pop out at us perceptually from a background demonstrating their relevance (with color, motion, sound and sex), so we will buy them (like the knowledge we 'acquire'). Market exchange and money reuse and misuse some of our gift-based cognitive processes, thereby not only blinding us to the original processes, but blinding us to the continued existence of the motherworld of which we are a part, and upon which money and the market are encroaching.

The co-existence of having-to-give, which is functional in the gift economy and having (or taking) -to-possess-or-exchange, which is the mode of the market, makes having-to-give vulnerable to appropriation and plunder by the market. In fact, having-to-give has very little defense against appropriators. It is perhaps this contradiction that is used as a rationale by patriarchy and paternalistic men to protect 'their' women against other men who are in the taking and dominating mode. In fact, there is very real and widespread danger for gift givers which has continued throughout history. Ways of addressing the danger collectively and peacefully do exist, however, and it would help if we could better understand the logically contradictory motivations perpetrators have for rape and plunder.[10]

---

9   And the gesture of pointing.
10   Perhaps the two levels of exchange and profit-taking promote rape and plunder. Only by understanding what the market does to the imaginary will we be able to stop this.

We need to validate the gift economy and maternal values for everyone including men. The social use of the maternal prototype in religious and spiritual terms (the unsubjugated divine maternal), and the understanding of nurture and nature as having-to-give, brings a collective validation of that mode.[11] Perhaps it once seemed that the market, the law and the separation of the domestic sphere from the market and public life could protect the vulnerable. However, it is quite clear that this is not the case.[12] There needs to be a discussion at a metalevel of the connections between economic violence and male violence, which can help us to collectively eliminate them so that participation in the motherworld can be made possible for all. Bateson called double binds 'schizophrenogenic'. We live with the contradictory injunctions 'give!' on the one hand, and 'take and dominate!' on the other, and our society is, indeed, insane. It is only by going to a metalevel and understanding these contradictory injunctions in a wider context that we can hope to resolve the double bind. Discussing gift-giving and exchange in language provides the wider context.

3.4 The gift and language lens

In the last century, semiotics moved away from the idea held by de Saussure[13] and his followers, that human language has a special importance among sign systems (glottocentrism). If we understand it as verbal maternal gift-giving and receiving, though, we can understand that language is central because mothering is central and language continues to put mothering into practice throughout life.

Language and gift-giving together form a lens through which we view and know the world. Thus language does take precedence for us in cognition, influencing our use of other (less maternal) systems of signs. This lens is what allows us to recognize other kinds of signs *as* signs and as parts of systems even though they may not be themselves the products

---

11   See, for example, the matriarchal Minangkabau of Sumatra who say "Just as the weak becomes strong in nature we must make the weaker the stronger in human life," Sanday 2002: 28.

12   Nearly 1 in 5 women (19.3%) and 1 in 59 men (1.7%) have been raped in their lifetime. One in 4 women (22.3%) have been the victim of severe physical violence by an intimate partner, while 1 in 7 men (14.0%) have experienced the same. http://www.cdc.gov/violenceprevention/pdf/nisvs-fact-sheet-2014.pdf

13   'Language is a system of signs that express ideas, and is therefore comparable to a system of writing, the alphabet of deaf-mutes, symbolic rites, polite formulas, military signals, etc. But it is the most important of all these systems' (Course p. 16).

of mothering. Biosemiotic and phytosemiotic phenomena, the genetic 'code' and hormonal 'messages', are understandable to us as signs and systems of signs because our mental glasses are formed both by material mothering communication and by a linguistic sign system that is based on mothering. This gives language a very central place in human communication and cognition. At the same time, the very versatility of the maternal gift pattern has somewhat disguised its core so that many structures that actually derive from gifting seem to stand alone.

In spite of our lack of consciousness of them, the basic lenses we use are produced by the maternal gift interaction and even though, at present, they are also altered by exchange, they continue to determine what we see. The overlay of exchange, as an anti-maternal filter on our maternal glasses (as artificial as clip-on polarized shades), eliminates both our knowledge of the maternal gift aspects of language and any consciousness of those aspects as a source area for projecting onto and understanding the world. Thus, we see ourselves as a species lost in the stars, a (mutually hostile and competitive) species that has nothing in common with its environment, which it, therefore, 'must' dominate in order to survive. Instead, maternal nurturing, maternal language and the projection of mothering onto our surroundings help to form the social interface between ourselves and the non-human but nevertheless nurturing motherworld. In this light, 'reality' is the giver side of our ecological and cultural niches of which we are the co-creative and inventive givers, receivers and passers-on.

Even if language is recognized as virtual mothering, we may still ask if human mothering – unilateral need satisfaction – should be attributed to (projected onto) non-human things. In fact, our projection of mothering onto Nature, the 'active' giving of the gifts of perception by the mother-world, makes up part of the gift lens and it remains as a factor in our understanding, even if we might not recognize it in that way 'scientifically', i.e. leaving aside humans (but what recognition and what science would there be without humans?).

We use the neutral and neuter concept 'code' instead of acknowledging mothering, so 'sign systems' seem to also be *sui generis* constructions that stand on their own. Perhaps some do, but we would not know them as sign systems or codes at all without our gift lenses and our own maternal gift-based sign system, language.[14]

If we look at the blue marble, our Earth from space, and take the broad ecological perspective, we can see how all the aspects of the environment

---

14   These lenses allow us to see sign systems as relevant, i.e. as gifts.

fit with each other, each serving as sustenance for some or many of the others in the web of life. We do not see this scientifically as mothering, nor at the individual level do we see mothering as an environmental 'fit'. Yet if we survive infancy, we have experienced that fit, and we are trained by experience to expect the part of our environment that is our human motherer to take the initiative to satisfy our needs. Our creative receptivity responds positively to these initiatives.

It is not a very big leap to generalize this expectation to other parts of our environment that are nurturing but less actively so. After all, in the womb the entirety of our environment was nurturing.

In fact, it is due to our creative receptivity that our surroundings may appear to take the initiative to satisfy our perceptual needs. Fluttering leaves 'call' our attention to them.[15] Bright colors 'leap out' at us. We are keyed to receive, to give attention to, what is new. We give some things more value by attending to them more. Our pre-conscious selective capacity picks out these more important elements and foregrounds them. Thus, it seems they take the initiative to come to us, to tickle our fancy, to say hello. Perhaps even more than other creatures, we live in a maternal perceptual '*umwelt*'. The way all the creatures and plants are delicately calibrated to all the others and each to its environmental niche lends itself to interpretation as maternal need satisfaction.[16]

We also alter nature to make 'it' respond to our needs, which also change and adapt accordingly. Thus, even *altered* nature is maternal. However, we have also invented a general and impelling economic-communicative need for money and we alter nature (and each other) again and again to make 'it' satisfy that need. This is causing huge distortions in the environment and in ourselves.

Earth-based philosophies, like that of permaculture, understand the all-round interconnectedness of living beings, micro-organisms, plants and animals, where each serves many different needs of the others and vice-versa. The African philosophy of *ubuntu* says something similar from the human point of view: 'we are all one." Native Americans call on 'all our relations'. Where the ego-orientation of exchange narrows the connection with others to our mutual egotism, the gift economy turns us

---

15 Psychologists like Jean Mandler (2004), find that infants give more attention to moving objects than to still ones.

16 Perhaps it would enhance our understanding if we use our maternal lens regarding other animals. The color of the flower is a signal to the bee that there may be nectar in the flower. It is a gift of the gift of nectar. What the bee is looking for is what the flower wants to give it. This is not so different from the motherer saying 'Dinner's ready!'.

towards others in a multi-faceted, need-satisfying way, and lets us see that they are turned towards us. The connections of words with other words are similar. As I will show, the connections depend on the needs of other words each word can satisfy. Projecting needs and gifts onto sounds (and graphemes) allows us to articulate the one world into the very many ways it can be relevant for humans and given and received by them.

3.5 Love me by facts

Non-verbal signs of all kinds nurture us as they do all other kinds of living beings. We humans receive and react to them in a very elaborate and intense way because we have been intensely mothered and because we continue to mother each other with language. Human non-verbal signs, postures, facial expressions, gestures, etc, can be nurturing gifts if the 'giver' can count on the other as a creative communicative receiver. We can also give off signs unintentionally, chemically, and kinetically, which others nevertheless receive, sometimes with undesired effects, because they are sensitive to their surroundings. Moreover, the black cloud means rain to us in a different way from other animals because our creative receptivity of sign gifts has been honed by mothering/being mothered and extended to many different kinds of nurturing. We have extended it also to meta-gifts, gifts about gifts. That is, the blackness of the cloud appears to have been given in order to give us something else: the idea of the probability of rain. It satisfies a need at one level and in doing so satisfies a need at another – because of the way we receive it (as mothered children).

Our capacity to receive perceptual gifts as gifts allows us to remain between signs and non-signs (Rossi-Landi 1992), to receive (and give) gifts as material nourishment *and/or* to receive them as communicative and giveable, potentially interpersonal gifts, which can also be passed on to others directly or by gifts of linguistic signs. Both sign gifts (including linguistic gifts) and material gifts are means by which we form human relations. The material gift-giving, first encountered in mothering/being mothered, creates the important patterns of giving and receiving, necessary for human communication.

The projection of the interpersonal gift patterns on to the world and our recognition of them there allow us to make what Victoria Welby called 'common sense', 'Mother Sense' (Petrilli 2009) of everything we perceive. Mothering could not be done by giving and receiving signs only, because the child would die.[17] It is this *sine qua non* of material nurturing that is the basis of human communication and language and, precisely because it is the basis, it leads us back to a material reality even when we find ourselves in a (postmodern) world that seems to be made only of signs.

A birth mother cannot easily be a linguistic or semiotic idealist; first, because she has the real body of the other inside her own real body and is responsible for its well-being even there. She is nurturing the child body-to-body before the child is born.[18] Then, once the child is part of external reality, she or someone else has to nurture h:er outside the womb or the child will die. This care that the motherer performs, as a realist, is itself propositional. It lays down in a material way the very grammar and inter-personal significance of the signs from which the linguistic/semiotic ideal-ist thinks it is impossible to escape.

The child's early giving and receiving in 'companion space'[19] with the motherer interactively constructs h:er ongoing *umwelt*-making process. Mirror neurons allow the establishing of common reactions and a common perspective. Through the shifting and reversal of perspectives from child to motherer and back, the child realizes the motherer is doing it too: s:he is taking h:er point of view as giver and as receiver. Pointing, s:he gives (without losing it) h:er point of view as perceptual receiver to the (m)other, who takes that point of view as well, creating joint attention, receiving the perception together.

The philosophical mind – body division, in which signs, which are seen as mental, have taken over, eliminated our understanding of propositional material communication among bodies – except when the bodies become signs.[20] If signs are mental, we 'solve' the mind-body problem by saying that all knowledge is mental. Everything we know is mind (instead, every-thing we know is the interactive child-and-motherer!). Signs do not seem to have a root in a non-sign world but function by referring to each other in systems, holistic networks of infinite semiosis. This rootlessness eliminates the idea of the motherer, the filling of needs and the gift economy. It elimi-

---

17 'Not words but acts!' says the child. 'Love me by facts!'
18 There are also choices she can make. She can eat healthy food, stop smoking and drinking alcohol. She can be careful not to lie on her stomach or fall on it.
19 Kenneth Wright (1991), following Lacan and Winnicot, talked about 'the space be-tween mother and child' Stein Bråten proposes infants' self-other 'companion space' (1998 [1992]). It is tempting to also reference in this context Fauconnier's (1994) and Fauconnier and Turner's (2002) 'mental spaces' in which 'blending' occurs.
20 Before the mind-body division there is a body-body division, when the child is birthed and h:er body is separated from that of the mother.

nates the transitive and transmissive interaction with the world of which knowledge as having-to-give is formed.

It also deprives signs of their deeper significance at another level, their ability to make a spiritual connection for us with the human community, the community of ancestors and the maternal all-that-is and it, thus, leaves the door wide open for the exploitation of language and other sign systems by the market and marketing, and sometimes even giving people a sense of language as the enemy.

For example, writer Andrew Gurevich quotes Orwell (1946), who calls words 'poisoned packets of arbitrary signification', and says 'rather than clarifying the link between truth and experience, our self-replicating linguistic memes obscure it, leading us along an infinite chain of signs and symbols. Signs and symbols that lead only to more signs and symbols. Over millennia, these linguistic artifacts accumulate over the surface of the ground of our being and cover it in reflexive, detached scraps of representation' (Gurevich 2012).

Instead, I propose that it is not language itself that is the problem but the postmodern philosophical and psychological conception of language as a kind of infinite semiotic metastasis, cut off from its root in the motherer-and-child interaction.

Mother-child altercentric intersubjectivity puts a healing other-oriented 'spin' even on non-linguistic signs, a 'spin' that less intensely and interactively mothered species presumably do not have. They would thus understand primarily through categorization. Our lack of recognition of the importance of mothering for epistemology places us in a mode of knowing that denies our species specificity.

Human semiosis has an altercentric directionality that allows signs to be shared (with a polarity of receiving and giving, slots and fillers). It is from the perspective of altercentric sign activity that we understand the world, i.e. receive its gifts and pass them on. Only from this interactive, nurtured perspective can we investigate, creatively receive and track the many different kinds of semiosis there may be even if at the same time we ignore the mothering that gave us that capacity. Even if it is true that, in Thomas Sebeok's sense, non-linguistic semiosis is everywhere, and that signs coincide with life itself, as now the disciplines of bio- and phytosemiotics are demonstrating, human signs have a social history both through the centuries and in ontogenesis. For us, they depend for their connectivity on early material communication.

3.6 Semiotics, mother sense and material communication[21]

Charles Sanders Peirce saw *agapasm* or nurturing love, as an important evolutionary principle, though he did not connect it with language as giving/receiving and passing the gift on. In our maternalist terms, though, Peirce's tripartite sign relation can be read as 'sign': giver; 'object': gift; and 'interpretant': receiver and re-giver – or perhaps I could say the interpretant is the receiver seen in its capacity to re-give, to pass the gift on to others.

A precursor of the gift perspective is Victoria Welby with her idea of 'Mother Sense'. Welby, who was Peirce's contemporary and interlocutor by correspondence, considered Mother Sense 'an a priori of language' and the 'necessary condition for the human signifying capacity' (Petrilli 2009: 139).

According to Welby scholar Susan Petrilli:

> Oriented by the logic of the gift, mother-sense is the originating source of self and of the human capacity to perceive life in all its expressions, to experience nature, the world at large, the universe in its dialogic relations of interconnection and vital interdependency among signs and senses. Gift-giving is structural to experience, knowledge and expression, and engenders the propensity for critique and transformation. (2009: 611)

Although Peirce recognized the importance of nurturing love, he did not integrate it into his concept of sign. Welby's Mother Sense complemented Peirce's extensive exploration of sign-categorization, providing the 'primal source of signifying processes' (2009: 580).

Von Uexkull's concept of the *Umwelt*, mentioned above, which is an important element in the current of semiotics centered on Thomas Sebeok's work, gives us an idea of the 'perceptual bubble' or picture of the world each species can have. According to Sebeok, humans can extend their *Umwelts* almost infinitely because they have a play of fantasy or 'musement' which allows them to imagine other worlds. I believe these other worlds (other

---

21 In their introduction to the book *Material Feminisms* (2008) , the editors Alaimo and Heckman pose the problem of postmodern feminists who conceive of reality as 'entirely constituted by language'. My answer to this is that the postmodern concept of language is erroneous and patriarchal because it has left out the unilateral gift. Understanding mothering as material communication and language as modeled upon it reveals the passageway between language and reality that exists from the very beginning. Language itself imitates (interpersonal) material reality in this sense. Thus, it is not looking at 'reality' in a different way that will solve the problem, but looking at language in a different way.

possible environmental niches) cannot be imagined without the frame of maternal gift-giving and creative receiving, internalized and hidden from the conscious level though it may be. That is, materially, linguistically and perceptually, maternal nurturing creates the social gift lens through which humans view and construct their *Umwelts*. Language as a collective projection of mothering, makes our *Umwelts* maternal and shareable, and transforms the possible worlds we invent into possible commons.

Some signs are biological matter, like DNA or hormones, and we mentally investigate them, perhaps recognizing a kind of material molecular, genetic, hormonal or neuronal giving/receiving communication at the biological level although we are not recognizing the giving/receiving cognitive model that happens at the level of life practice. We are blind to a whole level of life that we are actually already living even though we use it as a lens and partially recognize it even when it is projected into asocial areas.

I would agree with Barthes (1967), Baudrillard (2001[1988]) and many other semioticians that there are complex sign systems of material goods such as garments or furniture. However, the giving and receiving of material goods is communicative in its own right at the level of nurturing practice. Codes and sign systems on their own are not sufficient to explain communication. Caught in the exchange paradigm, semioticians and philosophers do not consider giving directly to needs, especially to others' needs, and the creative receptivity of those others, as fundamental. In fact they do not see communication as the satisfaction of others' needs at all. If communication is only the satisfaction of our own needs for self-expression, the interpersonal connection becomes obscure. Each communicator only perceives the other as part of the 'external world' upon which s:he operates using the tools of the sign system.

There seems to be no communication *prior* to signs. Instead, material nurturing is prior to nurturing with signs and lays the groundwork for it. Then, when we satisfy the others' communicative and cognitive needs with verbal and non-verbal signs, there is already a connection. Language is a specific and complex construction of verbal gift-giving while non-verbal and non-human signs outside of that construction are also understood by humans because they have been educated through maternal gifting. The success of this semiotic nurturing is testable in the comprehension of the others. If they understand, we have indeed satisfied their communicative and cognitive needs. Their non-verbal signs as well as their verbal replies, with which they satisfy our needs in turn, let us know if this is the case. This benign feedback mechanism is altered in *quid pro quo* exchange, in that each instrumentalizes the need of the other, the one for the product, the other for the money. The feedback that is the proof of the probable satisfaction of the other's need is given only by the equal exchange itself.

All this causes a defect in our perspective that makes it appear that material communication, the importance of which is mainly non-sign in that it creates bodies, is ... nothing.[22] Thus, we remain in a universe of signs with no exit into life, just as we remain in the market economy with no exit. Everything has to be represented in a sign. Everything has a price. Everything has to be represented in money. TINA: There is no alternative. We can do material exchange, which 'exists' because it has monetary representation, but not gift-giving, which is materially unrepresented because it is free, and so ... does not exist.[23]

Even a critic of market exchange like Marx did not see unpaid labor as producing value. Because it is unpaid, it is not abstract (i.e. not abstracted in that way) (see section 8.6). It seems in capitalism that exchange value defines labor as such. That is, labor only exists socially, for others by being directed towards its representation in money or in another product, or in a sign. Gift labor does produce gift value as we will see in section 8.0. That is, it implies the value of the receiver. Satisfying needs creates the material bodies of the community and, because it lays down the basic patterns of interpersonal relations, it creates minds as well.

Thus, when gift-giving is confused with exchange or no distinction is made between the two, as in 'gift exchange' or 'communicative exchange' there is not just a terminological difficulty but a difficulty of categorization/ cognition and a difficulty *in res*. The market is also material communication but of an alienated kind. It is embedded in a context of unrepresented gifts, which it does not recognize but which, once we attribute an independent, proactive character to gift-giving, prove to be the unacknowledged source of the profit that motivates the whole system.

The market is a collective cognitive mechanism, a way of knowing, which is also a way of not-knowing, denial and constraint. It addresses all the products that are brought to it in a way that replaces the (pre-conscious) maternal selection of the perceptions and events that come forward from the external background to our consciousnesses; it weighs their value with respect to each other and performs its own selection. It judges value quan-

---

22   As if nothing exists without money.
23   This is like saying men and women are all equal according to the male norm, (which carries equality within it). Outside of both, however, and beyond the male norm, remains the maternal norm, the original gift-source of both market and signs, the gift-source of humans of all kinds and genders.

titatively, including exchange values and excluding free gifts, but like a person in denial, it is dependent on what it denies. Exchange value is thus a partial or 'layered' representation of the total value of the commodity of which some other (gift) layers are invisible.

In capitalism, the exchange value of the commodity contains the value of the gifts of housework, surplus labor and free natural resources, which are not monetized until the final exchange of the commodity with the consumer. Gifts are concealed by labeling the labor they require 'low cost', or non-existent, non-labor ('mere activity'or even 'leisure'). Many gifts and services are unquantifiable. All the gifts are hidden behind the binary face-to-face transaction of exchange – yours or mine – and the binary understanding of the transaction itself – gift or exchange (but it's a steal!). Not only is the market cognitively dysfunctional in this way but it imposes this duplicitous judgement of economic value as a model for knowledge, especially for knowledge by categorization, while actually it is free mothering/gift-giving that lays down the transitive propositional processes of human cognition and commmunication and is their original model. In fact, the ways we presently understand knowledge and market exchange are similar in that both use binary category judgements that hide gifts.

What actually happens is that motherers take proactive, other-oriented gift initiatives towards children. As altercentric children, we require this altercentricity of others in order to survive and to arrive at the stage in which we can be said to know. What we know in the beginning is this original interactive model itself, which, at the time, is providing much of the experiential basis of our knowledge. That is, mothering and being mothered, not the market, is the cognitive model. It lays down the way we know, and gives rise to an original gift-based episteme (see Kuokkanen 2007). Without this model, we could not know or even imagine chemical, hormonal, neuronal or genetic giving/receiving 'communication' or 'sending and receiving of messages'. Codes and sign systems would make no sense to us.

3.7 The conduit metaphor

The cognitive linguistics movement began in the early 1980's with the critique of the 'conduit metaphor' by Michael Reddy (1993 [1979]), who showed that in English there are hundreds of metaphors about communication that use the idea of the conduit. These, like 'getting one's idea across' and 'conveying one's thoughts', 'sending a message' were considered erroneous despite *vox populi vox dei* because language at the time was seen as tool-using[24] and because the transfers seemed to be unlike the real world where giving something to someone means the giver doesn't have it anymore. My own short answer to this is that tool-using can itself be seen as a kind of giving. For example, we use the hammer as a tool to give the nail to the wall. Moreover, in a successful gift economy, we would live in abundance in a maternal commons, and we do experience abundance linguistically because indeed we do not lose the word-gifts we give to others but can re-create and re-combine them at will.

With language, we give each other what we already have (have-to-give) in abundance (because we can always remake it), but we decide when to give it and to some extent how to rearrange it. This giving is significantly different from exchange. We have a need for another to give us something we already have also regarding the *way* and the *timing* with which s:he gives it to us. By giving something arranged in combination with other elements and in a specific context, we satisfy others' cognitive and communicative needs in a new way, perhaps stimulating new needs. Listeners and readers also need the speaker/writer's energy, h:er initiative, in order to call their joint attention to something and to create a human relation to it with h:er.[25] From our linguistic capacity, we can understand something of what it would be like to live in material plenty even if we don't have any experience of it in present reality. It is because we live in an exchange economy where gift-giving is unrecognized and scarcity is considered normal that the conduit metaphor seems unacceptable.[26]

From Reddy's work on metaphor, George Lakoff and Mark Johnson (1980) began their far-reaching investigation of metaphor that in many ways revolutionized the study of language and cognition. Reddy, Lakoff and Johnson argued that words are not conduits for meanings and that ideas are not contained in words, to be transferred from one person to the other. Reddy, in fact, thought that the sentence provides a kind of common blueprint for meaning. From the critique of the conduit, Lakoff and Johnson began their focus on embodied metaphor that started the cognitive linguistics movement.

In contrast to the metaphor of a conduit, an understanding of words as

---

24 Reddy wanted to encourage this Wittgensteinian interpretation.
25 If we are identified with each other through body mapping, what the other gives us perceptually is something we have ourselves. H:er face is given to us but we have our own faces. We smile in response to h:er smile and we know how h:ers feels by feeling our own. S:he gives us a word and we respond by giving it too. We feel it on our mouth. 'Ma, ma, ma'. Each repeated syllable maps onto the next.
26 The neutral postal metaphor seems preferable.

communicative gifts and services that satisfy the communicative/cognitive needs of others allows us to think of a transmission, without the meaning or idea being 'contained' in the word(s). In fact, the needs belong to the listener, and by giving words to satisfy them, the speaker creates a temporally interconnected and foregrounded assembly of satisfied needs in the consciousness of the listener. At the same time, by satisfying the listener's communicative needs, the speaker also automatically satisfies h:er own need for a relation with the listener regarding something. The words are gifts, and therefore, relational tokens, which the listener, like the speaker, uses to establish nurturing human relations and consequent (shared or parallel) mental organization regarding some kind of perceptual or conceptual gift. One 'gets one's ideas across' not by sending them through a conduit but by satisfying others' needs. We will see that there is an image schema of the gift that functions as a kind of mould underlying the construction, not of tools, but of relations (that organize the mind).

CHAPTER IV

SATISFYING COGNITIVE
AND COMMUNICATIVE NEEDS

4.0 The structure of material communication

George Lakoff and Mark Johnson started a kind of philosophical revolution when they began to revise the concept of metaphor, recognizing it as a cognitive device coming from common human experiences of the body. They continued to affirm (2001) that 'the corporeal or spatial logic, arising from bodily experience, is exactly what provides the basis for the logic of abstract thought'. It would have been more accurate if they had said '*inter*corporeal logic' and '*inter*corporeal bodily experience'.[1]

Lakoff and Johnson introduced and made popular the idea of 'image schemas', basic patterns that come from the implications of interactions between the embodied mind and the environment (yet somehow the motherer is not usually considered part of the child's environment). Some of these schemas are – UP AND DOWN – which map to other areas like 'up is good' or 'more is up' and PATH TO GOAL, which maps to areas like 'life is a journey' or 'love is a journey' or CONTAINERS, and going into or out of containers, which map to categorization. Lakoff and Johnson's work contains a vast collection of these image schemas and the metaphors deriving from them (Lakoff and Johnson 1980) and there has been much subsequent work on this subject (see, for example, Beate Hampe ed. 2005).

I believe the image schema that underlies both material and verbal communication is the interactive, interpersonal sensory-motor life schema of giving and receiving, first located not in the body of the child alone but intercorporeally, beginning in a moment in which the child has recently been part of the body of the mother, in the womb[2] and proceeding through the

---

1   The findings of the infant researchers would bear out the emphasis on inter-subjectivity.

2   Explaining the 'link schema' Johnson (1987: 117) says, 'We come into existence tethered to our biological mothers by umbilical cords that nourish and sustain us. But this physical linking is never the full story of our humanity, which

long period during which s:he is dependent on the mother's need-satisfying material gifts and services for h:er body's very existence. This is a complementary intercorporeality that is embodied in the individual and implies the body/mind of the other.

Independence (or autonomy) is actually a false ideal of patriarchy and capitalism, which does not recognize the constitutional interdependence of everything, beginning with the child and the mother. The child is first inside the mother's body and then is embedded in the material care that is accomplished by the motherers' body (and mind). Later, as the child grows older, s:he continues to be embedded more directly in the gifts of the environment and of society at large. Everyone is dependent on the gifts of air, sunlight, warmth, and all the products of Nature and culture (whether free or accessed through the market). What we call 'independence' in capitalism is really usually just efficient integration into and dependence on the market. Nevertheless, the illusion of independence is widely held and valued.

To me, studying the development of children without their intercorporeal experience is like studying the development of the baby kangaroo without considering the fact that it is living in its mother's pouch.

The cognitive psychology project itself usually excludes the mother-child interaction by concentrating on the individual child from the skin inward not recognizing that for anything at all to happen from the skin inward there have to be constantly renewed conditions of care from beyond the skin. Even if these interactions of care are registered in the individual body, each interaction implies the active body of the other.

Without the cultural centrality of the positive mother-child relation, gift-giving and receiving are eclipsed and read in a neutral manner as cause and effect, activity and passivity, according to schemas of agency, manipulation and motion that leave aside the gift initiative. I believe giving/receiving underlies these neutral schemas and our ability to understand them. In this light, agent-patient[3] and cause-and-effect constitute neutral depersonalizations of giving/receiving, but are understandable just because they are

---

requires a certain non physical linking to our parents, our siblings, and our society as a whole'. He goes on to mention a number of different kinds of linkages. Lakoff mentions the umbilical cord as well (1987: 274). Isn't the umbilical cord the prime example of a conduit? of giving and receiving nourishment? It is not just a string. Two entities are connected by a 'bonding structure'. I submit that the bonding structure is made by unseen or abstract giving and receiving.

3   By these terms I understand a person or thing that acts and one that receives or endures the action.

attenuations of that more basic and more significant model, a model that has extremely important psychological underpinnings for the child and that continues to function throughout life also as a cognitive lens.

What has confused researchers of language and of many other fields, including physics, is that cause and effect, agent and patient are seen as the primary and more general relations, of which giving and receiving are perhaps more specific cases. This indeed might be true for non-human knowers, but for young children, giving/receiving is primary and most important. The 'prototypical scene' thus would not be as Dan Slobin (1985: 1175) thought, a 'Manipulative Activity Scene,' understood as 'the experiential *gestalt* of a basic causal event in which an agent carries out a physical and perceptible change of state in a patient by means of direct body contact or with an instrument under the agent's control'. Rather, it is that human, universally-shared Nurturing Activity Scene: A satisfies B's needs. B receives the satisfaction of h:er needs from A.[4] This need-satisfaction may happen with the help of 'manipulative activity' but giving/receiving is the structure of the event, even if it is often carried out with movements of the hands.

Neither would 'conceptual primitives' be image schemas such as path, up-down, containment, force, part-whole, and link, as described by Jean Mandler (1992), following Lakoff and Johnson.

The original, 'conceptual primitive', interpersonal nurturing scene, or schema, which is necessary for the child's survival, is the basic kernel of human communication. From this original interpersonal scene, later scenes like Manipulative Activity and Figure and Ground and the various individually embodied schemas (path, containment, etc.), take their frame and significance.[5] Objects are given and prepared for giving through manipulation, and things come forward from a background as need-satisfying gifts. In fact, verbs like 'give', 'carry', 'put', 'throw', 'grab' and 'take', 'get', 'have' arise early in child language, and cross-linguistically, specifying various aspects of the nurturing as well as the manipulative scene.

---

4   Slobin (2013: 1175): 'Manipulative activities involve a cluster of interrelated notions, including: the concepts representing the physical objects themselves, along with sensorimotor concepts of physical agency involving the hands and perceptual-cognitive concepts of change of state and change of location, along with some overarching notions of efficacy and causality, embedded in interactional formats of requesting, giving, and taking'.

5   Terms like 'slots and fillers' may seem more appropriate in the Manipulative Activity scene than 'gifts and receivers' which are more appropriate to the earlier and more basic scene of mothering/being mothered.

My contention is that although children do perceive basic scenes like Manipulative Activity and certainly have physiologically-based perceptions of animacy, inanimacy, causality, agency, containment and support, all these are rendered significant for them (and for us!) because they are originally elements of the nurturing interaction in which the children are continually participating with their motherers, upon which they depend for their very survival and which are accompanied by shifting emotional states. That is, because our mothering/being mothered is so intense and long-term, it would weigh upon human development more than it does upon most other animal development (though perhaps whales, dolphins and elephants may be exceptions). Nurturing/being nurtured should be taken as the original paradigmatic scene or schema, which puts a 'spin' on the rest of our perceptual and conceptual relations to the world and each other.

Children's linguistic errors can also reveal the underlying structure of giving/receiving,[6] but linguists usually do not recognize that 'scene' as the original or deepest prototype. It is just because they do not recognize or even hypothesize the general importance of mothering and the satisfaction of needs that so many linguists agree with Slobin 'that the capacity to construct a human language in earliest childhood must, ultimately, be part of the genetic capacity of our species' (2013: 1244).

I do not disagree that genetic factors have a part in the construction of language, but the denial of the importance of mothering, and its cancellation as major factor in child perceptual and conceptual development and language, continually makes us overshoot the mark in evaluating the importance of the 'contribution' of genetics.

Closer to my own perspective is perhaps Tomasello's proposal that language comes from the 'human cooperative communication' that 'emerged as part and parcel of humans' unique form of collaborative activity' (2008: 172). Agreed. But where do communication and collaboration come from? Are they also only inherited products of evolution, or is there a situation in ontogeny that necessarily teaches social comunication, a moment in which biological survival depends upon prolonged social care given by others or another?

---

6   Slobin continues (2013: 1190): "As Bowerman points out, 'some languages do not formally mark the distinction between animate and inanimate goal that is observed in give vs. put'. She suggests 'that children's recurrent substitution errors may arise from deep-seated cognitive predispositions towards perceiving certain kinds of similiarities among events or relationships, regardless of whether these similiarities are formally recognized in the language being learned'... 'These predispositions are inherent in the structure of Semantic Space, and are available to speakers for reorganizations of their lexical and grammatical systems'.

Colwyn Trevarthen (2010: 120) tells us that infants 'are born with motives and emotions for actions that sustain *human intersubjectivity.* They perform actions that are adapted to motivate, and invest emotions in, an *imaginative cultural learning'*. In fact, infants are biologically programmed for the sociality that elicits nurture. The motherer responds socially to h:er socially-responsive child and indeed s:he h:erself was also biologically programmed for sociality as an infant and has learned socially from h:er own motherers (who also learned from h:er), as well as from h:er wider life experience, the specificities of the culture in which s:he lives. The categorization of mothering as instinctual has not only had the effect of denying mothers' and women's importance (and sometimes even denying them souls), but hides the social connection between nature and nurture that happens through nurturing and being nurtured socially.

Co-operation is learned just by engaging in altercentric giving/receiving in infancy. That is, giving/receiving is already co-operation, and role reversal and perspective shifting are among its prerequisites. Moreover, says Tomasello, 'human infants understand joint activity from a "bird's eye view" with the joint goal and complementary roles all in a single representational format, which enables them to reverse roles as needed. In contrast, chimpanzees understand their own action from a first-person perspective and that of the partner from a third-person perspective, but they do not have a bird's eye view of the interaction and so there really are no roles, and so no sense in which they can reverse roles, in "the same" activity' (2008: 179).[7]

The roles of humans can be understood as based on the image schema of the gift, with the shifts in perspectives among giver, gift and receiver. We might say that the first- and the third-person perspectives derive from the second-person perspective. 'I' derives from 'you and I' altercentrism, and 'they' is a depersonalized projection of 'you and I' giving/receiving onto others. Also, in joint attention, both (or all) of the attenders are in the receiver role regarding the same perception or experience as gift or giver and an ability to 'mind-read' in order to satisfy the needs of others is necessary for material communication, for sharing and for collaboration.

It is important to ground co-operation in the mother-child interaction because if we understand it as a genetic endowment, we cannot reason 'from is to ought' to justify it as a generalizable social principle. In fact, mothering is a weave of innumerable goal-oriented activities that are registered in the child's well-being or lack thereof. If the child uses h:er positive experience as a model for h:er own behavior, s:he creates human re-

---

7   Recall the 'tracking' of the grooming relations among pre-hominids.

lations of solidarity and emotional significance with others that motivate h:er to continue and to expand cooperation. S:he is altruistic because s:he has been treated altruistically. Tomasello and Warneken say that children behave altruistically, as shown by their recent experiment, because their parents have taught them to help others or because of a 'natural tendency to help other people solve their problems' (2006: 1302), but they forget the other-oriented work of the human motherer, which is always present as a potential model for the child.

This model is not taught, it is learned by participation and imitation, as the stuff of life, the 'way things are'. Also, if it is the case that even chimps in experiments can act in a helping way towards humans, reaching for things to hand to them, this might be because they have been trained in mothering ways by humans, or because their own long experience of being mothered by their chimp birth mothers has allowed them to 'catch on' to what their human trainers want.[8]

It is because we have an epistemology that does not recognize the fundamental importance of mothering that we have a society that does not recognize the ethics of care (Held 2006), or recognize the economic value of caregiving (Folbre 2001, Eisler 2007). Understanding mothering/being mothered as the core human experience would allow us to re-conceptualize both ethics and economics. It would also let us understand the nurturing human experience as the basis of meaning in life, of collaboration, and of the perceptual, conceptual and material commons. And of our ability to care for Mother Nature. And of a world without exploitation, poverty and war.

4.1 A maternal mould for language

> "The word falls", one is tempted to explain, "into a mould of my mind *long* prepared for it." (Wittgenstein 1958: 170)[9]

Many philosophers and linguists have believed that there is an underlying pattern for language, something that keeps a sentence from being a mere list of words. For example, Frege talked about 'complete' and 'incomplete', 'saturated' and 'unsaturated' parts of the sentence that must 'fit together to express a thought'. (M. Gibson, 2004: ch. 1). Sometimes the descriptions of this pattern sound very much like giving/receiving

---

8   The study of our simian relatives may be putting philogeny in the place of the mother in ontogeny.

9   Patricia Kuhl uses this quote to explain her 'motor theory' of language.

but the mother-child relation does not seem to have anything to do with it. Sending and receiving take the place of giving/receiving as a basic metaphor.[10] For example, catastrophe theorist René Thom describes schemas along these lines, as 'abstract representations of elementary spatio-temporal relations between entities'. He says they are 'templates, syntactic constituent structures, i.e. they serve a binding function'. There is a 'sender-position (abstractly understood), an Object-position, a trajectory-position and a Receiver-position; these positions function as semantic roles when represented in the mind, and the schema therefore functions as a syntactic *gestalt*, a configurational structure' (quoted in Bundgaard and Stjernfelt 2010: 59).[11]

Noam Chomsky believes there is a hereditary mould for language, the Universal Grammar of which the unification function Merge is a part. Instead, we are insisting, contrary to Chomsky, that a universal *social* mould does exist: maternal care, and it is universal because it is necessary for infants' survival after they are born. The mould should not be considered hereditary; it is social and its contents are poured and are set socially, through altercentric interpersonal practice. Many different kinds of things are given and received throughout life at many different levels. MERGE can be explained as a syntactic replay of the mother-child interpersonal schema. It is simply the giving of words to each other.

Cognitive linguist Leonard Talmy (2000: 409) talks about 'force dynamics in language and cognition' making basic the 'hitting' pole of the spectrum of gifting, the 'high transitive' (Vazquez-Rozas 2007) aspect of causation. Regarding schemas he says (2005: 200) that each 'schema that a closed class form represents is a "pre-packaged" bundling together of certain elements in a particular arrangement'.

Ronald Langacker proposes a basic 'billiard ball' schema:

> Where motion results in forceful physical contact, energy is transmitted from the mover to the impacted object, which may thereby be set in motion to participate in further interactions. Let us refer to this way of thinking about the

---

10　Even Jean Mandler's (2004) 'Perceptual Meaning Analysis' does not take into account that the first and most salient perceptions of the child must regard needing nurture and being nurtured and thus would be available for informing later action and path analyses.

11　In *Semio Physics*, Thom tells us 'The hypothesis put forward here is that only certain configurations of elements really make sense and can be used as a basis for an intelligible construction that allows linguistic description' (Thom 1990:vii-viii). My contention is that the salience of these configurations of elements derives from giving/receiving.

world as the **billiard-ball model**. This archetypal folk model exerts a powerful influence on both everyday and scientific thought and no doubt reflects fundamental aspects of cognitive organization ... Aspects of the billiard ball model correspond directly to the noun and verb prototypes. (1991: 13-14)

Like 'force dynamics', the billiard ball model functions according to the 'hitting' rather than the basic 'nurturing' aspect of gift-giving.

Adele Goldberg, the founder of 'construction' grammar talks about underlying argument structures that are matched by grammatical constructions (Goldberg 1995). These are 'structures of thought'.The one she investigates most thoroughly is the ditransitive construction with one subject and two objects, as in 'Mary gave Jane a cake'. I would say there are two transitive moments in that the subject 'Mary' as giver, gives the verb 'give' to the object, the receiver 'cake' and the noun 'cake' then becomes the gift that is given to the receiver 'Jane'. Thus giving, giving again, being given, receiving, receiving again and being transformed from receiver to giver to gift are all constructional aspects that function as 'structures of thought'.

As Reddy (1993) of the conduit metaphor suggested, the schema functions like a blueprint, which everyone already possesses and into which each of us fits the word gifts s:he has been given or is giving. From here it is a short step to the generalization and projection of this minimal structure onto Mother environment, the motherworld. Moreover we are all givers, gifts and receivers perceptually for each other.[12]

Although these thinkers and many others have proposed basic schemas of some kind, the schema of the maternal gift, the mother-mould has not been recognized. One reason for this is that the logic of exchange creates a blind spot towards the logic of the gift. Another is that most of the thinkers did not have the experience of being motherers themselves.

Many investigators of language, wary of 'naive realism', say there is no noun-verb structure 'in the external world'. From our point of view, this is not true because the gift schema is enacted externally – for each of us, other people are external – in material gift-giving and receiving both in early childhood, and throughout life in many ways and among people of all ages. It is also enacted in verbal gift-giving, which is at least partly external. That is, for the speaker or writer (the giver) the verbal product (the gift) and the listener or reader (the receiver) are both external, and for the listener, the speaker (the giver) and the verbal product (the gift) are both external, and, of course, they change roles. Moreover, as I said in section 2.4, we

---

12   If causation is a kind of giving, see below, are Gopnik's (2010) cognitive causal maps based on gift maps?

can track gifting among others (even bonobos do it). The gift schema *is* the noun-verb-complement structure on the external. And we know it because from infancy on, we enact and replay its roles ourselves materially and linguistically all the time and so do our inter-actors and interlocutors. If we believe the gift schema is projectible, (and it is if it is repeated on the linguistic plane), we can also project it onto the world and reverse positions and perspectives, with the world as giver and ourselves as receivers. That is, the arrow of gifting goes from the world to us, from the world to words, and not only vice-versa. Our exchange-based giftless and motherless theorizing does not let us see ourselves as creative receivers, as mothered children.

In this light, Chomsky's poverty of the stimulus hypothesis would be groundless because the schema of the gift first exists on the external. From this perspective, abundant stimuli for the patterns of grammar would come not from language itself but from the child's rich interaction with others, where the gift schema exists materially and interactively before it is schematized. They would also come to us from the environment, the gift aspects of which we recognize and creatively receive together with others in joint attention.

4.2 The image schema of the gift

Motherer-child giving and receiving is the basic human interaction because it is *the* original necessary interaction. This interaction and the abilities it requires and develops form the basis of material and linguistic communication. The image schema of the gift and the projection or mapping of it onto other levels[13] together with 'mind-reading' and 'joint attention' are the load-bearing processes of language for adults as well as for children. The relation-creating capacity of nurturing is transferred onto the verbal plane with word-gifts as relational tokens.

The capillary repetition of the mother-child intercorporeal interaction gives rise to a *pattern* of giving and receiving, which anchors and elicits sociality and emotions from the beginning. This pattern is charged with importance for the child in that it is absolutely crucial for h:er survival. Later, it also provides access to the experiences of other people, who have all themselves been mothered children, and whose early interactions have

---

13   The kinetic mapping that children do regarding the similarity of their postures with the postures of the motherer may be an early form of this ability to project patterns from one level to another.

therefore been formed and patterned in much the same way. The maternal interaction is also projected upon Motherers Nature and Culture, whose gifts we receive/perceive, elaborate and give again.

From this point of view, giving and receiving form the underlying schema of material and verbal communication, expressed and embodied in a routine that the child learns very early, a minimal play or script with three roles: giver, gift (or service), and receiver. This routine, which is repeated and elaborated upon in many different ways, is an extremely important but commonplace interpersonal intercorporeal experience that 'provides the basis for the logic of abstract thought' (Lakoff and Johnson 2002: 156). It constitutes an elementary structure that can have almost infinite variations.

The child can play any of the roles of the routine. S:he is a giver because s:he gives smiles, cries and gestures (as well as urine and feces), which are 'creatively received' by the parent. S:he is carried and birthed, given to life by the mother and is h:erself given by adults like a gift from hand to hand. S:he creatively receives h:er motherers' care of all kinds, as well as the perceptions and experiences that come from h:er surroundings. As s:he grows older, this creative reception sometimes means that s:he proactively (not passively), goes out to explore the world around h:er, crawling to reach the table, grabbing the keys and chewing on the book. That is, the creativity of the reception includes the fact that the child actively goes forward to receive the perceptual gifts of h:er surroundings. The motherer proactively goes to meet the child but s:he also sometimes refrains from acting in order to allow the child to explore independently.[14]

The roles of the dependent child necessarily imply the roles of the motherer. The role of giver of cries implies a receiver, and the role of being the gift given from hand to hand also. The role of infant receiver implies an actively engaged, attentive and repeated giver who is always 'mind-reading' the needs of the child, and is usually successful in satisfying them. The child can play these three complementary roles h:erself, and quite early can understand the other's part in the interaction because of mirror neuron simulations and because s:he takes turns and plays that part in another moment. S:he knows the roles by doing them.[15] Motherer

---

14   There are cultures where children are less in focus, customs like swaddling and extreme living situations like orphanages where the caregivers engage less with the children. Nevertheless, the child's basic needs have to be satisfied if s:he is to survive and this provides the basis of the schema.

15   Even if babies cannot 'mind-read' the motherer, the motherer's mind-reading abilities include interpreting the baby's cries – as an expression of hunger, for example, so the cries already satisfy the motherer's need to know.

and child alternate the roles and the perspectives and, thus, each can take the perspective of the other when playing the opposite role.

We can abstract the schema according to different emphases. The basic schema is A gives X to B. However, X is given by A to B and B receives X from A constitute the same schema from different starting points. One common variation on the schema is A gives directly to B when there is not a gift object involved but a service such as cleaning, dressing, carrying, etc. (perhaps a Manipulative Activity Scene). The unilateral giving/receiving changes in character according to the kind of gift that is given or service that is performed. Giving can transform into an activity with multiple steps as when for example, the motherer warms (gives heat to) the milk for the baby. Warming the milk is a service that is then transmitted as a gift of the warm milk to the baby.

The steps towards satisfying a need may be many. The motherer may have to buy the milk or keep a cow. In fact, there may be so many steps that the need is backgrounded, while the activities continue. The motherer may have to build a shed to keep the cow and take her out to graze every day. All this leaves an open-endedness to the chain of gift activities that may make them seem to be ends in themselves. In language the gift schema functions by satisfying immediate and extended cognitive and communicative needs repeatedly even if we never realize that is what is happening.

Relations of mutuality and trust arise from these need-satisfying, patterned interactions. The gift schema, thus, has positive relational implications. It becomes an integral part of the child's identity as a relational being and it is already part of the motherer's identity because the motherer h:erself (like other adults) learned the gift schema in childhood and continues to practice it in various ways. My hypothesis is that the interpersonal gift schema can be seen as a basic communicative-cognitive-linguistic structure which is projected onto different levels of life and language, and is modified and used in many different ways. At the linguistic level, verbal products are given and received, passed from one person to another, satisfying cognitive and communicative needs. The assembly of these verbal products into broader units by applying – giving – them to each other in syntax provides a way of constructing ad hoc linguistic gifts that are understandable by all because everyone who survives childhood has had to experience maternal care to some extent and consciously or unconsciously continues to play and project the roles of the gift schema and its variations throughout life.

Words as virtual gifts fit into a pre-linguistic 'mould', the image schema of giving/receiving, in which young children have had months of daily and even hourly and moment-by-moment full-immersion training by the time they begin to speak. The schema of the gift can be found and applied everywhere. Children experience it repeatedly. They can initiate it themselves and they can be its beneficiaries.[16] They can see it happening outside themselves among other people and among things. They can project it onto the world around them, laugh at the perceptual gift of the noise of the rattle or the sight of leaves moving in the wind. This interactive gift pattern is learned from experience and might even be considered a, or the, social basis for the neurological connections that facilitate language.

4.3 Shifting perspectives

We understand[17] mainly by receiving and potentially using, i.e. re-giving, words, ideas and perceptions in roles that are already there for us and have been functioning for both speakers and listeners since their early childhood interactions with their motherers. The speaker offers h:er words as relation-creating gifts, put together and patterned according to the gift schema and the listener creatively receives them as formed in this way. S:he knows who or what is the giver, who or what is the gift or service, who or what is the receiver in the sentence. Speakers and listeners can easily shift perspectives because they have played all the giving and receiving roles before in interpersonal material, gestural and vocal, verbal giving/receiving.

Brian MacWhinney has written at length about perspective shifting among the grammatical elements of a sentence (MacWhinney 2005). I believe these shifts are based on underlying shifts in perspectives among giver, gift and receiver that already take place in the material motherer-child interaction and are replayed in the image schema of the gift in grammar. In a transitive sentence, the subject of the sentence is the giver and has the perspective of the giver, the verb is the gift or service and has that perspective and the object is the receiver and has the perspective of the receiver. MacWhinney gives the example 'The

---

16   The gift schema is actually the best toy or the best game one could imagine!

17   The gift schema is not a code. It is prior to 'codification' a term that derives from cryptography and can be seen as a kind of translation of pre-existing words or bits of information into ever more artificial gifts. A code functions according to substitution, transmission and restoration of these. I discuss this process in the second half of the book. Like the DaVinci code, the code concept conceals the prototype of the mother.

boy hit the ball that rolled into the gutter'. We can attribute the role of giver to 'boy', gift or service to 'hit' and receiver to 'ball'. 'That' takes the place of 'ball' and is giver in the new clause, 'rolled' is the gift or service, 'into' specifies the kind of trajectory, and 'gutter' is the receiver. At another level, the speaker is the giver, the verbal product as a whole is the gift and the hearer is the receiver and these perspectives can also be taken, reversed and rearranged.

It is significant that in the mother-child altercentric identification, the perspective of each regarding the other has to be reversed 180 degrees, as Stein Bråten (2002) emphasizes.[18]

In the transitive sentence too, the perspective of the object (receiver) is the reverse of that of the subject (giver). Moreover, the subject is more active, because it initiates giving (like the human giver) while the object is receptive (like the human receiver), albeit creatively receptive – not passive. In the second part of the book I will discuss how we develop our psychological subjectivity by taking gift initiatives in language and life, initiatives that we enact on the verbal plane in the form and syntax of our sentences. Thus we are exercising our gift subjectivity verbally all the time when we speak or write. We are also exercising our receptive capacity as listeners/readers as well as in the formulation of the sentence 'object', but since the sentence itself, and therefore the object, is part of the gift initiative of the speaker, the object of the sentence perhaps appears to be more passive.

We project the gift initiative onto the subject of the sentence, so it corresponds to the gift initiative we have in speaking the sentence. We project the reception of the gift onto the object but, since we as speakers are taking the gift initiative to speak, the object does not correspond to what we are doing at the moment, but to what the listener is doing. In written communication, the subject's giving initiative still corresponds to the writer's initiative but the receiver is perhaps more active as the study of reading as interpretation shows.

The schema of the gift is sequential in that giving the gift usually precedes reception. In nursing at the breast or other services like holding, cleaning, dressing the child, giving and receiving are simultaneous. Still the motherer has to come to the child and there is a temporal sequence, before, during and after the need satisfaction. There is also a kind of turn

---

18   Bråten gives the example of the autistic child who is not able to respond with the mirror image of the adult playing the game 'Do as I do'. See below 5.6.

taking among words as to their place in the sentence.[19] We give them each a turn. This sequential character creates a brief organized time span with a beginning, middle and end. It also provides a way for us to give the words to each other inside the sentence, connecting them according to the gift schema, creating constants and variables, as in the early 'pivot stage' of language development. Some examples: 'more car, more cereal, more fish, more walk ... boot off, light off, pants off, water off' (Goodluck 1991: 76). We give morphological elements to words, which they then 'share'; that is, they agree as to case, tense, number or gender as if they were sharing joint attention regarding something (though we are actually sharing joint attention regarding them.) The sequence is complete when the gift to the other or the schema itself, or series of schemas, has been given and received.[20]

Some languages put the verb or the object first, and one could possibly hypothesize that this would cause a difference in emphasis. The gift or the receiver might be seen as more important than the giver – but this would require a Whorfian psycho-linguistic investigation, which is beyond my purpose at the moment. Variations of word order within languages do cause a change of emphasis as in the formation of the passive in English: 'The ball was hit by the girl', where the receiver of the action is put first. The relevance of the event is elaborated in a slightly different way.

The schema of the gift is presentational rather than representational. It has its origin in pre-verbal childhood *in res* and is played out over and over in adult gift behavior but also in the very acts of speaking or writing, as the speaker[21]/writer presents h:er word-gift schemas to the listener/reader. The 'present' aspect of representation is not so much a temporal present as Derrida thought, but has to do with the gift and giving (though as we just said there is a sequence of gift-giving in the sentence, a sequence, which indeed "gives-time").

The roles of the gift schema exist before language and also within language. Thus, the subject of the sentence is in the giver role (whether implicitly or explicitly expressed). The speaker h:erself is the giver of the

---

19   Trevarthen (1999) talks about the narrative structure of music: in the present, remembering the past, looking towards the future. Surely the same happens with giving and receiving. First, there is a felt need; then there is the giving and the receiving. Then there is the memory of it.

20   For more on the intransitive construction, see Part Two.

21   The time element is somewhat different for writing as Derrida showed. The interaction in writing is more like what anthropologists call 'tolerated scrounging', which seems less intentional than maternal giving. The relations established are less personal.

words and the phrase, right then, and persists as a model or reminder of giving. In commands, the subject can be elided in that the required 'giver', the subject of the action, is not the speaker but the other person: 'Go!', 'Sit down!'. The other is required to be the giver of that behavior.

In fact, perhaps we should replace the meta-linguistic grammatical terms 'subject', 'predicate', 'object' and 'complement' with terms like 'giver', 'gift or service' and 'receiver'. Thus, instead of considering these roles as abstract elements or categories to instantiate, we would consider them to be roles that we have been both playing and observing since childhood and that we can fill with many different verbal gifts. These interconnected roles form the original 'spatial, corporeal' and interpersonal (!) 'logic, arising from bodily experience' that 'provides the basis for the logic of abstract thought' (Lakoff and Johnson 2002).

Moreover, the 'parse tree' structures that are used to diagram sentences could be seen as bottom up instead of top down, with their 'roots' in an interactive script that all can perform, and that can be elaborated upon in many ways by applying aspects of the script to each other both internally to the schema and externally to it. The schema would be a 'deep structure', deep in the sense of early, basic and underlying, rather than a structure depending on abstract categories as the Chomsky of generative grammar suggested. It can be visualized as mapped horizontally rather than vertically.

speaker/giver   listener/ receiver

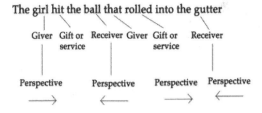

Figure 3: The gift 'deep structure'

Here the gift deep structure is repeated over and over – between the speaker and the listener, between 'the' and 'girl', between 'the' and 'ball', between 'girl' and 'hit' and with all of these 'the girl hit the ball' and between 'ball' and 'that', 'that' and 'rolled', etc.

4.4 Merging by giving and receiving

Words can be given to each other. A determiner can be given to a noun: 'the dog', that is, the speaker gives 'the' to 'dog', which receives it and they bond or merge.[22] 'The dog' is put in the giver role (as 'subject') and is given by the speaker a gift or service (verb), which it can give, for example 'chased'. A determiner 'the' is then given to another noun 'ball' and together they are put into the receiver (object) role. Many variations can be made upon this schema. More gifts can be given to each of the words in the different roles: 'big' can also be given to 'dog', creating the bonded series, 'the big dog'.

Objectifying words, linguists talk about 'slots' and 'fillers'. Instead I am subjectifying words, by describing 'slots' as 'needs' and 'fillers' as 'gifts'. Trying to visualize the way words are given to each other I thought of 'fillers and slots' as visual images of giving and receiving and I happened upon some pictures of cogs provided on Google.

Figure 4: Speaking and listening

Figure 5: Noun phrase with gift syntax.

---

22   In the mother-child interaction feeding is an important part of giving. The gift is actually incorporated into the body of the child. They merge. Nursing at the breast is a particularly good example because of the intimate intercorporeality. Words merge with each other in the same way that milk merges with the baby.

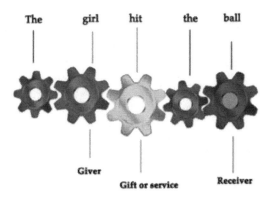

Figure 6. Sentence with gift syntax

It is the speaker/writer who is doing the giving externally to the sentence,[23] but internally to the sentence there are various gift acts that function as if the verbal components were doing the giving and receiving themselves. Thus, there are several levels at which verbal giving/receiving is taking place: the interpersonal level and the intrasentential level which is composed on the one hand of interverbal relations (words given to other words as we just saw) and on the other hand of the syntactic placement of words in the roles of the gift schema. Then there are correspondences between the levels. The subject of the sentence corresponds to the speaker, while the verb corresponds to the sentence-gift as a whole. The 'object' or 'complement' corresponds to the listener or receiver. Some verbs, that is, words that are in the gift or service role, can be given without the presence of a receiver. They do not need or 'take' an object: 'The girl laughed'. However, since the sentence itself is a gift from speaker/writer to hearer/ reader, the role of the receiver is always potentially available to exemplify or underscore that part of the communicative interaction. The trajectories that gifts can take as they move from one person to another can be elaborated as trajectories of motion of objects or persons from one place to another.

---

23 I use the word 'sentence' when I might better use 'proposition' or 'locution' to include the many segments of language that are not complete sentences and some that are wider or longer than sentences. However sentences usually provide complete gift packages and that is what I am trying to explain at present.

The end point of the trajectories are indicated by prepositional phrases that also take 'objects' or receivers in roles that at least sometimes correspond to the role of the receiver of the communication (listener or reader). 'The dog ran to the house'. The role of 'the house' corresponds to that of the listener to whom we speak. Anaphora allows us to replay the schema filling the gift roles with pronouns in added clauses and sentences. The dialogic interaction is permeated by gifts and gift schema correspondences.

The presence of the speaker/giver and listener/receiver also allows conversation to be made often of incomplete sentences, in that the giver and the receiver roles of the schema are continually underlined and understood by both interlocutors because they are playing them, taking turns giving and receiving their verbal gifts in 'vitality contours' (Stern 1985), or 'affect signalling gestural contours' (Trevarthen 2005) often accompanied by the perceptual gifts of emphasis.

Continuing in this brief exploration of some of the ways the schema can be re-applied: in recursion, clauses can be given to phrases, as in 'The boy threw the ball that hit the window'. The receiver in the first phrase becomes the giver in the second, where the anaphoric demonstrative pronoun 'that' is put in the role of the giver,[24] 'hit' in the role of gift and 'window' in the role of receiver.

Prepositional phrases can be given to the combined gift of subject and verb so as to complete a transposed gift schema. For example, in 'The dog ran to the gate' 'to the gate', is given to 'the dog ran' in order to complete the schema with a destination/receiver, a goal for the path. 'And' is a gift that is given to join two sentence-, phrase-, or word-gifts.

It has been noted by many anthropologists who have studied 'gift exchange' following Mauss (1990 [1923]), that the gift carries with it something of the giver and that it has a *hau* a spirit which arises in and through its circulation. In the world of verbal giving, the same thing applies, filling the sentence with a continuity and a sense of the speaker/writer as the words combine. Spoken words are filled with breath – 'spirit' – after all[25] (see below 9.6 on meaning). The *hau* that returns is the reply of the listener on the same topic, to which s:he usually adds something of her 'own'.

---

24   MacWhinney uses the example 'the boy hit the ball that rolled into the gutter' and he follows the changing perspectives. My contention is that the perspectives depend upon the roles of the schema of the gift.

25   Turning this the other way around, we can look at the *hau* as a linguistic effect on material gift circulation. Ie circulating gifts become like words, full of breath. The return of the gift to the giver through the circle is a kind of material dialogue.

4.5 Projections and implications of the schema

The image schema of the gift has important implications for epistemology. Humans are social knowers because we all identify and practice this basic pattern of material, nonverbal and verbal gift-giving in life and language. We can form a great variety of human relations with each other both materially and verbally by applying or attributing (giving) the schema to parts of the world, which we creatively receive/perceive as gifts and which we give again with word-gifts to others. If giving and receiving create relations among humans, we can also give on purpose in order to create relations. We give words to others in order to create specifically human relations with them regarding things.[26] Moreover, we project the gift process and the relations onto things, words and ideas. Then we recognize and receive them again as such and we can retain them in readiness to give them again to others (without losing them). Thus the knowing of *homo sapiens* is a product of the giving of *homo donans*,[27] not vice-versa.

We can use the schema according to different emphases. The gift structure remains relatively constant but can change in character and content according to the kinds of gifts given or services performed. As I just said, the service can become a two or three or many step activity as when the mother warms the milk for the baby or cooks and mashes the carrots for h:er. Each kind of gift or service, the warm milk, the mashed carrots, the feeding them to h:er, the bath, the clean clothes provides a qualitatively different content, different sensations and emotions, which create qualitatively different interpersonal relations in the moment.

Emotionally charged relations of appreciation, mutuality and trust arise from the successful unilateral satisfaction of needs in these patterned interactions that are necessary for the child's survival. It would not be surprising that the gift schema, therefore, would be deeply salient and memorable to the child. It becomes an important part of h:er identity, as it is already of h:er motherer's who learned it in childhood h:erself and has continued to use it in material, linguistic and other sign communication throughout h:er lifetime.

I believe that the image schema of the gift can be seen as a very basic and versatile communicative cognitive-linguistic structure, which is modi-

---

26 Many researchers would now say that these are relations based on 'social cognition'(Tomasello 2014). Anyway they are specifically human relations.

27 *Homo sapiens*, the wise or knowing 'man' is the scientific name of our species. I propose that call ourselves *homo donans*, the giving 'man'.

fied and used at different levels and in many different ways. At the linguistic level, the assembly of the various elements into units by applying (giving) them to each other and by giving them roles in the schema, provides a way of making or constructing verbal[28] products, which are understandable by all because everyone who survives childhood has had to experience and learn from the model and mould of maternal gift-giving. Morcover, everyone consciously or unconsciously continues throughout adulthood to play the roles of the gift schema and its variations both in language and in life.

At the most fundamental levels, breathing-in is receiving air and breathing-out is giving it. The heart pumps blood out to nourish the cells and the blood then circulates back to be oxygenated in the lungs. Perception is the receiving of perceptual gifts, which can be passed on to others with ostensive gestures or by giving words for them. We can also give ourselves purposely to others' perception, 'attracting' their attention. Every need-satisfying act of kindness or care can be seen as a gift and even within exchange, there are gifts, like acts of kindness, charity, immagination and art; at another level, giving someone a job, a loan or a discount can be considered a gift.[29]

After the child learns the roles of the schema through intimate interaction with the motherer, these roles also become evident to h:er (as they are to the adult), when others are performing them, as we mentioned regarding the 'Machiavellian hypothesis' where, for positive or manipulative purposes, primate spectators of grooming can follow the relationships among other grooming pairs. For humans, the ability to 'read' the actions of third parties in terms of the gift schema is an important key to cognition and understanding. Jane's giving to Sally and Sally's giving in turn to Sue and their consequent chains of relatedness are important elements of community formation. Such chains can be projected and extended to relations among non-human objects, their properties and interactions. I am saying that they are also projected onto interactions and relations among those special human-made objects that are words. The gift lens provides a way to understand many kinds of interactions as giving and receiving (including both material – the mason gives the brick to the wall

---

28   This 'construction' recalls construction grammar, which I believe is itself based on the gift schema via the building metaphor which has an unseen gift source. See below p. 201. Verbal products are the result of the work of gift construction for communication.

29   Much is being made now of teamwork and solidarity among corporate employees who satisfy each others' goal-directed needs. Similar solidarity occurs among military who are supposed to collaborate, serve and protect each other in combat.

and gives it cement to hold it – and verbal 'constructions'), which would not be available or communicable (giveable and receivable) without the nurturing interactive schema in which to insert them.

Projecting from a source to a target area, as happens with projecting from the source area of material gifting to the target area of verbal communication, can also be seen as forming a gift trajectory in the extended mode of path-to-goal. With this identification of projection as gifting it becomes possible to hypothesize that the gift relation is the kernel of all of the different aspects of communication. Even equivalence or correspondence between gifts on the two planes is a development of giving one for another and of giving again repeatedly, which results in the creation of the verbal plane itself. I believe I am able to say these things and expect some agreement because we all know much about giving and receiving already, which in a way, proves my point.

The completion of the gift transaction, the satisfaction of a need, can also be extended to the ascertainment of truth and lying. We understand whether Jane actually gave to Sally and satisfied her need, just as we know whether Jane actually gave to us and satisfied ours. The sentence 'Jane gave x to Sally' satisfies our cognitive and communicative relational need regarding gifts in the world if and only if Jane did give x to Sally. If she did not, the sentence does not satisfy our need. The gift schema did not take place on the reality plane so the sentence did not satisfy our communicative/cognitive need. If a sentence is true, it nurtures the receiver's contact with reality, h:er interface with the motherworld. If it is false it does not. If it is an intentional lie it nurtures only the 'giver', the liar, like an exchange.[30] If it is simply a mistake, it does not appropriately nurture either one.

The communicative/cognitive need regarding something can exist even if the thing referred to does not exist.[31] In fact, psychological needs for fantasy can be filled and can nurture the relation of the individual with the motherworld. Our communicative and cognitive needs also depend on the different kinds of possible commons, the topics we are trying to create and give access to.

---

30   This is very much the case now with advertising.
31   We can think of it as in the background of the thing we are attending to, the fingers that are not the index finger.

4.6 Two kinds of categorization

Another way of saying all this is that the gift schema is the hidden prototypical schema for language and cognition in a radial or graded category, and that it has been overshadowed by a one-to-many classical category with the idealized anti-maternal masculated male as its exemplar. The model of the nurturing motherer, who enacts the gift schema with the child, is already the prototypical model of the human for children generally, irrespective of gender. As a child grows up in capitalist patriarchy, binary gender categorization is established and the maternal prototype is overtaken and superseded by the model of the dominant father for all of 'mankind' and especially for males.[32] Binary categorization is established in the market as well, where the product is either free and valueless or exchanged and valuable. In the market, the schema of the gift is cancelled by the reflexive logic of exchange and the whole mode of graded categorization is cancelled by the 'classical' category of commodities in relation to the one-to-many exemplar of value, money.[33]

Since children's cognitive processes are also directed towards themselves, the kind of model they follow determine their self-concepts, which in patriarchal capitalist culture typically contain binary gender roles, constructed either upon the inclusive logic of the gift or upon the binary logic of exchange and domination.

---

32   See also Narvaez (2012) who speaks of the 'One mother'. An individual female reflection of the one-to- many male, she has to take all the 'dialogic positions' of the nurturing community that would have been. Narvaez says: 'Mothers today may be raised to be physiologically distinct from mothers in our ancestral contexts. Ancestral parenting practices mentioned previously build a brain that is fully prepared for deep sociality, garnering great pleasure from social relationships. In contrast, when a child is raised with greater isolation from others as in modern Western childrearing (e.g., not physically in contact with others throughout the first years of life, not breastfed for years), the brain is not wired up as well for social relationships and must learn to find pleasure in ways outside of deep social relationships. Mothers with this type of early life history may find it more difficult to attain the deep pleasure in being a mother and may be especially deflated by modern childbirth practices that greatly interfere with mother and child wellbeing and bonding, practices that are commonplace in the USA (e.g., drugging the mother, mother-child separation after birth, feeding newborns something other than breastmilk)'; see also Trevathan 2010).

33   And the motherer becomes the analog of property as Engels suggested. The cancelling of the maternal prototype does not happen with the matriarchal Minangkabau of Sumatra. The motherer is projected onto Nature as mother/ teacher (Sanday 2002).

The idea of graded categorization using prototypes was introduced by Eleanor Rosch in 1978 and has since been used extensively by cognitive linguists. Following along the lines of Wittgenstein's and Vygotsky's categories or complexes of 'family resemblance',[34] Rosch proposed the idea that categories are organized around a prototype having a variety of similarities with members, which cluster around it. No single common quality is shared by all the members as happens in the abstract 'classical' concept. Nor is there binary inclusion/exclusion. Thus, for example, the robin is seen as the prototypical bird for many people in the USA, with other similar kinds of birds clustered around it, while ostriches and penguins are on the periphery (see Lakoff 1987 and Johnson 1987).

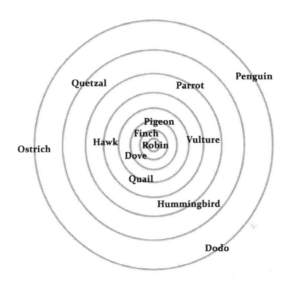

www.cervantesvirtual.com

Figure 7: Graded category.

---

34   The complex of family resemblance is like the strands in a rope mentioned by Wittgenstein – is a radial category a kind of cross-section of this? We leave out the fact that someone spun or twisted the strands. But even the family resemblance picture excludes the motherer.

Although Rosch investigated the prototype according to its statistical typicality in a *post hoc* way, the term 'prototype' carries within it the idea of 'original model' or term of comparison (as in the 2010 prototype Ferrari). When the human prototype is identified with the motherer, it retains this sense of primacy. Seen in this way a 'prototype' has the sense of imitability or even normativity that it lacks when viewed only statistically.[35] A prototype is an 'exemplar', that does not require a common property or essence among the items related to it. In fact, it is more like the Vygotskyian 'family name' complex or the Wittgensteinian 'family resemblance' than like a 'classical'[36] category per se. In a graded category there is a cluster relationship. The items are similar to the prototype and to each other in many different ways. Sparrows are like robins in size and shape while penguins are different from robins in size and shape but, like robins, they have wings and lay eggs even though they don't fly. Ostriches are even more different though they also have wings and lay eggs.[37]

The graded category is also more egalitarian and inclusive because the prototype can change depending on the culture and location. For example, for people in Guatemala the quetzal might be considered the prototypical bird, with parrots and toucans nearby and robins and sparrows on the periphery. Similarly, the maternal prototype can differ in many charactristics from culture to culture while continuing to be the original model of the giving/receiving interaction. Since the logic of other-orientation includes the other, the graded category with the maternal prototype will continue to be inclusive, while the classical category of Man is exclusive (sexist, racist, classist, etc.).

---

35 Lakoff talks about a 'generative category' (1987) in which a few elements have the capacity to generate many others. His example is the natural numbers 1-9 which generate all the others.

36 See Johnson's (1987) description of the classical category in his Introduction to the *Body in the Mind*.

37 Although the prototype relation seems clear at the base level of categorization, more specific levels seem to function according to more definite similarity. That is, we do not have much knowledge of individual robins. Our classification of them as robins would depend on our comparing them to an original exemplar, at least in the beginning. Actually, who can tell them apart? or penguins either?

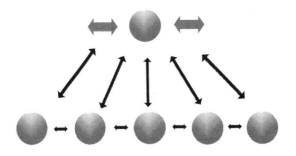

Figure 8: One-to-many classical category.

4.7 The maternal prototype of the human

Feminists, who have for decades critiqued the use of the term 'man' to refer to the human species, were/are taking their distance from the use of the male as the exemplar in a classical category of the human. However, they would, consistently with their principles, also challenge the male as the human prototype, the original or statistically most typical member of the graded category 'human'. In fact, particularly when we are dealing with categories regarding our own species, typicality judgments are usually ideologically determined. The reason the female motherer is not seen as the prototype in the sense of statistically central model of the human is socio-political. We have excluded h:er practically from this central position and we call the reasons for this 'sexism', 'matriphobia', 'mysogny', 'machismo', 'the war between the sexes'. If we do statistical sampling we find s:he is neither the exemplar not the prototype of the human, but a male figure is. The data are not neutral. In our society they are already skewed towards patriarchy and they are racialized as well.

Certainly for young children who are just beginning to form categories, their idea of themselves is tied to the motherer as their first model or term of comparison. For the child, the motherer, usually a female, is the model of nurturing, the source of the gifts and services that are crucial for the child's survival. The masculated male is the exemplar of a non-maternal gender, usually shorn of (evident) nurturing characteristics, at least in the Anglo-patriarchal West.[38]

---

38 Nurturing, giving and receiving are transposed and sanitized as in the typical father-son ball games, throwing and catching. Fortunately many men are now

For boys in patriarchy (and often for girls as well), the masculated male takes the place of the nurturing motherer as the exemplar of the category 'human'. This deprives the nurturing characteristics of their appropriate place of prominence in our concept of our species. With patriarchy and the market, the female motherer (together with nurturing, the gift economy and the image schema of the gift) is displaced as the exemplar or prototype of the human. At the same time, the classical categorization model displaces the graded or radial categorization model as well. The classical category requires a common property for membership, a necessary and sufficient condition. In the categorization of males, and therefore of human, this appears to be physiological, i.e. the penis.[39] The possession of this property socially implies the elimination of maternal giving from the behavior of its possessor at least in the patriarchal capitalist West. On the other hand, the possession of breasts, which are seen as the instrument of nurturing other-orientation, socially implies that women are more inclusive of others and more emotional, i.e. more responsive to needs than men.

If we took a meta-point of view and saw the female motherer as the exemplar or prototype or Lakoff's Idealized Cognitive Model, we would recognize one of her characteristics as her primacy: being the original model. This could restore to the definition of the word 'prototype' the sense of 'original model', which it loses from being taken as only a most typical item or statistical center.[40]

In a (usually non-Western) nurturing community, the motherers are many, as all turn towards the needs of children and each other. Thus, the values of care extend to everyone and it is commonplace for men to be 'maternal'. There are also men in the West who are nurturing and who, for whatever reason, haven't given up the maternal prototype of the human in spite of the crucial childhood and adolescent years (Chu 2014) in which

---

doing nurturing.

39   According to Marilyn Frye (2005: 43): 'The category MEN, sometimes in free variation with the sacred, transcendent and non empirical category MAN, has also been paradigmatic of categories. (Man is a rational animal) The feminist category WOMEN doesn't fit in the picture of categories in which the category MEN has this status'.

40   Lakoff (1987, 1987b) describes the Idealized Cognitive Model as the most typical or stereotypical of the members of the conceptual cluster. He problematizes the term 'mother' dividing its various senses from each other in order to use it as an example of a graded category. If we give back the idea of source to prototype and to mother, we reunite them so that the mother(er) can be the prototype of the graded category human. Otherwise, as Lakoff presents it, the category 'mother' is fragmented: divided and conquered.

'feminine' behavior is brutally discouraged by bullying peers. Moreover, there are also now feminist men who are consciously embracing maternal behavior. Many feminists defend men by saying that they are nurturing in spite of the evidence of widespread male violence. This defense depends upon biologism and essentialism directed towards men. I try to avoid these difficulties and my approach is different. I believe that all humans are originally nurturing, gift-giving and receiving, necessarily socialized by their interaction with the motherer(s). This original nurturing capacity is re-elaborated and borne out in language as verbal nurturing, which is not, however, recognized as such. Some humans, usually men in patriarchy, are socialized to turn against the mothering model. They unwittingly cancel and deny the importance of the unilateral gift and replace the agenda of mothering with an agenda of seemingly neuter exchange or with violence, as part of a false 'ideal' gender role. Moreover, they use language as a tool for domination. Then women sometimes nurture them more *because* they are male, i.e. because they are alienated in this way.

Indeed, the whole culture of patriarchal capitalism seems to tend towards patriarchal dominance by the 'ones' over the many. That is, even collectively,[41] it functions according to the idealized masculated ego and the classical concept model. This is particularly evident in racial domination and in the striving of a nation to be the hegemonic 'one' among the many nations. War is clearly a non-nurturing behavior and functions according to violence, exchange, reprisal and the denial of maternal gift-giving (except when using the protection of mothers and children and the motherland as the pretext for making the wars).

4.8 Inner speech and slang

There is an area of language in which we sometimes use single words, beyond schemas, and that is inner speech. Vygotsky (1962) saw thought as an internalization of external speech. Perhaps this evident private area of language use misleads us regarding the altercentric nature of language in that it seems that first we speak internally and then with others.

However in our terms, following Vygotsky, the gifts of language, which have been directed first towards others, are subsequently internalized. Our relational communicative needs, which would have been satisfied by others speaking to us, are satisfied by ourselves. In our internal mental space

---

41   See Stephen Ducat, *The Wimp Factor* (2004) on 'anxious masculinity' and war.

we 'mind-read' or 'scan' ourselves and satisfy the needs we find by thinking of word-gifts – or perhaps they simply emerge into our consciousnesses
seemingly unbidden (the result of our internal maternal selection/cerebral
statistical sampling and computation). However, we usually already know
our own needs quite well so we do not have to say many words or make
complete sentences internally. If we put a word in a role of the gift schema,
we can often do so without completing the other roles.[42] Much the same
thing happens for speech among intimates. Vygotsky gave the example of
a passage from Tolstoy's *Anna Karenina*, 'the declaration of love between
Kitty and Levin by means of initial letters' (Vygotsky 1962: 140):

> I have long wished to ask you something.
> Please do.
> This, he said, and wrote the initial letters:
> W y a: i c n b, d y m t o n. These letters meant:
> When you answered: it can not be, did you mean then or never?
> It seemed impossible that she would be able to understand the complicated
> sentence.
> I understand, she said, blushing.
> What word is that? he asked, pointing to the n which stood for
> Never.
> The word is 'never', she said, but that is not true.
> He quickly erased what he had written, handed her the
> chalk, and rose. She wrote: I c n a o t.
> His face brightened suddenly: he had understood. It meant:
> I could not answer otherwise then.
> he wrote the initial letters:
> s t y m f a s w h
> This meant: So that you might forget and forgive what happened.

He seized the chalk with tense, trembling fingers, broke it, and wrote the initial letters of the following: I have nothing to forget and forgive. I never
ceased loving you.
I understand, she whispered. He sat down and wrote a long sentence. She
understood it all and, without asking him whether she was right took the chalk
and answered at once. For a long time he could not make out what she had written, and he kept looking up into her eyes. His mind was dazed with happiness.
He was quite unable to fill in the words she had meant; but in her lovely, radi-
antly happy eyes he read all that he needed to know. And he wrote down throe

---

42   Chomsky says 'Is it the case, for example, that humans necessarily think in lan-
     guage?...when I think about a trip to Paris or a camping expedition in the Rockies,
     the few scraps of internal monologue that may be detected hardly convey, or even
     suggest the content of my thought' (Introduction to Schaff 1973).

letters. Before he had finished writing, she was already reading under his hand, and she finished the sentence herself and wrote the answer, yes. Everything had been said in their conversation: that she loved him, and would tell her father and mother that he would call in the morning. (Anna Karenina Pt. IV, ch. 13)

In inner speech we are satisfying our own communicative/cognitive needs *as if* we were another. We use the general social verbal means, the collective gifts for this purpose, a fact, which socializes and organizes our thought. However, we do not need to form complete sentences since we already understand many aspects of what we are thinking about. The need is already satisfied. We don't need to relate ourselves socially to everything in our internal (or external) context because much of it is already a given. We are already going through life with the accumulated gifts of the past ready to hand. We don't satisfy needs we don't have.[43] We can feel our own emotional tones, scan and shift our attention without verbalizing anything.

There is a very similar situation in the use of abbreviations and slang in face to face communication among friends. Even hints of non-verbal gestures can be enough to let the other person know something (for example, a 'let's go' head movement or an 'I don't believe it' gesture with the eyes). This is possible because the interactors are all mind reading each other and they are also jointly attending to the same situation. Their communicative needs are few because they are already embedded in the same context. In fact, our gestures (which we 'give to view') encourage others to 'mind-read' us. If we or they don't understand, we can always clarify with words.[44] For inner speech, if needs arise for more specificity or clarity, we can use a few words mentally to satisfy the needs for ourselves.[45] Also, because we are not speaking to someone else, we are not actually enacting the relation-creating, giving/receiving process with

---

43   This is quite different from cost/benefit calculation. We are not budgeting our inner words. We simply do not have a reason to tell ourselves what we already know.

44   The sign language of the deaf would require a thorough investigation in gift terms since the hands are organs of giving and receiving on a par with, or even more importantly than, the mouth and the ears.

45   Our subconscious usually seems ready to supply us with any words we need although, under pressure of a need at a different level, perhaps a psychological need, it can refuse to give us the 'right' word, thus creating a verbal symptom or sign of a problem, as Freud showed us. The wrong gift would thus come about through the conflict of needs at different levels, all of which the subconscious giver is trying to satisfy. On the other hand, 'hearing voices' in paranoia may be the internal response to an emergence of unconscious communicative needs of a 'distanced' self, an attempt to create the 'glue'.

another person. That is, the 'glue' of alignment with the interpersonal gift situation is lacking, so our internal speech can be 'unglued' – somewhat outside the form of gift syntax.

Writing, on the other hand, requires tracking the communicative and cognitive needs of imagined generalized readers (among whom the writer would also be included) and satisfying them with the help of relatively complete syntactical gift-constructions (which linguists consider constructions according to 'rules' of syntax).

Language users have all already engaged in context-embedded communication in the early motherer/child relation. Language is first acquired by the child at a time when the motherer has successfully learned to 'mind-read' and satisfy the child's needs. One could say their relation is similar to the relation of the lovers described in *Anna Karenina* or even similar to the internal speech of the adult. The context is given, in large part, by the motherer h:erself.

When children begin to say their first words, motherers usually scan the context to find the referent. There is an early stage of language acquisition, the holophrastic stage, in which children use one word to mean a number of different things. Even if the child is using the word holophrastically, however, the motherer is not. For h:er, it satisfies a more specific communicative need and she understands it as what the child is 'trying to say'. S:he receives it as a specific word-gift even if the child does not actually give it that way. If the child's holophrastic word is 'ball', one of the mother's specific communicative needs is satisfied, even if the child is not using the word specifically. The motherer usually tries to find what may have caught the child's attention and responds – gives it verbally again – in a positive and confirming way if the '(proto) referent' is the same as her own (she may say, 'Yes, there's the ball. Look at the ball'). S:he establishes a specific point where the attention becomes 'joint'.[46]

On the other hand, in teaching words by ostensive definition, a corespondence or qualitative equation is asserted between the single word and the prototype or exemplar of a kind, for example, by pointing and saying: 'That is a ball', where the extra-linguistic situation provides the context. Here the 'field' of the holophrastic word has been 'analyzed', internally divided (in the motherer's linguistic competence), 'articulated' by the presence of coexisting words and concepts, specifying the word gift, which is offered to the child.

---

46 This is already a kind of 'scaffolding' or 'zone of proximal development' (as Vygotsky says in other contexts). Motherers already do this when the infant cries.

The field of holophrastic 'ball' is reduced when the child realizes that h:er word satisfies a specific need of others, the need for a word-gift regarding balls, and that they have other needs, which are satisfied by other word-gifts (which might be 'throw', 'hit', 'boy', 'red' and countless others). Thus, s:he enters the 'pivot stage' in which s:he gives two words together, or one word to another, creating constants and variables: 'ball red', 'ball up', 'Daddy ball'.

The positive interpersonal gift aspects of language and language teaching complement and undergird the "implicit statistical analysis" that developmental neuropsychologists like Alison Gopnik (2009) propose as the process of language learning. She asks, 'How do any of us learn as much as we do about the world? All we've got are these little vibrations of air in our eardrums and photons hitting the back of our retina. And human beings know about objects and people, not to mention quarks and electrons. How do we ever get there? How could our brains, evolved in the Pleistocene, get us from the photons hitting our retinas to quarks and electrons?'.

Both innatism and the appeal to statistical learning detour around the model of maternal material nurturing. From very early on, we do already know about language, objects and people, not just vibrations of air and photons, because language, objects and people have a crucial relevance for our survival. They nurture us and we also nurture them.

Children and motherers are privileged with respect to scientists. A motherer would already know or guess from h:er experience with the child – make a 'statistic determination' h:erself – what part of the experience had caught the child's attention, and s:he would specify or elaborate the word-gift in that direction – 'Yes, the doggy is playing with the ball'. 'Yes, the ball hit the window'. 'No, you can't have the ball', etc., with appropriate pointing and pragmatics.

The child's holophrastic field of 'ball' is eventually delimited by other words (other qualitatively different little gift vibrations of air). The delimitation happens syntactically semantically and contextually, dividing the holophrastic field into more specific gift areas.

4.9 Prototypes and family resemblance

In the nuclear family, the motherer has a graded or radial relation with the members of h:er family, which is not based on identity but on giving and receiving in many different ways. S:he fulfills h:er job description as center of the family by h:er ability to nurture a number of others. S:he gives milk to the baby, meat or tofu and potatoes to the adults, strained soup to the old people, cakes to the neighbor. If s:he lives in a close community or an extended family s:he receives in turn from others. The[47] identity of the family is actually based on h:er and in turn h:er identity is shaped by h:er practice. S:he includes others by recognizing their needs and by giving to them, not just by categorizing or judging them according to similarity and difference. However, there is also similarity: members of the family can be like h:er in a number of ways, physically and in their activities. The father and other family members can also care for the children and older children can care for younger ones and each other. Nevertheless, the female motherer usually remains the central nurturer. In philosophical 'family resemblance' categories, however, this gift-giving figure is absent and physical similarity seems to be the only criterion even if there could be some functional similarity as well. The fact that the motherer is the origin for the child and constitutes a multifaceted original prototype, is not considered. This elimination is sociopolitical, ideological. It is caused by patriarchy and the market.

Thus I would like to restore the dictionary definition of 'a first or preliminary form from which others are copied' to the use of the word 'prototype' in cognitive linguistics by asserting the female motherer's centrality or typicality. That is not all. I want to restore her as the prototype of prototypicality itself. Nevertheless, I am wary of hypostatizing the 'one mother' of the nuclear family. As Narvaez suggests, a nurturing community would provide multiple 'dialogic positions', similar perhaps to positions in a graded category, while the nuclear family's 'one mother' has to cover all of the 'phantom' dialogic positions by herself for the child.

---

47   This is similar to the functional 'collaborative' complex of knife, fork, spoon, or perhps fire, pot and food. Family members create a family identity by giving to each other, and they become the same kind of gift for others.

Figure 9: Smith Brothers Family Resemblance.
Reprinted from *Cognition*, 13/3, Sharon Lee Armstrong, Lila R. Gleitman,
Henry Gleitman, "What some concepts might not be", Figure 3, "The
Smith Brothers", 269, May 1983, with permission from Elsevier.

This picture used to explain conceptual family resemblance (Armstrong, Gleitman and Gleitman 1983), leaves out the female motherer and even the possible daughters. In fact, the nurturing basis for actual family resemblance (necessary for children to survive into adulthood), is not recognized. When we use a visual similarity that eliminates the female mother (and which probably is concerned more with breasts and genitals than facial hair), we also leave out the interaction of giving and receiving as the salient aspect of the prototype. The Smith Brothers recall Peter Pan's Lost Boys without a mother or even a Wendy.

Figure 10: Put the mother back in the picture.

Having been mothered is a common but usually unseen factor for all these boys. And there are often daughters in families as well! Ropes, threads and the strands they are made of also do not come from nothing. Rope-making and spinning (usually 'women's work'), the complex twisting of the strands, is a long-term repetitive labor that keeps the strands together. Similarly, the work of usually female motherers keeps families together, and the mental work of knowers keeps categories together, associating their members with each other, even when their physical resemblance may not warrant it.

(Female) motherers and mothering have usually been excluded from the metaphors that are used to elucidate mental processes, or they have been made neuter as in 'mental conceptions'. When they are used, they are sometimes infected with patriarchal negative values of submission and domination. The 'mastery' of a subject, the 'pursuit' of knowledge, understanding as 'grasping' and minds as 'sharp' and 'penetrating' are examples of interpretations of the process of knowing as masculated and aggressive.

One example of patriarchal metaphorical inclusion of women in linguistics is the use of the terminology of 'ancestor', 'mother', 'daughter' and 'sister' in naming the parts of the sentence in a relation to each other called 'c-command'.[48] These relations are of dominance of the 'ancestor' over the 'mother' and the 'mother' over the 'daughter' and of coequality with the 'sister', a term that is equally dominated by the 'mother'. It is really striking that dominance, a particularly patriarchal capacity, is supposed to create 'binding' and is attributed to the metaphorical mother rather than giving. Dominance, in fact, requires the person who is dominated to give gifts to the dominator, and especially the gift of h:er will. It overturns the *egalitarian* maternal nurturing relation. In the terminology of c-command, nurturing/gift-giving is denied in favor of a transitive relation of domination, which passes from ancestor to parent to child (should we think cycle of violence?).

We must restore the mother(er) as the original (inclusive, non-dominant and non-binary) multifaceted prototype of the human and consider nurturing as the most important activity for the survival of the child. Ensuring the survival of the child is a relation-creating and confirming activity, which remains in the memory and the make-up of all of us as mothered children as we become adults and nurture each other linguistically and materially in adult ways.

Thus, it seems warranted to leave aside the model of dominance and investigate all kinds of human activities as kinds of giving and receiving and their variations and projections.

---

48   These terms were used in 'government and binding' theory by Chomsky and
      many others.

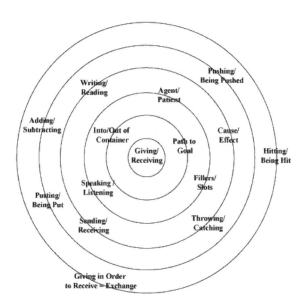

Figure 11. Graded category with giving/receiving prototype.

Cognitive linguists have extensively discussed 'basic' schemas like putting something into and out of a container and path to goal.[49] By restoring the maternal prototype, these can be reinterpreted as extended, attenuated and perhaps disguised derivatives of the gift schema. Receiving is often something coming into a container and giving is often something going out of one, even if the container in question is only the giver's or the receiver's own hand or body or proxemic space.

Path to goal can be seen as the trajectory of the gift itself as it moves from giver to receiver. The giver can be seen as the start of the path, the movement along it as the movement of the gift or purposeful activity of the service, and the goal or point of arrival as the receiver. From this, other kinds of attempts to achieve goals, such as working towards them can also be seen as gift trajectories. If the goal is conceived of as getting something in the future, one can be seen in the present moving or working towards it as giver at the beginning of the gift trajectory, gift or service in the process and receiver at the end, playing all the roles oneself, taking their different

---

49   Schemas are often rendered in small caps but I have used regular type for them throughout the book.

perspectives, foreseeing and remembering them as well, creating a minimal narrative structure (see Mark Turner's 'small spatial stories', 1996: 13).

The projection from source to target can be seen as a gift itself in that it is useful as a means for cognition and language, because we are capable of creatively receiving it as such. We can view it from the outside, tracking it as an interaction among gifts (see 2.4 above), as a trajectory which in this case traces a path from the reality plane gift (world-gift) to the plane of the verbal gift (word-gift). Moreover, if we can look at the world, taking its perspective as a giver, we can see ourselves as receivers of its perceptual and conceptual gifts, and our words as secondary receivers that we use to give again, giving them *for* the gifts of the world.

Both the movements into and out of a container and path to goal are schemas that propose the gift schema in a neutral register of transitivity, where it does not appear to be an explicitly maternal or nurturing interaction. In our society, evidence that boys are masculated, i.e. trained away from the maternal prototype very early, is that they typically play with toy vehicles, which (apart from also being phallic symbols), allow them to practice moving something (like a gift) along a path to goal, 'giving' without giving, while girls traditionally continue to practice overt nurturing with dolls. The displacement of the gift onto cars and paths makes the schema appear to be neutral,[50] without a maternal character and available to all. Girls can usually play with cars without challenging gender expectations while boys who practice the maternal role by playing with dolls are traditionally considered effeminate.

Thus there are games close to the nurturing prototype like children's pretend tea parties, and those a little farther away like the path to goal trajectories of boys (and girls) playing with trucks and cars. Ball games, throwing and catching, or throwing and catching and hitting as in baseball, attempts to arrive at a goal (give the gift) competitively, in spite of an obstacle – baseball and football, chess with its many complex trajectories, and games of war, combining trajectories of hitting or pretending to hit in order to give or pretend to give, death. It is not my purpose here to explore all possible gift-based games but only to suggest that many games are indeed based on gift-giving and its extensions. Perhaps with this proposal we can put the mother back into the picture of family resemblances. That is, *pace* Wittgenstein, giving and receiving with its variations in hitting and

---

50   Unfortunately boys also play with toy guns, with giving the negatively transformed trajectory of the bullet, the gift of death. They substitute 'high' transitivity for 'low' transitivity.

paths-to-goals could be seen as the hidden maternal prototype of the radial family resemblance category of games.

At another level, as adults of all genders, we come out of the containers of our houses, travel in vehicles to other containers, the buildings where we work. Or we travel from one city-limits container to another city-limits container, or from one nation container to another, crossing borders. It is not just on the highway of love that we travel metaphorically (as Lakoff and Johnson say) but on the highway itself that we travel materially, as rematerialized gift metaphors.

4.10 Gifting or just self-expression?

In the description of language using the maternal gift lens, speaking or writing can be seen as satisfying the communicative or cognitive need of the other, while, through the lens of neuter and neutral exchange, speaking or writing becomes mere self-expression, interpersonally intransitive, a kind of 'giving' that ethologists and anthropologists would call 'display' or maybe 'costly signalling' (Gurven et al 2000).[51] Consequently, understanding becomes 'grasping the intention' of the speaker rather than receiving a gift. The speaker's 'mind-reading' of the listener's communicative needs and h:er proactive satisfaction of what s:he believes they are, is not considered. One partial exception to this criticism is H. P. Grice's (1989) Cooperative Principle, at least at the level of conversation. However, his recommendations are framed as rule following, or maxims, while I am saying that satisfying communicative and cognitive needs by unilateral linguistic gift-giving is the way language *functions*. Individual words satisfy cognitive and communicative needs of others and they are organized by syntax which is a construction of word-gifts given to word-gifts at that level. Taking another step away from the gift framework, Sperber and Wilson (1995) have thoroughly integrated Grice's work into the exchange paradigm applying cost-benefit to the communicative interaction (see 8.2 below).

The maternal gift process has three basic parts or moments, the giver, the gift or service, and the receiver with h:er need. Leaving out the receiver as a key element in this process, while concentrating only on the giver makes us look at gift-giving as an ego-based process, done for the good

---

51   But see the infancy researchers on intersubjectivity and dialogism, for example Stein Bråten ed. 1998.

of the giver, as happens in exchange. The transitivity of the gift process depends upon the actual transmission and the (creative) reception and use of the gift by the receiver. The more passive the receiver is considered, the more active the giver appears. When the receiver is eliminated, the giver stands alone and, in fact, without a receiver, the idea of the speaker (or writer) as giver soon fades and the interactivity of language is placed in the background. All the creativity seems to occur on the part of the person who is 'generating' sentences. S:he is no longer a giver but just a neutral 'agent'.

It is through the lens of exchange that speech can appear to be just the exercise of an innate capacity and that speaking seems to be just the satisfaction of one's own need to express oneself. It is in this area that Chomsky's 'linguistic creativity' resides, in that each person is said to be endowed biologically with a language capacity that can be almost infinitely exercised. There is no satisfaction of others' needs in the innatist model, and no acknowledgment of the contribution of the model of material mothering. It is interesting that the very kind of material economy that Chomsky might embrace politically is excluded from his linguistics. This is perhaps because in our academic culture, maternal material giving/receiving, the nurturing 'making' of the body of the other, is not considered (categorized as) a kind of communication.

Lacking the emphasis on giving to needs, we consider the speaker as actively generating or constructing h:er sentences and the listener (perhaps) as actively interpreting them but, in spite of the fact that we have to use the language of the other in order to be understood, we do not see the speaker as in touch with or satisfying the communicative and cognitive needs of the listener. Nor do we see the interpretation and understanding of the listener as h:er completion and fruition of the satisfaction of h:er needs by the speaker.

We can say the same kind of thing about Wittgenstein's 'For a *large* class of cases of the employment of the word "meaning" – though not for all – this way can be explained in this way: the meaning of a word is its use in the language' (2009: 43). It is not the use as such but the satisfaction of the need of the other that is the completion of the linguistic communicative act. Words are verbal gifts that are specific to the needs they satisfy. Even in those relatively rare cases when one does speak for mere self-expression alone and for h:er own benefit, s:he understands through the satisfaction of her own communicative needs with words which would satisfy the needs of others.

Descriptions of the world based on semiotics, for example, Charles S. Peirce's tripartite 'sign, object and interpretant' (Ponzio and Petrilli 2005), usually omit the mothering frame and have no concept of the subject of language (speaker or writer, and even the grammatical subject) as the giver.

While this can function well in such areas as biosemiotics or phytosemiotics and even at the level of the genetic code, (maternal) giving and receiving are a necessary part of human language, which is relational and community-oriented in a sense that non-human sign systems are not.

However Peirce's tripartite schema does to a certain extent include an actual movement from one point to the other as well as a passing-on of the focus of attention or perspective. Peirce's account is opposite Chomsky's: there is little attention given to the 'giver' and most of the activity is concentrated in the 'receiver', the interpretant, which in turn, becomes a sign and is received by another interpretant, etc. Though[52] the interpretant relation captures the 'passing it on' aspect of the gift, needs and maternal giving to satisfy them are not part of Peirce's tradic relation. As we have seen above (in section 3.6), Peirce's correspondent and friend Victoria Welby did try to introduce the concept of 'mother sense' as a basic part of the functioning of language (Petrilli 2009), in spite of much opposition by the male establishment of her day. This suggestion was not taken up by Peirce. In fact, the lack of the giver in Peirce's description of the sign (sign, interpreter, interpretant), makes it appropriate for application to non-human scientific contexts like bio- or phytosemiotics, where there is no human giver. Human-initiated sign activity is gift activity and requires a giver. Even when we say 'the sense of a sign is another sign' somebody is providing that sign and the other sign and so on in the chain of signifiers, suspended for the moment from the communicative and cognitive needs of any specific receivers.

---

52   Peirce's idea of the interpretant leads to infinite semiosis because it is concerned with similarity and difference rather than need satisfaction. See below p. 235 on Marx's extended relative form of value. In the gift register 'passing it on' creates community.

CHAPTER V

EXPLORING GIVING

5.0 Benefactive 'give'

The word 'give' itself has not been ignored by linguists. John Newman (1996) made an extensive study of the word and collected a number of essays of other linguists in his edited volume (1998). However, all of these studies 'of the role ordinary human experience has in shaping linguistic structure' (www.johnnewman.org/research) leave aside the fundamental importance of maternal giving and the gift economy.

Newman says, 'In referring to an act of giving I will mean, in the typical case, an act whereby a person (the GIVER) passes with the hands control over an object (THING) to another person (the RECIPIENT)'(1996: 1). This objective way of describing giving presents as basic a scenario which occurs after early maternal gift-giving, when people, including older infants, are able to receive things with their hands. It leaves out the fundamental maternal action of breastfeeding, for example, and services like cleaning and clothing the child. Newman discusses various 'domains' within the frame of of GIVE-type verbs: 'the spatio-temporal domain, the control domain, the force-dynamics domain, and the domain of human interest' (1996: 37). He diagrams the scenarios of the various different senses.

For example, following Langacker he diagrams 'give' as a movement from an 'energy source' to an 'energy sink'.

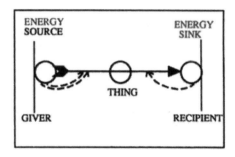

Figure 12: The force dynamics of Give from Newma (1996).

The various senses of 'give', as listed by Newman, should not be seen as equally important. Rather I believe they are clustered around the original need-satisfying 'benefactive' sense, which Newman sees as part of the 'human interest' domain. It is this benefactive sense of giving that is the prototype: the original gift is life-enhancing, given to satisfy need(s) and make the child grow. It is this successful benefactive interaction that is relevant, indeed crucial, for the survival of children and that is therefore the emotionally charged psychological prototype.[1]

Acts of giving that diverge from the prototypical act, such as simple giving and receiving with the hands, transfer of control, force dynamics, and those at a more complex level, such as gifts of munificence without a specific receiver, gifts of 'tolerated scrounging', gifts without a specific giver, divine gifts, gifts to strangers, even exchanges and gifts that harm instead of help (see 1.16) can all be seen as informed by and located at varying distances from the central maternal need-satisfying giving/gift-receiving prototype, which is 'benefactive'. Newman says there is 'a further dimension of meaning to GIVE predicates and that is the dimension of meaning which has to do with the ways in which the participants are advantaged or disadvantaged by the event' (p. 51). My contention is that it is the way par-

---

1   I mentioned that Lakoff (1987: 74-84) by proposing that the concept of mother is a cluster without one main model leaves the nurturing prototype out of the picture, denying its centrality. In this, his approach is similar to Newman's lack of emphasis on the benefactive character of 'give'. I hope my term 'motherer' can avoid this difficulty somewhat.

ticipants are advantaged that makes the giving/receiving interaction fundamental and prototypical. The way they may be disadvantaged is a variation, which I will discuss in the next subsection.

The restoration of the maternal prototype provides and maintains an original – prototypical – image schema that we can call upon to understand a graded category of actions.[2] That is, giving and receiving can be used as the original model of transitive actions and services: pushing, throwing, carrying, baking, washing, looking, making, planting, speaking and on the receiving side, getting, taking, catching, hearing, harvesting. Actions such as getting and taking focus agency on the receiver side of the schema (the passive voice focuses the interaction on the receiver). Many of children's earliest words, not surprisingly have to do with getting,[3] as they themselves have so often been in the receiver role in the gift schema. This should not be read as egotism but simply reflects the point of view of the role. Moreover, most children's early words have to do with the gift scenario if not with the whole transaction itself. These can include things the child wants, as well as ways of giving and receiving, etc.[4]

For adults in our society, giving is often made neuter and neutral as doing, which can also be made more forceful as hitting; receiving is made more active as getting and taking or more static as having or more passive as recipient of force.

As I have been saying, linguistic giving and receiving can be added to the graded category of mother-child giving and receiving. The speaker or writer gives linguistic products and the listener or reader receives them. Together they use the word-gifts to create human (species-specific) relations with each other and other humans regarding world-gifts.[5] The words

---

2   This has not been understood because by taking the male as the prototype of the human, we have taken attention away from mothering and even played down mothering in the study of child development.

3   In a study of 11 infants from between 9 and 15 months of age and their mothers by Daniel S. Messinger (1998): 'Infants were more likely than their mothers to request objects and less likely to respond to requests for objects, suggesting a relatively acquisitive style of interaction. Nevertheless, the children's "offer" gestures seemed more prosocial, accompanied by gaze and smiles, while the "request" gestures were not'. See also, Tomasello (1998).

4   Ninio (1999:644) says 'the semantics of the earliest combining verbs and of the grammaticalized inducers of transitivity seem to revolve around what in a different context is called "object relations" (Klein, 1957). All these verbs deal with the literal and metaphoric ingestion and ejection of an object by a human being'.

5   I use these terms word and world in a somewhat different way from philosophers of language terms 'word-to-world, world-to-word' from whom I have taken them.

are given. They go out of the container of the mouth and into the container of the ear, out of the containers of head, hand and pen onto the paper, or out of the container of head and hand into the container of one computer and through the gift trajectory of the Internet into another, and finally into the container of the eye of the beholder.

Humans in particular can understand signs this way because, however much we ignore it, we have been intensely mothered and have developed the gift schema, a maternal practice and a giving/receiving lens as well as graded categories with mothering as the prototypical interaction.[6]

Language is mothering at a (meta) level, giving by and about giving. It is virtual mothering. It is simulated giving and receiving in the medium of sound or writing, giving verbal gifts, which are themselves organized according to gift principles. Language is a collective maternal synthetic *a priori*, continually being constructed as we speak. It is a legacy of our infant altercentric interaction, extended, stretched, diluted (partialized, expanded, given, given to, given from, given forward at many levels) but still functioning on the basis of nurturing, unilateral giving, receiving and turntaking throughout our adult lives. Philosophers, who use language as their main instrument, touchstone and explanatory key even to the exclusion of the world around them, remain confused because they do not see its central maternal gift *benefactive* aspects. The engagement with the world, which begins in infancy together with the motherer and is later replayed on the verbal plane, satisfying others' cognitive and communicative needs, is the source of the solution to philosophical problems regarding the relation between world and word.

This source has been invisible because unilateral giving has been invisible, and that is because exchange and its paradigm have occupied our collective focus, intervening like the cuckoo in the robin's nest (the nest of the prototypical bird).

Language is not a member of a graded category that has exchange as its

---

6   While the sun does not shine intentionally to give us light, our perceptive apparata have developed to use the sunlight so that we can creatively receive it and see (and plants have evolved photosynthesis to use it to grow). We respond to this by saying that the sun gives us light. We learn this giving-receiving schema from our interaction with our mothers and use it to understand many things including the interaction between the sun and the Earth and the sun and ourselves. Does my cat remember the warmth of her mother when she sleeps in the sun? Maybe, but she cannot replay the gift schema of her mother's care linguistically with the sun in the role of the giver. So she cannot tell us about it, maternally satisfying our communicative needs in its regard.

hidden prototype. Nor is it a member of a graded category that has a neutral give-receive scenario as its hidden prototype. Instead, altercentric maternal giving is the hidden prototype of a graded category in which language and the neutral give-receive scenario are near members and exchange is a peripheral member among other peripheral members (like hitting, see below). As we shall see in Part Two, exchange is actually a (secondary) derivative of language, a projection of the process of projection, of changing planes, of simulation itself. As such it proposes giving-without-giving, which creates a second lens, a second and more artificial (real time) *a priori* structure through which we reorganize and distort our (gift-based) perceptions.

Even though it is obvious that children learn language at a time when they are being intensely mothered, as adults in patriarchal capitalism, we do not usually imagine that our understanding might be based on the model of that early interaction. Our capacity for knowledge and language is attributed instead (at least in this place and time) to neutral and (mostly) neuter biological 'inheritance' (a gift word!), and to interactions among neurons rather than interactions among people. Looking at the world around us we filter out the benefactive motherer and h:er maternal structures and use giftless reifying lenses when we consider language and heredity as well as all kinds of experiential 'event structures'.

Some of the neutral members of a graded category clustered around the unacknowledged maternal giving and receiving prototype are cause and effect, where for example, one object transfers motion or force to another (see Hume's and Langacker's billiard ball models), and agent-instrument-patient, where the receiver is seen as passive, not creative. Cause and effect and agent-instrument-patient are considered basic to cognitive mapping and they are neutral (or neuter), that is, non-maternal. They may indeed *be* non-maternal but we understand them because, as mothered children, we use the roles of giver, gift, receiver in which we place cause and effect or agent, instrument and patient even if subsequently we rightly de-anthropomorphize them.

I do not want to say that cause and effect and agent, instrument and patient do not exist as such but that we understand them because they can be inserted in the gift schema, which, in their case, has been depersonalized. They rest on maternal giving-receiving, which continues to function as a hidden schema even in the very language with which we describe them. They are located at a distance from the giving prototype but still remain in that graded category.

Or if we located them upon a continuous spectrum of gifts these interactions, which are giftless, might be placed somewhere closer to the extreme

of Newman's 'adversative' pole.[7] That is, they would be equidistant between positive and negative with perhaps an ideological effect validating
the negative pole just because giving is ignored.

If path-to-goal is seen as a derivative of the trajectory of the gift, and
time is understood in terms of path-to-goal (Lakoff 1990), time can also
be seen in terms of the trajectory of the gift. Lakoff discusses the points of
view regarding time, whether it is coming or going or passing by. These
points of view can also be seen as those of the receiver, the giver but also
the onlooker or tracker of the gift motion according to the direction of its
trajectory, and they recall MacWhinney's shifts of perspective in the sentence (see 4.3). The onlooker perspective tracks gifts among others rather
than re-enacting giving and receiving as happens in the schema of the transitive sentence. Similarly the perspective of an onlooker-narrator guides
the narration, which with its beginning, middle and end, is a kind of time
trajectory deriving from a gift trajectory (and then the whole story itself is
a gift from the narrator to the listeners, which takes time to tell).[8]

Experience can be a gift when it is relevant and shareable. We turn our
joint attention towards some event, receive it together and can give it again,
recounting retelling the story in our own words, from beginning to end. I
discussed pointing at length in *For-Giving*, and will discuss it more later
but here I will just mention that it is path-to-goal giving of something to the
gaze of the other. Also, fingers held back are a backgrounding with respect
to the pointing finger that is given and giving – indicating metonymically
– the path to the goal (pointing can be seen as iconic, an exosomatic representation of the classical exemplar-to-many concept form – see chapters 15
and 16 in my *For-Giving*, 1997, on pointing, joint attention and patriarchy).

5.1 Nurturing vs force

Looking at 'adversative' as the independent opposite of 'benefactive'
does not allow us to see harm as a negative derivative of giving.

Studies on transitivity beginning with Hopper and Thomson (1980) distinguished between *high transitivity* as force, exemplified by verbs like 'hit',
'break' and 'kill', and *low transitivity* as exemplified by verbs like 'take',

---

7   'Slots' and 'fillers' have the same denatured neutrality, but recall a sexual met-
     aphor, which is also a derivative and disguise of nurturing gifts and needs.
8   It is interesting that as researchers on infancy say, protoconversation provides a
     narrative envelope for experience.

'carry', 'put', 'get', 'have', 'give', 'want'. Later researchers, such as Ninio (1999) and Vazquez-Rozas (2007), have challenged this approach, because it characterized high transitivity as more prototypical than low transitivity:

> ... there are no sound arguments that support the attribution of a greater cognitive importance to the events expressed through highly transitive clauses as opposed to low ones. On the contrary, both the acquisition and the textual frequency data lead us to think that the clauses that configurate the most relevant cognitive model are those characterized by rather low transitivity. (Vazquez-Rozas 2007: 30)

Vazquez-Rozas continues:

> As Goldberg (1998: 207) indicates in regard to verbs like *put, get, do* and *make*, the fact that these 'light' verbs, which are drawn from a small set of semantic meanings cross-linguistically, are learned earliest and used most frequently is evidence that this small class of meanings is cognitively privileged. (Ibid. 30)

The most 'prototypically transitive' verbs are those having to do with the actions involved in the processes of giving and receiving, of nurturing, rather than those having to do with physical causation and force. Velazquez-Rozas quotes Ninio, who says that the children's first verbs 'codify meanings that are pragmatically important for the children like the wish of obtaining an object (*want, get, give, take, bring, find*), the creation of an object (*make, do*), the perception of an object (*see, hear*) or the ingestion of an object (*eat, drink*)'. Ninio says, 'The concept underlying prototypical transitivity both cross-linguistically and developmentally is, thus, inclusion in and exclusion of objects from the personal domain' (1999: 647). In our terms this 'translates' as receiving and giving.

Because force, or at least 'gross motor activity', appears to be more salient than nurturing, it may also appear more prototypical, more basic. Nevertheless, the interaction of giving/receiving is actually more important and more prototypical because it is necessary for the child's survival, even if it may sometimes recede into the background while people attend to other things. The later confusion of transitivity with exchange, with the non-nurturing and contingent *quid pro quo* transfer of equivalent properties, obscures the primacy of the unilateral gift relation. Force, the causative transfer of energy of active agent upon passive object, takes the place of milder gift-giving in the foreground of attention. When there is a response of force as well, there is often an escalation into an exchange of blows until one makes the other 'give up', i.e. stop hitting and submit to the winner's unilateral higly transitive activity.

Thus material giving and receiving also functions as the schema for harmful 'highly transitive' actions like attacking, hitting, kicking, hurting, beating, shooting and killing. These activities, which can be seen at the edge of the graded category of giving, constitute the opposite of benefactive maternal giving, and therefore, may seem to be appropriate behavior for boys and men who are trying to distinguish themselves from the mother in order to achieve a masculated identity. Fathers, who underwent the same kind of socialization in their youths, serve as models in this for their sons while motherers and others sometimes 'benefactively' nurture and validate violence as an aspect of the masculinity of their 'boys'. This is a pathological configuration for both women and men and it is contributing to wars, economic exploitation, and the destruction of the planet and all her creatures. It is important to recognize this as part of the diagnosis of the disease of patriarchy.

Nevertheless the intention behind verbal gift-giving is always fundamentally 'benefactive' in that word-gifts are given in order to satisfy the communicative and cognitive need of the other for a human relation with the speaker to something. This need satisfaction can be used in negative ways, however. If the speaker says 'Bitch!' the listener knows s:he is establishing a relation with h:er to a female dog. However, she also knows that this positive relation is being used in a negative way in that the word is being given to refer to her – her communicative and cognitive need regarding dogs is being satisfied - but is being used to misname her in order to denigrate and offend her. The negative attack is made using the means of the positive need-satisfying word-gift.

Moreover, the lack of a structural distinction in language between giving and force creates a problem. 'The girl fed the cat' and 'The girl hit the cat' have the same positive gift-based structure. The transitive structure looks neutral because it serves the whole spectrum between nurturing and violence.[9] However, positive relational bonds come from giving and receiving not from violence, so the bond-creating and functional aspect of the transitivity must come from giving to satisfy needs rather than from hitting to hurt, and to satisfy the hitter's need to dominate. Even if the situation referred to by the sentence 'The girl hit the cat' is negative, the sentence

---

9   We say com *muni* cation, not com *culpi* cation. Passing on the gift – Peirce's interpretant – is positive, while passing on violence is negative and has a different interpersonal significance.

itself is positive in that it is a verbal gift made of verbal gifts satisfying the listeners' communicative and cognitive needs. Similarly, 'the girl threw the ball,' which appears neither positive nor negative, functions according to the positive need-satisfying initiative and impetus of the gift schema.

Children's survival depends on adults giving to them, not on their hitting and dominating them. Giving and receiving, thus, have a fundamental positive survival value that hitting and being hit do not have. The transitive communicative structure depends on this positive need-satisfying transfer rather than on a negative transfer of energy. While 'cat' has a need or a linguistic 'slot' for being both 'fed' and 'hit', cats have a need for food and not for being hit. Even neutral or neuter transfers that might be seen in terms of Langacker's 'energy source and energy sink' function because they can be assimilated to the prototypical maternal benefactive schema, not vice-versa.

All these considerations point towards making giving rather than hitting or objective transaction the prototype of the graded category of human communicative interaction as expressed in language and towards making the motherer rather than the masculated male the the prototype of the human.

Interactions (event structures) like cause and effect or agent and patient, and schemas like path to goal seem to belong to a category with a neutral and neuter transitive prototype. Instead, I believe they have a common source in positive maternal giving/receiving and are clustered around that prototype at various distances in a graded category.[10] They are neutralized and attenuated versions of giving/receiving, altered, watered-down or on steroids. Yet they derive their explanatory capacity from their consonance with the gift schema and their interpretability using the gift lens.

The prototype of giving informs other activities that seem neutral and neuter such as putting, moving, going, making. These illustrate aspects of giving, such as putting something in someone else's hand, moving it from here to there, going in a gift trajectory from here to there, or making something to give. There are also actions that leave needs in abeyance and concentrate on the process: walking, talking, seeing, doing, or creating. There are activities that can be part of the long-term process of need satisfaction, for example, planting, gardening and harvesting crops that will eventually be used to satisfy needs. Another widespread special case is giving perceptually, giving-to-view, or display: showing, manifesting, touching,

---

10 Even the description of metaphor as mapping from source to target, brings with it a neutral appearance but which maintains the image of shooting ('target'), or hitting rather than giving.

gesturing, dressing, or emanating. All of these activities and many others seem *sui generis* if the core of gift giving is taken away.

Linguistic forms where the 'gift or service' destroys the receiver as in 'the girl ate the cake' or (as I have been saying) 'the man shot the burglar', can be placed in the same graded category, though they are only partially similar to the gift prototype not in this case because they are diluted, but because on another scale, they are destructive or violent.

Thus 'low transitivity' 'Mary fed the cat' is more in alignment with the gift prototype for grammatical transitivity than what is considered 'high transitivity' as in 'John hit Mary'. Hitting appeared somehow 'high' ('up is good'), more transitive, than feeding or giving. That is, negative 'gross motor activity' appeared more transitive than peacefully satisfying another's need. Instead, satisfying a need, which is closer to the gift prototype is more transitive than hitting someone, which is farther away from the prototype in the graded category.[11]

Even if the event in the world to which a sentence refers harms the 'receiver': 'the girl hit the cat' the relation between the speaker and listener and among the words themselves is one of positive satisfaction of needs. The description in terms of slots and fillers avoids this issue by providing something of a neutral metaphor but, in this way, the particularly positive side of verbal need-satisfaction is rendered invisible. Whatever the negative charge of the words or the sense of the sentence, the 'glue' that holds the words together and the reason the sentence is understandable (the unity of the proposition), is the positivity of the need-satisfying gift relations.

Our lack of recognition of positive giving/receiving as the basic image schema for communication and transitivity not only makes us misunderstand language but works as an obstacle to the practice and validation of giving in other areas of life. We do not see maternal benefactive giving as functional but only as the expression of a kind of *sui generis* sentimental morality or even of weakness, submission, masochism, and sacrifice. Because language itself is conceived without the motherer, it seems that it is neuter and neutral and that it makes no judgments on whether it is used to help or harm.

The over-emphasis on exchange and force, together with the denial of the importance of mothering/being mothered influences all of Western thinking. It leaves the way open for the foregrounding of (high transitive) patriarchal violence, war and exploitation, while canceling the importance of ('low' transitive) gift-giving and care.

---

11   In patriarchy hitters often hit givers, which perhaps makes them seem superior
      – at least to themselves – because their actions are "more transitive" – stronger
      and more relevant.

On the other hand, exchange itself and especially monetized exchange, can also be seen as a linguistic derivative, and we will discuss this in the second half of the book, again with some excursions into malestream philosophy and linguistics.

As I have been saying, capitalism and patriarchy have created a filter that excludes these connections from academia, from philosophy, linguistics, economics and science and perhaps even from feminism. Assimilation into the capitalist market has freed some (mainly Northern Anglo) women, myself included, from domestic slavery and made them able to compete on an equal basis with men. Unfortunately, this has not solved the social problems created by patriarchal capitalism, which have only grown more dire.

The fact that language can be used to harm does not alter its basic positivity, however, nor does the fact that there is 'high' transitive hitting alter the basic benefactive character of the transitive gift schema. The schema of the unilateral gift is fundamentally life-oriented, and it is learned from the model of mothercare that gives life to the child as it provides the sustenance and substance of h:er body. Language and mothering understood in this sense could provide a basis for badly needed life-enhancing choices since for many, the traditional ethical rationales have ceased to be convincing and the ethics of care have not (yet) taken hold. Perhaps the lack of traction happens just because those who are trying to justify moral behavior do not recognize the negativity of market exchange.

Revealing maternal transitivity as the prototypical schema of language as well as of economics provides a widespread example of the logic of the gift and begins to generalize mothering, making it easier to recognize gifting rather than hitting as the basic human interaction.[12] From another point of view, perhaps the existence of the binary opposition so common in Western thought (and so heavily criticised) allows us to consider the poles together and so to neutralize both giving and hitting (understood as nurturance and violence) to a more neutral spectrum of transitivity of agency or activity and to see the different degrees of transitivity just as values of more and less along a spectrum of 'relevance' (a kind of neutral valence of an item or event).[13] What is relevant is 'maternally' though pre-consciously selected as likely to satisfy a need or to cause one (e.g. to avert a danger). There is also the very positive side

---

12   Interestingly, in societies where gift-giving coexists with exchange like the Minangkabau, the spiritual prototype of the mother maintains the gift culture (in spite of its co-existence with patriarchal Islam). (Sanday)

13   The exclusion of the positive gift character of items and events at these various levels feeds the more specific denial of gift-giving by the market and the appropriation of gifts for profit.

186 The Gift in the Heart of Language

of naming or announcing negative but extremely relevant things like 'Fire!'.

We must also consider the negative – and positive – aspects of *taking* as a more active variation on receiving, which is located on the same spectrum of relevance – although receiving is not to be considered less positive than taking. 'Patience' as simple submission to agency is perhaps neither positive nor negative. These are neutral interactions but they are still informed by the gift prototype and understood through the gift lens and all contain the positivity of the communicative gift. In the case of 'patience' the need that is satisfied is a need for a neutral term but the satisfaction of the need itself is positive and transitive.

Even just the fact that we can talk about neutral or negative interactions revives their positivity for us – and we really can't imagine them without that – as if they were Kantian things in themselves.

5.2 Games, laws and rules

As we saw above with family resemblances, there is also a gift interpretation that would link a number of diverse games. For example, a little girls' tea party game is pretty obviously gift-giving and a group throwing and catching a ball is pretty clearly a variation on giving and receiving and giving again. If hitting is a high transitive kind of giving, hitting the baseball that is thrown is an intervention of one kind of altered giving onto the trajectory of another. Then there is a path-to-goal trajectory of runners around the bases. Football is an attempt of one team to give the football to the container of the goal by kicking, carrying and throwing it in spite of opposition – kicking, throwing, catching and and grabbing – by the other team. Basketball uses a different kind of team effort to give or prevent the gift of the ball to the basket/receiver by bouncing and throwing. Tennis is unilateral giving-by-hitting and turn-taking receiving and giving back. It starts with a 'service' and requires a 'return', terms that are now used instead of 'giving in turn' by child development researchers (see Harvard Center on the Developing Child 2009). Even chess is a complex combination of gift trajectories, paths to goals of 'eating' or capturing the other pieces by force (of argument). In golf, the club (perhaps a phallic index), sends the ball-gift to the hole. Shooting at a target is somewhere between hitting and projecting onto a target. Shooting at animals ('game') or at other people gives them the 'gift' of death! (see Vaughan 1997). To puzzles (as needs), we try to give the gift of solutions.[14]

---

14 There are many games made in the exchange frame such as the prisoners' dilemma 'game', which is actually a test. These mainly make people strive to be the one

Our concept of games may be based on family resemblance as Wittgenstein said, but it mainly leaves out the prototype of the mother as does his concept of language games.[15] In fact if language is based on the image schema of the gift, language games would be extensions of maternal gift games, even those that function according to displaced hitting.

Much of material culture can also be seen as variations on a theme of mothering. The cup and its handle are two gifts, satisfying two needs. One for containing a liquid, the other for a way of holding the container, giving the (meta) gift of the gift. ('Handle' is also illuminating slang for a name, a nick name or username). Similarly, there is the handle of the pitcher that contains (the communal gift) liquid that is poured into various cups. The knife is a pointing index that cuts, the fork is a little hand, the spoon is a pointer and a cup. Then there is the key, inserted perhaps phallically into the vaginal keyhole as in the gift of heterosexual intercourse. Following this train of thought we come to slots and fillers again, the linguists' way of describing what I am calling needs and gifts.

Seemingly neutral exchange, the market and the rule of law that protects them, are usually more acceptable than the rule of patriarchal violence as such. However, exchange changes the other-oriented logic of giving into its ego-oriented opposite and confounds the difference. The market allows and promotes economic violence, disguises, discredits and exploits gift-giving, and makes an egalitarian maternal gift economy impossible.

The law is a construction that validates the market and keeps it safe by controlling illegal violence with greater legal violence (systemic higher transitivity?). The masculated values of competition and domination merge with the psychoeconomic ego-oriented values of the market and form the motivation of greed for 'infinite' accumulation of gifts of money and power – infinite along a spectrum of monetary relevance. The seemingly neutral law is constructed on an analogy with exchange, promoting an equation of value of crime and punishment[16] meant to control violence, a difficult job especially in the absence of the maternal prototype of benefactive giving.

The gift schema is not rule-governed but reality governed. A gives x to B and B receives x from A are aspects of a basic multilevel interactive

---

who receives more gifts by mind-reading the other player and calculating how much to keep, give or share. They are definitely 'Machiavellian'.

15   The same can be said of those who base their understanding of culture on language games (e.g. Lyotard (2004|1974|)).

16   Like exchange proper, which cancels the gift, justice as exchange attempts to cancel the transitive valence of the violent crime (the denatured gift) by imposing payment.

function, which brings with it a number of implications. This function is
not made of rules but of roles – the schema – which is enacted at many different levels, and which can be repeated and modified in many ways. The
schema is a kind of basic interactive 'module', which is simple enough to
be learned in infancy from the necessary participatory life experience of
being mothered, but we elaborate upon and continually use it throughout
life. The gift schema precedes rules and it precedes the law, which is based
on rules imposed by force, and which punishes by using varying degrees
and kinds of violence as the price of wrongdoing or rewards by giving gifts
(or sometimes just the gift of indifference) in return for obedience.

Though Chomsky's grammar rules are not rules in the sense of
laws,[17] the gift schema is not rule-governed at all. It is a root of language that comes from the way things (and people) function, the way
humans make ourselves by giving and receiving, interacting with things
and each other and projecting these interactions. Apples are not red
because of a rule and it is not because of a rule that we say 'red apples'
but because of an extended use of the gift schema on the cognitive and
on the (virtual gift) verbal plane.

We cannot recognize the gift schema in language because the gift economy has been taken over by the exchange economy in which we live, which
takes its sustenance and profit from the unacknowledged gifts of all. In
this context, when we come upon the unilateral gift in language we turn
our eyes away and explain it in some other more neutral way such as the
following of innate rules, or sending and receiving packages, or putting
contents into or taking them out of a container, or sending things through
a conduit. Alternatively, following Wittgenstein (and Reddy), we call upon
the use of tools as the source domain, not even imagining that tools can
also be interpreted in terms of giving and receiving.

Not recognizing our own anti-maternal masculated bias, if we do actually notice unilateral giving, it appears to be an impossibly difficult
moral undertaking of individuals or an instinctual dedication of mothers
to their children and thus hardly something accessible to all as the basis
of language. Or, we may accuse givers of ignorance, of hidden ego motivations or of destructive compulsions to self-sacrifice. While these and
other negative interpretations may occasionally be true, especially in the

---

17   Rules of grammar in the sense of generative grammar are not like any of the sorts
      of rules or laws in ordinary life: rules of etiquette, rules of chess, traffic laws, or
      laws of physics. They are unconscious principles that play a role in the production
      and understanding of sentences (Jackendorf 2003). See also the Searle and Chom-
      sky controversy in the New York Times Review of Books 2002.

context of scarcity created by the market, unilateral giving and receiving and turn taking are commonplace in mothering and being mothered. We are all mothered children because at least some mothering is necessary for our survival. Thus, it is probable that mothering gift-giving and receiving, form the original prototype of human interaction rather than something less widespread and more occasional like following rules, sending and receiving packages, hitting or using tools.[18]

5.3 Slots and fillers

We have been saying that the 'slots' and 'fillers' that linguists see as explaining adjectival 'attribution' or the 'merger' of words with each other, can be understood in gift terms. 'Slots' can be understood as 'needs' and 'fillers' as 'need-satisfying gifts'. That is, 'red' can be given to 'ball' because 'ball' cannot express redness on its own and so has a need for 'red'. On the reality plane also, qualities can be seen as belonging to (having been given to) things, which have the 'female property' relation, having-to-give – which is different from the private property of patriarchy and the market, established by contract. Meaning has to do with this readiness or verging on giving, this having-to-give of things, words and people, and is an extension of maternal free property. This is the motherworld, the invisible country, the still unrecognized commons of nurturing reality, which is made inaccessible to us by the market, private property and patriarchy.

That 'needs' and 'gifts' of words in syntax are called 'slots' and 'fillers' by linguists follows the objectification and neutering of everything in market culture. Instead, what I am proposing is a conscious anthropomorphizing, a projection of mothering and being mothered onto everything as a process or even *the* process of cognition. While this process may transform and extend into a variety of others in adulthood, they nevertheless remain anchored in the deep source of the motherer. The first level continues to

---

18 Producing something gives the gift of form to matter, which receives it, according to Aristotle who realized this but saw it in terms of the male imprint of form on the matter of the fetus (see Irigaray 1985). In other words, the metaphor of paternity for production overtook the metaphor of the unilateral maternal gift (which was and is already form). The source area of the father/owner (combined with the sexual and economic source domain where the forced gift overtakes the free gift) overtook the source area of the mother and child (see Irigaray and also Luisa Muraro 1991).

determine all the others.[19] The objectification of receivers as 'slots', and of gifts or givers as 'fillers' can be traced through other analogies such as 'male' and 'female' electric plugs and sockets, keys and locks, or the toy, Lego®, with its protrusions and holes. In fact, autistic children who do not seem to understand linguistic 'merge' – witness the stacking and endless series of items they construct – are helped in their language ability by playing with Lego® toys. Their therapists may not have acknowleged their transposed gift aspects however.

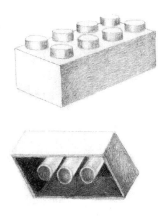

Figure 13: Lego slots and fillers.

If need is seen in terms of a lack, we could apply a Freudian interpretation to this objectification, in that the 'female' is supposedly 'lacking' and requires the 'male element' to fill the lack. I am not talking about Oedipal needs and constructions here though, but about needs for nurturing, nourishment and holding, and the early human 'merging' coming from that. However precocious sexuality is, it does not precede or preclude the need for the nurturing, which ensures survival.[20] It is important to recognize that,

---

19 See Daniel Stern's stairstep analogy. I believe we have identified adulthood with the exchange paradigm, which children in capitalism usually have to embrace in adolescence. In a gift economy our experience as adults would have a greater continuity with our experience as children. This does not mean we would never grow up, but that being grown up would be less lonely, less individualistic, less competitive, etc.

20 See Kristeva, but also look at how how the exchange framework undermines her concept of mothering.

following the logic of exchange, the heterosexual metaphor overshadows the metaphor of giving/receiving, and obscures the view, making giving/receiving unrecognizable. Thus, the terms 'slots and fillers' are neutralized and neutered heterosexual images, which themselves may be understood as a transposition or attenuation of giving/receiving.[21]

5.4 Construction seen through the gift lens

There are many more issues in the study of language that can be seen differently in the light of giving and receiving and the gift schema. I will just touch briefly on a few of them here to show how they can be viewed from the mothering perspective. Recapitulating: in the standard or typical transitive sentence, the subject (noun phrase) of the sentence can be seen as giver, the predicate (verb phrase) as gift or service and the object (complement) as receiver, and each has its own perspective. In English, it matters which is which as in 'dog bites man' or 'man bites dog', though word order in many other languages is organized differently.

In the speech situation itself the giver, speaker (or writer) gives word-gifts to the receiver, listener (or reader), which satisfy the receiver's need for a means to create mutual human relations with h:er to things, ideas, or perceptions. The speaker is the giver, the verbal product is the gift or service, and the listener is the receiver. The interpersonal situation matches the intrasentential situation and both match the mother-child altercentric giving and receiving (economic-communicative) pattern of interaction.

As we saw above with philosophers like Wittgenstein, Frege, Thom and Chomsky, this possiblity of an underlying preverbal schema seems to shine through various descriptions of the way language works.

Adele Goldberg, founder of constructionism says of Ninio (1996) that

> [Her] account seems to assume that the semantics of the verbs match the semantics of an independently existing "combinatorial property" and that it is this correspondence that results in the verbs' early use in the construction. The combinatorial property and its associated semantics is in effect a schematic construction: a pairing of form and meaning. The account seems to assume,

---

21 Many factors and images, such as these, conspire and collaborate to hide gift-giving in our society because there is a need to disguise the gift aspect of profit. Otherwise, in the gift frame, those who supply profit with their gifts would be empowered to refuse and those who 'make' profit could not so easily justify it to themselves. The needs of others would take precedence because as human beings, they, too, are givers and receivers.

therefore, that a construction exists prior to the first verbs being used in it; verbs whose meanings match the constructional meaning are used earliest. We might call this the Match Proposal. (Goldberg 1999: 207-8)

We have an abundant store of giveable word-gifts and can always learn more, and we can make endless gifts of gifts, giving the gifts of words while replaying the roles of the gift schema in our sentences. The roles of the image schema of the gift are transferred into the transitive grammatical constructions of language. We can also recognize them on the external where the man is biting the dog or the dog is biting the man.

The indirect object (di-transitive) construction, can be seen as the variation on the gift schema in which there are two steps in the giving as we saw above, where the mother warms the milk (a service to the milk, which passes through[22] as part of the gift to the receiver) and gives the warm milk to the baby. Sentences of the type, 'Mary baked the cake for Sue', function the same way. We can look at this as a shift in perspective in the sentence, but also, on the reality plane, there is a series of perspectives in our and Mary's attention that focuses both on the cake and on giving it to Sue, which is expressed with 'for', which takes the dative case, from Latin *dativus*, from *dare*, to give. The perspectives follow the roles of the schema, as I said above.

Construction grammar is informed by the source area of building, which actually itself contains gifts and services that we do not see as such. We mentioned using the hammer to give (through hitting!) the nail to the wall. The foundation of the house sustains the floor, which gives the wall a place to stand. The wall serves to hold up the roof. The tool-use that, since Wittgenstein, has been called upon as an analogy for language, can also be seen in terms of the gift: fire gives heat to food, the chisel releases the statue from the stone, the needle guides the trajectory of the gift thread, the potter's wheel spins the clay and helps the potter give form to the pot in which the food is cooked and served, etc.

Our prehistoric ancestors made axes and arrowheads by hitting stone on stone and then hit animals with the weapons, bringing gifts of food to their communities. Others searched for and creatively received plants and wove baskets, giving reeds over and under to other reeds, so they could contain and carry gifts, as the ancestors walked along their paths to goals. They devised ways of giving fire to stones which passed on the gift of heat to food (see Wrangham 2009), etc.

Since gift-giving has been eliminated in our society as a key for inter-

---

22   Housework passes value from the worker's surplus labor to the capitalist.

preting the world, tools and constructions are typically seen as neutral and gift-less. We can restore to them an interpretation in terms of gift-giving, however. Constructions are made so that different parts of a whole sustain (give to) each other in different ways and this happens in sentences as well, as linguistic constructionists say, but that is because building itself is a variation on giving and receiving. Since the gift has been taken out of the source of the metaphor (tools and building are both seen as belonging to masculated identity, by the way) it has also been taken out out of the 'target', the mapping of building onto language, both as tool use (Wittgenstein) and as sentence construction (Goldberg, Tomasello etc.).

The above interpretations of constructions may appear anthropomorphic, especially to people who are affected by *anthropomorphobia*, but my point is just that there is an early original projection of giving and receiving onto the world around us, which lets us understand it in terms of what we ourselves do together with each other (and, in fact, we are part of that world).[23]

I contend that Jakob von Uexkull's perceptual bubble is filled with aspects of mothering and being mothered for humans, but that then the secondary lens of exchange filters mothering out so that we no longer perceive what it is that we are projecting and responding to. Like bats that send out their cries and perceive the reverberations, we project giving and receiving onto the world and then perceive it there. Then we use that knowledge to construct things by placing them in new gift relations to each other. But in our society, we cancel our knowledge of the source.

Making buildings and using tools are transpositions of extended gift relations onto the external, which are aided by the understanding, which we achieve by projecting the schema of the gift onto the world (even though we don't realize we are doing it).

The field of construction grammar is complex and computational and it is not in my scope to discuss it extensively. I will just content myself here by mentioning the gift interpretation of the source of the construction metaphor and suggesting that giving and receiving can also be found both in the source and in the 'target'. In this, as in so many other aspects of linguistics, language and life, it seems to me that the same important piece is

---

23   In this regard, it is interesting to look at Michael Reddy's own analogy for communication of one person's giving a blueprint to another who constructs the meaning from it. The gift schema functions as a blueprint, which the other already has. Words are gifts that are given to the other placed by the speaker onto the blueprint of giving (the gift structure is repeated at different levels). The blueprint is an indication of how to construct by adding gifts to gifts, parts of the schema to each other at different levels. This is done in constructing buildings, too.

always missing, the gift schema, the interactive maternal prototype, which is necessarily at the beginning of human ontogenesis.

New/old understandings, coming from the environmental movement and indigenous peoples, see all of life as connected, every creature nurturing other creatures in many different ways. I believe that here as with many other types of investigations, we understand the connections because our *Umwelt* is formed and shaped by gift-giving and receiving but we do not describe it in this way because the exchange paradigm has been imposed upon the gift paradigm and hides it. Thus, in our descriptions, we talk about 'being connected' rather than about the giving and receiving, which cause the connections among humans as well as among non-human things (but we recognize the connections because we have been mothered).[24]

5.5 Gifting as an alternative to computation

Computer science, neuroscience, and the various combinations of the two, have provided more new ways of understanding human communication that leave aside mothering. Input and output of data and the transfer of packets of information through computer 'languages' seem to take place beyond nurturing. Afferent and efferent cells giftlessly convey nerve impulses throughout the body to their destinations in the central nervous system and return. Epistemologies based on these new sciences bring with them the absence of the deep maternal gift (and of perspective shifting informed by giving and receiving).

For cognitive science and child development psychologists, the big breakthrough was the idea that the brain 'is a kind of computer' (Gopnik, Meltzoff and Kuhl 1999: 21). Instead, I believe that the brain functions according to a kind of mother-child altercentric interaction, and so do the computers we have invented. Computing is a way of functioning we can understand only if we already have an at least unconscious understanding of communication that recognizes the fundamental importance of gifting. The image schema of the gift, which develops from the patterns of physical, psychological and linguistic nurturing in early childhood, repeats, on

---

24   If we multiplied the tick's experience thousands of times to allow it to be nurtured by many different kinds of things, and if we also made it capable of taking the initiative to nurture others in innumerable ways, we would bring it much closer to our experience of the human *Umwelt*. However, that world has already been shaped by the significance of mothering and being mothered materially, and again by mothering and being mothered in and through language.

the 'external' interpersonal plane, processes that are possibly even similar to the interneuronal processes in our brains.

The social-experiential frame of the gift allows us to recognize the processes that are its extensions and dilutions – as I said above regarding physical cause and effect, and agent and patient. Thus, we can understand the transmission of impulses of neurons within that frame, even if from a point of view external to mothering they are not maternal gifts. It simply happened, in the great mix of things, that evolving humans created interactions on the material plane of nurturing that were somewhat like the processes of their brain functions (and somewhat like the fit of creatures with their environmental niches and like chemical and atomic processes of combination). Then they were able to project nurturing to create a frame within which they understand a great many other things, including neuronal activity, computer communication and languages. Since they do not recognize mothering/gift-giving, they use some of its motherless communication analogies such as sending and receiving chemical or hormonal messages or postal packages of information, to describe the processes they actually though unconsciously identify by using the mothering/gift-giving frame.

The 'scientist in the crib' (Gopnik et al 1999) is the child who is being mothered, and learning to be mothered and to mother in many ways, to receive and give again. S:he is developing h:er creative receptivity to receive the same cognitive gifts others receive. Hypothesis testing is trial and error about who gives what to whom – or just what gives to what. You cannot feed the chair however much you try though you can feed the cat. To some extent, the authors recognize mothering but do not go further than analogy:

> Grown ups are themselves designed to behave in ways that will allow babies to learn. This support plays such a powerful role in the babies' development, in fact, that it may make sense to think of it as part of the system itself. The human baby's computational system is really a network held together by language and love, instead of by optic fiber. (*ibid.*: Intro)

> Other people may also play a particularly important role in how the brain gets shaped. Even bird brains seem especially tuned to receive information from other birds, particularly nurturing birds. (*ibid.*: 195)

It seems that the scientists come near to the recognition of the importance of gift-giving but since they have a different theory they do not go into it deeply enough. In fact, 'one advantage of having a theory, for scientists as well as children, is that it lets you know what you should pay attention to' (*ibid.*: 156). This is indeed the crux of the matter. There has not been a widely shared theory based on mother-child gifting, so attention has not been paid to it. I will be talking about this more below in Chapter 8 with regard to the collective elaboration of relevance and value.

The technology-based computational lens makes linguistics (as quantitatively assessed or produced re naming), a description of the gift relations of syntax, again without giving any importance to gift-giving or to needs. Claudia von Werlhof discusses the capitalist patriarchal replacement of giving birth by 'alchemical' technological creation. Not only birth but also nurturing is replaced by this alchemy in neuroscience, linguistics, economics and philosophy.

Even if it is true that, as these scientists say, we unconsciously do statistical sampling and calculate the probabilities of word occurrences, if we are to understand and use them, we still have to put them in gift schemas and give them to each other syntactically in order to satisfy other people's communicative and cognitive needs. The words occur together because we put them in those relationships. Beginning in childhood we are often giving them and receiving them together with the perceptual gifts of our environmental niches and this gives them an emotional charge that makes them memorable to us. The words occur together because we are talking to each other about gifts and giving in our common surroundings.[25] That is why they are more or less probable in any occasion. It is what the statistics are due to.

Brian MacWhinney proposes perspective tracking and shifting within sentences and he also espouses the competition model of meaning or role assignment. I believe this appeal to competition would be unnecessary if we understand that word-gifts are fitted into a basic schema with variations. In the computational mode, he talks about the 'cue weights' that help determine the choices as to which lexical items are allocated to which roles in the sentence. These cues can be morphological or depend on word order, etc. From a 'human interest' (Newman) point of view, instead, since we are always tracking who gives to whom and what gives to what and their perspectives in the external world, we would be just as clever on the verbal plane as well. Listeners/readers are not passive; they are creative receivers. They actively seek out affordances, and they put themselves in position to 'grasp' and use what is being given to them in such a way that it satisfies their communicative and cognitive needs as it has been given to do, thus creating the relation of mutuality with the speaker/writer regarding something, at least for the moment. The realms of word gifts and of world gifts are not separate but are mutually perva-

---

sive even if we can distinguish a vocal or written or gestural language plane from the 'rest of life'.

The benefactive relation of *giving for* (giving a word-gift to another for a world-gift) is more emotionally salient than computationally assessing cue weights, and less abstract as well. Our experience as mothered children anchors the understanding of giver, gift or service and receiver, which anchor the perspectives of actor, action, acted upon, making it easy to identify which role is which among words and among things, as well as among other people. The 'cue weights' regard these preset schematic positions and roles. Morphology and word order derive from the positions with different regularities in different languages. The original unity is the material gift level from which the many languages of Babel continue to emerge according to the linguistic and lived history of the particular community.

According to MacWhinney's 'competition model', the words that we hear 'compete' to occupy the various grammatical roles. Instead, I would propose a model of 'cooperation' according to which words have gifts for other words, and which words can receive from other words, depending also on morphological and positional cues: what they sound like, where they are, which other words they 'agree' with, but mainly on what they mean. World-gifts are already connected to the word-gifts we use because we are giving the word-gifts to others for them (and those word-gifts have been given to us for something similar in the past) and this giving and receiving is emotionally salient.

World-gifts also give to and receive from each other and us. We track the givers and gifts, who gives what to whom and when and how. No dominance or competition is needed to tell us which combination or role is more likely. We track and enact the cooperation, even if we discard possibilties that are less consonant (that is, even if some possible word-gifts lose the 'competition'). The co-existence of a variety of choices does not necessarily mean they are in competition with each other. Rather, they constitute an abundant reserve of alternative gifts. These gifts also determine or 'educate' the needs they satisfy. 'Horse', 'charger', 'steed' or 'nag' satisfy somewhat different needs of the listener depending on the context that is also created by words that satisfy and educate a variety of other needs. 'She mounted her steed' is more probable than 'she mounted her nag' because 'mount' is appropriate to the cognitive need that arises regarding the kind of horse that is meant by 'steed' and vice-versa 'steed' is appropriate to the cognitive and communicative need regarding the kind of action referred to by the verb 'mount'. The distinction among different kinds of horses causes the education of different communicative and cognitive needs in their regard.

The competitive model is like the fitting of goods to needs in the marginalist economics approach, where from the individual point of view, one has to decide which goods to buy, which needs to satisfy with the limited money available in one's budget. Investigating what the market offers, one chooses the most appropriate product at the right price. In the competitive frame that product 'wins' the competition.

The gift model is like the giving of gifts to needs directly in the gift economy and it functions more by giving attention to the needs than by calculating competitions among the possible gifts. It is not cost-benefit and does not come from scarcity but from abundance. Nevertheless it is benefactive and perhaps even maximally benefactive in that the speaker/writer chooses the most appropriate gift to satisfy the need of the listener/reader and the listener/reader embraces the gifts allowing her needs to be satisfied and educated. 'She mounted her steed while he rode his nag' tells the receiver a story about the relations between the two people as well as the two horses. This does not depend upon the competition among possible terms but upon a choice among abundant possibilities of gifting.

Of course morphological and syntactic cues are still important but the listener would be asking herself, what is the speaker giving me and how and why, not abstractly calculating the cue weights in order to receive neutral words – i.e. words that are not gifts. Without the idea of nurturing and needs perhaps competition seems the only relation that holds among alternatives for interpretation and understanding. Instead, from the gift perspective, we see them as being offered as possible gifts to give and to receive according to a collaborative, benefactive, cooperative or companionship-model.[26]

Since giver, gift and receiver are also the perspectives in the speaking/ hearing or writing/reading situation itself, their omnipresence there would also give them priority as cues over more neutral understandings like actor and acted upon or other neutral schemas.

Children learn about the affordances, the need-satisfying aspects of their surroundings and they also learn about the affordances and need-satisfying aspects of the elements of the stream of vocal sound surrounding them. Their cognitive and communicative needs develop and become specified to the world gifts and the word gifts that satisfy them. New needs arise that can be satisfied by new words, but can also be satisfied by new com-

---

26   Perhaps also a model of care economy or a partnership model (Eisler 1988). The theory of conceptual blending brought forward by Mark Turner and Giles Fauconnier (2002) is perhaps more cooperative than competitive but it is also dependent on non maternal processes and explanations. 'Blending' would be gifts given to each other, creating new gifts. Giftless blending lends itself to computation better than maternal gifting does.

binations of words using the gift schema. Preconscious statistical analysis could have a function in identifying and satisfying needs. However, surely the frame of the gift would overide a frame of statistical sampling and the calculation of probabilities for conscious social interaction.

Finding competition, which is a typical and negative mode of patriarchal capitalist interaction, as a basic mode of linguistic thought gives it a status as permanent, objectifying it and ratifying its practice. While it may explain some of the neurological facts, these are already ideologically selected and described to exclude nurturing. I am trying to offer alternative gift-based explanations and to locate them in the context of a world that exists but is unrecognized to our great detriment.

To a certain extent, there is still a perceptual and conceptual commons, owned by no one and everyone, which is similar in its accessibility to the gifts of language. Unfortunately, this motherworld, this perceptual and conceptual commons, is being privatized and commodified by capitalism, corporations, nations and academia in much the same way that the gifts of nature and culture are being privatized and commodified. The lexicon, our linguistic commons and collective inheritance, which provides the stored and accessible linguistic gifts of words and syntax and the gift processes with which we form our individual and group identities, is now being used in Machiavellian ways to force us to buy and to comply. Perhaps philosophers past and present have had difficulty in understanding the positive relation between the linguistic and the perceptual/conceptual commons, because like everyone else, they themselves have been deeply immersed in a world in which the material commons have been enclosed and in which society functions according to the relations of patriarchy, private property and the market. Competition for scarce resources and for winning the prize of wealth seem to be human nature.

The relations to and through the perceptual/conceptual and the linguistic commons are established in childhood prior to the child's understanding of private property and exchange and they continue to function as such throughout life.[27] In the gift-based 'domestic sphere' the motherer's relation to h:er property is usually 'having to give' (see 3.3). S:he is a kind of outpost of the motherworld, a member of the vanguard of the gift economy trapped in a web of capitalist patriarchy that does not acknowledge h:er existence.

---

27 Some perceptions are denied to poor people – see for example the walls around the property of the rich. But there is also much display – 'look but don't touch' – as well as jargon and 'exclusive' language.

5.6 Joint attention and alternating perspectives

As I have been saying, we project the maternal giver onto our surroundings as the motherworld, justified by the fact that the mother is our first (and most proactive) environment, so we can also understand perception itself as a gift, something we (creatively) receive from the outside. We can create commonality with each other by participating together in the reception of the same gift perceptions. Joint attention to something is joint creative reception of that perceptual gift. Two or more people perform the receiver role of the gift image schema together, when the surroundings are placed in the giver role (both as Motherer Nature and as Motherer Culture) and the object, event or idea to which the perceivers attend is in the role of the gift. Calling the attention of the other to an item is a kind of secondary giving (the singling out and therefore giving, of the perceptual gift, the *gestalt*). We give it to the view of the other by pointing at it (which backgrounds the rest). The gift 'pops out' as salient (Chiarcos et al. 2001). Each of the perceivers is aware that the other person is also playing the receiver role in the schema, with the perceived item as the gift. Each also receives the gift of the perception of the other as receiver and realizes s:he is similar to h:erself because at the moment s:he has that role regarding the same thing.

We also jointly take the perspectives of those who give and of those who receive the gifts and services evident in the world around us (the gifts to gifts). I mentioned Brian MacWhinney's perspective-taking in this connection above. In a transitive sentence, the point of view shifts from subject to verb to object, i.e. from giver to gift to receiver. The shifts in the points of view depend on which role of the gift schema is in focus. MacWhinney's example, 'The boy hit the ball that rolled into the gutter', illustrates how the perspective transposes and changes from one sentence element to the next. But these are gift perspectives. The giver looks forward, the receiver looks back (and the perspectives are reversed in turn, in speaking and writing sequentially). 'Boy', 'looks forward', 'ball', 'looks back' with the valence reversed. Both speaker and listener (writer and reader) can 'track' or 'jointly attend to' these perspective shifts in the sentence.The speaker has received the perception of the event. S:he becomes a giver, taking the initiative to satisfy the communicative and cognitive needs of the listener for the means of a relation to the boy, to the hitting and the ball, the rolling and the gutter, which are seen in an (extended and articulated) gift schema relation, and s:he uses the word gifts that are appropriate to them.

In experiments on 'mirror reversal in face to face imitation' in which children are asked to 'do as I do', an ordinary child is able to reverse perspectives 180 degrees without a problem, while autistic children fail to do so (Stein Bråten 2007: 118). If perspectives have a grammatical function, the lack of ability to reverse perspectives would logically carry over into language difficulties in autism.

If giver and receiver perspectives exist in the sentence according to the schema of the gift, the difficulties some autistic people have with speech and their use of echolalia might have to do with their inability to put the gift

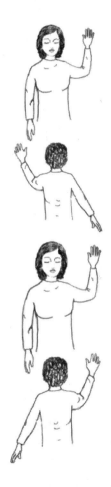

Figure 14. 'Do as I do' raised hands experiment. The one above is 'normal' reversed perspective mirroring. The one below is autistic 'echo' mirroring.

schema into practice in life. They would thus be unable to take the perspective of the receiver as the reversal and complement of that of the giver both interpersonally and in the sentence where the grammatical object-receiver is the reversal and complement of the subject-giver.

Giving sentence gifts allows speaker-giver and listener-receiver to track the gifts that are taking place in the environment just as our primate ancestors tracked the grooming, nurturing relations among the members of their group. It is an extension of 'Jim's relationship with John' that is, of 'who is giving what to whom'.

5.7 Glances at some Chomskian issues

5.7a Linguistic creativity
The linguistic creativity that Chomsky talks about is not an end in itself. According to the gift perspective, it is not just verbal expression, exuberance or munificence. We create linguistically in order to satisfy the communicative needs *of others* for a relation with us to something and it is on the basis of this satisfaction of needs that we also develop and communicate new ideas. Our creativity is other-oriented and need-directed, not just an unlimited capacity for production as an end in itself.

5.7b Poverty of the stimulus
Chomsky's (1980) 'poverty of stimulus' question does not arise if we realize that language is built on life and that it is fundamentally other-directed, and need-oriented. The 'actual life processes' (Marx) of maternal gift-giving and receiving thus become the abundant stimulus for giving and receiving in language.[28] We also see and track other people giving to and receiving from each other so generalizing giving and receiving from human beings to other parts of our environment is not such a big step and vice-versa, since other people are themselves parts of our environment (as we are for them).

---

28   Marx's insistence on the material basis of life justifies us in looking at material communication, giving and receiving as the source of grammar rather than appealing to genetic inheritance. For example, in *German Ideology* he claims that: '...men (sic!) , developing their material production and their material intercourse, alter, along with this their real existence, their thinking and the products of their thinking. Life is not determined by consciousness but consciousness by life' (1964: 46-7). I am saying that first of all they alter their thinking and its products to the extent that they make them into language.

Moreover, there are naturally obligatory gift relations in the external world that are analogous to relations among words. Just as we cannot in any proper sense successfully give milk to a chair (just try it!) or to a canary, we cannot say 'colorless green ideas'. To a little child who knows nothing about the ways things work it may seem completely arbitrary that food goes in our mouths instead of our noses and water is poured into glasses and not onto tables. Chairs give us a place to sit not a place to stand. Many children experiment with doing things the other way. While these are not rules per se because they come from the nature of things, they are patterns children learn to enact and respect.

What we mistakenly call 'grammar rules' are similar. They are patterns that come from the 'nature' of the way words are given to other words, which depends on the ways we nurture and are nurtured and the ways things are given to each other in the world around us as well as in the particular language we speak. The ways we give things to other things are basically pre-established (no milk to the chair), and the ways we give words to other words also. If we do it differently, people will not understand and probably someone will correct us. Soon we learn what to give to what; that is, how a 'construction' based on giving and receiving works in our native language.

Children learn how to do proper sentence constructions by experiencing and experimenting with the world, with the grammar of objects and of social relations, that is, with the possible gift relations among objects and among people as well as among words. A child may throw food on the floor but the floor does not eat it. S:he can suck on the doorknob but no milk comes out. S:he can try to take h:er sister's toy but h:er sister will not give it. Some gift actions may be forbidden by rules and by possible consequences. Don't put your finger in the socket! Patting a strange dog may cause him to bite you. However, most kinds of gift relations are understood by exploration and experience. A child actively exploring the environment is learning what kinds of perceptual gifts it provides, its 'affordances' and how to receive them. Similarly, word-gifts take their patterning from the kinds of pre-linguistic material gift patterns that exist among humans, that are projected onto the world. Language is understood because it is based on the gift patterns that are already established in mothering/being mothered. This is not 'conventional' in the proper sense because it does not require an act of agreement, but it is a common process of knowledge.

Gift giving and receiving permeate the world we live in. They provide an interactive interpretative map that leads us to treasures of all kinds (in an environment that is at least minimally nurturing), awakening needs we did not know we had, by the taste of different foods, the warmth of sun-

light, the wetness of water. Our environment's 'rules', if we have to call
them that, are light and do not constrain but facilitate us. They are based on
needs and what satisfies them rather than on laws we must follow. Moreover, we are able to take the perspectives of other people and of things in the
environment as givers, as receivers and as gifts.

5.7c Questions, linguistic and metalinguistic

The importance that Chomsky and many other linguists attribute to
linguistic and metalinguistic questions places us already in the middle of
the denial of needs and gifts. Questions are used when mind – and behavior – reading fails. Otherwise, they are not needed. Like economic 'effective demand', which represents the need (and, therefore, the product) in
money, questions overtly represent a communicative or cognitive need.
If we ask 'what is the subject of a sentence?', we can answer 'a noun
phrase', or with an example, 'what is the subject of this sentence: "the
cat chased the mouse"?', we can answer 'the cat'. The speaker or writer
is expressing or filling a listener's or reader's imputed need to know. The
focus of the joint attention is the noun phrase or 'the cat'. However, in
the sentence itself, 'the cat chased the mouse', the question has not been
asked. Rather the speaker has given the gift of the sentence to the listener,
mind reading h:er communicative needs regarding that situation in which
the cat chased (gave chase to) the mouse, and thus, by satisfying those
needs, creating a human gift relation with h:er to the event, the cat, the
chasing and the mouse, however fleeting.

Thus, the subject of the sentence does not answer the question 'what?'
because the question is not asked. Instead, it is a word-gift given freely by
the speaker or writer who has altercentrically guessed the communicative
need of the listener/reader and taken the initiative to satisfy it, placing the
word-gift in the giver – subject – position in the sentence schema. Mind-
reading the others' communicative needs is not usually difficult because
they are similar to what the speaker/writer's own needs would be in that
circumstance if s:he were the other. Shifting perspectives allows correc-
tion for differences. That is, the speaker might say 'the gray cat chased the
mouse' if s:he thought the listener might not know which cat did it. By taking the perspective of the other, s:he understands the need without asking
a question. However s:he can also ask a question: "what did the gray cat
chase?'. In this case s:he is expressing h:er own cognitive need, asking for
a specific linguistic gift that will put h:er in relation to a world-gift. There
is no purely linguistic way to satisfy h:er need to know. The person who
wants to answer the question, satisfy the need, has to receive a perceptual

gift from her surroundings (or from the linguistic context) and pass it on to the listener. There is a difference between examples and practice, abstract *langue* and concrete *parole*.

The image schema of the gift provides roles in which the different word-gifts of the sentence may be placed. However, these roles are more meaningful and dynamic than simple slots or blanks to be filled in. The speaker/writer actively gives the gift by placing the subject in the giver position, speaking/writing the words 'the cat' and adding 'chased' and 'the mouse', the gift or service and the receiver roles. Each role has its own perspective, which involves the others as well.

5.7d Recursion

The mystery of recursion can be clarified by considering each new anaphoric subject as a giver, the initiator of a new gift schema, taking the receiver in the previous phrase as the proactive giver in the subsequent one: thus, the gift schema can be given again and again, nested and renested as in the traditional nursery rhyme:

This is the dog that worried the cat
That killed the rat that ate the malt
That lay in the house that Jack built.
This is the farmer sowing his corn
That kept the cock that crowed in the morn
That waked the priest all shaven and shorn
That married the man all tattered and torn
That kissed the maiden all forlorn
That milked the cow with the crumpled horn
That tossed the dog that worried the cat
That killed the rat that ate the malt
That lay in the house that Jack built!

'Dog' is given, then 'that' is given in a new giver role. 'Worried' is given in the gift or service role and 'cat' in the receiver role. 'That' is then given in the giver role for 'cat', 'killed' in the gift role and 'rat' in the receiver role etc. The perspectives shift accordingly.

5.8 Intentions

Linguistic communication requires a basic intention to satisfy others' needs. We know their communicative needs by 'mind-reading', putting ourselves in their places, taking their perspectives, figuring out what it is they do not know and giving them the word-gifts that people in their/ our linguistic community give for that kind of thing. Thus, we have a basic underlying need-satisfying intention that we do not recognize as such but is the *sine qua non* of speaking and writing. However, it is not so much the reading of the speaker's 'intention' by the listener as many linguistic philosophers think (see Searle 1983) that provides the key to communication, but the mind-reading of the listener by the speaker. This recalls the process of maternal altercentric need-satisfaction in which the other (not the self), is the focus of the attention. We guess what the other needs in order for h:er to relate h:erself to something as a gift or given, that is, to track world-gifts to world-gifts (like the pre-hominids tracked gifts among the members of their communities). If we can tell by mind reading that s:he is looking for a door we can say 'door' and point. Or we can say, 'there is a door to the yard in the next room.'

If, instead, we think of the listener as grasping the intention of the speaker, we put the speaker (giver) in the position not of one who is intentionally satisfying the listener's needs but who is offering something – a product – external to the listener, which the listener must grasp and which is used to influence more or less manipulatively or didactically what s:he thinks. Thus, the relation that is established is not the basic nurturing relation of mutuality but a kind of power relation (or one of argumentative force) that varies according to the occasion. The intention is a kind of non-nurturing path-to-goal motivation. H. P. Grice (1989), and more recently Sperber and Wilson (2004), are perhaps exceptions. However, Grice's positive relations are based on maxims and the cooperative principle, which are more or less contractual, and Sperber and Wilson use a cost/benefit framework for determining relevance. 'Human cognitive processes ... are geared to achieving the greatest possible cognitive effect for the smallest possible processing effort' (1995: vii). Their contention that 'the relevance of new information to an individual is to be assessed in terms of the improvements it brings to his representation of the world' (*ibid*.: 103) does seem to regard the satisfaction of cognitive need. However, the importance of communicative need, the satisfaction of which creates relationship, is not recognized and the cost/benefit framework leads them into the market camp.

Not just sentence meaning but word meaning and sentence construction are due to both communicative and cognitive need satisfaction taken (or given) together. Perhaps I should borrow John Austin's title, *How to Do Things with Words*, and change it for my purposes to *How to Do Things with Verbal and Non-Verbal Gifts*. That is, speech acts depend not on 'force' of argument or other so called 'high' transitivity, but on the implications of nurturing in a context. Words are gifts and metagifts that participate in gift constructions.

Material gifts can be used to create psychological leverage, as the many books on gifts and exchange show. We use them to pledge and promise, as with engagement rings, or to seal the change of marital status, as with wedding rings. We also use gifts as 'conversational' opening gambits and questions in teasing temptations, plumbing the depths of others' needs. We use them to establish power relations and relations of subservience. However, there is an important difference between material and verbal gifts, deriving from the fact that linguistic gifts are infinitely abundant and we do not lose them when we give them, while material gifts are lost to the giver and are usually difficult to replace (due to the scarcity created by the market). As Yvette Abrahams (2007) says, 'Not having private property and land was a basis for the Khoekhoe gift economy, because if I have enough and you have enough, then the gifts can take on a social symbolism'. In abundance, the question 'why did s:he give me that now and in that way?' takes on a different character from that of the same question in scarcity.

The listener or reader sees or imagines some perceptual or conceptual situation in which the elements can be placed in a gift schema as indicated by the sentence or wider text. S:he tries to identify what perceptual or conceptual gifts are being passed on to h:er through the word-gift constructions s:he has received. The sentence gifts have elicited h:er attention in their regard and they, therefore, emerge as relevant, 'popping out' from the background of (almost unlimited) possibilities. Then they become, for the moment at least, the objects of joint attention, the gifts that speaker and listener, writer and reader receive together.

This view is quite different from the view of intention as a manipulation of the beliefs or the consciousness of the listener/reader, even if in fact, it can change h:er consciousness, directing h:er towards world-gifts by giving her word-gifts. It provides a conscious rather than a preconscious selection of perceptual gifts.

Sometimes the speaker's intention is seen as the kind of giving that anthropologists call 'tolerated scrounging' (Blurton Jones 1987). That is, the receiver is allowed to do the 'uptake', to 'pick up' whatever s:he finds of the speaker's constructions, and use them if s:he can 'grasp' them and what they are for (as s:he would do with tools in the world). This 'tolerated scrounging' description is more appropriate perhaps for writing/reading than for speaking, but even in writing, the reader's communicative and cognitive needs have to be investigated, understood and satisfied by the writer. The writer guesses these needs, which are also aroused, educated and elicited by the context that is created by the writing itself. The needs are also affected by a common 'encyclopedia': what the reader can be expected to know about the world. Moreover, the writer can read the minds of h:er readers in a general way as members of groups and communities (children, academics, bloggers, pop music fans) with a variety of experiences more or less like h:er own. We address this gap between ourselves and others, in general, by saying we know how words 'are used' – that is, in our terms, what communicative and cognitive needs we and others can (probably) satisfy with them.

If we can create relations with other people by satisfying needs, giving and receiving material gifts and services, we can also create relations with them by giving them verbal gifts. These are not relations of debt and obligation but positive relations of mutuality and joint or shared attention, like the positive relations we created by giving and receiving with our motherers in early childhood.[29] Since the gifts of language are usually much easier and faster than material gifts for individuals to produce, give and receive, the relations created thereby are not usually as intense and binding as are the relations created by giving and receiving material gifts. Nevertheless, satisfying each others' cognitive, communicative, metalinguistic and emotional needs linguistically affirms mutual recognition and a kind of species specificity, a common identity as humans who are part of a linguistic community with joint access to an epistemological commons.[30]

5.9 Some consequences of this approach

An epistemology based on altercentric gift-giving and receiving can be constructed by viewing language in the ways indicated above. This would also lead us to understand perception as the reception of the perceptual gifts of our surroundings and to embrace the mother and the mothering Earth as matricentric indigenous people do, with gratitude.

An epistemology of this kind could inform and support a movement towards a gift economy. It would allow us to become conscious of the gifts we are already giving and receiving as motherers, as children, as women and

---

29   See Meltzoff (2011: 54): 'The Like-Me Framework provides the initial foothold for interpreting others as bearers of psychological properties commensurate with one's own, but further development is neeed for acquiring the mature theory of mind encompassing beliefs that directly conflict with/contradict one's own'. That is, positive commonality is established first, before conflictuality.

30   Specialistic jargon privatizes this commons and makes it inaccessible.

men, as indigenous peoples and colonized peoples, and even as colonizers and capitalists, as Motherer Earth and Children of Earth. It would allow us to see that the market is actually a small and alienated mechanism that floats upon the gifts of the many and indeed is parasitically dependent on them.

We have been led to believe since Aristotle that reason, *logos*, is an abstract rational process that has very little to do with mothering. Through the centuries, the image of the dominant patriarch and of money as standard of value have combined to create the phallic model of the human.

Instead, if we take the image schema of the gift as a basic structure of language and of economics, we can understand *logos* as an abstraction from the mother-child interaction. The so-called 'faculty of reason' does not exist on its own but is derived from the image schema of the gift.

When the verbal gift takes the place of a material gift, giver or receiver in one of the roles of the schema there is signification because the schema and that place in it are attributed to and 'received from' the part of the world whose gift representative is taking that role. The gift schema on the virtual level of language and the level of the 'real world' interpersonal gift schema are structurally the same. They align and function in similar ways at the different levels. This is not so much a picture, or even a moving picture theory of language, but as the words say, a re-gifting, a re-presentation.

Masculated Western philosophers, who have been made to renounce maternal gift-giving as part of their gender identities, have not been able to integrate it into their epistemologies. Presentation – gifting – is problematic for them so they have difficulty with re-presentation.[31] From a feminist maternalist perspective we can affirm prior gift-giving both in the sense of motherer-child nurturing and in the sense of the giving and receiving of perceptions. This prior giving and receiving is continuous with and part of the contemporaneous context created by all the linguistic, perceptual and material giving and receiving in which adults as well as children are usually engaged – but without knowing it (see ch. 3).[32] There are indeed many different kinds of presentations, which can be re-presented, but their importance to humans, their relevance, harks back to a maternal gift origin, upon which our survival as infants depended.

---

31 See cynical postmodernists like Baudrillard, Bourdieu and Lyotard. Some philosophers, like Derrida and Marion, put God as the Gift or the Gift as God (Horner 2001) in the place of the maternal giver.

32 In this light, the motherworld is pregnant with meaning – without ever having been inseminated! S:he 'parthenogenetically' creates all the gifts that satisfy our needs for goods, for perceptsions and for means of communication. We do not have to plow and plant, just gratefully gather what is given.

There is also co-respondence in the sense that mother and child respond together, both to each other, dyadically, and in joint attention regarding one or many 'thirds'. Their shared re-presentations co-respond to presentations on the reality plane.

Moreover, the schema of the gift can be elaborated and turned in many different directions and dimensions. It can be expanded to a large scale – the safe home is a gift to the family. A dinner is a gift as are each of its components, even each of its bites or mouthfuls.[33] A song is a gift, its melody and rhythms and all its words are gifts. The singing is a gift and the concert in which the song is sung is a gift. The world can be seen as the giver and we the receivers or vice-versa, or the gift itself can be seen as giving. And the word is also a gift (we are not looking at metonymy here – a relation of a part standing for the whole, but at gifts made of gifts – harmonic composition, like the golden mean). We are in Ali Baba's treasure cave, which we reach by using the magic words 'Open sesame'. Sesame from Arabic 'sim sim,' the tiny seed, seme, semiosis. Sim sim: the double unilateral gift of repeatable similarity[34] (not GMO) and it is on two planes.

The area of life that is verbal gift-giving is made of sound-gifts (and sign-gifts and written word-gifts) that can be placed in the schema and its schematic variations. In the next chapters, we will describe these word gifts as the virtualizations (means of virtual giving) for others of things in the world around them. Children go through a period in which they learn many word-gifts per day. At first, they may only have a vague idea of what they are ('fast mapping'), but at the same time, children are also learning about the things in the world for which the words are the virtual gifts: how things are used, given and received, (their 'affordances') how they give (in an extended way) to each other and how people receive them as material, perceptual and conceptual gifts. Importantly, children also learn syntax, that is how to make the words they speak give to and receive from each other virtually. In this way, each child eventually creates h:er own linguistic plane ('virtual gift plane'), on a par with that of others so that the people speaking the same language all use the same gift 'syntax' and inhabit the same (giveable) world.

If we were only giving gifts virtually, combining them syntactically in language, it would be just an abstract exercise. However, we actually give

---

33   Wrangham's (2009) theory of cooking as the spark of evolution can be called on here. Each ingredient in the pot is a gift to the soup, like the words in the sentence. The soup is a gift to those who eat it.

34   See Frank Keil (1992: 247) on the 'Original Sim'. I am saying instead that there is not an original sim but an original sim-sim and that makes all the difference.

them to others when speaking or writing (even though we don't lose them). The proof that words are gift constructions for others comes when others receive them, understanding what we say. They can do this because, like us, they need the words in their gift constructions, to form relations with us regarding all the gifts of the world.

The rejection of mothering has altered epistemology (and the episteme) and so has distorted our perspective on who we are as a species, how we know, and what we should do. It alters our idea of who we are as knowers, making us believe we are isolated individuals, lonely sapiens addressing an alien world with merely biological perception, which we somehow translate into a biologically 'inherited' grammar and language capacity with which we demonstrate our non-maternal creative exuberance. Moreover, without the roles of the gift schema to guide us, we become the cogs of an economic machine that ignores, exploits and destroys the motherer in all of us, and Motherer Earth as well, leaving aside the altercentric transitive aspects of knowledge and covering them with denial. This makes it necessary to explain knowledge in some other way, ergo, 2500 years of Western philosophy. Because they do not go through socialization to be members of a non- or even anti-mothering male gender, women, even if they are not birth mothers, are not originally masculated, and therefore, often find it difficult to embrace masculated philosophy. Their life experience in which they willingly or unwillingly do unilateral giving also does not receive much clarification from that philosophy. Fortunately, some men also escape or overcome their masculated socialization.

Sexism really depends on the fact that many women are (or have the capacity to be) biologically and socially mothers, not just on the fact that that their bodies are different from men's. Misogyny is "misomitry", a hatred and suspicion of mothering generalized to all women, and a rejection of the creativity and importance even of one's own childhood. There are many psychological reasons for this, which have been widely discussed among feminists. I have mentioned some of them above, in discussing the term 'masculation'. Both genders forget and disbelieve the experience of being mothered because the market economy distorts (and forgets and disbelieves) it and because, like our mothers before us, we are forced to live in artificial scarcity within which giving is difficult. Even if we have enough resources personally, others live in deprivation and we cannot practice mothering towards them without sacrificing our own small abundance. We cannot give it nor can they accept it easily without shame and embarrassment because of the ruling mores that over-value exchange.

Unfortunately, most of us forget our motherer-child experience because the exchange-based patriarchal culture cancels the prototype of the mother for the human and replaces it with a patriarchal male exemplar and a male god or gives us a neuter scientific and technological universe from which the gift economy and mothering have been exiled. This is a universe whose explanations begin downstream from gift-giving, with cause and effect, agent and patient, force, even path to goal, thus making it impossible to generalize mothering in its explanatory capacity. Yet we continue to function anyway according to the elaborations of the altercentric maternal interaction patterns because they are what works, what makes us tick.

In spite of our excellent science, we are basically misreading everything. In the next section I will try to explain in detail how and why. This misreading would not matter so much if it were not leading us to the destruction of each other and the planet. As icebergs melt and hurricanes abound, it is urgent for us to understand what we have been misreading and why.

PART TWO

THE ENIGMAS OF LANGUAGE
AND OF EXCHANGE

CHAPTER VI

THE VIRTUAL PLANE

Now that the idea of the gift in language as been introduced, new aspects of exchange can be seen. If exchange and its giftless epistemology occupy the whole field of vision, there is no background against which to contrast and emphasize its relevant aspects, so many of them go unobserved. With the gift forming the background, the picture looks very different. This part of the book will focus on exchange, especially monetized exchange, to show how it derives from another important aspect of language and how it alters and alienates our human potential, creating the apocalyptic consequences that are now upon us.

6.0 Language as virtual gift-giving

My hypothesis is that beyond gift-giving there is another originally positive aspect of language that has developed into market exchange and has become over-emphasized, creating a mechanism that programs us to become *homini economici,* with the motivations of ego-orientation and greed that fuel the expansion of the market.

As Marx says (2009:300), 'The anatomy of the human being is the key to the anatomy of the ape. But the intimations of a higher animal in the lower ones can be understood only if the animal of the higher order is already known. The bourgeois economy furnishes a key to ancient economy, etc'.

From this backward-looking point of view, we can see that the virtual worlds we now invent with computer technology are developments of the specialized area or level of life that was established perhaps as early as the Pleistocene by the primordial re-giving of gifts in language. In light of the virtual worlds it has now developed into, we can consider that spoken language is a life area[1] or 'level' of virtual gift-giving that takes place in the medium of the voice.[2] The virtual gift-simulation is not created by pixels,

---

1 Usually it is made up of 10,000 to 30,000 words for each individual.
2 The medium can also be gestural as in the manual sign language of the deaf (and, of course, the hands are also major protagonists of giving and receiving).

i.e. visual computer images, but by modifications of sound. The medium of the voice exists for the child from h:er birth in h:er crying and babbling and it provides the expression of emotion, timing, and interactive coordination between child and adult (see Bertau et al 2013). The plane of vocal sound is also already present and emotionally charged when children begin to make word-gifts with it because they have been using it themselves and have been listening to their motherers making word-gifts with it even from before birth.

I will use the characterization of language as 'virtual gift-giving' for the kind of difference language has from the rest of 'reality'. Language is the 'virtualization' of gifts in the service of gift-giving, of passing (perceptual, conceptual, experiential and relational) gifts on to others. It is the creation of a virtual gift plane made of sounds, that is, of puffs of breath passing through the larynx, which have become phonemes distinguishable by the linguistic community (just as present virtual reality is a mostly extra-somatic 'addition' to the 'real' world, language is a mostly extra-somatic 'addition' to the motherworld made of gifts). The medium of the human voice is more specific, more subtle, more widely available and more manageable, than is the medium of the electronic virtual world. It is charged with emotion and has possibilities and constraints that the electronic virtual world does not have.[3] On the other hand, we can understand the electronic world as a development of the change of levels of gift-giving that originates in language.

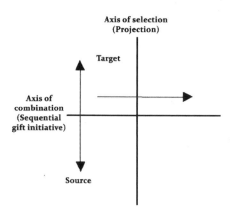

Figure 15: The vertical and the horizontal axis.

Alternatively it can be graphic as in writing, where marks, left by the hands, are gifts for delayed perception/reception.

3   On the other hand, the virtual world has been made relevant already by its programmers, often using sex and violence for that purpose.

I read these not only as selection and combination, metaphor and metonymy but as substitution and contiguity/transitivity.

The transposition of a gift from one plane to the other, its 'virtualization,' is accomplished by giving virtual word-gifts 'vertically' for non-verbal perceptual and conceptual world-gifts. The result of this 'vertical' giving is the creation of the vitual plane. Given to each other and together with logical connectors in gift constructions the resulting collection of these word-gifts forms the language and constitutes the virtual 'plane' that is already in existence when each new speaker learns to implement it, giving virtual gifts in the medium of h:er own voice.

Virtualization is a kind of path-to-goal projection of gifts from one plane to the other. The focus moves from a potential object of joint attention to the voice and back (perhaps even enacting a potential 'like me' relation between things and words?). The term 'virtualization' is useful because it makes explicit the move to an alternative vocal 'reality' and to the construction in that reality of relations that are similar to those in the mundane world. It is broader than naming, which is only the giving of a specific word-gift for a world-gift. 'Virtualization' can be used to indicate not only naming but the projection and replay of schemas and combinations of schemas in the other medium.

The capacity to virtualize and give (or re-give) word-gift constructions in sound begins later in childhood than material gift-giving and receiving and is less essential for survival. Even though it is very pervasive, this transposition of gifts is perhaps not as deeply embodied for the child as is the original gift schema because it appears later in the child's development.[4] Still, during h:er first year, the infant probably begins to realize that h:er own voice satisfies h:er motherers' needs to know about h:er (when s:he cries or laughs, for example), and that many of the sounds h:er motherers make can satisfy h:er own relational needs. As s:he begins to understand and register this emotionally, s:he can receive the motherers' sounds as gifts and by imitating h:er, begin to give them again as word-gifts starting at around 18 months of age.

The creation and implementation of a virtual plane of need-satisfying items, vocal sounds and patterns of gifting that are similar to the ones used by adults in h:er community, gives the child an ability to give and receive, to share, that would be far beyond h:er years if only material giv-

---

4   The motherer does do things for the child, in h:er place. S:he gives h:er things s:he can't reach and s:he may give things to others for h:er. S:he gives h:er one thing instead of another: a spoon to put in h:er mouth instead of the car keys.

ing and receiving were available to h:er. It is in this sense that language
nurtures and scaffolds gifting intelligence. It 'teaches itself' to children,
and teaches them thinking (see Lakoff and Johnson's 'logic of abstract
thought'), based on the material giving and receiving in which they are
necessarily already engaged.

We can look at virtualization also as a kind of schema derived from
the gift schema in the sense of giving for: giving something for something and to someone. There are, thus, at least two main kinds of schemas and the one derives from the other: the schema of the gift and the
schema of virtualization.

Because it appears later than gift-giving and receiving in the child's development and is less essential for survival, the schema of virtualization
is not as deep and actually would not bring with it the same explanatory
capacity as the schema of the gift. Material giving and receiving has to take
place repeatedly from the very beginning, and although it is often accompanied by the voice, by the child's vocalizations and the motherers' child-
directed speech ('motherese'), it is not yet language. The verbal plane is
created when the relational aspects and logical consequences of material
gifting are transposed into the accompanying vocal gifting, taking place
through and among sounds (repeatable segments of the vocal stream).

After the first tentative beginnings in their second year, children learn
quickly and usually have a vocabulary of some 500-1100 words by age
3 and 3000-5000 age 5 to 7 (http: //www.talkingkids.org/2011/07/how-
many-words-should-my-child-be.html). Together with their motherers
and others, they altercentrically co-create and re-create the vocal word-
gift plane, using word-gifts that have been passed down to them by the
linguistic community.

Material giving not only comes before the virtualization/verbalization
of giving but it continues throughout our childhoods and indeed throughout our lives. However, it is not surprising that the only period in which
humans seem to be capable of learning a first language corresponds with
the period of childhood during which they are most intensely nurtured.
Moreover, children who do not learn language, like Genie (Rymer 1993),
often have not been adequately nurtured and have endured abusive parenting situations. They have missed the period of maternal material communication in which adults give to children unilaterally and children engage in
altercentric gifting interaction with them.[5]

---

5   It is interesting how feral children like Victor of Aveyron are subjected to (ex-
     change-based) reward and punishment teaching, rather than to unilateral verbal

Language is added onto things as a virtual world is added on to a life world. It creates a virtual gift plane in which human relations are constructed regarding things and ideas through the implications of verbal need-satisfying giving/receiving. In order to access this plane and act upon it, the speaker (or writer) takes the initiative in giving a verbal gift to the listener (reader). Each verbal gift initiative requires one or many moments or acts of virtualization (though we become so used to doing this that we hardly notice it).

The act of virtualization, which happens repeatedly, is built on and is developmentally subsequent to the schema of the gift. We can see it as a projection (or mapping), a giving of gift giving from one plane to another, the projection from a source (material giving and receiving) to a target (acoustic giving and receiving). Although, like other projections, its trajectory is invisible, this projection of giving can be recognized as another instance of the transposed or extended gift schema: path-to-goal. Thus, the gift schema can also be considered the basis for the schema of virtualization.

The schema of virtualization becomes important on its own even though it inserts itself into and is permeated by a situation in which the schema of the gift is already operating in many areas and in many emotionally important ways. Speakers and (later) writers project and transpose the gifts from the non-verbal to the verbal plane, where they can give them again verbally to others, satisfying others' and their own evolving cognitive, communicative and relational needs. Listeners and readers receive them as such, and joining their attention to that of the speaker/writer, turn that attention towards the perceptual and conceptual world-gifts for which the word-gifts are given. Then they project gifts and gift relations into the medium of sound themselves in their turn, carrying on the conversation (we displace our solitary perception, add the word that comes up and immediately we are accompanied.)

When we focus on something as relevant to others (and to ourselves among them), as a perceptual gift on the reality plane, we access a virtual gift, a word, which can be given again for it on the linguistic plane. If this is a kind of thing (world-gift) that has been identified as relevant by others generally in the past, the linguistic community has usually already provided a verbal gift for it. That is, the community has given it a name, a word-gift (passing it on to others and to us), which we learn. If the collective importance or relevance of the thing, event, idea has not crossed a

---

and material gifting that they might imitate. For example Genie was punished, rewarded and manipulated in the many unsuccessful attempts to teach her to speak (Rymer 1993).

certain threshold and been registered as such by the community in a name, we can combine word gifts in a sentence in order to express it as a gift to others in a contingent way. That is, we give several word gifts together in order to satisfy the listeners' communicative need(s) in regard to something. This process retroacts by satisfying also our own need for a common relation, a kind of companionship.[6] The communicative need is a need for a common (cognitive and communicative) relation to something, a need of the listener, which the speaker mind-reads and fills, using combined word-gifts as means. By giving these word-gifts to the listener, creating with h:er a relation to some perception or conception, the speaker creates a relation with the other in which s:he h:erself is also included. This satisfaction of the other's cognitive and communicative needs provides and implies a shared receiving of the gifts of the world, which is similar to the mutuality that is established in the relation of giving/receiving and of joint attention with others, beginning in early childhood.

Naming can be seen as our giving (following and participating in the community's giving) of a (long-term, repeatable) gift on the virtual plane to the gift on the reality plane. Then we can give the gift on the virtual plane, the name, again and again for the reality plane gift[7] (which cannot give its name to others by itself, even though now it has it to give).[8]

I am now giving the name 'virtualization' to the giving of a verbal gift for a perceptual or conceptual gift. The previous sentence is a speech act and an example of what it says!

On the virtual plane, the word-gift maintains much of the human relation-creating capacity of the material gift even though its form is completely different. Many new things can happen in the virtual gift world and many other things are impossible. We can create human relations of mutuality (companionship) to flying above the clouds or to a nightingale singing thousands of years ago or to the idea of a better world. However, we cannot eat the bread we give each other verbally or hug 'the baby'. Virtual sound or written gifts are not material gifts in the sense that they do not satisfy material needs directly. Nevertheless, the relational consequences of mutuality, solidarity and positive expectations, which take place with giving

---

6   Trevarthen now says the relation between child and mother is one of 'companion-ship' and Bråten believes the child has a virtual mother from the beginning.

7   Mothers give *for* children. Things don't give their names even though they have them because they dont speak, so we give the names for them. We give the names for the children to the things and to the things for the children. Children are like things in the beginning in that they don't speak either.

8   This is similar to what we do when mothering small children.

and receiving, material nurturing, are preserved, at least to some extent, in the satisfaction of communicative needs.[9]

In a way, like money and commodities, verbal gifts are not gifts, but unlike them, they do not contradict giving. Word-gifts momentarily suspend the need to give material gifts to create mutual human relations regarding them, by being given in their stead in the roles of the gift schema.[10] They are given in the same direction as are material gifts: towards the other. In exchange, money and commodities are given in opposite directions (money in exchange inherits this directional capacity from language while contradicting it).

Once the plane of language has been formed for the individual within the group, the virtualization process itself, the moment of the change of planes, giving one kind of gift for another, is a very commonplace process, part of every linguistic act. In fact, it is so unremarkable that it is taken for granted, a given, and often even considered innate.

We could write the roles of the virtualization schema as 'A gives X (the word gift) for B'. If we put it in the gift schema, we add 'A gives X for B to C',[11] also implying 'B gives X by means of A's giving it' or 'B gave X to A, and then A gives it to C'. So this is another variation of 'if A gives to B and B gives to C, then A gives to C' and 'C receives X for B from A'.

Perhaps a good example of giving-for in another context is learning to read by sounding out the alphabet. We learn to give an appropriately voiced puff of air, a phoneme, for the letter and then to give the puffs to each other, 'blending' them to make the word: p-a-t, p-e-t, p-u-t, c-a-t. Each word-gift as a whole is then given for a different aspect of the world (which cannot give it on its own). It is an aspect of caring for the world to give its word-gift for something. Motherers often speak for children in this way ('the baby is tired'). Sentences and other meaningful sequences are formed by giving words to each other in a way that is somewhat similar to giving sounds – phonemes – to each other, as in 'pat the cat'.

The lexicon is a collection of word-gifts that can be given for world-gifts

---

9   Like 'activation contours' and 'flow patterns' with 'vitality affects' (Stern 1999) and protoconversational emotional 'contours' or 'envelopes' (Trevarthen 1999), the material gift has a narrative contour, of beginning, middle and end. Likewise, the sentence or paragraph or conversational segment has a contour.

10   We do not have to give a cat to someone but can give the word 'cat' to create the relation.

11   To some extent this schema also serves not only the word but the whole transitive or intransitive sentence. These relations are similar to those in Peirce's tripartite definition of the sign, see here immediately below.

and that can be combined with each other, 'merged' by gifting the words to each other in various ways.

The creation and use of elements of the virtual verbal gift plane is what philosophers call 'representation', a term that has aroused much controversy. We will see below that the controversy is largely due to the contradictory nature of monetary representation, which imposes a mutually exclusive relation that takes the place of the mutually inclusive relations created by both verbal and material gifting. Monetary representation deeply warps our thinking about representation generally, making it seem giftless, abstract and drastic.

6.1 Substitution or accompaniment?

Substitution in the sense of *aliquid stat pro aliquo* – something stands for something else – has been considered an aspect of the sign since St. Augustine. It is discussed in terms of a dyadic or triadic relation ('something stands for something to someone in some respect or capacity') by semiotician Charles S. Peirce (1931–58: 2.228). Recently, the idea of infinite semiosis (a holistic network of signs or in language, word-gifts), has taken the place of substitution as an explanation of how signs function. In our terms, infinite semiosis is an infinitely repeated virtualization schema. As such, it has replaced the schema of the gift in explanations of language influenced by exchange.[12] Marxist semioticians may remember that Marx's 'extended relative form of value' shows us a similar chain or network of substitutions when commodities are not seen in relation to the general equivalent, money, but only in relation to each other as particular equivalents.[13]

I will discuss this similarity more below and will show how the extended relative form and the general equivalent form, as well as substitution itself, take the place of the schema of the gift as models for our understanding in economics as well as linguistics.

---

12   Umberto Eco's recent book (2014) presents these non-maternal alternatives in the title *From the Tree to the Labyrynth*.
13   'the relative expression of value is incomplete because the series representing it is interminable. The chain of which each equation of value is a link, is liable at any moment to be lengthened by each new kind of commodity that comes into existence and furnishes the material for a fresh expression of value' (Marx 1996 [1867]: 42).

To substitution, I would like to oppose the idea of 'accompaniment',[14] in that the verbal plane does not actually take the place of the non-verbal plane but accompanies it and word-gifts do not take the place of world-gifts but accompany them. The need to communicate linguistically about something is added to other needs regarding that kind of thing. Satisfying this communicative need creates a human relation that is added to the other human relations that might be created using those things directly. We almost always need relations with others regarding things even if these relations may sometimes be negative. Even the need to be alone or unrelated is still a need regarding relations.

Words are not substitutes in the sense that they actually take the place of things (as money does), but in the sense that they are added onto the gifts of the world; they go along beside them in a companionable ('altercentric' or perhaps 'like me' way); they represent or regive them on another relatively self-consistent 'plane'. The vocal verbal plane is a plane of alternative gifts and giving accompanying the material plane, the purpose of which is basically relational.[15] One plane does not take the place of the other altogether. The presence or absence of things at the moment of speech (or writing) thus becomes to some extent irrelevant to their re-presentation, and to their interpersonal relational aspects on the verbal plane. We humans can relate ourselves to each other and to things in their presence and in their absence (and this opens up a wide space for the imagination).

Verbal giving creates this 'new' plane of accompaniment and cooperation. Our collective product, language, cooperates with life, and we cooperate with each other using it. Nevertheless, just as when we cooperate with each other, we take each others' places in roles, word-gifts take the place of non-verbal gifts (and sometimes of other verbal gifts), in the roles of the gift schema and in those of the virtualization schema as well. Since the roles remain relatively stable and the things and the words that occupy the roles change, they do take the place of (substitute for) other words and other things in the roles, at least temporarily.

Understanding it in this way, as different from and prior to mutually exclusive exchange, we can recycle the idea of substitution without suggesting that there is a binary relation between what is 'substituted' (the

---

14   Mothers and children also accompany each other. From the child's point of view at least, their relation is not usually either/or but both/and. See Bråten's self-organizing dyad and virtual other (1991), and Trevarthen's companionship relation (2005: 11).

15   See also the use of the voice in mother-child relations, the regulation of attention, and tension.

referent), and its 'substitute' (the verbal gift, its 'virtual other') or, though both have gift characteristics, that there is a one to one mirror (*wieder-spiegelung*) relation between words and things.[16] The lens/filter that makes evident gift roles and relations among things, together with the placement and replacement of words in gift roles, allows the speakers and listeners, (and writers and readers), to relate themselves to each other, to their words and to what they are talking about in similar mutually inclusive ways. They enact the roles themselves as they share the giving and receiving even though they are only doing it on the verbal 'accompaniment' plane and even though one person is speaking/writing/giving and the other is listening/reading/receiving at the moment. Words follow the good example of their users and share themselves with each other also, satisfying each others' needs, bonding felicitously for the moment.

In 'malestream' philosophy under patriarchal capitalism, we tend to put words into the roles of the virtualization schema without recognizing that there is a gift schema at all. We also believe that virtualization, which is verbal, comes before giving/receiving, which is both material and verbal. Ignoring the gift schema, we explain everything according to the schema of virtualization, interpreting it as naming (and renaming) and categorization (property, containment), while viewing logical consequences as based on inclusion in or exclusion from categories.

Nevertheless, the purpose of linguistic virtualization is giving virtual gifts and the virtualization relation itself does not function according to exclusion but according to accompaniment. In the definition and naming also, the word-gift does not replace the world-gift, the word 'dog' does not replace dogs but only suspends the need to give them to the other person in order to form human relations with h:er regarding them. It is also used instead of some phrase like 'a four-legged animal that barks and wags its tail' but does not exclude or cancel it, and can occasionally be used together with such a phrase in a definition or explanation.

Language (speaking or writing) is the virtualization of gifts in the service of the giving and the re-giving of (perceptual, conceptual, experiential and relational) world-gifts on the virtual verbal plane. Similarly 'virtual reality' is a supplement made of images accompanying the real world. A living language requires the continual communicative re-creation of a vir-

---

16   The primary repetitive relation between children and others is not a mirror relation but a mirror or empathy neuron relation of simulation with another before a relation of reflection in a mirror-object of a pre-existing self. Moreover, mimicry is mimicry of the other. If anything, the relation between words and things would follow this human path, not the path through the objectual mirror.

tual gift plane made of phonemes, words, word-constructions and texts.

Gifting verbal gifts on the verbal plane, we create relations with each other and to the world-gifts without having to give the world-gifts directly. In fact the world gifts can be absent. Two axes[17] are formed that are similar to the substitution and contiguity (metaphor and metonymy) axes depicted above.

The two planes work together like the vertical and horizontal cocomponents of a traditional loom, creating the warp and weft of the textile. The vertical, projected gift of virtualization is enlivened and organized into meaningful segments by the horizontal interactive movement of gift-to-gift transitivity.

However even in the virtualization schema, there is a giver– the speaker or writer – though we often forget h:er. Since language is a human (maternal gift) process, a human agent (maternal giver) is required.[18] There is also a potential receiver. The virtualization schema seems more easily decontextualized than the gift schema. The receiver's need in relation to the context can be left aside. However, if we say word y = object x, we are giving y for x, because x cannot give the word y, itself. In this process, we are also bringing forward x, because the other, who understands this relation, having experienced it h:erself, can search for what it is that we have given h:er the word for, and this amounts to our having given it to h:er attention.

In this process, the speaker/writer is actually passing the gift on, giving it to others to hear and to view. Giving something to the attention of the other is an artifact of virtualization, through a one-to-many relation both on the virtual and on the reality plane (see below 6.13). Speaking/writing is not just intending or doing, but is actually giving. The speaker/writer is not just an aspecific agent; s:he is a giver who satisfies the other's communicative and cognitive needs. The receiver is not so much 'grasping the intention' of the giver as s:he is experiencing the satisfaction of h:er communicative and cognitive needs while creatively engaging in the interpretation of the giver's gift constructions. The child is not just an 'agent' but a giver of adult verbal gifts long before s:he is able to be a giver of adult material gifts. S:he does not just perform speech acts

---

17 These axes are possibly a projection of the embodied schema 'up is good', which itself may come from the adult being taller than the child and picking h:er up as well as from the fact that speech comes from our breath through our mouths which are above the rest of our bodies.

18 There are now, of course, robots and computers that speak. They are virtual humans, virtual givers. See Kristeva's insistence on the human agent.

but gives virtual gifts, which satisfy others' needs and so s:he is a gifting subject. S:he is not primarily a dialogical self but a giving and receiving self. That is, dialogue is taking turns giving and receiving and it happens both materially and virtually (verbally).

Virtual giving and receiving, turntaking dialogue is grounded in an already existing structure of material giving and receiving in which the child has participated many times every day since birth. The formative capacity that researchers attribute to dialogue is actually first created by material giving and receiving 'dialogue'. The continuity between the two planes makes them mutually informative. When this is not acknowledged, the analysis is skewed and incomplete. Mental and verbal work are seen as primary instead of material work, and the connection between the virtual and the material world is lost. The use of the term 'exchange' instead of 'giving and receiving' covers up the evidence of the gift structure on both planes.[19]

6.2 Virtualization and intransitive sentences

As we said, virtualization continues to be done in all our linguistic activity. Its very ubiquity makes it difficult to identify. However, the virtualization schema becomes evident in another way when it is 'replayed' on the plane of language itself in intransitive sentences. This occurs in the definition where the *definiendum* is given to the listener or reader for (or to take the place of) the *definiens*, which is also given. In 'a cat is a four-legged animal with a long tail and whiskers', 'cat' is the *definiendum* and 'a four-legged animal with a long tail and whiskers' is the *definiens*.[20] Giving the name 'cat' suspends the speaker/writer's need to give 'a four legged animal

---

19 One good example of this is Maria Lyra in *Dialogic Formations* (2012). She describes a 'give and take' game between mother and child in terms of 'exchanges'. What she sees as 'abbreviation' of an 'extension' of dialogic interaction, I would see as games of decontextualization/generalization and clarification of giving and receiving and an elaboration upon it. Perhaps I could say they are games of schematizing giving and receiving in which it becomes clear to the child that the basic pattern remains throughout the variations. Moreover, s:he is already receiving and giving care materially on a daily basis with h:er motherer(s). These games might be seen as a transition to virtualization. In fact, one kind of gambit is feigning giving, giving not giving. Also, showing is giving to view, not to take. And I mentioned the game of peep-eye or 'boo!' in which the adult makes h:er face pop out towards the child). See also Wittgenstein's games.

20 See my *For-Giving*, 1997, and discussion here below p. 233.

with whiskers and a long tail' to satisfy the other's communicative and cognitive need regarding cats. The other's need is now satisfied by 'cat'.

We continue to reuse the virtualization schema in many ways, not only in naming and the definition and in intransitive sentences, but in copula constructions (with the verb 'to be'), in propositions about existence, in translation, in teaching languages, in cryptography, etc. The verb 'to be' is the word-gift with which we explicitly if unconsciously re-give the gift of virtualization, which is its referent. Instead of giving the words directly to each other as in 'the gray cat', we say 'the cat is gray', creating predication – as if the listener needs to know that we are virtualizing this quality of the cat as having some special relevance of its own.

The use of the voice in early childhood to convey emotions makes it particularly appropriate for it to be the material of words that are used as value accents (Voloshinov 1974) of relevant world-gifts. With the voice, we give the gift of emphasis, of relevance, of value, so that others know what we are giving them to attend to. We care for the world for them and we care for them regarding the world.

Speaking functions to bring forward relevant aspects of experience. Since rhythms of breathing change with exertion and excitement, the volume of the voice is appropriate for emphasis. However, emphasis can also be created through syntactic variations, which words we give to which, when we give them and how (Chiarcos et al 2011). In English, we can play on the two schemas for emphasis, giving 'gray' directly to 'cat' or enacting the virtualization schema 'the cat is gray'. Our choices of which to use provide emphasis also because the listener/reader makes similar stylistic choices in h:er turn.[21]

We virtualize what is selected as relevant, what we and others need or want to create human relations in regard to (by satisfying the others' communicative need), so virtualization/naming itself carries a particular relevance.

There is actually quite a difference between transitive sentences, where the gift schema is embodied in the grammatical form, and intransitive sentences where the gift schema is foreshortened, and the virtualization schema is displayed. The differences between these two forms are often overlooked. Perhaps this is because the intransitive sentence as a whole ('the cat is gray') is also a gift to the listener even if it does not function according to the transitive gift schema internally (as does 'the gray cat' or 'the cat chased the mouse'). Transitive and intransitive can combine,

---

21 We can also use figurative language and metaphors extending the virtual plane a little: 'the ash-colored cat' or 'this cat is the color of a rain cloud'.

of course – one kind of phrase can be given to the other – 'the cat that chased the mouse is gray.'

Similarly whales look like fish but they have a different ancestor. Like the transitive gift schema in language, whales' ancestor went into the sea after being on the land (after being material gift pattern, the gift schema became verbal) while fish and their ancestors have always been in the water (the virtualization schema and its derivatives have always been verbal). Now this intransitive virtualization schema has become embodied ... in commodity exchange.

6.3 Definition, virtualization and the copula

Like the image schema of the gift, the image schema of virtualization is versatile and is used in many ways. As in the definition proper, the ostensive definition, for example, 'that is a cat', suggests a substitution (a change of planes), by equating the demonstrative pronoun 'that' and 'cat', usually accompanied by pointing at a cat. Then 'cat' takes the place of 'that' and of the object of the gesture of ostension for the language-learning listener.

Although we can repeat the process of virtualization again and again for different items, naming them *ad infinitum*, these word gifts on their own do not form a sentence, a circumstance that gives rise to the philosophical problem of 'the unity of the proposition,' which I discussed above.

Naming alone, even sequential naming, is not language. The virtualization of gift schemas and gift connections are necessary for the emergence of meaning and the creation of a 'proposition'. We have seen the functioning of the gift roles in creating transitive propositions, but what about intransitive ones?

In 'the cat is gray', 'is' is a step up to a meta level, regarding the gifts in the sentence, which says 'the gift I am giving you is just the virtualization of this aspect [gray] of the [cat]'. There are languages that don't use the copula but in English saying only 'the gray cat' is incomplete: it seems we are going to give another or different gift schema with 'the gray cat' in the giver role.

The proposition with the copula 'is' is a way of giving, of attributing, the predicate to the subject. That is, the subject is not in the giver role but is seen as receiving other verbal gifts given by the speaker. This is giving by virtualizing. The motivation – giving– is the same and the effects are similar but, as we said, the two processes are different and have different origins: in one or the other of the two schemas.

Actually, the virtualization schema and the gift schema are mutually supportive as they are enacted by the speaker or writer. 'That is a cat' justifiably takes meaning and sequentiality from the gift schema because it is also the explicit giving of the word 'cat' for the cat to the listener (and it is a service for the cat who cannot give h:er name to the listener by h:erself).

In language teaching, giving the name is satisfying the listener's metalinguistic need for a word-gift regarding something. In the ostensive definition, 'that is a cat,' the virtual gift we initially give for the |cat| is the demonstrative pronoun, the generic gift 'that', which is replaced by the word-gift 'cat'. The virtual gift for this act of replacement (its virtualization) is 'is'. The listener receives the word-gift 'cat', which s:he can use again, give again, to others fo: |cats|.

Giving something in the place of something else continues to be a kind of giving, if something or someone can receive it. The speaker or writer is the giver of the sentence as a whole and the listener or reader is the receiver of the sentence as a whole. Inside the transitive sentence, the subject is the giver of the verb (the gift or service) while the object is the receiver of the verb. Inside the intransitive sentence, the receiver is the subject to which a predicate is 'attributed' (given) by the use of the copula. In 'the gray cat chased the ball', the gift schema is played out: 'the gray cat' is in the role of the giver, 'chased' is the role of gift or service and 'ball' in the role of the receiver. In 'the cat that chased the ball, is gray', the pronoun 'that' is given to and for 'cat' as the subject (giver) of the verb 'chased' in the clause, where 'ball' is the receiver and then 'gray' is given to 'cat'. There are changes in perspectives of giver, gift and receiver throughout these sentences as I noted above.

In the ostensive definition 'that is a cat', there is a replacement of 'that' by 'cat' and together they are given to the listener as a moment of virtualization, satisfying the listener's need to know the virtual verbal gift for that kind of animal. In 'the cat is gray' there is only an attribution or giving of 'gray' to 'cat' and both together to the listener.

If we do not recognize that there are gifts on the two planes of world and words we cannot see speech/writing as the transfer of giving onto a virtual plane nor can we see the use of the copula as a replay of virtualization on the virtual plane itself. Because we do not attribute enough importance to material giving, the processes of virtual giving, of virtualization, of the reenactments of the gift schema and of the virtualization schema and even the use of the verb 'to be' continue to be misunderstood even if we practice them all the time.

It is the influence of exchange, which as we shall see, is a derivative of the virtualization schema, that discredits giving/receiving and makes these linguistic processes mysterious. The mystery is also both an effect and a cause of the deeply problematic position of women, motherers and the gift economy in Western (and now worldwide) patriarchal capitalist society. The erasure of the gift paradigm by the exchange paradigm hides the explanations that the gift paradigm would provide with the result that we do not understand how to create our common humanity as adults even though we are doing it necessarily as infants and in caring for infants.

Without the recognition of the primacy of gift-giving, philosophers lose the connections between world gifts and language, the functioning of which appears to depend on what I am calling the virtualization process alone, leaving aside the original gift schema. Language becomes a 'faculty' with no social connection to material nurturing or to the motherer. The human relational aspects are hidden, though they continue to be elaborated in practice. Transitivity seems to be just another category.

Without the maternal relational model, connections among the virtual verbal items themselves are mysterious and are thought to be 'governed' by rules, which perhaps are given by heredity, located in brain 'modules' and/or accessed by statistical sampling. Accordingly, the relations among humans are also thought to be created by rules of behavior, which perhaps limit or enhance biological drives, or they depend upon the exchange constraints of debt and obligation, while unilateral giving and receiving, which actually do create the relations spontaneously, are usually invisible, and when visible, are discounted as unimportant, discredited as profligate or over-praised as saintly. This has the negative effect on economics that it leaves the field open to the justifying figure of *homo economicus*, which validates the heartless accumulative rush to the top, domination by the few, and the impoverishment and subjugation of the many.

The new infant psychology, which, at last, is beginning to look also at the behavior of motherers, is making important new contributions to an alternative view of the human. The connection with the gift economy has not been made, however. Material nurturing seems less social and more corporeal than verbal nurturing, so perhaps less interesting. Yet, its importance for survival makes it the foundation of any transposed patterns of nurturing that the child later develops, including nurturing with the voice.

The child's crying satisfies the motherer's need to know the child has a need. The 'proprioception' of the child's own voice first in crying and then in murmurs of satisfaction accompanies h:er experience of need and nurture, while the motherer's voice often accompanies these interactive moments as well. By satisfying the child's needs the motherer gives value to the child by implication, showing s:he is relevant to h:er. S:he often speaks and sometimes sings to the child during these interactions and h:er voice traces their different moments and tempos. The emphasis of the voice thus is associated intimately with the emotions of early material nurturing and the voice continues to give value to the child and to shared experience with the motherer even when no material nurturing is taking place.

The giving and receiving of material nurturing is the first human interaction, the opening gambit of life itself. As I said above this does not imply that the child is passive. S:he participates in the interaction and understands the motherer's giving through h:er own responses, 'like me' body mapping and mirror neurons. Unilateral giving lays down the first step and when the child is able s:he imitates this step by giving unilaterally h:erself. S:he does this gesturally and vocally, turntaking with the motherer, taking the initiative to give and to respond in protoconversations.[22]

It is important to remember that the child is also giving materially if unintentionally from the beginning – feces and urine. The production of feces can be an event that involves the rhythmic effort of the child's whole body, and thus be quite emphatic. Urinating requires less effort but nevertheless is accompanied by specific sensations. Both follow physiological tempos. The caregiver has to 'receive' both these material 'gifts' of the infant unilaterally and 'take care' of them according to the child's timing.

The giving and receiving of nurture and its byproducts between motherer and child constitutes a material dialogue from the very beginning of life outside the womb. Does this demonstrate that human experience is 'innately dialogical' (Gratier and Trevarthen 2007)? I don't think so. The dialogue derives from the way things have to be in order for the child to survive but the patterns of experience are just that; they come from re-

---

22 I do not know if the child associates the food she has eaten with the feces she makes. Feces actually have a good smell when the child is receiving only breast milk (personal experience). Freud's connections among feces, gifts and money seem strange and only applicable after the child is potty trained. What about the cultures where potty training doesn't happen in an oppesive way? http: //nacd. org/newsletter/0409_pottytraining.php
'[I]n the products of the unconscious—spontaneous ideas, phantasies, and symptoms—the concepts *faeces* (money, gift), *baby* and *penis* are ill-distinguished from one another and are easily interchangeable' (128). 'Defaecation affords the first occasion on which the child must decide between a narcissistic and an object-loving attitude. He either parts obediently with his faeces, "sacrifices" them to his love, or else retains them for purposes of auto-erotic satisfaction and later as a means of asserting his own will' (p. 130). In *From the History of an Infantile Neurosis* (1918b [1914]).

peated experiences. They do not have to be genetically pre-programmed and, in fact, the child in the womb does not have these experiences because s:he does not have a space between needs and their fulfillment. There is no giving and receiving because h:er needs are already filled.

The material nurturing of the child by h:er motherer(s) already implies that the child is valuable to h:er (or them). To see the effects of the lack of this implied value, one has only to consider the desperate psychological as well as physical condition of children who are not individually nurtured.[23]

Thus the interpersonal elaboration of value originates with the value given to the other in the earliest material 'dialogue' with its tensions and tempos and continues also with the accompanying tones, rhythms and emphases of the voice. This is important in the understanding of relevance and value, even economic value, as something that is originally given through nurturing, accompanied by the voice. Then it is also attributed through linguistic gift-giving of which the voice is the virtual medium and the early modulations of the voice are the precursor.

6.4 Giftless thinking

Without the idea of the gift, the perception or circumstance resulting in the proposition 'the cat is gray' seems disconnected from the phrase itself, which appears to be only a *sui generis* verbal activity. The question as to why it was said seems not to be relevant to its meaning so it is available to be used as an example without a context. Not only words but sentences can be taken by themselves and appear to be arbitrary.[24]

From the gift perspective instead, we see the origin of the process as a perceptual or experiential gift received by the speaker/writer from h:er surroundings, which s:he is unilaterally passing on to others with a word-gift construction, satisfying their cognitive and communicative needs. Others have these needs, which arise from the relevance of the ongoing context, even when they are not themselves conscious of them. The speaker mind-reads the listener, identifies the contextual relevance

---

23   http://www.huffingtonpost.com/maia-szalavitz/how-orphanages-kill-babie_b_549608.html

24   In the Saussurian sense, they appear to be unmotivated as well, without a similarity, but we are saying that there is a similarity in that they are gifts on the two levels, and also that the psychological motivation for speaking is a gift-based motivation. We do not see any of this when we isolate a sentence for investigation or just use it as an example of a proposition.

and the word-gift and syntactical needs of the other. If cats are relevant at the moment, s:he gives the other the word 'cats' to create a gift relation with h:er to them. S:he does not use the word 'dogs' because that word satisfies a different communicative need of the other.

These are also the others' needs for a relation with h:er, the satisfaction of which creates at the same time a relation for h:er with them, regarding the perceptual or experiential gift.[25] Predication with the copula 'to be' is a use of the virtualization schema for the attribution – giving – by the human speaker/writer, of one virtual gift to another virtual gift inside the sentence, a predicate to a subject. By understanding the perceptual gift as received, we regard its origin, the world-gift (which is also a perceptual 'giver' on the external) as continuing to have that perceptual quality to give without losing it. In saying 'the cat is gray', we virtualize the world-gift cat and we virtualize her grayness – because she has it to give and gives it to us to perceive. Would we even have virtualized – and given – the word 'cat' if we had not had something to say about h:er, some other relevant gift to give?[26] If I say 'the gray cat' it is not clear why I am giving you these verbal gifts at the moment. The schema is incomplete. If I say 'the cat is gray', the psychological motivation must be that I think you have a need to know this now, and therefore a need to receive this ad hoc gift construction made with the virtualization schema. That is, virtualization with the copula is used not just as and end in itself but for us to give each other something relevant.

The verb 'to be' is a virtual gift of the gift of the virtualization process itself, a kind of meta-moment, a virtualization of virtualization concerning parts of the sentence, which contains it.[27]

The use of the virtualization schema in the definition, which I mentioned above, may appear to substitute the *definiendum* for the *definiens* though it doesn't really. 'A small friendly feline animal that says "meow"' still exists as a possibility in the language and can be said any time, even though we don't need it and now use 'cat' more often instead. They are not mutually exclusive.

'Is' is also used to virtualize together gifts that are given to each other on the reality plane, stacking word-gifts without substituting one for the

---

25 Although this satisfaction of the other's communicative need has positive consequences for the speaker/writer in that it creates h:er relation to the world-gift as an accompanied relation, it is not an exchange.

26 But children who say the name of something, 'cat' for example, do it as a way of knowing it, which involves having ('acquiring') the virtual gift to pass on.

27 We shall see the similarity of this moment with the substitution of commodities by money in exchange.

other: 'the cat is gray', which we described as the 'attribution' (gift-word) of 'gray' to 'cat,' expresses the fact that on the reality plane the cat has the 'property' of grayness, which has originally been given to her (and passed on to our perception) by Motherer Nature, Motherer Reality.

The cat does not keep her 'property' but shares it with us. [Gray][28] is the 'property' of the [cat], the reality plane, a world-gift, a perceptual property, which s:he 'has to give'. S:he 'has it to give' to our perception and we receive it without h:er losing it, just as we give our words to each other and to the listener/reader without losing them. Our expectation and experience of perceptual and linguistic abundance facilitate our sharing in this way. The explicit giving of one virtual word-gift to another on the linguistic plane implies the giving (or already accomplished gift) of things on the reality plane to each other.[29]

With our virtual gift sentences, we satisfy the needs of the listener/reader regarding the cat but not the needs of the cat except in the sense that cats perhaps do need a specific virtual gift relation to humans, which is provided when humans talk to each other about them ('Please feed the cat!'). Even if cats have a communicative need, we have to satisfy it for them, as we do for all listeners. However, as happens for most everything else that is not human, there are many of our linguistic communicative needs cats cannot satisfy, though they satisfy our perceptual needs and a few of our communicative needs with vocal and with nonvocal signs.

Thus, 'that is a cat' is an example of an elaboration of the virtualization schema itself, of accessing the virtual plane. It follows the same process as the definition I mentioned above. On the other hand, 'the cat is gray' is virtualization used for attribution, for verbally re-giving the perceptual gift of the gray color that the cat has received and has available to give on the reality plane. We usually confuse these two functions of 'to be'.

This use of 'is' in the ostensive definition is also a specific giving of the verbal gift, 'cat,' which is a gift to the cat (of h:er human language generic name) as well as to the human listener.

Without the idea of gift-giving, the functioning of language appears to depend on virtualization – this transfer of planes – alone. If we only say

---

28   Brackets are used by linguists to identify things that are on the non verbal reality plane.

29   It is just this ability to receive and understand the aspects of our environmental niches as gifts that allows us to collaborate, pass them on to each other, attend to them jointly and eventually add to them by modifying them. For example, cooking food, which had important effects on our physiology in pre history (Wrangham 2009).

one word, for example, 'cat', we are giving one virtual gift for one particular perceptual gift, or for the category 'cat' but we have abstracted both the word and the perceptual gift from their contexts so they are not being seen as given by anyone or anything to anyone or anything. They have no further relevance, no value is given or received through them. That is, they have no relations (almost as if they were in the background). Without other verbal givers and receivers, it looks like there are no gifts.

We have been saying that gift-giving creates relations among people and among words. Does virtualization itself create relations? The fact that we are able to access the verbal plane, to produce a virtual item in the gift role of a reality plane item, makes us similar to each other and, thus, would allow us to include ourselves in the same category. But this categorization is not enough to explain how linguistic communication functions. The virtualization has to be done in order to satisfy the communicative or cognitive need of the other. When that is done dynamic relations of roles are created among people and among the gifts of different kinds.

The unavoidable basic intention of linguistic communication is to satisfy the cognitive and communicative needs of others by giving them word-gifts. This is a generic intention and it is not by grasping it that listeners/readers understand the specific segments of language they are being given. Understanding what is said has to do with creatively receiving the other's verbal gifts and aligning our relations with them as receivers and givers. In doing this we may indeed grasp the speaker's specific intention but it is the gift structure, not the intention that carries the communication.

We perform the act of virtualization in order to give its product but if, ignoring giving, we think there is only a *sui generis* process of naming something or saying or writing a word, we do not understand how the words are connected to each other. Without the gift schema, the virtualization schema on its own would not be enough to create meaning and communication. If, like virtualization itself, actions of the verbal plane – naming, saying, speaking, telling, even writing – belong to the graded category that has giving as its prototype, they are kinds of giving and it is from this that their relevance to humans, their significance, derives. Unfortunately, as I mentioned, they can also function according to the negative transposed gift, hitting.

Contemporary mainstream (malestream) linguistics, and philosophy, especially epistemology, concentrate on the virtualization aspect of language but ignore the schema of the gift (or now they may relegate it to the category of neuron activity). Therefore they look at words on their own as individual signs of various kinds and affirm that they are related to each other by rules[30] or that they merge as 'slots and fillers'. Taking words out of context and considering them on their own is a process that indeed removes them from the image schema of the gift at most of the levels in which it occurs. Then an explanation of the words' connections with each other when they are in context, goes missing.

In contrast, our more 'organic' (and more feminist maternalist) approach sees the connections among words as similar to the connections among people. Both derive from giving and receiving begun in the motherer-child dyad. At the level of material gift-giving, the experience of needs and the positive and justified expectations of their fulfillment by the motherer creates the basis of the child's life and h:er relations with others. This involves the image schema of the gift, which functions also in language, with the virtualization and transposition of gifts to the verbal plane and the ongoing creation and satisfaction of cognitive and communicative needs. The variety of the kinds of gifts at both levels creates a multiplicity of contents for a limited number of different kinds of connections. The regularities of these kinds of connections are what we call the syntax of individual languages, mother tongues.

The definition is an attempt to give the gift of the word to other(s) through several steps of virtualization, by which we/they are led to identify the world-gift referent as a part of the perceptual/conceptual commons. However, if a word is taken out of context and has no relations with other words in a sentence we cannot usually tell what relational need of the listener it is supposed to be satisfying at the moment, if any. It is outside the schema of the gift except for the enunciation or mentioning of it. Thus it is connected to the world gift only cognitively and as represented by a possible exemplar[31] of its kind or category.

If in philosophical discussions we enact the schema of virtualization with only a single word, for example 'cat' we may be giving one virtual gift for one particular perceptual gift, or for a category 'cat', but we have abstracted both the word and any possible related world-gifts from their contexts so they are not being seen as given by anyone or anything to anyone or anything. That is, they have no 'interpersonal' gift relations since those relations come from giving and receiving. They are outside the gift schema

---

30   Perhaps women, who are supposed to be more 'relational' than men, can understand these relations better, not as rules but as expectations of solidarity of different kinds constructed by giving and receiving need-satisfying gifts and services. Also, see E. B. Pashukanis (1980[1924]) on law as derived from commodity exchange – and I would say ultimately from virtualization.

31   I will be discussing exemplars in concept formation in subsequent chapters. See also my article 'The Exemplar and the Gift' in *Semiotica* 148 (2004): 95-118.

though they may still have relations of identity and difference, which are part of the virtualization process.[32]

The conception of codes and codification, coming from one-to-one constructed correspondences between words and signs or other words, developed originally by the military for the purpose of concealing meaning, hides gift-giving in a similar way. Cyphers privatize the virtual verbal area, building a second virtual language and restricting the giving/receiving of the words and messages to only a few potential receivers who have the specifically altered communicative needs that are satisfiable by those revirtualized gifts. Although it has been used extensively by semioticians and linguists and with practical success in artificial intelligence, the concept of code is inappropriate as an analogy for understanding language because it is based mainly on the process of virtualization and ignores the schema of the gift.

Without sentential givers and receivers, it looks like there are no gifts. Since gift-giving and the relations formed by it are ignored in our society in favor of 'neutral' monetized exchange anyway – the virtualization of not-gifts in the medium of money – gift-giving does not come to mind as an explanation for meaning. Thus, the virtualization process seems to function by itself especially when words are decontextualized and taken singly as examples. We may say we 'apply' a name to something, or even 'give' it a name, but, in any case, just by isolating a word to examine it, the whole interpretative register of gift giving is usually left out.[33]

There are some uses of words alone that do function as communicative gifts, of course. For example, by yelling 'Fire!' or 'Help!' we are satisfying others' need to know (that there is a fire, or that we need help.) However, if we point blank say even something simple like 'horse', we satisfy the listener's need for the relational token regarding horses but the listener cannot tell what contingent need of h:ers we are satisfying. Our other-oriented motivation is obscure. To satisfy the listeners' contingent need, we have to give gifts to gifts syntactically. One can also say a word louder or softer but the change in decibel level does not by itself give any extra gift except to show an increased degree of relevance.

The same happens with the loss of meaning that comes through repetition. When I was a child, my friend and I used to play the game of saying

---

32 We may also submit it to a kind of substitution 'test': if something is similar to something else, it can take the place of the other.

33 In a way, if we 'give the name for the kind of thing', we are serving the kind of thing by giving its name to others. If we deny the dynamic and even the existence of the gift schema, this way of characterizing it becomes invisible and seemingly uninformative.

the same word over and over: 'car, car, car, car ...' after only a few repetitions something strange happens and the word becomes meaningless. The reason, as I finally understood it, is that after the first two or three repetitions, there is no longer any need the word is being used to satisfy so there is no gift. That is, there is meaningless excess.

6.5 Relations created by giving and receiving contrast with exchange relations

In the by now extensive, mostly Western, philosophical and anthropological literature on the gift, it is generally recognized that gift-giving creates and confirms positive human relations (see Hyde 1979).[34] These relations are not created by exchange/categorization but by transitive gift-giving. The kinds of relations that are created in language are similar: transitivity creates relations of combination and connection[35] while categorization facilitated by virtualization, now influenced by private property and exchange, creates mutually exclusive relations among the different kinds of items categorized.

Giving verbal gifts made of gifts creates a core of egalitarian, nurturing, cognitive and communicative relations among people regarding the gifts of the world, including direct and indirect emotional and personal identity relations. As well, there is an understanding of a kind of 'social grammar' in groups regarding who gives what to whom and when (Yan 1996).

The constrained reciprocity, debt and obligation typical of the market are not necessary for the functioning of relation-creating, turn-taking material and/or verbal gifts. We can understand what the other person says even if we do not reply. The reader is typically in this situation.[36]

---

34 'a bond precedes or is created by donation and ... it is absent, suspended or severed in commodity exchange' (Hyde 1979: 80).

35 Adequate connection has not been made between indigenous social gift-giving, maternal gift-giving and the important mutual cognitive relations giving/receiving creates between motherers and children. Nor has the connection been made with verbal gift-giving and the human (and syntactic) relations that are created by giving and receiving word-gifts. Nor has the feminist philosophy and psychology of relations and the ethics of care (see, for example, Virginia Held 2007) made these connections among care, mothering as material communication, indigenous gift economies and language.

36 Writing is a sort of revirtualization of sound, made in a 'more material' medium. See below the discussion of Denise Schmandt-Besserat (1992) and the development of writing in the Middle East from exosomatic tokens. Gestures made with the hands are in a different kind of virtual area, proxemic space. The hands are, of

While I said that word-gifts do not take the place of world-gifts, (instead they accompany them), there is no doubt that money takes the place of things in exchange, when the things are commodities, i.e. not-gifts. But similarly, words are not the material gifts for which they 'stand,' and which they accompany; like money, words cannot be eaten or worn. In a sense, they are also not-gifts. Yet we use them to create nurturing human relations among ourselves to things in our surroundings. We mutually include each other by giving each other words while we mutually exclude each other when we exchange commodities for money. We even continue to include each other by talking while we are mutually excluding each other in the process of exchange.

The gift schema is simple and for this reason as well, it can be elaborated in many ways. The schema of exchange, based on the embodied schema of virtualization is more complex. 'I give you this *and* you give me that' is very different from 'I will only give you this *if* you will give me that'. Using contingency to create leverage between the two moments changes the perspectives entirely and the whole picture as well.

Exchange is complex because it contradicts the gift schema, which we are using all the time in many ways even if unwittingly. At the same time, it is structurally composed of the gift schema doubled back upon itself, made contingent and used for leverage. This process contradicts and alters what would have been a gift trajectory, taking away many of its positive implications while permitting the physical transfer of the commodity in spite of the mutually exclusive relation of private property. The bilateral contingent transaction hides the straightforward unilateral gift transaction that would have been (and in this sense, it does take its place, 'overwrites' and usurps it). Additionally, monetized exchange replays on the material plane what on the verbal plane is a functional linguistic process, and it splits the reified virtual 'verbal' gift object, money, from the material would-have-been-gift object, the commodity, while the one materially takes the place of the other.

This reified process is used not for accompaniment and unifying communication as happens in language, but for mutual substitution and separation, in order to maintain private ownership, thus opening the way for competition, accumulation and domination.

---

course, important in gift-giving. In fact, we embody in our hands the 'exosomatic' representation of the one-to-many concept formation, with the pointing finger as exemplar and the other digits as the many, held in abeyance.

6.6 Structure and superstructure revisited

The linguistic virtualization process, which is necessary for verbal gift-giving, has become gift-denying, monetized exchange and a fundamental part of the economic structure of the market. As a result of this embodiment, monetized exchange broadcasts itself back into our minds onto our ideas about language and the world in general, renaming, discrediting and concealing gift processes, making it appear to philosophers and the rest of us that virtualization, categorization and rule-following are the primary linguistic processes. The ideological projection of the incarnation of virtualization in exchange denies the importance of the gift initiative for the formation of human subjectivity. The projection also denies gift giving as an economic motivation in a patriarchal capitalist mode of production and distribution now developing into patrio-corporatocracy (if corporations are juridical persons they are anyway not maternal persons). The ideology of exchange promotes the practical discrediting of gift-giving and gift-givers, particularly mothers, and, by association, all women (including those who are not mothers), as well as non-dominant, gift-giving men.

The schema of monetized exchange coming from the schema of virtualization replaces the altercentric maternal communicative schema of the gift not only practically but as the explanatory key for everything.

Thus, it is not just Western patriarchy, capitalism and corporations, but the market itself, monetized exchange, C-M-C, (commodity-money-commodity), which is responsible for the oppression of mothers, of women and of all gift-givers, of workers and of the unemployed, and especially of indigenous people practicing gift economies.[37]

The economic structure of the market is based on the logic of exchange/virtualization, while the structure of the gift economy is based on the logic of the gift. Each of these constitutes an economic base that has its own superstructure of ideas, though the two superstructures are intertwined because the two bases are presently combined. One way of behaving, exchange, dominates. One mode of distributing, giving, nurtures the other mode. The complex web of these economic interactions, taken together with their many permutations, is what we call capitalism. The ideology of capitalism combines hidden gifting and over-visible exchange. It promotes

---

37   C-M-C influences and is influenced by the oppressive construction of gender in
      the West. There are some indigenous societies like the one in Juchitan, where
      women have dominated the market to their own relational ends. Their involve-
      ment in exchange is offset by their very frequent, even daily, gifting festivals
      (Bennholdt-Thomsen 1989).

the transposition of gifts into something else, a monolithic and contradictory material 'language' made of commodities and money, in which money is the value exemplar and the reincarnated word while the totality of commodities make up its 'semantic field'.

It is not surprising that exchange encroaches on gifts everywhere, commodifying every source of gifts: from the selling of human beings as slaves or wives (over whom the owners' control can be total), to the seizure of the commons of the land, to the commodification of land and minerals, energy, water, seeds, fertilizer, species, traditional practices, genes and finally the selling of adults and children for slavery, war, sex and body parts. To this may be added the insidious commodification of desire through advertising and of opinion through propaganda. What is surprising is that the gift-plundering mechanism of exchange is actually very simple and yet people are fooled by it. I believe its derivation from virtualization/naming in language (where it is benign), explains our vulnerability to its perverse influence on our imaginations and our actions.

Let me also hazard the suggestion that the time-honored Marxian distinction of structure and superstructure might be understood as the mapping of the linguistic schemas of giving or of virtualization (source) into the economy (target) as giving or exchange and their further mapping as economic schemas of material communication, either gift or exchange (source) onto other-centered or ego-centered behavior of individuals, groups, corporations or nations with their correspondent accompanying ideas and explanations of the world (target).

In fact, if a schema such as PATH TO GOAL can be understood as informing such an important experience as the passage of time (Lakoff and Johnson 1980) surely the deep schemas of interpersonal gift and virtualization/exchange would be even more powerful. The economic structure would determine the ideological superstructure, not only because it influences day-to-day behavior, but because that behavior itself is often the implementation of the gift or of the exchange logic that externalize themselves in practice and also in ideas (both directly and as embodied in practice).

If this description of the projection of exchange into our ideas is accurate, we need to investigate it so we can understand what is happening and know what to do. In fact, even from this brief description, we should conclude that money is in itself a harmful influence. Monetized exchange replaces the human economy (and logic) of gift giving, while it exploits, dominates and hides it. It does this by using the logic of linguistic virtualization to mediate the reversal of gift giving, transforming it into exchange.

Those who want to create new social forms should avoid money of any

kind in the long term because replaying the linguistic virtualization process on the plane of material provisioning, halting the free flow of goods
to needs, feeds back negatively into our psychology. Presently, monetized
exchange is expressed in the ideology of *homo economicus*, while gift giving appears to be only sacrificial, a vulnerability to plunder. As feminists
and economic activists, one conclusion we must draw is that we should oppose the economy of the market and all its permutations and developments
instead of 'empowering' women and gift-giving men to assimilate into it.[38]

In the nineteenth century, many people wanted to improve the lives of
the slaves, give them better food, clothing and houses. On the other hand,
there were the abolitionists who wanted to eliminate the institution of slavery (Richard Wolf). We need to think like the abolitionists about our patriarchal capitalist institutions, including money and the market.

The attack of Western culture on indigenous peoples has been ferocious
but some of these societies have survived and continue to function according to maternal egalitarian communicative gift processes (Goettner-Abendroth 2012). They have still not accepted the incarnation of the virtualization process and the replacement of giving by exchange. Although they
have often been deprived of the abundance that would have been passed
down to them by their tribal ancestors, they continue to provide living
models of gift communities beyond the market for the people of all nation-
alities who are now searching for alternatives to patriarchy and capitalism.
They demonstrate that it is possible.

6.7 Extra-somatic tokens of ideas

When money was invented, this one to many externalized and standardized exemplar of value began to validate the abstraction and generalization of the exchange process. Long before the first coinage of money in
Lydia around 600 BC however, other kinds of tokens had appeared. Some
very interesting work from archaeology provides an illuminating point of
comparison for money and language. Denise Schmandt-Besserat (1992)
discovered the importance of the numerous small clay tokens that were
produced in the Middle East from 8000 to 3000 B.C.:

---

38   Short term, women do need to survive and thrive, and it does seem that women
      on the 'inside' of capitalism do make changes. However, we need to make sure
      that reform in this sense facilitates total radical social change in the long run
      rather than short-circuiting it.

> Tokens were counters used to keep track of goods with each token form standing for one specific unit of a commodity.... It is now well established that, in the fourth millennium BC, the tokens were an accounting device used by the Mesopotamian temple administration to record entries or expenditures of goods offered by worshippers during monthly religious festivals. Presumably, their function was similar in prehistory, when they served to collect and administer communal goods and, as such, were the backbone of a redistribution economy. (Schmandt-Besserat 1992: 170-83)

So it seems that at first the tokens were ways of keeping track of items that were given and received, and that particularly as 'dues to the collectivity', required contributions to the temple (not-exactly-gifts and IOU's). Later as temple tributes and then commerce increased, they became a means of accounting in trade. There was 'an entire repertory of interrelated types of tokens, each with a corresponding discrete meaning. The tokens, therefore, represent the earliest non-verbal code, or sign system for transmitting economic information'. Nevertheless, Schmandt-Besserat does not draw a connection between the tokens and money (in fact, coined money developed much later, millennia after the tokens were no longer in use) but sees them as important in the development of writing in Mesopotamia around 3300 BC.[39] The tokens were part of an oral culture, and she compares them to spoken words, each of which has, in Saussure's terms, a *signifiant* and a *signifié*. Each token abstractly or figuratively represented one of a kind of product or animal and was given in its stead (almost, we might say, as if there were a different kind of money for each different kind of product and a token or 'coin' for each product of a kind).

According to Schmandt-Besserat, each token stood for one unit of a good: a vase of oil, a sheep, a large or small container of grain. There was no plurality or numerosity (so there was no one-to-many generalization, no 'general equivalent'). A number of items had to be represented by the same number of tokens. There were only '...noun concepts.

---

39 'The transition from counters to script occurred about 3300 BC when tokens, probably representing a debt, were stored in an envelope until payment. These envelopes in the shape of a hollow clay ball hid the tokens held inside. The accountants, therefore, impressed the tokens on the surface of the envelope before enclosing them, so that the shape and number of counters could be checked at all times without breaking the envelope ... Finally the three-dimensional tokens had been replaced by two-dimensional impressed signs, that conveyed the same meaning'. This would have introduced the one-to-many aspect as the same sign would have represented any or all tokens of that type. Writing introduced the one to many aspect that tokens did not have. Also the 'envelopes' are a lot like our category – containers: 'types' containing 'tokens'.

The system had no symbols for verbs, pronouns, articles or prepositions. Unlike spoken language, the token system made no use of syntax'.

Figure 16: Tokens identified by Schmandt-Besserat.

Much of what Schmandt-Besserat says about the tokens as extra-somatic instruments of abstraction, would hold for money also, and for similar reasons.

Even though money is one-to-many while the tokens were one-to-one, there are many similarities. Like the tokens, money has no syntax. It is a three dimensional exemplar of value, which can be increased or decreased quantitatively (as with the decibel level of the spoken word). Coins and bills are 'stackable', kept together in one place, representing a certain quantity of value. And material money is available for anyone's perception; it is not a private mental image of an exemplar.

Money, like the tokens, abstracts the 'data from the verbal context' and from 'body language'. Like the tokens its 'significance' never varies and it abstracts from 'subjectivity' (Schmandt-Besserat 1999: 25). This recalls Sohn-Rethel's (1978) idea of money as an abstract thing, a major element of the 'exchange abstraction', which is an abstraction on the reality plane, and which he saw as the basis of the concept of substance in Western Philosophy. The tokens as representatives of not-gifts: required tributes, dues or debts, would have been very early examples of instruments of the 'exchange abstraction'. Schmandt-Besserat sees the positive side: 'tokens prompted new cognitive skills to manipulate, scan, evaluate, scrutinize and analyze an account. This in turn, allowed new ways of abstracting data. Whereas words consist of immaterial sounds, the tokens were concrete, solid, tangible artifacts, which could be handled, arranged and rearranged at will' (Schmandt-Besserat 1999:25). Very much the same thing can be said for material money. The token system facilitated counting and abstracting the relative values of different items. Similarly for money.

The characteristic of money that it is a store of value is foreshadowed in the tokens, which had the important aspect of 'permanence' and could be kept for any length of time as evidence of a debt paid or to be paid for example. They could also be easily transported – another of the advantages that money also provides. 'The Neolithic accountant ... took an active part in decoding the visual information encoded in the counters. This necessitated the acquisition of new cognitive skills that capitalized upon the visualization and physical manipulation of data. In turn, these new techniques fostered further abstraction of the data according to such variables as type of goods, value and number' (*ibid.*).

I am citing this work at some length because the existence of these tokens in daily life for some 5000 years in the Middle East is intriguing to say the least, but also because of Schmandt-Besserat's claims about their influence on cognition.

The writing and the literacy to which the tokens eventually led have been credited with even more capacity for cognitive change and for similar reasons, as has writing with other origins like Chinese and Meso American writing. Two popular writers on the negative cognitive effects of writing in the 'West' are Schlain (1998) and D. Abram (1996). But it is also important to take into account Haarmann (1995) on writing in the prehistoric Danube region. The Danube script would have been contemporaneous with the tokens but prior to Mesopotamian hieroglyphics.

An interesting development in the nineteenth century was the initiative of Sequoyah, the Cherokee man who, on his own invented an alphabet of

86 characters for the Cherokee language. He had originally thought that he would need to make a symbol for every word (somewhat like ideograms) but finally invented an alphabet for syllables. 'He had also observed white people write things on paper, and he had seen books; and he knew that what was written down remained and was not forgotten. He had attempted, therefore, to fix certain marks for sounds, and thought that if he could make things fast on paper, it would be like catching a wild animal and taming it' (Foreman 1938: 28).

Perhaps writing was necessary for the development of money. That is, the conceptual one-to-many aspect of letters to phonemes or syllables of written to spoken words, or of an ideogram to what it represents had to be made externally explicit before the one to many re embodied exemplar, money could come about. Words, money and writing are much more general than the tokens. They are not just one to one.

The referents of the tokens were probably not giveable gifts though they were not yet commodities. They were tithes, debts owed to the community or to the ruler or to the temple.

If the tokens, and writing had such an important influence on cognition, how much more influence may all-pervasive exchange for money be presumed to have? Moreover, what is the cognitive effect of the electronic dematerialization of money now? its reabsorption into language and the mind?[40] Tokens were equivalents but they were not general. Money is a general object, the 'general equivalent'.

6.8 The structure of Marx's general equivalent

Long ago, I realized something that over the years I have found to be very important. Money is the 'offspring' of language. By looking at it this way, we can correct for the differences and look back at language and concept formation (or 'categorization') in the light of what they have 'become' in a different environment. While philosophers generally believe that we cannot get outside of language to look at it, that there is no external 'Archimedes point', this view of money as a 'descendent' of language can overcome that difficulty to some extent. We take the point of view of the progenitor to compare it to the offspring and vice-versa. Even though

---

40   We might also see spoken words as extra-somatic perceptual/conceptual tokens made of sound. And writen words as tokens made of graphemes. And even pointing is an external embodied icon of deixis that is available for all to see and perform.

we are using language to do it, we can investigate money and look back at language from that point of view. Money holds up a mirror to the mind, though it also distorts and reverses the image – as indeed a mirror does. We can use this constructed 'outside-inside' vantage point to understand the function of language in categorization. That is, we can see how money also categorizes, and then look back at language from money to see if indeed language categorizes that way. Many of the differences we have to keep in mind and correct for in this process have to do with the function of money in mediating private property, while language, as we have been saying, mediates gift giving and the perceptual and conceptual commons, the motherworld, 'having to give'.

In order to begin this discussion, let's look very briefly at Marx's characterization of money as the general equivalent.[41]

Marx begins *Capital* (1996 [1867]: 26ff) by discussing how it is that commodities can be exchanged for money. He starts by putting products in an equation of value with each other and goes on to show how the two sides of the equation, a relative and an equivalent side, are equated/related. The products in exchange on the relative side are called 'commodities' while the one commodity that is used in a stable way to occupy the equivalent side is what we call 'money'. The very fact of being exchanged on the market divides the commodity's value into use value (whatever the product is used for), and exchange value (the amount it is worth in exchange). There is a process of development of 'the money form' in which the equivalent generalizes. Products are not exchanged for each other directly but all are exchanged for money or vice-versa, money is exchanged for each of them. So there is not an endless series of products, such as a coat = a quantity of linen = a quantity of whiskey = a number of pairs of shoes, etc. Rather there is a series of equations in which a quantity of coats = a quantity of money, a quantity of linen = a quantity of money, a quantity of whiskey = a quantity of money, etc. In this way, the item in the equivalent position generalizes, and Marx calls it the 'general equivalent'. He describes several steps in this generalization, from the 'relative form of value' to the 'expanded relative form' to the 'particular equivalent form' to the total or expanded, 'general equivalent' form. These are all derived from or are elaborations of the simple equation between two items: x commodity A = y commodity B.

---

41   On the other hand, perhaps this look at the language-'parent' can give us a confirmation of the nature of the money-'child'. That is, perhaps it can help confirm Marx's characterization of money. Both language and money are methods of communication, however intensely distorted and distorting communication with money may be.

Anything that repeatedly and exclusively occupies the equivalent position in the equation could be the general equivalent because it would become general. Different kinds of things have occupied that position historically, like shells or cattle in early societies but, as we mentioned above, in about 650 BC in the West, metal coins issued by states began to be used for the purpose.[42] The use of one type of three-dimensional object repeatedly in the equivalent position, with a polarity between itself and all other commodities (Marx says like the polarity between the Pope and all Catholics), allowed it to express or represent the value of each of the items in turn in exchange, and thus to become itself constant and general.

I believe that Marx's explanation shows how the exchange of commodities for money is actually a reenactment *in res* of the way we form concepts, the way we generalize using an exemplar and words. The schema of exchange, as I have been saying, is the schema of virtualization materialized and 'rotated' onto the 'horizontal' plane. When one item repeatedly occupies the equivalent (the 'virtual') position with respect to many in the relative (the 'real') position, it becomes general. We will try to show that money is actually the 'exosomatic' incarnation or externalization of the one-to-many process of generalization in the formation of concepts.[43] In fact, it was this that Marx was describing, long before the idea of culture as 'exosomatic memory' or tools as 'exosomatic organs' became popular (first broached by Lotka in 1925) and long before the hypothesis of the 'extended mind' was made by Clark and Chalmers (1998). It seems clear to me that, apart from everything else one may say about money, this replay of the generalization process extra-somatically should be a cause for alarm. Moreover, this is not just any generalization but the generalization of value itself![44]

I just mentioned Alfred Sohn-Rethel, who studied Marx's analysis of the commodity and money in-depth, and developed the idea of the exchange abstraction and its influence on abstraction in philosophy (1978). His friend George Thompson (1972) wrote about money as the

---

42 These have had an evolution from (electrum) to copper, to silver and gold to the modern replacement of metal by paper money and finally now electronic bank money.

43 I am talking about the classial concept here, with an exemplar, not the graded or radial category with a prototype. Later, we will see how these two kinds of possible concept structures are related.

44 The importance of sex for everyone has allowed it to be used to manipulate us through advertising. Concept formation is even more basic than sex, but we do not recognize it because of the different dimensions and different emotional investment or lack of it.

model for the Parmenidean One.[45] Recently, Richard Seaford (2004) has traced the influence of money on philosophy in ancient Greece in more detail (and see Meikle (1995) on Aristotle and exchange). Gift economy supporter Charles Eisenstein (2011) references Seaford's work in his book, *Sacred Economics*.

Perhaps the most interesting of the authors investigating the relation between money and ideas is Jean-Joseph Goux (1990 [1978]), who discussed the various forms of one-to-many general equivalent structures such as the Father, the King, and the Phallus. I found his work very useful in constructing a theory of patriarchy (Vaughan 1997). The difference between Goux's theory and mine is that I have a different starting point. I put (classical) concept formation first and looked at the different general equivalent structures, including money, as variations on that cognitive structure.[46] I used an experiment by Vygotsky on concepts that showed the way children developed one-to-many conceptual reasoning through successive stages, and seemed to demonstrate the similarity of concept formation to Marx's description of the formation of the general equivalent (Vaughan 1981). If this similarity is real, the relation of money to commodities writes large on the material plane a mental process of abstraction.

As Sohn-Rethel proposed, it deeply influences philosophy. Moreover it creates a model on the external that continually broadcasts itself back into the recesses of our private minds, and into the ways we are conceiving of consciousness and of our own thought processes. The ancient Lydians, materialized part of their linguistic cognitive process as money in order to 'represent' (virtualize) value and give while not-giving. However, patriarchal structures were already in act. Croesus, who is said to have invented money, already as a king, embodied a one-to many patriarchal form (as did the warring chieftains referenced by Seaford (2004: 75) who parcelled out the meat of rituals and the victory feasts on skewers that may have been the metallic forerunners of coins. That is, money in-

---

45 'The Parmenidean One, together with the later idea of "substance", may therefore be described as a reflex or projection of the substance of exchange value... the money form of value is a factor of cardinal importance for the whole history of philosophy' (1972: 301).

46 The development of prototype theory has offered an alternative to the 'classical' concept form, which would allow for thinking to occur without it. We will be discussing Plato's and Aristotle's Third Man Paradox and Russell's one-over-many 'regress' below. Recent writers about one-to-many structures like Virno (2004) and Negri and Hardt (2000) speak of 'multitudes' though they do not recognize the one-to-many patriarchal structures in the families and in the individuals who make up the multitudes.

carnated or embodied a cognitive form that had already been embodied in male dominant social structures. Whatever the historical origins of Western patriarchy this second incarnation could only solidify the power of the one-to-many patriarchal-and-monetary form at the expense of more egalitarian matriarchal ways of living.

Surely there were ways that cognition already worked before money. I believe these can be found in mothering-being mothered and its legacy in the transitive structures of language.

As I have been saying, cognitive psychology recognizes both the 'classical' exemplar model and the 'prototype' model for concepts. Recently, other types of models have also been used such as the conceptual blending model (Fauconier and Turner 2002), the construction model (Goldberg 1995), the competition model (Bates and MacWhinney 1989) and statistical sampling (Gopnik 2010) as I mentioned. The areas they address are all somewhat different from the structures addressed by first two models.

Vygotsky (1962 [1934]) thought that what he called the 'scientific concept', the exemplar-to-many classical concept model, which was learned by children in school, was the culmination of a development of which 'complexes', which we can identify with the family resemblance and prototype model, were an earlier stage. However, perhaps we should see the scientific or classical concept as a way of organizing thought that developed under the influence of money and patriarchy. To Vygotsky, the 'scientific' abstraction seems to be progress, but it is appropriate for the formation and mediation of mutually exclusive abstract categories and leaves behind the more inclusive prototype model. However, abstract categories are relational, not static containers for Vygotsky. They are composed of a consistent relation between the many and the one, which implies a common relation among the many as well. These positive relational configurations are understood in contrast with relations to other categories which they are not, and which are represented by other words (with one-to-many relations) within a given linguistic totality.

Both money as general equivalent and the classical or 'scientific' concept are formed by creating a 'polar' relation between one item and all the others. For Marx, this is the 'excluded commodity' gold, and in Vygotsky's experiment, it is one named item of a kind that is held constant as the exemplar. If monetized exchange is an externalization of this abstract way of forming concepts, it is potentially broadcasting this aspect of the way we think back to us from beyond the mind. This would explain to some extent the influence of money on our behavior, our desires, our philosophy and other aspects of our thinking, but it is dangerous for us also because we don't usually know that it is motivating us. Like an addictive substance, the General Equivalent spreads its toxic monolithic form into our individual psychology as well, where the 'one' can become the dominant 'I' with the many related to it (so that we internally no longer appear to be multifaceted 'polyphonic' givers and receivers or the linguistically validated subjects of gift initiatives but are driven to be the ones in control). This concept form riddles society with patriarchal power structures. J. J. Goux (1990 [1978])explains these structures in a Lacanian sense as phallic general equivalents but here we see them as different one-to-many classical concept forms proliferating from or emphasized by money, which is phallic and conceptual and as means of exchange, cancels maternal gift-giving.

Goux called his book *Symbolic Economies*, and many of the different structures he proposes are not actually economies except in a symbolic or figurative sense, as in 'libidinal economy'. My own project is to uncover the conceptual structure that underlies all of them, which then also can be found in the originally 'non-economic' area of language. My contention is that the monetary general equivalent is the material 'incarnated word'[47] and the process of monetized exchange is an extra-somatic 'real abstraction', a replay of this cognitive-communicative concept process on the material plane. Goux's general equivalent structures can be seen as proliferations in many fields of the one-to-many concept form validated by the 'real abstraction', in which money is the exemplar of value. In fact, what his work is describing is the structure of capitalist patriarchy. It is necessary to put the monetary general equivalent concept form at the center, however, in order to understand it as the incarnation of a mental process with the many repercussions that Goux identified.

In this way, we can understand how patriarchy and monetized exchange support each other and infect our minds, our reason and emotion, our thinking and our thinking about thinking.

Capitalist patriarchy has attempted to erase the practice and the knowledge of gift-giving in the context of indigenous peoples, in mothering and childhood and in capitalist society at large. Nevertheless, gift-giving forms the ground upon which the negative figure of exchange emerges, and I am pencilling, or shading it back in.

If the 'classical' concept form is influenced by its embodiment in money and vice-versa, what is the alternative for philosophy – and for life? I believe it is possible that graded categories with prototypes are sufficient for

---

47   The structure of money broadcasts itself into religious thinking as well.

reasoning, and for reasoning about reasoning, especially if they are liberated from their similarity to private property (where each 'one' owner has a binding relation to h:er many different kinds of property, not of identity – though the property makes up the owner's 'substance'- but of control).[48] The different kinds of giving and receiving relations that the motherer prototype creates with the various members of families and communities, constitute a web in which the motherer is source but not an abstract general equivalent and not dominant. S:he is related to all the others according to many different perspectives, polyphonic voices, ways and positions as they are to h:er and to each other. H:er relationality as prototype is quite different from the monological patriarchal voice of authority, the 'one' voice that silences and controls the many others.[49] The child's self that develops in relation with h:er is not the Cartesian monological 'I' but a multifaceted (material and) vocal giver and receiver.

This monetary exosomatic concept process functions as a kind of magnet for us, distorting our beliefs and desires. Aspects of the process, specifically the general equivalent position, become invested with other psychosocial aspects like phallic dominance, greed for money, political ambition, corporate and national hegemonic aims, reinfecting our thinking over and over with one-to-many hierarchy and validating it. The classical concept is perhaps only a more streamlined (or perhaps a more rudimentary) form of the graded category. Nevertheless, as an externalization of this concept process monetized exchange has a dangerous potential for providing the template for many of our most negative motivations. I will continue to discuss these aspects extensively below.

6.9 General equivalent addiction

Both the material plane substitution of the schema of the gift by the schema of virtualization/exchange and the substitution of gifts by commodities and money burden and bias our thinking. We need to understand them so that we can not only demonetize our economies and our conscious-

---

48   Although Vygotsky saw complexes as an early stage of development, Wittgenstein described the family resemblance concept, which was similar to Vygotsky's complexes (and to the graded category), as the basic concept structure for adult thinking in language as well.

49   Is this one reason why 'male' monological modes of speaking prevail over 'female' multiplicity and inclusiveness; the voice of money prevails over the voices of gifts? Is this why women are not heard while men are?

nesses but liberate ourselves and humanity from exchange and the market altogether. It is not enough to say that money stimulates greed and it is good to live without it. We have to understand the complex reasons why.

We need to understand the powerful influence that the existence of the 'extra-somatic', 'externalized' concept process can have on our ongoing 'internal' conceptual processes and on our understanding of them. Having externalized part of our concept process into money, now we are internalizing money, feeding its form into our thinking and into our idea of thinking, poisoning ourselves with it, addicting ourselves to it and to the one-to-many ego position that success in capitalism can provide. This a structural addiction: to a concept structure and an ego structure and it is not the same as addiction to accumulation except in the sense that having more gives us greater access to assuming the 'one' position.

This linguistic/virtual character of monetized exchange makes it easily feed back into our thinking, permeating our communication and our interpersonal relations. Exchange is the linguistic virtualization schema, materially and 'horizontally' applied, in a way that contradicts gift-giving. The virtualization schema is rebroadcasted from the external economy back into our minds and we use it as the interpretative key for everything (and we call it 'reason'!). Abstract inclusion/exclusion, categorization, identity and difference, all of which are aspects of exchange for money, become moments of the ideological social nexus, the commonplace interactive matrix. In this framework, transitivity is mysterious. Gift-giving is eliminated or relegated to an independent moral sphere as an individual virtue or ethical penchant, or it is seen as weakness, servility.

The challenge to material money that virtual money on the Internet poses, is that it makes its conceptual and 'immaterial' aspect more evident. This allows us to perceive the conceptual aspects more clearly in a defetishized way.

As I have been saying, the linguistic virtualization schema involves the giving of one kind of gift for another (word for world) while the enactment of the gift schema actually gives the virtual, perceptual and conceptual gifts at various levels, satisfying the receiver's cognitive and communicative needs. There would be no purpose in linguistic virtualization without gift giving, and there would not be an abundant repertory of giveable word-gifts without virtualization in sound or writing. It is because virtual verbal items can be given and received that they can be relevant and that they can be used in sentences to pass on the gifts of the relevant perceptions, conceptions and ideas to which they 're-fer' (to which they bring us again).

The *raison d'etre* of the market is just the opposite. The virtualization of commodities into money puts a general item in the place of a particular one and both are given in order not to be given. Thus, the kind of communication that follows upon monetized exchange is not gift-giving but a variation on the virtualization schema, which has to do with augmenting or diminishing the relevance of the virtualized item ... its value. This is registered in the polyemphatic 'voices' of the commodities, which all cry out, expressing themselves in the one word, money, with its scalar decibels.

If Western culture has been negatively influenced and distorted by the exosomatic incarnation of the concept process in money-and-commodities, it is very important for us to know this distortion is happening so we can do something about it. However, as part of our understanding, we need to identify the mental processes that are being distorted, and learn how they might be restored. As happens with research into substance abuse, it is necessary to look at the addiction to the general equivalent with the goal of finding the non-addictive position.The importance of giving and receiving for cognition and communication needs to be clarified as the baseline from which exchange is a deviation.[50]

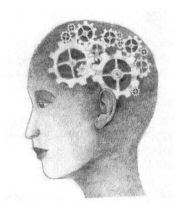

Figure 17: We think in concepts using words.

---

50   Susan Carey, following Quine (1960), says that our conceptualization is done by
      bootstrapping. The cover of her recent book, *The Origin of Concepts*, provides an
      image of the issue. However, the ground beneath our feet is always the gift-giving
      that we have learned not to see, or we might think of the ground as a glass floor.

Figure 18: There is a collective projection of
the one-to-many concept form into money.

Figure 19: There is a collective projection of the externalized
money concept back into the individuals' minds.

Then the externalized money-word-concept form feeds back again into
hierarchies as transfer of one-to-many onto individual men/heroes/divas/
shooters (and other top positions: judges, government officials, CEOs, best
in show, internal dominant egos).

Figure 20. Hierarchy, the one to many classical concept form,
influenced by money and incarnated in patriarchy.

*6.10 Using the general equivalent structure to understand language and
vice versa*

In spite of the negative aspects of money, investigating the development
of concepts, and comparing money, concepts and language, can help us understand how abstract concepts can develop from graded concepts through
the development of the polarity of the exemplar. The exosomatic concept
process provides an example of some of the workings of the mind outside
the mind, available to the view of all. In this it has some of the advantages of contemporary brain research, which also gives us knowledge of the
workings of the mind outside the mind. Both are appeals to the movements
of matter to corroborate mental events. One is social, extra-individual,
while the other is buried in the brains of every individual.

Money, the exemplar of value, also functions as a sorting device, a tau-
tological test[51]: if you can exchange a product for money, the product is
exchangeable, and as such at least for the moment, it is not a gift. This
test does not take into account the satisfaction of the need of the other
(except for the common need of everyone to exchange, which overrides

---

51   Like saying, 'If she is not a witch she will float'.

all the other needs, framing them as 'effective demand'). Thus, the market imposes upon us one giant material category of commodities sorted by using one giant all-knowing exemplar/word, money. The market itself functions as a rigid 'classical' category in which the confrontation with the money-exemplar is used to exclude irrelevant characteristics (creating an internal polarity in its members between relevant and irrelevant, valuable and valueless)[52]. Gifts are not relevant as such to this category for they are by definition not exchanged. This is one reason they are not seen, even if they continue to be given[53] as free labor and indeed as I have been saying, the promise of receiving free gifts actually motivates capitalism (and probably patriarchy as well). This magician's trick is aided conceptually and linguistically by considering unilateral gift-giving 'aneconomic', or an 'externality', as well as by renaming the gifts 'profit' and by separating the public and private, the market and the domestic 'spheres'.

As I was just saying, money has both the character of the exemplar and of the word. It functions in the role of the exemplar of a classical category to which all its members are compared and found similar with the consequence that they are then found similar to each other as well. At the same time, money functions in the role of the word, the virtual gift, which can be given for things as their name, in this case their quantitative name. Looking back and forth from language proper to money as a one-word-and-exemplar 'language' allows us to compare the two and to understand each with the help of the other. That is, correcting for their albeit considerable differences, money can be understood by comparing it to language and language can be understood by comparing it to money.

For example, without the reference to the exosomatic concept, discussions of the classical concept type often make use of examples like 'A triangle is a geometric figure with three sides' and 'A bachelor is an unmarried man' to give perfect definitions where the 'intension coincides with the extension'. All A is B and vice-versa. These examples seem to show that the name 'triangle' is simply applied or given to the category-container |triangle|,[54] which includes all of its members. Examples are brought

---

52   The same binary process opposing relevant to irrelevant qualities was evident in Vygotsky's (1962) experiment.

53   Many gifts are given at a higher logical level, not to the individual other exchanger but to the market itself. These are material gifts like housework including the free work of shopping, both necessary for the market. Giving these gifts gives value, credence and respect ... to the market.

54   These examples bring with them a heritage of sexism. The triangle as a geometric figure has backgrounded the importance of the female pubic triangle in pre-

only to 'illustrate' the categories, which have common qualities or 'essences' and are understood as containers. These categories are static while Marx gave a description of the development of the general equivalent as dynamic, and Vygotsky gave an account of dynamic processes in which mental concepts develop and change at different stages, using a polar exemplar and the 'guidance' of the word. In the next sections, I will discuss how the word-gift functions as a verbal exemplar and implies the similarity of members of a kind to each other just as would a non-verbal exemplar placed in a position of comparison like the general equivalent. In fact, if we are not sure what a word means we can imagine an exemplar of the category or ask someone to describe one.

6.11 Money – the materialized word

In the virtualization of world-gifts by word-gifts, we change planes, and we do the same when we give money in the place of commodities. Money forms a social area that runs alongside commodities while language forms a virtual gift level that accompanies us in relation to each other and the motherworld. Money takes the place of commodities, 'reflecting' their value in equations of value, and it is a structural part of the process of market exchange, which as a whole takes the place of gift-giving as our 'social nexus' or central mode of social interaction.

The mutually exclusive human relations created using money in exchange for private property are the opposite of the mutually inclusive relations created using language. With language, we give to and receive from everyone, creating common relations to the world. In exchange, we usually create our 'common' relation one-to-one, dyadically as in the mother-child relation, but it is common only in being mutually exclusive. Both parties have the explicit right not to share the product or the money with each other or anyone else.The way money functions is very similar to the way the schema of linguistic virtualization functions except that money – *aliquid* – actually takes the place of or stands for the commodity – *aliquo* – in a binary, mutually exclusive way.

Money functions as a one-word material language, and it is both a material and a virtual exemplar of value. It has only one gift to re-give (represent): the contradictory gift of the not-gift, the exchange value of the

---

historic art and life, and the gendered opposite of 'bachelor', also backgrounded, is the negatively charged 'old maid' or 'spinster'.

commodity, and it is itself continually given to take the commodity's place. Money is stuck at a meta-level because the kind of 'gift' it re-presents is so contradictory. It is also one word-not-word and it can change and combine only in quantity – decibel level – to become more or less relevant!

The economic equation of value contains a polarity between the relative and the equivalent position and money is always in the equivalent position.[55] Similarly for language, words are also always in the equivalent position. There is a unidirectional virtualizing path-to-goal from things to words. We start with things (and experiences and ideas) for which we give the words to the other to make them 'for h:er'. We satisfy the other's need for a connection to us in that regard. The construction of linguistic gifts is facilitated by the asymmetry of world-to-words, relatives to equivalents.

However, when with money and with writing, counterparts of vocal language were placed in the non-verbal world, the asymmetry between world-gifts as relative and word-gifts as equivalents was obscured. Still as derivatives of language, even written words (given for sounds) and ideograms (given for ideas) and money (given for commodities) remain in the equivalent position while the things for which they are given are relative to them. Moreover, as I mentioned above, the fact that we can relate words to other words as relatives to equivalents in the definition: "A cat"(equivalent) is "a domestic animal with a long tail and whiskers" (relative), is so commonplace that it hides the unidirectionality as well and we hardly notice it. On the other hand, positions of patriarchal power (the king, the general) do function as general equivalents in the world.[56] The embodiment of the money-word is just the permanent assumption by gold (or other money material) of the equivalent position on the material plane.

Money as general equivalent is monolithic (though it has many orderly 'internal' parts) and it is the measure of exchange value. Its instances are given to each other (merged) only quantitatively in addition and subtraction representing quantities of the value – the common quality of not-gifts – increasing or decreasing in relevance, like economic decibels.[57]

---

55 If monetized exchange is the embodiment of the linguistically mediated concept-forming process, looking back at language (the ancestor) from the point of view of money (the descendent) we can see more clearly what the ancestor is. That is we can notice this characteristic of language, that it remains equivalent (except in a case in which a metalanguage is being used).

56 They are installed with Austin's performative speech (and symbolic) acts, 'I crown you king'.

57 But we have no collective tympanum even the highest decibels could shatter. The 'listener' cannot establish a common relation to the 'speaker', because s:he cannot

Exchange for money is like the virtualization schema in naming – but it does not name gifts. It names only commodities that are not-gifts like itself, valuable and exchangeable, while words do name things that are gifts like themselves, relevant and giveable virtually.

Exchange gives value to itself and to commodities and money through categorization and mirroring. It might seem to be a moment of economic dialogue but it is not dialogue, only economic naming, the kind of naming that one would use to satisfy the other's cognitive need as to what something 'is called'. This economic identity and its logic are put in the place of turntaking, giving/receiving dialogue. The communicative (community-making) need is not satisfied but deeply altered to produce a 'community' of mutually exclusive individuals. This contradictory community of exchangers competes with the community based on gift-giving and wins, because it successfully cancels the prototype of the abundant mother, together with the variously giveable abundant commons, the motherworld.

The word-and-exemplar-to-many concept pattern established by money and patriarchy seems almost to create a neuronal pathway for social domination. Thus, we have oligarchical dynasties like the Bushes whose family resemblances consist of money and power. It is as if by this use of money and patriarchy (and even intensified by the dematerialization of money), we were creating a social slot or series of slots for dominant families to fill. Already the one percent, the CEO's have incarnated the one position. In the US and elsewhere, we seem to be readying ourselves for domination by 'first' families, hereditary dynasties, of manies made up of ones-over-manies.

Though these families and these ones do have a lot of power and manipulate public life, they are really an expression of the manipulation being wrought on our social consciousnesses by the flow of intentionality or energy or motivation along deeply scored tracks of incarnated concept patterns. These tracks unconsciously determine the powerful also, as well as motivate them. Until we identify the patterns and deal with them, they will keep on surreptitiously programming races, religions and nations to wage wars of domination, corporations to form monopolies and young men to become 'ones', shooters of many.

The monetary not-gift element is always in the equivalent – word – position to which the would-have-been world-gift element is relative. Thus, it incarnates – makes extra-somatic – not just the word but the whole world-gift-word-gift process in a gift canceling mode. Money is a mirror of the value of the relative item, but since it is itself a not-gift, it does not reflect

---

"hear" or remember – keep – the money 'word': 'speaking' it, s:he loses it.

gifts. The gift aspect of the commodity does not come forward. It is not relevant (as, instead, it would have been in language). There is no gift-giving 'like me' bridge in the buyer-seller dyad but only a 'like me' mutual opposition and exclusion. In fact, one might say that the buyer-seller dyad is an adult replay of the mother-child dyad with gift-giving eliminated.[58] Then, as a mirror of value reuseable by others, money is given again to reflect the not-gift character of the next commodity. Words are given and given again as gifts and they re-enact gifting as they are given to each other in syntax. Money is given in exchange as a not-gift and repeats or reflects the relevance of not-gifts, when given in again exchange.

Money reflects the paradoxical 'common property' of exchange value, as the common quality of exchangeable private property, which each owner has but which is not usually given and received. On the other hand, common gift property requires both having to give, and actually giving and receiving.

In the world without gifts that money manages, we see everything as neuter and neutral, ungendered and abstract. Words seem to have no connection with the world. We see them in the image of money as giftless signs traveling along pathways and trajectories of, to and together with other signs, creating infinite semiotic chains. Neuter science operates on a seemingly neuter (mother-denying) and neutral (gift-denying, non-benefactive) world. Everything is relevant to money and money 'making'. The social movements that oppose this mentality call on moral values, but they still do not see the central importance of the values of the mothering economy and of the motherworld. Nor do they see how the seemingly neutral sciences, including linguistics, psychology, economics and even physics (Mirowsky 1989) by their neutrality constitute apologies for the market and back up the elimination of the motherer and the gift. Exchange imposes one kind of value – exchange value – and distorts (or hides or just does not compute) any other kind of value. Even outside the exchange transaction, the focus on money socially discredits all kinds of gifts and gift values, while capturing as many of them as possible for exchange purposes.

This is the case even if money itself can be given as a gift in philanthropy or extracted by forcing others to over-work or over-pay. In its rarified atmosphere, money shows that the particular aligned relations, not of direct

---

58 The baby is relative and the motherer is equivalent but they can take turns, and change places. S:he is an equivalent that gives while money is an equivalent that does not give (or grow, nor do we make it). We only add (give) other amounts of money to it.

giving/receiving in this case, but of joint attention, are very strong, even binding because we collectively concentrate our focus on this one thing (exchange value), and leave aside everything else. It is not an agreement of solidarity but a mutuality-in-antagonism that is imposed on us as our common ground every time we exchange. The market price seems to be the result and the mediator of the joint attention of everyone.

Perhaps it is just the constant repetition of this contradictory mutuality that eliminates the positive mutuality of the gift relation. We accept it because we do it all the time. Our capacity for selective attention allows us to concentrate our gifting within an inner circle while billions of other people starve.[59] Exchange is able to eliminate the gift and the consciousness of the gift because it is backwards co-muni-cation; because the money-word is only internally and not externally articulated: assembled and disassembled, it stands alone without 'slots and fillers' for other 'words' (even currency exchange with other national currencies is only another virtualization, another substitution). It stands alone because it stands as the judge of the quantity of the social relevance – the exchange value – of innumerable instances of not-giving and because in spite of this, money is the one thing that is constantly given and received (transferred). It is also the one concept exemplar that seems to stand on its own (though supported by myriad gifts), even if in equal and giftless exchange, either the buyer or the seller usually gives an unseen gift of profit to the other one.

While a commodity is not a gift, in the store, in the exchange abstraction (as Sohn-Rethel saw), it is semi-virtual, it cannot be used, but its perceptual qualities are emphatically given-to-view in the store window or picture (or television 'store window'), and forced on us in advertising and media so that we associate this perception with its sign, logo or name and price. Because of corporations' and their own need for money, advertisers 'give' us the perception and the name of the commodity again and again. They create a need for it by priming a lack, which we have to give them money to satisfy. They play the cognitive/communicative gift process backwards artificially creating the need and then calling for the money 'word', making us choose to come forward actively to give the money 'word', to buy the product.[60]

---

59   I say this not to 'guilt trip' anyone (guilt is part of the exchange paradigm, preparing to pay for a wrong done). Many people, myself included, are shaken by the enormity of the task of systemic change. In fact this book is an attempt to address the general problem. That is what we need to do, the gift we need to give: understand the system accurately enough to successfully change it.

60   They function like our internal self-motherers, bringing forward the perception, giving us its name ... but in order to *make* us 'choose' to buy it.

This weird material virtualization process of exchange for money influences everything, while it cancels and discredits giving. Giving is hidden and re-routed as profit; it is also partly integrated into exchange, where it appears as a moment of sales and gimmicks in the process of marketing (as in special deals and discounts). Selling and buying are the moments of material virtualization and de-virtualization of products, when their place is taken by money; all of the products have the same qualitative (but potentially different quantitative) 'name', their exchange value expressed in money as their price. All of them are specified as quantities of that virtual gift of the not-gift, providing them with an exchangeability, which replaces the giveability they do not (or must not) have as private property.

If a word is a virtual and, therefore, in a sense, a dematerialized gift, and money is a rematerialized word, money can also be re-dematerialized, having an existence that is doubly virtual. That is, it can become merely a fleeting electronic impulse, a sign on a bank's computer screen (a sign whose main relevant relation is, indeed, that it can be substituted by another sign as in infinite semiosis).

Exchange is the linguistic schema of virtualization, which has been re-embodied and appears to us to be primary,[61] taking the place of the gift schema in that regard as well. Exchange even seems to be embedded in our linguistic capacity itself. Because it is derived from linguistic virtualization, which, when we ignore giving, appears to be the origin of language, exchange is easily projected by researchers into early childhood, into preverbal mother-child relations, into protoconversations and full-fledged ones, and it is also mapped metaphorically onto language as the 'exchange' of words, information and ideas. As I have been saying, the blanket-use of the word 'exchange' instead of 'giving and receiving' hides the important distinction between the two; challenging it can sometimes be a relatively easy introduction into a discussion about their differences.

6.12 Commodity fetishism and the 'like me' bridge

Marx discussed the 'polar' positions in the equation of value in that one side is made equivalent, the other relative. However, language already provides this distinction because word-gifts are in the equivalent position with

---

61 Many experiments have been done with apes to see if they can exchange, perhaps supposing that if they can't, exchange may be the distinguishing feature of the human species.

regard to world-gifts as relative. The great variety of word-gifts, which
are also polysemic, in combination, can 'reflect' or virtually give again, an
almost infinite qualitative variety of world-gifts. In contrast, the equation
of value between commodities and money is an abstract mirroring in the
single respect of exchange value. In this, it is unlike the all-round interactive identification that happens in the mother-child 'like me' relation.

One result of the material virtualization process is the 'fetishism of
commodities' where the relations between things take the place of relations among people. But we should ask, just what relations do they take
the place of?

I believe these, too, are the 'like me' relations described by Meltzoff.
Infant psychology can illuminate something that Marx's metaphors were
getting at long ago. Where the child discovers h:er similarity with h:er
motherer (and, therefore, with other humans), the commodities 'discover'
their similarity with the general equivalent (and, therefore, with each other). This identity as 'quantities of exchange value' then allows commodities to enter into the altered communication, exchange, that takes the place
of maternal giving and receiving as the main social nexus.

As bearers of commodities participating in an adversarial non-nurturing
relation, the exchangers are abstractly similar to each other. They move
beyond their adversarial stance by asserting in an equation, the qualitative
and quantitative identity of their commodities and money, as quantities of
exchange value. These equations of identity of value are abstract and very
different from, but still recall, the interactive motherer-child identity.

I have been thinking about one of Marx's footnotes in the first chapter
of *Capital* for a long time. It has helped me to understand some important
issues about identity and subjectivity as influenced by exchange. Explaining the relation between commodities in the relative and the equivalent
positions, Marx says:

> In a sort of way, it is with man as with commodities. Since he comes into
> the world neither with a looking glass in his hand, nor as a Fichtian philoso-
> pher, to whom − I am I − is sufficient, man first sees and recognises himself
> in other men. Peter only establishes his own identity as a man by first com-
> paring himself with Paul as being of like kind. And thereby Paul, just as he
> stands in his Pauline personality, becomes to Peter the type of the genus
> homo. (1996 [1867], note 19: 54)

But Marx is wrong. 'Man' does come into the world bringing a looking-
glass, a mirror, with h:er. The interactive, intersubjective 'mirror' is the
motherer in h:er altercentric relation with the child. Each simulates the

other's experience with h:er mirror neurons and the child reflects the motherer with h:er 'like me' mapping. This is typically an altercentric mapping of nurturing in which each is relevant for the other (nurturing also each other's perceptions).

It is an aspect of fetishism that commodities seem to use the 'like me' interaction to find their commonality. Marx's prescient analogy differs from the infant-motherer scenario, in that it places two men – not mother and child – in the roles of the commodities (not-gifts), but it also differs because the relation is used for discovering the relative commodity's identity by finding an exemplar of its exchange value category in the body of another commodity (no maternal nurturing is taking place but only an identity is being affirmed through this categorization as a value). The equivalent commodity is the general equivalent, money, and the identity of the relative commodity is 'externalized' as a specific quantity of that money. This is its specific exchange value, which functions as the exemplar of the qualitative and quantitative category of which this relative commodity (as value) is a member (and proven to be a member by the exchange itself).

This kind of commodity categorization is understood long after 'like me' mapping and the transitive logic of giving and receiving in ontogenesis have developed children's subjectivity and language. In fact, the logic of equal exchange produces its own kind of human identity by imposing the quantitative virtualization-categorization of the commodity and the interaction of its facilitators over nurturing intersubjectivity, displacing it. Both the market and the imposition of patriarchal masculation on boy children deny the nurturing mother-child altercentric identification, which is at the origin of human interactive subjectivity and of gift value.

The relation between commodities and money takes over and replaces the altercentric 'like me' bridge. In the process of market exchange, money, the 'type of the genus' of value, becomes general, the general equivalent; it is the exemplar for the category. It does this in the very moment in which it cancels the gift or pushes it into the background. The general equivalent steps forward; it pops out; it shines on its own. Not only for products but even for humans, 'objective' evaluation by money takes the place of the mind-reading, caring motherer, the responsive other, the initiator of relevant gifts, who in the nurturing interaction gave value to and was known and imitated by the child (no longer do we say 'what are your needs?' but 'what are you worth?').

If the market is the totality of exchanges, it is also the totality of these fetishized 'like me' bridges. Market equilibrium is the compendium of them all under the rubric of the equation of supply and demand. The market logic contradicts the logic and the experience of the formation of altercentric intersubjectivity. Since we engage in exchange all the time on a daily basis, we are used to it and do not suspect that it is dangerous. We ignore it at our peril though. By following the market logic we are socializing ourselves, through the interactions of our products, to be asocial *homini economici*. Our selves as *homo donans et loquens* are in service to our selves as denizens and unwitting artifacts of monetized exchange. We nurture our selves and our products, not each other. We want our money to grow. Neoclassical economics uses this psychological development to explain the economy that produces it. The self-interest, reward and punishment, cost-benefit, scarcity-based model of the human is an integral part of the exchange paradigm. Behaviorist economists and psychologists generalize exchange and project it everywhere including into childhood so that giving and receiving are invisible or the individual is even seen as punished by having a need and rewarded by its satisfaction (or punished by giving – cost – and rewarded by receiving – benefit). The interpersonal relation is extraneous (but is a means to the reward or punishment).

Psychology, sociology and economics all make exchange a basic part of human nature. Finding exchange among animals, from pigeons and mice to monkeys seems to give it a primordial source (while at the same time the researchers disregard human mothering). Altercentrism is invisible or made to seem irrational. Rationality is narrowly defined to coincide with exchange (and with categorization as cost or benefit), leaving out the necessary rationality of gift-giving transitivity. The invisibility of gift-giving in language abandons the field of explanation to cognates and corollaries of exchange. In society at large, some of these are: retaliation and vengeance, justice as payment for crime, the system of grading in academia and other hierarchies of judgments of individual worth, bureaucratic categorization, lying, advertising and propaganda, and all the various one-to-many structures and the laws that uphold all of these. In the case of the investigation of language, some of the cognates and corollaries of exchange are representation, definition, categorization, identity logic, quantificantion, computation and statistical sampling, etc. In both cases, the similarities are probably due to feedback from exchange for money, the exosomatic concept form. These corollaries may be illuminating and helpful within the social context of the market, but because they leave aside giving/receiving they are all at least partly dysfunctional or inaccurate. The influence of the feedback is different in the two cases, perhaps more direct and emotional at the level of society and more cerebral and detailed at the level of the study of language, where the topic, language, is part of the original source of the projection.

6.13 Sounds of language. Two exemplars

A number of philosophical problems have arisen in Western thinking due to the elimination of mothering from epistemology and to the over emphasis on patriarchy and exchange. I feel it is necessary for me to address a few of them at least briefly. They are: the relation between words and the world, the relation between type and token, and the issue of resemblance nominalism (Russell's regress).

In spite of its negative effects, if indeed exchange is the incarnated concept process and money is the rematerialized word, we can use this embodiment to better understand language and concepts. With the possibility of this intermediating perspective in mind we can revisit the philosophical problem of the relation of words to the world and of the world to words. As I have been saying, there is a relation between world gifts and word gifts *as* gifts. However there is also a second relation that money and exchange help to illuminate.

After seeing the parallel between Vygotsky's experiment on concept formation and Marx's development of the General Equivalent many years ago (Vaughan 1981), I have tried to think back and forth from money to concepts and language, which precede money in the history of the species and ontogenetically in the history of every life. I realized already back then that if money is the descendent of language and functions like a materialized single word, which is given to someone for a commodity-not-gift, we could turn this relation around and consider single words (except, perhaps, proper names and logical connectors) as, like money, general equivalents. Each word would thus have a one-to-many form like money. I could see this in Vygotsky's concept experiment, where he used both words and things according to what he called the 'method of double stimulation'. There, comparison with the exemplar implied the similarity of the members of a kind to each other, as 'guided' by the words that named them and in contrast with other objects that had different names.

However, I was worried that there might not be a real fit between the terms of this comparison between words and money. Several important differences disturbed the completion of the puzzle. Words are virtual gifts in the medium of sound while money is virtual in a non-acoustic material medium. This creates a perceptual and cognitive break between the two, and makes their similarity depend completely on unrecognized abstract patterns. Moreover, money is really one specific kind of thing while words are legion. Then, there is the question of perceived 'size'. Material money seems so macroscopic and evident; it is of long duration; it can be weighed and handled, while, in comparison, words, made of breath, seem tiny, fleeting and evanescent.[62] There was much to correct for in fitting the pieces of the puzzle together but I continued to try. In order to make them fit, I had to find a somewhat different view of language, which I did, following my hypothesis of money as an embodied 'word'. I realized that spoken (or written) words are material things, too[63] and that, unlike most other kinds of things, we have to learn not only to recognize them but to make (reproduce) them as well.

In fact, there is an exemplar[64] – to – many function with the sounds of a language just as there is with things. We cannot imitate most of the things we see but beginning in infancy at 3-6 months we can repeat ('da, da, da') and imitate sounds.[65] Our own and others' phonetic patterns are thus exemplars, which we unconsciously recognize and try to match (proof that we recognize them is that we imitate them.) Even as adults, we still hear variations and deviations when someone pronounces words in a way that is unusual for us. If we learn each word by comparison to a vocal exemplar (maintaining the sense of original model), and recognize non-verbal things in the same kind of way, there are two kinds of exemplars, one virtual and verbal, and the other non-virtual and non-verbal, to which we attend. One would be the first or most prominent instance of the phonetic patterns of a word to which some other sounds are compared and recognized as similar and instances of the same word, while still other sounds are compared and discarded as different. The other would be the first or most prominent instance of a kind of thing (to which other instances of that kind – and intances of other kinds – are compared). Even if the two levels are different because we can easily reproduce the word but not the thing, these two exemplars would be related to each other precisely in their one-to-many functional character. Word and thing would each have the (cognitive) 'polarity' Marx talks about regarding money as the General Equivalent.[66]

---

62 It might seem that the idea of words as general equivalents could not account for synonymy and polysemy but actually a number of different kinds of 'manies' can be related as many to a single virtual equivalent 'one' (for example, 'crane' can mean a bird, a kind of machine, or sticking one's neck out).

63 'Agitated layers of air', Marx says.

64 I will use the word 'exemplar' here for brevity but realize it can be taken as one end of a spectrum of which the other end is prototypicality, depending on what kind of concept form we are discussing.

65 There has been a large amount of work recently on infant phonetic and phonemic perception. See Kuhl et al (2008) and see the work of Tomatis (2004) on the fetus listening in the womb.

66 Like the positive and negative poles of a magnet, Marx says (1995 [1867]: 55).

When we speculate that 'words take the place of things' (*aliquid stat pro aliquo*), what we are getting at is that the exemplar of a word (related to other instances of the same word), takes the place of the exemplar of a thing (related to other instances of the same thing or kind of thing),[67] in virtue of its exemplarity. Each is the 'one' in a relation of one-to-many polarity.[68]

With practice, it becomes unnecessary for us even to imagine an exemplar of a kind of thing, because the word takes over the (polar) 'one' function of implying the similarity of the many members of the category to each other. In case of doubt about the meaning, we can always point to a material exemplar if there is one in the vicinity or imagine or describe one if there is not, but usually that is not necessary. The virtual exemplar, the word (which is also the momentary present 'one' exemplar of all the possible instances of that word), makes the connection among the members of a kind in place of the non-verbal perceptual exemplar. Similarly, with abstract ideas like justice or beauty; even if they dont have one exemplar, the word maintains the position of implier of their similarity.

Perhaps this exemplarity of the word is enhanced by the fact that the speaker usually maintains a consistent pronunciation of the word even if s:he can recognize it as the same word when others say it somewhat differently. We can also hear ourselves (and others) speak mentally. We can produce a mental sound image of the spoken or unspoken verbal exemplar.

In addition to this, there is the miraculous fact that the word is something that can be in many places at the same time. That is, in its many instances, it is one word. This is because other people use it the way we do, as the virtual exemplar (and virtual gift) for things of that kind. The particulars of their personal images and experiences of non-verbal things of that kind may be quite different from ours, but for them, as for us, the word (name) maintains a relation of similarity of these images and experiences of things to each other. People don't usually need a material exemplar or its image anyway except in language learning or occasionally for jogging the memory. The word, as a particular combination of phonemes, is the virtual exemplar[69] of a kind of thing. Its phonetic simi-

---

67   Both something as an individual seen in its object permanence and something in its generality as related to others of the same kind.

68   Usually, the way we each say a word, in our own idiolect, is that word for us. It can also be taken by other adults or by children as the prototype or model they imitate.

69   The mutual exclusion among words in Saussure's *langue* and the mutual exclusion of private property make the word seem more like an exemplar than like an open ended prototype. The idea of *langue* as a system of mutual oppositions,

larity to other instances of the same word is usually even stronger than the similarity among the members of the kinds of things it represents. The word, therefore, helps to emphasize and maintain this similarity[70] (see below on the resemblances of resemblances).

Other people have the same one-to-many word-gift exemplar, which is similar to our own, even if they don't have the very same individual thing (world-gift) as exemplar of the category.[71] Their extra-linguistic exemplar only has to be one of the same kind but they – and we – usually don't even need an exemplar because the word serves that function instead. Perhaps you originally used your family dog as an exemplar of dogs for the concept and the word 'dog' and I used my family dog as my exemplar. But the word 'dog' as virtual or substitute exemplar implies the similarity of all dogs to the exemplar dog and to each other, so that now we don't even need to think of a material exemplar because we have been given the virtual (substitute) exemplar, the word. If we ever need to, we can think of an exemplar or even just of an example, of any item of that kind.[72] Usually though, the category, made up of all its members, remains in the background, and the word functions as the virtual exemplar.[73] I believe this is the 'mechanics' of how words work to categorize things: this exemplar quality of the word an-

---

shows how the strict one-to-many aspect of the word is held in place by the fact of its not being any other word.

70   Autistic writer Temple Grandin (Thinking in Pictures, 1995) says animals think in images – that is, I would say, pictures of exemplars. They do not have the word-exemplars to which to relate them.

71   'many people see a generalized generic church when they hear or read the word steeple. Their thought patterns move from a general concept to specific examples ... Unlike those of most people, my thoughts move from videolike, specific images to generalization and concepts. For example, my concept of dogs is inextricably linked to every dog I've ever known. It's as if I have a card catalogue of dogs I have seen, complete with pictures, which continually grows as I add more examples to my video library' (Grandin 2008: 11).

72   Looking at this in terms of the type-token distinction we can say that one token is placed in relation to all the others as equivalent (exemplar) and is substituted by the word as equivalent (virtual exemplar). In this way the type is constructed. Then the equivalent token goes to join the others, while the word remains as the vitual exemplar, implying the similarity of the members of the category to each other (the implication does not have to be as strict as in the classical category). The name comes from the fact that statistically enough people have seen the similarities to call a kind of thing by a name rather than using a description. What we call the type is thus just this constructed relation among the tokens in relation to the word.

73   Usually in philosophy the exemplar is hypostasized, and the set made into a container, disguising the construction process. Where is the type that is the exem-

chors it to an exemplar of the things it virtually represents (re-gives). Thus, the exemplar of things of that kind is not necessary for most purposes, so it 'evaporates' as a 'one' and drops back into the many.

Anything of a kind can be taken as an example or instance for the moment. It is an instance that would be related to the exemplar as similar if the exemplar were there, but the word is there in the place of the exemplar, so the instance is not an exemplar but only a member of that kind.[74] It is one-of-many instead of one-to-many. The 'ladder' of the reality plane exemplar has been kicked aside. And we only see the virtual exemplar sitting on the roof – usually linked with others that are sitting there, too, in a sentence, so no longer looking like an exemplar at all but rather like part of a whole jolly crew. The relation of things to each other within a category is maintained by their common relation to the word as their virtual exemplar (or prototype if it is a graded category), so there is not an endless signifying chain, as with Marx's extended relative form of value (as we saw above). From this perspective, contrary to the beliefs of postmodern and other contemporary philosophers and semioticians, language is not an endless self-referential system.

Words are related to the world in two ways, cognitively and communicatively: as the substitute exemplars (or prototypes) for at least once-perceived (or even once-imagined) world-gifts (i.e. exemplars of things) and as virtual gifts that can be given for them on the linguistic plane. We know which kind of thing a given word refers to because, at some time, we encountered an exemplar of that category and the word and the thing were connected in their exemplarity. We have learned which verbal exemplar takes the place of which non-verbal exemplar or prototype in the maintenance of that category. We have the verbal exemplar because it has been given to us by others and we use it to give again to others to satisfy their communicative and cognitive needs regarding that kind of thing. The virtual gift is an actual verbal exemplar. That is, a virtual exemplar is not "just" a kind of conceptual marker, which helps us to construct categories and keep them together. Rather, it also a gift that has a use in satisfying communicative needs and in creating human relations to the items for

---

plar of the concept 'type'? Haven't we just surreptitiously introduced the image of an abstract container?

74   This backgrounding effect is important for autism because autistic people do not do it. Their minds are crowded with detailed images. Unlike animals and autistic people 'a normal person's brain uses the detailed raw data of the world to form a generalized concept or schema, and that's what reaches consciousness!' (Grandin 2005: ch. 2). They filter out much more than autistic people and animals do.

which it stands and whose similarity to each other it implies. If words did not have the capacity to be gifts, we would have very little use for them, and they would therefore not even remain long in our minds as virtual exemplars. Thus, the social maternal use is at least as important as the internal conceptual use in the creation and function of language, and in everything that language makes possible.

When we think about the meaning(s) of the word, we explore the various aspects of the world-gifts for which that word is the virtual exemplar. The world-gifts in regard to which a common relation is constructed among people by means of the word-gift, are relevant. That is, they are preconsciously selected and, thus, 'pop out' from the background as sources of perceptual and conceptual gifts that humans can receive and pass on to others. These gifts are brought forward into attention by the use of the name, their word-gift/virtual exemplar in combination with other word-gifts in sentences and in discourse. Their relevance can itself be seen as a gift at another level, and it is part of what we call the 'meaning' of the word.

6.14a Type and token

We can look at the type/token distinction in terms of the exemplar to many relation.[75] Philosophers usually say there is a type, a category, or abstract object, a universal of which each token is an instantiation. But from our perspective here, a type is just a generalization from tokens, reified. It is the two-level, one-to-many relation with the non-verbal exemplar elided. The type/token gamut in this perspective would be simply the foregrounding of a binary polarity, a relation between an exemplar and the many-of-a-kind after the exemplar has already subsided into the many, due to the presence of the word as substitute exemplar. It is a process involving the word as exemplar and the thing as exemplar, both of which, however, are suspended or ignored for the moment. We do not think of a process of generalization in act but hypostatize the result as a universal, an abstract category, making it static and timeless.

When we are talking about a particular thing, we take it as one of many: 'that cat chases mice'. We do not need an exemplar-to-many relation to identify the type: cats, because we already have it, both for the particular (the token), that cat, and for the kind (the type): cats. The word 'cat' takes the place of any exemplar cat to which all individual 'token' cats could be

---

75   See discussion of Marx's footnote on the king and his subjects p. 296 below.

related, but which is now not necessary, since speaker and listener have already established that relation (between them to something) using the word 'cat' as verbal exemplar.

The word 'cat' functions both in referring to cats in general, the 'type' and in referring to any member of the category, any 'token' cat. It is therefore not really appropriate to talk about the 'type/token distinction'. Instead, it might be better to talk about the exemplar-to-token(s) generalization process or established relation. This is not the relation of containment inside a category container. Nor is it the encyclopedia of everything that can be said about cats. Rather it is an exemplar (and substitute exemplar) -to-many relational cognitive structure around which perceptions, memories, notions, ideas and knowledges about cats can cluster, a structure around which mental processes can be collected and focussed.

This structure appears to be a container because it 'receives' these gifts. A better image than the container is a 'growth medium' like a string in an experiment for growing crystals in a saturated solution. The connection is made from the combination of two perspectives: one-to-many and many-to-one, each of which implies the other (and includes also many one-to-ones).[76] If we ignore the structure, the 'type' can appear to be an abstract idea, a sort of ectoplasm, of which tokens are dollops, 'instantiations,' or a generalization by fiat without a process or structure. The container of private property is always available as an underlying catch-all metaphor.

Our ability to switch perspectives, one looking at many, many looking at one, gives us roles that can be identified in others and a 'span' between them that seems to be a type. This shifting of viewpoints is actually quite commonplace. We do it with gift or virtualization schemas and all their possible extensions and variations: 'the girl fed the cat' or MacWhinney's example 'the boy hit the ball that rolled into the gutter'. That is, we have lots of practice. Discussing the category 'cat' though, we shift perspectives between a word as 'one' and (having elided the world-gift exemplar) things as 'many,' creating a potential relational space to which we give the name 'type'.

The word-gift maintains the equivalent position, with regard to which the world-gifts are relative; it must do this in order to be the equivalent and substitute of the non-verbal exemplar.[77] Patriarchy has invested the equiva-

---

76   Like our 'Machiavellian' ability to recognize when others give to others establishing relations between or among them.

77   I believe that what as mothers we can still see is that the relation between item and exemplar is a variation on the 'like me' relation.

lent position with power over the many and the market has incarnated the exemplar/word as money in exchange for commodities. A mental process (of binary perspectives), the one-to-many, many-to-one relation forms not only categories but the structure of hierarchy and of monetary value in patriarchal capitalism. It is the structure of the concept (the way we take those things together) that has been incarnated in the money-commodities form and so broadcasts itself into society and back into our minds.

Money is a particularly good example of the problems with the type and token relation. As a whole, money is made of many tokens. Each denomination is a different quantity but then would each denomination be a type? In any case we seem to accept that all these strange, repetitive, numerically-identified objects are part of one 'type', money, which is one with regard to the many commodities that are exchanged for it.

In spite of all its 'manyness', money is one, very much like the monotheistic god. And there are those who worship it. Now also its diversification and dematerializations into computer notation, the bank issuance of credit-based money, credit cards, bank cards and money machines, cell phone price-scanners, etc. have splintered the monolithic money 'type' and made it a new kind of 'many,' leaving room for alternative currencies. What effect this strange new one-to-many is having on patriarchy is not yet clear. Money is not monolithic anymore (nor is masculinity). As important as money is for us, this diversification of mediums is like clear water. We hardly notice it, but it has the potential for eroding the monolith.

The privileging of the equivalent 'one' position: of words, of money and also of things in the world, taken as non-verbal exemplars, is an important element in classism, racism and sexism, and now in the oligarchy of the banks. If anyone was wondering whether the one-to-many cognitive structure is just an abstraction, the proliferation of these examples in social life should convince h:er of its reality. The 'elite' exemplar can be the father over the family, the monarch or president over h:er subjects or citizens, the CEO over h:er corporation, the corporation over the population, the banks over their debtors and depositors, the owning 'upper' class over the other classes, the white race over the other races, the Northern over the Southern hemisphere and the male over the female gender.[78] Goux's one-to-many general equivalent structures come forward again. Now divas and presidents, newscasters, talk show hosts and charismatic leaders attempt to personally incarnate this one-to-many relation and reap its benefits. Lone self-made 'exemplar' shooters give death to the many in schools, offices,

---

78   These are 'intersectionalities'.

movie theaters, military bases and youth camps, while sovereign nations assert their exemplarity by attacking and dominating as many other nations as possible. Technology comes to their aid so that one can kill many with single bombs, and one drone driver can abstractly from one country destroy many enemies and civilians at wedding parties in another with the use of one (index) finger upon a button.

One-to-many and many-to-one are the structures we find at every turn in our society. The way these structures fit together at every level and determine the whole is what we usually call 'the system'. They are embodied 'universal(s)'.

6.14b Resemblance nominalism: beneficial regress

Philosophers addressing the problem of universals and particulars have seen an infinite regress to which it leads as a negative circularity that renders probematical the relation of resemblance or common properties among things. Perhaps there is a positive aspect to the regress, however. In the light of our discussion of the General Equivalent, we can look at the specific type of Resemblance Nominalism that finds similarity through the resemblance of the many-to-one, what (with remarkable inconsistency) is called by some authors a 'paradigm', by others a 'paragon' or what still others and I myself call an 'exemplar':

> …what Resemblance Nominalism says is that what makes things have their properties is their resemblance to other things. There are two ways in which Resemblance Nominalism can be developed. One can say that resemblances to all white things make white things white. Or one can say that resemblances to certain privileged white things make white things white. These privileged things are called 'paradigms'. Paradigms are supposed to 'hold a class together' [Price 1953: 21-2). (Roderiguez-Pereyra 2004: 644)[79]

This relation is similar to the one-to-many general equivalent relation between money and commodities. That is, it is by comparison to the 'paradigm' or 'paragon' or 'exemplar', money, that the similarity of commodities as 'quantities of exchange value' comes forward (much as a perceptual gift 'comes forward' into focus) and is recognized. The many exchanges with this exemplar in the equivalent position, bring forward (make vis-

---

79   Of course what I would say is that it is not primarily similarity that gives things their properties but the fact they are gifts which things have to give. They are also rather similar, in graded ways.

ible or relevant) the 'common quality' of the exchange value of the commodities at the same time and in the same process that the generality of the equivalent is formed.

Both areas of resemblance nominalism, regarding words or regarding money, presumably run into this problem of infinite regress, which has been investigated by philosophers from Plato and Aristotle to Bertrand Russell and beyond:

> The regress is as follows. Consider the white things. According to the Resemblance Nominalist what makes them white is that they resemble each other, or that they resemble the white paradigms. But what makes their resemblances resemblances cannot be, according to the Resemblance Nominalist, that they all share a universal of resemblance but it must be that they resemble each other, or that they resemble a resemblance paradigm. So there are second order resemblances, namely the resemblances between resemblances between white things. But what makes these second order resemblances second order resemblances cannot be sharing a universal but it must be that they resemble each other, or that they resemble a second order resemblance paradigm. So there are third order resemblances, and so on. The regress arises because each level of the regress is a product of the application of the Resemblance Nominalist account to the preceding level. The regress is said to be vicious because it prevents Resemblance Nominalism from completing its account of what makes white things white in terms of resemblances. (Rodriguez-Pereyra 2004: 645)

Because money is a rematerialized word used to materially name the value of commodities and take their place in exchange again and again as equivalent in the equation of value, it unites the character of word and exemplar (which he is calling 'paradigm') exosomatically (this is a purely social incarnation. As Marx says, there is not an atom of matter in value). What we are dealing with is a collective casting of the money material into the role of exemplar of the social quality, value.

In contrast to other kinds of things that we have to recognize without being able to make them ourselves – we recognize a cat without being able to make one – we are able to actually make words which sound like those of others, using theirs' as models. This is an ability that takes some time to develop in early childhood (see Ted Talk, http: //www.ted.com/talks/deb_roy_the_birth_of_a_word.html) but once acquired it becomes much easier and children have a 'word spurt', learning some five to fifteen words a day.

A spoken word is a phonetic combination that others can always potentially imitate, thus it is always potentially an exemplar (a 'paradigm'):

for imitation, a copiable model.[80] In fact any time a word is spoken, the variations in pronunciation (having various kinds of sociocultural associations) can be imitated or avoided by the hearer and corrected by the speaker. We also have mental sound images, memories or collections of memories of speech, which we can use to guide our imitation and further speech if necessary.

The same issue of resemblance arises with words that arises with things but more so, if words only exist by virtue of their resemblances to and differences from other words as Saussure said, while most things in the world have a permanence and function beyond their immediate appearance.

The relation between the exemplar and the many imitations or instances is somewhat different when it takes place among words and when it takes place among things. The word that is being used at any given moment can be taken as an imitable exemplar. Other instances of that word (how many other people worldwide are speaking/hearing or writing/reading the word 'cat' at this very moment?) can be seen in the 'relative position', while the present word is in the 'equivalent position' as imitable. But as I said above the words are all in the equivalent position regarding things. When we think of the name of something we do not make the word relative to the thing as equivalent but we think of what word the thing is relative to.

While exchange implements the substitution of the equivalent item for the relative item, the relation of instances of the same word to each other is not that of substitution but of accompaniment as I said. In fact, a present word[81] is also related by similarity to all the other instances of that word in the language that are being said or have been or will be said by others and which, when they are spoken, will be potentially imitable exemplars, in the equivalent position, for others. We are not usually conscious of this and in fact, when we are speaking or writing, the other instances of that word collapse together, and we take them all as one word, while their different instances subside into a manyness that remains in the background.

In the same way, when we want to say what things are, we call on something as an exemplar. We give an ostensive definition: 'that is a horse'. By this we imply that all the things that are like this animal are horses and we

---

80 My children laughed when I said 'yestedee' in my South Texas fashion. They would repeat it to tease me, rejecting my phonetic model as an exemplar for themselves. They liked 'yesterdaaay' as sung by the Beatles rhyming with 'far awaaay'.

81 Derrida would say that focus on the present word is logocentrism and that instead there is no exemplar relation of the word, but that it is related to other words by 'différance' in a Saussurian structure of differences without positive relations. In this he recalls Marx's general relative form of value.

call them 'horses'. That is we use the speaker's word 'horse' as a present
potential sound exemplar (to which all the other instances of that word are
related by similarity) when we are talking about them. Thus[82] we have two
resemblance relations and two exemplars, verbal (the word 'horse') and
non-verbal (a horse) each of which has a relation of similarity to other instances of the same thing or kind of thing (instances of the word 'horse' or
of horses) just because at the moment they are being considered that way:
that kind of attention is being given to them.[83]

The repeated use of exemplars establishes the equivalent position,
which both words (regarding both other words and things)and things (only
regarding other things) can occupy, a position, which they can be placed in
or removed from mentally.

When an ostensive definition is given: 'that is a horse', both the word
'horse' and the horse are in the exemplar – equivalent position. 'That' is
relative to 'horse,' but as an equivalent of the world-exemplar horse, it is
empty and is replaced by 'horse'. They have this invisible relational similarity to each other in that each stands as one to many. They resemble each
other as exemplars even if (as words and things) they don't have any other
resemblance to each other. For both the word and the kind of thing the resemblance has a content: the other instances of that word, said or written by
others in other moments and contexts and the other instances of that kind
of thing in all their materiality and specificity in other moments and contexts.[84] The relation of similarity of the instances to their exemplar implies
their relation of similarity to each other both in the case of the words and
in the case of the things, though the contents of these resemblances do not
themselves resemble each other on the two levels. In the case of spoken
language for example, all the resemblances are made of sound, while the
resemblances of world-gifts are of infinite variety.

The resemblances of words to each other on the one hand and of things
to each other on the other hand *only* resemble each other as resemblances,

---

82   The spoken word is always imitable by the hearer, and in a situation like the os-
     tensive definition the listener may repeat the word. When we have an extensive
     vocabulary, we may associate the form of the word, the sound itself with the
     things it stands for, in that we imagine it has the sense, or the quality of the world
     gift in it, as 'horse' may seem full of the essence of horseness.
83   Similarly when we are socially considering gold as money, as Marx said.
84   Or the specificities of an idea or a quality, are sometimes also indicated or remem-
     bered with a material exemplar or emblem, like the scales for the idea of justice.

while they have different contents. Thus[85] the exemplarity of the word can take the place of the exemplarity of the thing in the world but it can do so just because it resembles it as an exemplar.

The infinite regress Russell and other philosophers have found here is benign. The resemblance to each other of the exemplar-to-many structures connects the different levels at which they occur. It is not negative but part of what actually makes the relation work; it is a second kind of 'glue' that keeps words and things together.

Viewed in this way the question of universals (or properties) is not so much philosophical or logical but cognitive. It is not negative for cognition that the logic is circular. The regress itself is a peculiarity, which has an 'affordance' that is helpful in connecting one 'realm' to the other.[86] Moreover the existence of paired realms with a plurality in each makes it unnecessary to have any permanent exemplar on either level.

Once the verbal exemplar, the name, has been given and a non-verbal exemplar identified, the name takes over the role of exemplarity for the category implying the similarity of the members of the category to each other. This implication of similarity is what allows us to use the word 'horse' to represent the whole general category of horses (or any member of the category). If the category becomes unclear a new non-verbal exemplar can be found or a mental image called to mind, but this is not usually necessary. What H. H. Price aptly calls the 'aristocratic' category structure (Rodriguez-Pereya 2004) subsides into an 'egalitarian' category

---

85 These relations do not fall prey to the circularity of resemblance nominalism because their resemblances do not altogether resemble each other. The resemblances among words have to do with their imitability by the speaker (or perhaps, writer) while the resemblances among things do not. How similar really are instances of resemblance among red things and instances of resemblance among stars and among acts of kindness?

86 When discussing the image schema of the gift above, we saw that there were numerous repetitions of it at different levels. The word is a gift, syntax is gift-based – the schema replays at the level of the sentence, between and among words. The sentence is a gift given by the speaker to the listener. The relation of joint attention of the speaker and listener to the non-linguistic gifts and schemas brought forward by the sentence make them receivers and givers (passers-on) of these gifts. These resemblances resemble each other and also may be seen as resembling the resemblances of the exemplars. Perhaps what we should look for is the way they are aligned, as in the 'golden mean'. The infinite regress functions not like a hall of mirrors but like a little mirror capsule, a construction validating our generalizations, a bubble, and we are ourselves the generalizers, don't forget. The difference between mirror and 'like me' relation is that the (m)other is indeed different from the self and can have other needs.

structure because the word takes over the one to many role of the 'aristocrat'. Thus it is unnecessary for a non-verbal item to become an exemplar, (an 'aristocrat') permanently. This is very useful because it permits
each person to have a different original non-verbal exemplar (for example, h:er family dog), and even to forget the original, while maintaining
the similarity among the items of a kind in relation to the substitute exemplar, which is the word.

The capacity of word-gift exemplars to be given to each other in the
roles of the schema, in the construction of the sentence, also makes it
necessary for the images of their original non verbal (world) exemplars to
disappear to some extent and new examples or instances to be imagined.
'The red ball' elicits an image of a red ball while our original exemplar
of a ball may have been blue. In order to think of the red ball we have
to leave aside the blue one. We may understand without thinking of any
images but if we need to think of them (to focus our attention for example), we may also merge (or 'blend') internal images by giving them to
each other in our *dark* or open (non autistic) 'mental space' (Fauconier
1994) at the same time that we 'merge' words by giving word-gifts to
other word-gifts.[87] If we had to keep the same original exemplar for the
category in mind we could not do this, so it is better for the ladder to be
eliminated.[88] The suspension or elision of the original non-verbal exemplar is an important part of the functioning of linguistic categorization
and the formation of concepts.

Moreover anyone can say the word 'cat', with any kind of emotional
expression in almost any context. And any cat (or image of a cat) can be
used as the exemplar on the reality plane if one is needed. The character
or role of exemplar – one to many – can be attributed to any 'one' (so the
concept is 'egalitarian' also in this way).[89] For words this one to many
exemplar character is held in place by the contrast with all the words that
it is not[90] (and thus with the things for which those words are substitute
exemplars). For things a similar contrast exists between the things of a

---

87   See Fauconier on blending of the grim reaper – a provisional exemplar who has
     taken over the place of Frau Holle.
88   Psychological experiments test the memory of original exemplars (Murphy 2004)
     and so are misleading in this regard.
89   Though some exemplars are chosen politically, ideologically: the use of the
     masculine pronoun and the word mankind, identifies the male as the exemplar
     of the human. Those who are not like the exemplar are not really human. The
     concept remains 'aristocratic'.
90   According to Saussure's idea of *langue* as a system of differences.

kind related to that word and all the other things of kinds they are not, kinds which are backgrounded (aided by the words' mutually exclusive relations with each other).

We mentioned the prototype relation above, where the similarity implied by the 'one' is not strict, but multifaceted as in a family resemblance. Thus there may be different pronunciations of a word 'horse', from Cockney to Texan to East Indian, but as the name, the verbal exemplar for horses, these pronunciations are taken as one, and they all imply the similarity of horses to each other (Wetzel 2009). And there can also be different kinds of horses: Mustangs, Percherons and Thoroughbred race horses, but they are clustered around an exemplar (or prototype) a kind of horse in the culture and for the individual (though the robin may be the prototypical bird in EuroAmerica, the emu might be considered the prototypical bird in Australia and perhaps the penguin in Tierra del Fuego). The differences between the verbal and the non-verbal planes and internally to those planes, are quite evident. There is no confusing 'horse' perceptually with a horse. On the other hand the above process can occur many times with the same word as verbal exemplar, making the word polysemic – some examples: 'horse' in English can also refer to the knight in chess, a saw horse, a nautical term for a kind of cable, a mining term for a mass of rock with a vein of ore (Oxford English Dictionary).

The connection of the word with what it represents is thus 'arbitrary' as Saussure says but it is not as he also says, 'unmotivated,' not without a process involving resemblances. The structure of the resemblance of things in the world to an exemplar and therefore to each other resembles the structure of the resemblance of words to a verbal exemplar and therefore to each other.

Although the relation between words as exemplars and things of a kind is important to our understanding of language and thinking, it would not function if words were not also virtual gifts and if we did not receive and perceive gifts from our surroundings. Word-gifts make perceptual and conceptual world-gifts giveable again (re-presentable) *to others*.

Words are given for things in their capacity as exemplars, but they are also or mainly given as gifts, used to satisfy cognitive and communicative needs, which are needs to to know and needs to form positive human relations regarding some relevant thing(s) or kinds of things. In this capacity they also satisfy each others' needs for modifiers, specifiers and determiners so that together they can step away from their position as general (equivalent) exemplars and participate in a present piece of communication and knowledge sharing (the creation of the linguistic and perceptual commons). Saying 'the gray cat' allows each word in the phrase to be given to the other words (many languages tell us which words have been given to which by having them 'agree' for example in gender and number: 'Le bambine carine accarezzavano il gatto grigio'). The words have these needs, which are 'instrumental' needs because they also have to satisfy the human communicative needs for clarity regarding which words give or are given to which, and what is put where in the gift schema.

6.14c Pointing, joint attention and beneficial regress

Above I mentioned that joint attention constitutes the reception of a perceptual world-gift together with another. In my book *For-Giving* I also discussed the gesture of pointing. Thinking about the index finger back then, I discovered to my surprise that this gesture is a perfect icon of the one-to-many exemplar relation in that the index comes forward as the exemplar while the other fingers are held back, and therefore they form in the hand, the 'many', which are similar to that 'one', the pointing finger. There is backgrounding as well as foregrounding. The index finger is an exemplar because we are using it that way. By pointing we pick out something on the external as a possible exemplar and invite the other's attention to accompany our own. The hand with the pointing finger is the exemplar of the identification of exemplarity, and (barring disabilities) we all have two hands, which we can and often do use that way. Pointing fingers resemble each other and the things at which we point also potentially resemble other things of that kind. The resemblance among pointing fingers and the resemblance among things of the same kind resemble each other – except that we make the gesture of pointing while we do not make the exemplars-and-the-many (though we do consciously or unconsciously make the focus itself and thus also the backgrounding). Pointing is perhaps the first somatic (but also external, extra-somatic[91]) 'incarnation' of our internal concept-forming exemplar-to-many process.

The different moments in which we point and the different moments in which we attend to something also resemble each other. Repeated pointing at different things abstracts and generalizes the pointing activity itself. The other fingers are backgrounded, and the other things, of that kind – and not of that kind – are backgrounded so the whole hand with one pointing finger

---

91   For each of us other's indexes are extra-somatic, though we may identify with
      them by body mapping.

and the other fingers drawn back resembles the *gestalt* in which something 'comes forward' ('pops out') to our attention as relevant.[92] Not only do we have an index finger that we can use to indicate an exemplar, but we have two of them, though we don't usually use one of the two. The other one resembles the one we do use. The pointing finger and its companion index on the other hand, provide a concrete image of resemblance that is always accessible. The lead finger is the exemplar, the one that takes the initiative. It comes forward for the gaze of the other and towards the external item-exemplar, 'giving' it to h:er by directing h:er attention.

The relation between the pointing finger we use and the one we don't also resembles the relation between the external exemplar in focus and any other exemplar of the same kind of thing. Pointing is a ubiquitous bodily icon of a process of resembling resemblances, which philosophers still do not usually focus on or understand as such. Pointing is embodied cognition, not very abstract abstraction. And it is done early – beginning around eight months of age – by babies.

6.15 Virtualization and resemblance nominalism

Money is a one-word virtual-material language, expressing a single kind of contradictory gift, the not-gift of the value or (general) relevance to all of a would-have-been-gift-now-undergoing-exchange. The 'giving' of money in the process of exchange cancels the gift by the return of an equivalent, and thus, it also cancels the gift value that would have been transmitted by satisfying the need of the other with the product. The value of the receiver is not implied if the product is only given in order for the 'giver' to receive its equivalent. However, the use value of the product remains and is only suspended for the time required to complete the exchange transaction.[93] After the exchange has taken place, the buyer has the use value at h:er disposal. S:he can use it for h:er own sustenance or pleasure or for someone else's or s:he can give it away or waste it or s:he can sell it again. When s:he uses it for someone else or gives it away, the product acquires gift value again, but is not part of a longer social chain of giving as it could have been if the product had originally been given and not exchanged. Its gift implications disappear during its trajec-

---

92 Look also at the 'come hither' gesture with the index. And the coming forward baby game of peek-a-boo.

93 This is the moment of Sohn-Rethel's 'exchange abstraction'.

tory to and through the market. Detached from giving in the market, the materialized money-word takes on the characteristics of the logical forms it influences.

Russell's infinite regress seems to be incarnated in coins and bills, in their resemblance to each other and the resemblances of their resemblances, not to mention the king's (or president's) face on the coin re-enacting his role as one-to-many. Coins and bills have to be standardized and not counterfeit. Their resemblances have to absolutely resemble each other and it is partly this that makes them recognizable. Marx saw gold as the necessary money material because its resemblances do resemble each other. Gold is all one thing, as can be seen when its pieces are melted down and recast. It also comes forward from a background, calls attention to itself as relevant by its color and shinyness – as if it were taking its own maternal gift initiative towards us.

The resemblances of each denomination of money resemble each other within the denomination, and the resemblances inside one denomination are different from those inside another. But then of course the resemblances of each denomination resemble each other in so far as they are resemblances. The currency of one country hangs together by the resemblances of the resemblances it has in common – as the material gift of the not-gift, the mediator of the 'commons' of the mutual exclusivity of everything. Each country has a currency and these currencies are also mutually exclusive and have to be equated and exchanged for each other: 'translated' according to the changing daily rate.

In the 'type' of pennies, it is clear that any one exemplar subsides into the many. We can say that pennies of a certain number are categorized again as nickels, which are categorized again as dimes. (They may be inside several different category-containers while inside one pocket container.) We can also say that the many of pennies reaches a decibel level of intensity or relevance (value) at which they receive another name and a new exemplar, the nickel, which corresponds to the new 'denomination'.

Isn't money itself an example of the infinite regress of resemblances of resemblances resembling each other? Each increasing denomination is a higher level of this. All pennies resemble each other and all their resemblances resemble each other and all nickels resemble each other and the resemblances of the pennies resemble the resemblances of the nickels, dimes, quarters, half dollars. That's what makes them jingle in our pockets. That's as far as coins go. Then there's paper money – the dollar bills resemble each other and resemble the resemblances of the other denominations (we can see the same faces on them, and that they resemble each other or indeed are identical).[94] What a maniacal artifact! No wonder money has now re-dematerialized!

Standardized products are similar. They stand out on the shelf in the supermarket because they are the same. They are like money, and they all have the same price.[95] The prototype, graded or family resemblance form is different from the classical exemplar-to-many form because many of its resemblances do not resemble each other very much. They are also full of content, qualitatively various, not abstract though they may become more abstract or sketchier as the items included get farther away from the prototypical center.[96]

Between motherer and child, there is not so much a common quality or property as a common feeling or attunement, sealing the altercentric relation of accompaniment. The 'family resemblance' that we saw above comes not only from the similar appearance of the members but from the fact that they have been nurtured by the same person and have established an altercentric 'like me' bridge with h:er, which makes them more similar to each other. Their very existence comes from the fact that they were birthed and (most probably) nurtured by the same person. That is perhaps the original common quality: the shared access and 'property' of belonging to each other that comes from giving/receiving together, i.e. a positive emotional content of body mapping and the 'like me' bridge with the same motherer. So here the model or prototype of the knower is the nurturer-and-receiver at the beginning of the commons rather than the money-judge exemplar, discriminator of categories and private property.

Actually the idea of 'properties' of things is, like Marx's fetishism of commodities, a projection of these early human relations onto things. We attribute to things the common property, a kind of sharing that, as adults in capitalist patriarchy, we no longer do with each other. The institution of private property both founds and confounds the metaphors of sharing and property in philosophy. This is also because once again the source area of

---

94   And remember the importance of the face for infant interaction and for philosophers like Levinas (and bourne out by mirror neuron research).

95   It is the same with numbers since the resemblance of any 2 with another 2 resembles any other 2 or pair of twos or other numbers. Or 3 x 5. The resemblances resemble each other but they have different 'contents'. Infinitely expandable. See section 10.2 on 'plus one' as receiving one.

96   Do mother's and child's resemblances resemble each other? and if not, is this why mother can be prototype not the exemplar? The resemblances are constructed through body mapping and projection. This is the 'original sim' – original similarity – that David Cheal talks about and denies. It is constructed in Meltzoff's 'like me' bridge.

the metaphor doesn't include giving and the maternal commons, the motherworld prior to or beyond the market.[97]

Money is the exemplar in the classical concept, and vice-versa, the classical concept is externalized in money. The gradedness of the 'graded category' has been subsumed into money and remains visible only in quantitative gradients. Money is the owned property that denies maternal gift-giving and replaces it with exchange (see below the similarity of the categorizing ego to money).

We also saw above how, on the verbal plane, words can be relative to other words as equivalents. For example, they are relative when they are in the definition, in which the *definiendum* is the equivalent and takes the place of the *definiens*, which is relative (but which itself is an alternative equivalent of the world-gift). The whole definition itself, of course, takes place on the verbal plane, in the equivalent position. This asymmetrical circumstance, i.e. that words are in the equivalent position, has an important function in cognition.[98] However, not recognizing that this is 'only' an element of a cognitive-linguistic process may lead to linguistic idealism: the belief that words and concepts are all we can know.[99]

This belief brings with it the social privileging of words over things, mental over manual labor, and verbal mind over non-verbal body. The 'real world' non-verbal exemplars and collections of manies appear to be irrelevant. Thus the paper money-word also seemed to be enough, without the material exemplar of gold and now money has been subsumed, transubstantiated, beamed up, not only into the 'less material word' of paper but into the still less material medium of electronic bank accounts. Now these banks, with loans, debt and money 'creation' have the power of command over the many as those who can 'speak' or not 'speak' the immaterial

---

97   The use of the term common 'property' though brings to mind a significant object – perhaps the penis or the milk-bearing breasts – which the mother and the boy child do not (and will never) have in common, while the girl child will eventually have breasts.The mother as prototype is the one with whom we share body mapping. As we differentiate from her we can't share the body map, like penguin or ostrich do not share the body map of the robin. The same for the boy with the penis and the mother with breasts.

98   Writing is extra-somatic in a way that vocal language is not and its external existence perhaps disguises the assymetry.

99   And the creation of the world by the word of God. But it is not the word that creates the world but the body, especially the body of the mother: what the word is *about*. Of course the world is different for creatures that have language and those that don't because of the detailed maternal mediation of the community, the means for whichlanguageprovides.

money-word, and this ability may have life or death consequences for 99% of the human beings concerned.

6.16 Classical and graded categories

The products compared to and exchanged for money really did and do have one common quality: the fact that they are exchanged instead of given. The relation of money to commodities as a streamlined exemplar-to-many, is a material incarnation of the classical concept. It regards only one necessary and sufficient quality because it is focussed on one contradictory meta-interaction: exchange. This is a meta-interaction because it regards the common relation of private property, and changes individual owners while maintaining the quality, value. The relation of commodities to money as general equivalent is that of the members of a classical category to their material exemplar. The material-virtual exemplar is the specific quantity of money, which functions as their name, expressed verbally in a price.

The price is a number-word-gift for an amount of money, which is spoken or written and given to the buyer to satisfy the buyer's cognitive need to know how much s:he must pay for the commodity.[100] The amount of material money that is given, embodying the price, is the exchange value in the form of the material-virtual money-word. When the transaction takes place, not the virtual verbal exemplar but a quantity of the actual material exemplar, money, has to be given as the gift of a not-gift to the seller. The adversarial relations require it. While mutually exclusive proprietors are each in a kind of prototype-to-many relation to their possessions (which are related to each of them in a variety of ways), they are also all related to each other through the common need to exchange. They need an instrument at this meta-level to mediate all the exchanges. This is a single instrument, valid for all and quantitatively varied, money. The general equivalent is thus the exemplar of a classical concept relation in contrast to the many (prototype-to-many) private property relations it serves to mediate. In the same moment that it replaces private with public and the many with the one, it provides the transition between one's own property and that of another.

100　The common relations we have as givers and receivers as well as the content of these relations in our joint attention to things, show that like others, we also belong to the same graded category of interactively self-construcing humans who construct this commonality and prove it on the moment. Exchange for money also has a semblance of this possibility but if you don't have the money or the product you can't do it.

This unseen conceptual configuration in our economic life has the potential for deeply influencing our thinking. It can validate abstract philosophical figures like the classical concept over more concrete ones like complexes and private property and both of these over need-satisfying communicative gifts and the cognitive and the material commons.

The potentially very broad general equivalent exemplar character of the word when taken alone – given alone – is placed in a tension with its use in the gift schema, given as a gift at the moment together with other words in a sentence to satisfy the communicative need of the other. That is, combining virtual word gifts in the sentence particularizes the general equivalent character of each word (which is also its general giveability as an equivalent), gives it and makes it give and receive together with particular other words for the moment. However, each word maintains a connection with all its other possible uses in that it is always giveable again, available to be said or written again. Grammatical markers and logical connectors also specify what kind of gift each word is within that sentence gift 'package'. The general word-gift is particularized when and because it is made to play a role in the schema of the gift, a role that is common to all speakers and listeners (and writers and readers) on both planes. On the other hand placing a term in the schema of virtualization can express its generality: 'cats are felines' or attribute properties in more particular uses: 'cats are good mousers' and 'that cat is a good mouser'.

The 'encyclopedia entry' regarding a given word is closer to our minds than it would be if we were not using that word. The generality of the word when given alone is actually constructed by the many particular gifts and services for which it can be given[101] and the various uses in sentence-gifts that the linguistic community makes with it. Individuals can invent or coin a word like 'cybernetics' or 'masculation' or a phrase like 'creative commons' and use them as if they were already general. Then other people take them up and they can become general.

---

101   This is the 'social cognition' aspect of language, which gives a sense to the motor theory Patricia Kuhl talks about, or any mainly neurological theory of language.

CHAPTER VII

MONEY, PROPERTY AND EPISTEMOLOGY

7.0 Owning and knowing

At a certain moment the individual commodity stands in front of all the others as their equivalent for its owner. The general equivalent takes place of that commodity, just as the word takes the place of the individual's private exemplar of some kind.

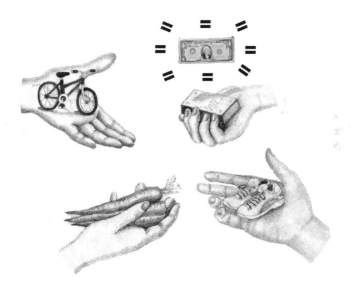

Figure 21: The individual with h:er commodity as equivalent of all others and money replacing it as equivalent (really the public social exemplar replacing the private one!).

Thus, the bridging of property is done in a somewhat similar way to the bridging of mutually semi-opaque minds, by giving to the other a social exemplar that functions as the equivalent of the private exemplar (for property, the social exemplar is money, for language, a word). But the bridging of property in a context of patriarchal competition and greed makes the minds more opaque and often intentionally deceptive, while the original bridging through giving and receiving in the maternal dyad and later through language creates the transparency and mutuality of social ways of receiving/giving the knowledge of the world and of each other. Filling the image schema mould with word gifts and giving it again to others so that they can turn their attention to the world-gifts, which can be organized in that way, is also a great interactive and mutually constructive game.

Instead in the bridging of private property and mutually opaque separate minds through the virtualization schema of exchange only a short-term abstract equivalence is put into effect. In the general equivalent, money, characteristics of the word-exemplar and of the world-exemplar are united. This unity causes some peculiarities. For money, which stands alone without belonging to a lexicon of similar material exemplar-words, there has to be a consistent polarity between the money material and other commodities. Otherwise, money would not be able to generalize as the equivalent (exemplar). That is, the money-word does not have a context of other substitute exemplars surrounding and particularizing it as do words in the language.[1] But it actually does have a context of mutually exclusive private proprietors – we are saying that that property is like a prototype-to-many relation based not on similarity but on ownership – and this is social relation also, which money rises above and mediates. As an identity relation regarding the property relation, money-to-many is meta to the property relation and it is more streamlined and abstract. Every proprietor uses the general equivalent as equivalent of all the others' products rather than h:er own product as equivalent. This process is similar to using a word instead of one's own private mental exemplar in order to communicate about something.

In marginalism's market where money is considered only a numerary, commodities appear to have value as tokens of an ideal type or as items that share in a universal; but the general equivalent character of money is

---

1   At least within a single nation. Anitra Nelson (1999) talks about the tension between commodity money and nominalist money with which Marx was grappling. From our point of view that is a tension *in res*, in the thing itself, because money has merged both the character of the word and of the one-to-many exemplar of a kind.

ignored.[2] That is, the commodities' resemblance to a general exemplar of value is not acknowledged, and they simply seem to be like each other as values inside the conceptual 'container' of the market: they seem to have the common quality, 'value' in an 'egalitarian resemblance nominalist' way, just because they resemble each other. The common quality seems to be without a source or structure, except for the choices of the buyers. This egalitarian resemblance nominalist approach reifies abstract value, giving it a kind of object permanence as a 'property' of commodities and money, or abstracts it, rather than abstracting labor as its source. This approach misunderstands the exosomatic concept in the same way that it misunderstands the mental concept.

For Marx, the value (or we could say relevance or salience) of commodities, which makes them exchangeable, and indeed imposes their exchangeability, comes from labor and is expressed in the general equivalent (the exemplar of exchange value). This labor is the work of everyone for everyone, which is abstracted because it has to go through the exchange process, the gateway of the ego-orientation of the many. The exchangers' desire for property or their need for money 'brings the property forward' as relevant, to be given in exchange, in the sharing of not sharing.

The conventional type/token frame hides the one-to-many generalization process I have been discussing and the issue of relevance-value. We seem to 'own' in our minds the general types, the containers into which the tokens fit. At least we have access to them. Like other knowers, we 'acquire' and 'possess' the concept, i.e. the container with its contents. We confuse knowing and owning (they rub off on each other). We take the perspective of the owner to be the perspective of the knower. Instead the knower has received what s:he knows and has it to give without losing it. Or at least s:he did before the imposition of intellectual property rights.

There seems to be an idea of concepts or categories as a kind of property relation – or family relation – of categories to a 'one' prototypical owner/knower: ourselves. However, in private property relations, the human owners are mutually exclusive, in concepts, there is only a hidden potential exemplar-to-many relation and the human knower 'owns', or has and can manage, all the concept-containers and their contents, which s:he can juggle or apply or rearrange. H:er category 'red things' intersects with her catego-

---

2   Money even seems unnecessary and unjustifiable, just a fact the market could do without.

ry 'balls' and she has the new category container 'red balls'.[3] H:er category 'grim' merges with h:er category 'reaper' in a 'mental space'(Fauconnier and Turner 2002) and s:he has the image of the bringer of death.

7.1 Money as the individual thinker

I think we can make a case for an imperfectly blended metaphor[4] located in the mental space of our self-concepts. This would be an image of the individual thinker as h:erself the general equivalent, the 'money–head': exemplar, judge, evaluator and categorizer in the hidden concept exemplar/prototype-to-items 'property' container relation inside our own minds (see Goux 1990 on capital).

The decontextualization of words in philosophy and the decontextualization of money in the market are repeated in the decontextualization of the individual. S:he is internally the knower-owner, the buyer and the seller, the giver, receiver and allocator of the items in h:er categories. But s:he also takes on the characteristics of h:er instrument. S:he is measurer of value, discriminator of gift/not gift. S:he holds within h:er inner-self a whole storage area of property-category-containers that may intersect or overlap but do not give to each other except when s:he brings them up front in a mental space and merges them with each other. These containers are the mental representations of types, full of tokens. Is s:he internally a store then, with many container bins or shelves full of possible tokens of kinds? S:he gives them to others by exchanging them for money-words at the cashier.

I think (categorize), therefore, like the money-word and like Being, the existential predicate, I am. I belong to the super-category of those that are. I am a token of the type 'Being', like a token of the type 'money'. How much of it am I? What am I worth?[5]

---

3   Actually her ability to manipulate and arrange these categories just means that without realizing it she can come up with an imagined exemplar and a bit of encyclopedia for each category if necessary to supplement the word, its name. S:he can also recognize different kinds of things as given to each other, the color red as given to the ball and the word 'red' as given to the word 'ball'.

4   The theory of conceptual blending brought forward by Fauconnier and Turner describes the combination of ideas as a neutral process of blending. I believe blending results from ideas' being given to each other, and I trace our capacity to do this giving and receiving back to the mother-child model of nurturing interaction.

5   The one-to-many form fits perfectly with patriarchal figure of the father-to-the-many of the family, the king-to-the-many of the nation, the one at the top that others strive to imitate, the father whom the Freudian sons attempt to kill in order to

The possible ways of knowing: as interactive body mapping, as process-es of socially guided generalization, as giving/receiving and the giveabil-ity of what is known, are superseded ('overwritten'), by an imperfect but widespread metaphor of categorization as property, the ownership/know-ership of abstract categories, while the owner/knower h:erself is one-to-many regarding her 'acquired' knowledges but also as one of many similar knowledge-property owning and communicatively 'exchanging' selves. The experience of giving/receiving being is superseded by the category of being (and of being an owner and a knower). The more and the fuller category-containers one has, the wiser and the better 'in-formed'.

7.2 Abstracting economic value

The polarity Marx finds between money and other commodities is nec-essary for the market. Outside the market, the polarity doesn't have to be as emphatic among other kinds of things related to their exemplars because words maintain the relation. Words are always identifiable as things of a specific kind, gifts on a virtual plane, in the 'equivalent posi-tion', recognizable as spoken or written or gestural sign language (each with its own sensory mode of virtuality). Moreover, following Saussure, words exist in a *langue* of other words, which are all related to each oth-er by mutual exclusion and reciprocal delimitation. Money has no such *langue* to which to belong externally.[6] It remains a one-'word' language, a singular social phenomenon as the rematerialized (and now re-demate-rialized) word-exemplar for the category of commodities with exchange value as their 'common quality'. It accomplishes this by its 'internal' division into a material quantitative progression, a material *langue* of sequentially organized numerical units.For Marx, the generality of the equivalent commodity (gold at the time), is constructed by its repeated use as the exemplar of value with regard to all other commodities. As such it is able to express in a single medium the general and abstract char-

---

take his place. I discuss the figures of the one in patriarchy at length in *For-Giv-ing* and attempt to show how they bolster each other. The one-to-many form of m(one)y particularly bolsters the one-to-many forms of patriarchy and vice-versa, but this allows for some 'evolution' witness electronic money and the changes in heterosexual and homosexual family identities, roles and definitions.

6   Though of course each national currency does exist in the context of other nation-al currencies. Each 'word' for value 'translates' into all the others, with the same qualitative 'meaning' in different quantities.

acter of the value of all the commodities, assessing each one with regard to every other.[7] It is as if the virtual plane were made of only one material word, one sound, a cry that can be varied quantitatively.

That commodities have a common equivalent becomes important in another way when the equation between the general equivalent and the many is turned around and the singularity of the money is reflected in the many items as their one common quality, exchange value.[8] The alternation of selling and buying makes each take the perspective of the other, turning the equation around. Using money in exchange elicits the common quality of all these commodities because their owners' need for money and the need of the buyers for commodities is leveraged and intensified by scarcity. We say that the commodities are the same because they have the same equivalent. Then, turning the equation around (shifting our perspective to look at both sides of the equation so that we see the many from the point of view of the one and vice-versa) allows us to say that the relative commodities all have the same equivalent because they have something in common – their exchange value. For Marx, this is their abstract labor value,[9] the relevance of the remunerated (not-gift) labor plus the leveraged surplus (gift) labor of the many. The many are related to the one exemplar as their equivalent. Then, in a third step, shifting perspective we see the one equivalent reflected in the many as their one common quality, (labor) value.

We do the same thing with words, exemplars, and things of a kind, turning the equation around, and identifying the common 'properties' of the many, which we also call their 'essences'. In classical concepts, these are the 'necessary and sufficient' characteristics, which are identified by comparing the many things of a kind repeatedly to a single exemplar. However, words are not mono-logical like money. They exist in a plenum of other words. Most of the time they are polysemic and they come to us in contexts of gift constructions with other words (which makes all the difference).

---

7   It is because the exemplar and the items in the category have to be of the same kind to form a concept that money has to be a commodity for Marx. Otherwise it would not be the exemplar of the concept of things having value. But it also has the character of the word as the substitute exemplar,the virtual gift-not-gift, which takes the place of the commodity, and this is shown when gold is replaced by paper.

8   And perhaps we do the same as proprietors, reflecting on the ego-building 'mine' quality of all we own.

9   Analogously, what Vygotsky considered to be the true concept stage superceded a pseudo concept stage that had only to do with matching. Thus the common quality was found by comparing the many with a single equivalent. In this case the common quality is exchange value.

The one abstracted relevant common quality, value, reflects the singularity of money, which as one *aliquid* stands for many *aliquos* again and again. Insofar as commodities have this quality of value, they are all the same and are reciprocally substitutable, 'like peas in a pod', Marx says. This is the case because they are all destined for exchange, a material interaction that brings forward their value as abstract labor and makes it relevant (makes it 'pop out', come forward, as salient). In fact, abstract labor and exchange value as such would not exist without the exosomatic concept process, the real abstraction, which is just the practice of exchanging products (commodities) for money.

7.3 Perspective shifting

I discussed MacWhinney's perspective shifting briefly above, and mentioned his finding that the different instances of grammatical functions involve taking different perspectives. I proposed that the perspectives of the grammatical functions can be seen in terms of giving and receiving. Borrowing MacWhinney's example, 'the boy hit the ball that rolled into the gutter', 'boy' has the perspective of the giver, 'hit' of the gift, and 'ball' of the receiver. Then 'that' assumes the perspective of the giver again (because it is given for 'ball') 'rolled' of the gift and 'gutter' the receiver. In this sentence, we trace the gifts and the perspectives together. The perspectives of the gift schema are different from perspectives that are only visual. In fact, giving and receiving are interpersonally emotionally and kinetically grounded. The perspective of the giver is other directed, investigating the needs of the receiver, while the perspective of the receiver is directed towards the giver in expectation of the fulfillment of h:er need. There is also the perspective of the gift which is moving from one to its destination in the other. Think of the baby being passed from the arms of one person to the arms of another. All of these perspectives are registered in different emotional and bodily states.

However, as I said above, the situation is different for a copula construction, an intransitive definition or an investigation of the meaning of a single word, which are more abstract and focussed on the schema of virtualization itself, on giving an alternative gift. There we can take the perspectives of the one or of the many as just mentioned with money, buying and selling.

Given infant altercentric interaction and mirror neuron simulation of the feelings of the (m)otherer and the importance of mind-reading and joint attention for early communication, taking the perspective of the other is a very early and pervasive skill. Though we probably always privilege the human other, if we can take the perspective of the (m)other who looks back at us and gives to us, can we not take the perspective of the thing we look at or point at? That is, the perspectives of others and of ourselves past, future and in possibility, the perspective even of the words we speak and of the things about which we speak, word-gifts and world-gifts, the ones and the manies, and switching points of view, the manies and the ones?

To illustrate the general equivalent relation Marx says in a footnote, 'such expressions of relations in general, called by Hegel reflex categories, form a very curious class. For instance, one man is king only because other men stand in the relation of subjects to him. They, on the contrary, imagine that they are subjects because he is king' (1995: 54, note 22). Here the point of view shifts from the one to the many and the many to the one, while each attributes an opposite 'reflex' active defining capacity – perspective – to the other.

Thus there would be perspective shifting in the schema of virtualization as well as in that of the gift, with a result not of transitivity and merging but of reciprocal characterization and delimitation as with the king and his subjects.[10] And similarly for the perspectives of money and commodities.

While we are shifting perspectives from the one to the many and back in the market, we engage in the abstraction of the common quality of value. For example, we say that the reason why all the commodities are related to the one 'excluded commodity', money, as their equivalent is that they all have a common quality, value. The one is projected upon the many in the singleness of the value quality, expressed in money, and the many are projected upon the one in the variety of its quantitative divisions. Each is understood from the perspective of the other, even if it is actually the human perceivers who are doing the looking, 'tracking' them.[11]

If this is the case with the perspectives regarding commodities, what is the perspective regarding people whose work is a commodity? Like the king's subjects, they believe their work is valuable because money is its exemplar. Those whose labor is free consider it valueless because it is *not* related to money as its exemplar. The virtualization of work in money leaves out work that is unvirtualized, making it uncognized, unknown but nevertheless able to be owned by the 'head' of the family or the capitalist.

---

10   That is, categorization.
11   A similar projection happens with the motherworld in that we can take not only our own perspective's as speakers and listeners but the perspectives of the things we talk about.

7.4 Money is mono-logical

The money-word is mono-logical and has a special place of its own in society, decontextualized from verbal language by its material incarnation. Some uses of single words for decontextualized philosophical examples are similar. On the other hand, in inner speech or in conversation with intimate friends, the use of single words depends on a deep embedding in and knowledge of the context.

When it is outside the interconnected roles of the image schema of the gift, a decontextualized word is 'free' to be used in the philosophical investigation of the process of naming-virtualization, and as a verbal exemplar in a conceptualization process. This makes it available for us to establish or assert its relation to other instances of the same word, and to the non- or extra-linguistic gifts it re-gives. However, the very extraction of words from their contexts takes them away from the realm of the satisfaction of needs. It removes them from most of the interpersonal communicative needs they might satisfy at the moment, from the needs of world-gifts to be spoken about, and from the 'combinatorial' needs the words might have, and the needs of other words that they might satisfy syntactically. Thus, the philosophical decontextualization of words is another way in which gifts are hidden. It creates a situation in which the gift aspects of words are not visible because, indeed, they are no longer functioning in the usual way at the moment.

Let's take the example of a philosophical discussion of a decontextualized word. I said above that the definition is a replay of the process of virtualization within language itself. The classical philosophical example of a definition is 'a bachelor is an unmarried man'. The *definiendum* 'bachelor' takes the place of the *definiens*, 'unmarried man'. This sentence might be used in language teaching, to satisfy someone's need to know what 'bachelor' means. But here it is just being used (probably by a philosopher) as an example and potential one-to-many exemplar (for those who might need it) of a 'perfect' definition, where the 'intension' and the 'extension' coincide.

If the enquiry is not being made in order to know what word to use instead of 'unmarried man' or how to use the word 'bachelor,' but ontologically, in order to know what a bachelor 'really' is, the question itself asks for the 'essence' of the bachelor (Carey 2009: 9). That is, like the question, 'what is a woman?', it places 'bachelor' in the 'one' position, asking what are the 'many' related to it as their virtual exemplar, and why. It implies that they share a common quality that makes them all look like each other and not like something else. They all have something – the same thing – to give, a certain kind of relevance. Isn't even the question itself made in the image of money, commodities and value? What is the necessary and sufficient common property, the relevance, the 'value' of bachelors or of women that makes each group have a single word as its name?

The 'essence' of women in front of the general equivalent money is that they have the capacity to give birth and do gift-giving, which the general equivalent does not have (even if we do say that investments 'bear fruit' and that the economy 'grows'). But the question itself is an artifact of exchange and money in our society. The view of all women as having a maternal 'essence'[12] is only the appearance of an alternative economy seen through the filter of the hegemonic exchange paradigm, narrowed down to a common quality of women in binary heterosexual gender opposition to non-maternal masculated men. With prototypes, there is not a necessary and sufficient common quality but several qualities, not equally shared.

The items in the graded category have different kinds of similarities and values, but they all have a similar relevance as participants in a family and in a family resemblance. There is still a many-to-one relation of items to a prototype but it is less streamlined and abstract than the relation to an exemplar (general equivalent). Property is a variation on the theme of prototype-to-many, where the one father-to-many sons excludes the maternal prototype and indeed becomes the owner of his 'chattel'.

7.5 *Money as a devirtualized word*

Having looked at words as general equivalents, virtual gifts and verbal exemplars, let's look back one more time at money as a devirtualized word. Language precedes money historically so it cannot be the other way around. That is, words as such are not virtualized money (though we could make the case that that is what prices are). Money has both the character of exemplar of value and of gift-not-gift. It is *aliquid* given in the place of *aliquo*: in place of products, which are (would-have-been) gifts, transforming them into commodities.

The contradictory gift of not being given – everybody's private property is mutually exclusive in the same way – gives rise to a common need for a mediator: a gift-not-gift that can be given instead: the material/virtual not-gift, money. Private property has created a kind of material solipsism (a 'new extraneousness'), a separation among humans that has to be bridged by a special devirtualized material means of communication; therefore,

---

12   See gasoline as '*essence*' in my article in Vaughan ed. 2004.

the virtual and the material exemplar have been collapsed into each other. In Marx's terms, one member of the category of commodities is socially selected to be the general equivalent: the exemplar against which all the others are compared.

The commodities' common quality – value – is an (*ad hoc*) social quality that is invisible as such, and depends on the social use – exchange – to which they are being put. They would not be recognized as having that quality except in terms of an exemplar – money, which, in this case, is always present in the exchange in the (very) moment in which it is necessary for that common quality to be evident. We have seen that exchange is a kind of backwards elaboration of the gift, a giving in order not to give, using the virtualization schema. Now, exchange has become the behavioral norm and money as the exemplar of value has the status of norm of that norm.

Money is part of the change from collaborative joint attention to mutually adversarial joint attention, (and from an inclusive nurturing 'mother' prototype to an exclusive, competitive, dominant 'patriarchal' exemplar of the human), from qualitative to quantitative, and from gift to exchange. When we hand over money, we are doing giving that is not-giving, giving that is almost virtual. This is why we need an almost virtual material object (a not-gift) to give. We can still actually give away money, however, which everybody needs for exchange.

The need for money is a privatized material communicative/cognitive need, a distorted legacy of linguistic communication. The transition from language to money and exchange in the market is the transition away from the motherworld as a having-to-give, which is mediated by virtual verbal gift-giving, to the world of private property as having-to-keep (not-to-give), and having-to-get-more (to take), mediated by exchange. That is, it is mediated by exchange for one re-embodied, de-virtualized general material 'word'. The process of exchange categorizes products as economic values in exchange, not-free, qualitatively identical (as not-gifts) in their relation, for everyone, to the same devirtualized 'word', but potentially differing quantitatively. The two aspects of words, a) as exemplars and b) as gifts, are transformed in money into a) money's capacity to be the general equivalent and measure of value and b) its capacity to be the means of (giving/not-giving) exchange.

Prices are the linguistic virtualizations of quantitative aspects of the common quality of commodities in terms of ordered sets of quantities of the exemplar of value. Placing things in this incarnated and decontextualized linguistic process abstracts their common quality, which can then be quantified. What commodities have in common is that they are gifts-not-gifts.They are nurturing gifts (and services) that have been distorted and transformed, made not-nurturing for the moment. Their relation to a single exemplar leaves aside all their other particularities and qualities, the variety of all the effort that has gone into making or doing them in ways that are directed towards others' needs. What they have in common is that they are products of abstract(ed) human labor for others, products of human 'mind and muscle' made for satisfying the needs of others. In the market, these others are others in general.

This abstraction of the common quality is made necessary because all the need-satisfying goods already available are caught in the mutually-exclusive private property relations of the many to the many. Instead, the products of labor on the market are momentarily suspended from the intransitive ego-oriented not-gift property character. They are held in abeyance, in the exchange abstraction until their common quality, the special way they are relevant – as abstracted labor for others – is acknowledged and the money-word is given up for them.

Similarly with language, I have a perception or experience that I want to share with you but you are not attending to it. I give you a word-gift for it, to satisfy your need for a specific means to that attention, and, by receiving the word-gift, you relate yourself to that perception or experience, which is no longer mine alone. By giving and receiving the word-gift, we share a relation to it and to its world-gift. By giving the money-word in exchange as a not-gift, we share a relation to it and to the commodity as the gift of a not-gift. We share our mutual exclusion, the relation of ownership of each to h:er private property. This is similar to our mutual exclusion as private minds, non-communicating owners of our private perceptions and experiences. There seems to be an analogy here with autism as I mentioned above referencing Temple Grandin's description of autistic thinking as having a mind filled with pictures – in our terms, of mental image exemplars – usually not related to words and not generalized or made generic. Instead of generalizing she says, she has a file of specific images. On the other hand, the 'normal' generic image may be a statistical prototype, the image of an average item, which might arise when the word (the sound exemplar), has taken the place of the image of the particular material exemplar, which is therefore no longer needed and can subside into the many as I described above.

On the other hand, as I have been saying, there is an analogy between private property and prototype-to-many graded categories, with the owner as prototype, not based on similarity but on ownership. The common quality of the possessions is that they are property of that person. Then the exemplar-to-many relation of money to commodities supercedes the property relation for the moment of the exchange.[13]

According to Saussure, words in the *langue* are mutually exclusive – like property owners. They can only have that property or that meaning because others don't. I propose that this exclusion is overcome by the use of the verb 'to be', the copula, which is used to attribute – give – word-gifts to each other. The difference between the verb 'to be' and money is that money itself remains private property, so that when it is given, it is given up, lost to its previous owner. In language, on the other hand, we can give the verb 'to be' without losing it.

Since private property owners do need to access the property of others anyway, and have to give others access to their own, they have a communicative need, a need to give and receive and to establish a common though mutually-exclusive human relation. They do this through exchange, the giving of not-gifts. In order, to make this possible they need to know what gift they are establishing their relation with each other in regard to, i.e. what the 'referent' is. That is, they have a cognitive need regarding the common quality of value of the product they want to buy or sell. This is also a need for quantitative cognition: a need to know 'how much?' Money is a communicative instrument that, as means of exchange and as measure of value, satisfies both communicative and cognitive needs. It functions as a material word that is also the exemplar of exchange value.

Commodities and money do have the common quality of value-in-exchange, and we implement the moment of categorization by giving one for the other of them. Their exchange value is their relevance within the total social process of the market, that is, their would-be gift value within this strange area of the not-gift. In the attribution of economic value, there is a frame change from mutual exclusion back to 'normal' communication so that from a meta-level, we look at the 'gift character' or relevance of this commodity-not-gift. Thus, we are able to reply to the questions 'what is it?' with the answer 'a value' and 'how much' with the answer 'x amount of money' as its price.

In the German ideology, Marx and Engels give a definition of language as 'practical consciousness as it exists for other men (*sic!*) and for that reason alone it really exists personally for me as well' (1964:

---

13   Money as a classical category supplants many prototype categories, abstracting from and standing for them. In this case, the prototype owners themselves are the manies. Money is to commodities as owner is to property, but, with money, this is not an ownership relation but a relation of substitution and standing-for. However, in both, there is polarity between relative and equivalent positions.

42). The practical consciousness receives its characterization according to what it is for others.[14] We could say, for example, that practical consciousness regarding cats exists for others in the form of the word 'cat' and, therefore, really for me as well; it also exists as the word 'cat'. This is very similar to labor for exchange in the market. A particular kind of product requires a certain amount of labor time given the level of productivity and of the development of means of production. That is, Marx's 'socially necessary labor time' (what it is for others and, therefore, for me). It is virtualized in money of a certain amount, the price of the labor, and subsequently, the price of the product.

If work were not being done for the market, it would not have to be quantified but could simply take place until the need was met. Planting could be done until the field was planted, weaving until the cloth was made. Food could be offered until the receiver was no longer hungry. The scope of the work would be in the satisfaction of the immediate or intermediate need, the use the other makes of the product, the gift value attributed to the other and the gift value of the product for the other. This is meaningful qualitative value that circulates, and by circulating transmits not just use value but gift value.

Instead the work of production for the market becomes what it is for others as expressed in the price as a quantity of money and 'therefore for me' also, it is that amount of the money-exemplar-word.

We all engage personally in the exosomatic concept process. From the point of view of exchange, we say 'we are not givers, we are exchangers of not-gifts. Our products as not-gifts are worth x.' From the point of view of the money, we look back at the commodity and we see its relevance, the highlighted quality it has in common with all other commodities, its value as a quantity of the labor that has been abstracted through its relation to this money equivalent. We give the commodity a money name, a linguistic virtualization of a quantity of money, a price, according to what it is for others in the society, and therefore, for ourselves. Then we have to give up the actual embodied quantity of money-exemplar-word in exchange. We are all engaged in the virtualization of giving as not-giving and our very engagement and communicative instrument are part of the process. We access a meta-level to name the extent of our mutual exclusion, but it is so singular and contradictory we can never elaborate it in other ways. We are collectively performing a real abstraction, implementing the embodiment, the exo-somatization of the concept form.

---

14   Similarly a child can understand what things are by seeing how the motherer reacts, what they are for h:er.

We focus our whole society on this material naming , abstraction and categorization process even though there is still the motherworld of gifts being given all around it. Unfortunately, to our great detriment, the motherworld has been made 'unimportant' and has been relegated to the background, outside the valued category.

7.6 The holophrastic word

I believe we can say that as a material 'word' money is 'holophrastic' like the words of very young children or even like the danger cries of some animals.

Holophrasm is an early stage of speech in which the child uses only one word with a very wide meaning. For example s:he says 'ball' to mean a variety of things: 'there is a ball', 'give me the ball', 'red ball', 'John threw the ball', etc. The gift of red or the schema of giving or throwing is there, it is pertinent and even motivates the act of speech, the communicative gift initiative, but it is not virtualized. For the child, the holophrastic word by itself covers a whole field of meaning. S:he has not yet projected the gift relation onto the relations among words as syntax, nor is h:er word 'ball' delimited by a vocabulary of many other words. Animal cries are similar and can communicate a range of emotions.

When the commodity is bought and sold, the money-word, which is given for it, holophrastically covers the whole field, referring not only to the monetized materials and labor the product contains but to the gifts of nature, of housework and surplus labor as well.

For the money-word, what would have been gift-based syntax has been limited to quantifiability through assembling and disassembling different 'denominations' of money by addition and subtraction, giving to and giving from quantities of coins and bills. There are also no other 'material words' that would delimit its semantic field, as would happen if we had one kind of money for food, another for clothes, another for technology, another for labor, for example, or even more specific monies, for apples, oranges, robins and ostriches, bachelors and black and white swans.[15] Moreover, exchange for money enacts the virtualization schema, while it contradicts the gift schema, except quantitatively in its arithmetical operations like addition and subtraction. The money exchanged in retail virtualizes the cost of the product and the retail costs, but the mark-up, the profit margin which is the

---

15   These monies would be similar to Schmandt-Besserat's ancient tokens.

motivation of the sale, is not independently virtualized. Here quantitative 'blend' in the retail space is more complete than qualitative conceptual and linguistic 'blend' in mental space (à la Fauconnier). The sum, which is the virtualization of the cost and the profit blended together conceals their difference. One portion is an exchange and the other is an unacknowledged gift from the many, i.e. from the buyer, the housewife, the worker, nature and the people of the future, to the people in the chain of sellers.

The 'semantic field' of the holophrastic money-word is wide enough to cover the whole market, but it can be specified quantitatively to cover a single commodity. The money-word varies as to 'volume' but whatever the 'decibel' level, it overtly or 'consciously' excludes gifts while at the same time it actually covertly transmits them through the process of exchange.

Money is a holophrastic word and value is its volume, its decibel level. Commodities are its semantic field. Children's holophrastic words do not have gift relations with other words. In fact, at that stage the young child has not learned syntax. But s:he does know how to cry and increase the volume.

Linguists studying protolanguage in the development of the human species also study the danger calls of primate species. Vervet monkeys for example have different warning cries for danger from eagles, snakes, and leopards (Seyfarth et al. 1980). These cries are also holophrastic 'words' with a very general meaning of danger. Perhaps it is exactly this that money is for us, a material cry, warning us. In fact the word 'money' comes from name of Juno Moneta, Juno the warner, whose temple was near the mint in ancient Rome.[16] What does money warn us about? Not leopards or snakes or eagles but the other exchangers. With money, we warn each other about each other – ourselves – as predators. The 'cry' communicates the potential danger of loss by cheating and hidden plunder. Our vulnerability to loss can increase almost infinitely. The more we have, the more we have to lose.

The amount of monetary value of the commodity is the amount of danger to us from the other's desire for it (to have it as a gift or to steal it), which s:he cancels by giving us the money, the material holophrastic word – forewarned is forearmed – in order to get it. The buyer gives voice to the degree of the seller's alarm, which the seller has expressed in the price. Owning high value objects like diamonds demonstrates a person's ability to control the means of warning.

The quantitative combinations and disjunctions of the money material allow us to specify the decibels, the amount of the danger of one product

---

16   In 396 BC, Juno's sacred geese in her temple on the Capitoline hill warned the
       Romans of an invasion by the Gauls. Thus Juno became the 'warner'.

relative to that of others. The volume, the amount of the warning covers not only the 'equivalent' amount of value of the product – what it cost, or what it is worth if we keep it for or from others – but also the gifts it 'contains', internally, quantitatively articulated. The warning is other-oriented only to the extent of our equality with other self-interested exchangers. It is our common cry of uncommonness. We become addicted to it though, to the danger and the *force du frappe*, the power it gives us.

On the other hand, language surrounds and pervades the use of the money-word (like pearly nacre around a grain of sand), and we could not even haggle without the endless verbal discussion of everything, from our families to the weather, to the differences in quality of the products, to who bought similar products yesterday, where and for how much, etc. All of the qualitative values involved in the transaction are expressed in different qualities, different words, the qualitative 'value accents' of language proper. In market society, we actually have two languages, one is this one-'word' holophrastic material language and the other is multi-word verbal language proper. We use language proper for transmitting to each other the infinite gifts of our experience of the world, while holophrastic money is used in the non-nurturing market to transmit not-gifts. That is, money is a material language embedded in and delimited by some verbal language, (though it does not matter which particular language). However, with the commodification of language and the dematerialization of money, the holophrastic material word is now creeping out of its boundaries. The recent commodification of linguistic gifts in advertising and intellectual property, as well as the revirtualization of money through credit cards and banking technology, have enhanced this remix of virtual characters.

In the development of child language the holophrastic word is soon surrounded by other words so the semantic fields diversify. The vervet monkeys have several different cries for different dangers but in market society the one money-word dominates an entire area or level of life, while language proper continues to function in the others. Words limit each other and they limit holophrastic money (as their 'other') – because not only is it not part of the motherworld commons, it does not refer to it but only to the 'commons' of mutual exclusion of property. It warns of the danger of the others for each according to the quantity of value – social relevance in exchange – of the commodity in the ungiving niche that has been created by us for ourselves as an artificially ungiving species.

But what is the money word's referent? Just the product in the moment of exchange, the not-gift compared to all the others, caught in the moment of virtualization when the thing becomes relevant enough to name.

The other's Medusa face reflects our own and turns us both to stone, so commodities and money are related to each other instead of to us. They act out the 'like me' bridge while we are reified. They satisfy each other's cognitive need: 'how much?' and allow their bodies to be brought forward. While their communicative (community-forming) need is just to be replaced by that warning.

Holophrastic usages in adult language are also short cuts to communicative performance, pragmatics that 'achieve the bonus of sustaining multiple levels of linguistic expression of our social identity, thus preserving an invaluable feature of the social-interactional system of our primate ancestors' (Wray 1998: 65). If in our language, we are still using some of the devices our primate ancestors invented, we can also incarnate them in money. Far from seeing money as progress, we should look at it as atavistic, a reprise of even pre human protolanguage.

Then the cry itself, the material scream, becomes the object of desire (and addiction), because with it one can manipulate the will of the other (my desire calls forth your desire as in sex). And it demonstrates the 'superiority' of the one who owns it – who has it to give.

But perhaps we scream louder and louder with our money satisfying the other's cognitive/communicative need to know how much we want the object, like a child crying louder and louder for a toy. Although the child doesn't always get the toy no matter how loud s:he screams, usually a high enough volume of the money-word will achieve the purpose. Everything has a price.

If humans are a nurturing species, the use of the holophrastic word money is a species specific danger signal regarding our own and other people's *pre*-human non-nurturing, indeed, predatory behavior.

Money has had to replay the exosomatic one-to-many concept-virtualization process as a kind of collective theatre. Thus, this material holophrastic word has itself grown in importance as the object of our desire and as the 'one',[17] the exemplar of the not-gift value of everything. Money had to be a physical object to serve as material exemplar of economic value because value is not a substance, nor even an 'energy', any more than relevance is. Value is a collective implication of antagonistic, not-gift relevance, dangerous for the group and for the individual (for others, and therefore, for me). On the other hand, non-economic relevance itself is also an implication, an implied social quality that emerges when we talk about almost anything.

---

17   Is this the detached Lacanian Phallus of the mother? Her No(m), Her Law? The Law-not-Law of matriarchy and gift-giving? of the goddess of Willendorf? The generalized abundant (m) other.

What is relevant is pre-consciously pre-selected for us; it is salient; it 'pops out' (Chiarcos 2011).[18] The implication of something's coming forward is that it is relevant, important, perhaps a gift initiative, a potential positive gift and the bearer of mutual relations, an object of joint attention at which we can point. Our pointing finger itself pops out as something relatable and 'giveable' to others, i.e. an instrument of giving. The volume of the holophrastic money-word pops out also but hardly for our good.

In the early childhood gift economy, relevance is intimately connected to the emotions and to the interactive, interpersonal body. Exchange among adults allows detachment. In the market, exchange value itself, not emotion, forms a hierarchy of emphasis or relevance, where the most is the strongest or biggest or loudest. The emotion is not felt but it is distanced and displaced onto the quantitative scale of exchange value as expressed in money. It is a a cry of infinite decibels for which we have no ears. But we can weigh its 'volume' kinetically with gold, silver or coins, or virtually with numbers in our online bank accounts. And we want it.

The field of meaning of money (its 'semantic field'), is the totality of commodities on the market; the field is 'analyzed' and specified quantitatively internally into amounts given for each particular commodity (and any one of a kind of commodity).

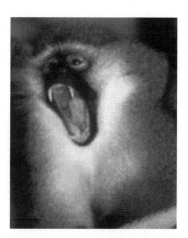

Figure 22: It is a cry of infinite decibels.

---

18   'Ah boo' say the motherer's friends to the baby, putting their faces forward into h:er proxemic space.

With no syntax and no semantic competitors or complements at the same level, money covers everything that has exchange value, the whole field of production of goods in that one aspect. The monetary holophrastic cry is a word but the listener cannot learn it. It is a relational lever, a proto-word with a very broad but unique semantic field. Like the logicians' example 'triangle', for the classical concept, its intension corresponds to its extension. All the products directed towards expression in money have the common quality, exchange value, and only those products have it (similarly all triangles and only triangles have three angles).

CHAPTER VIII

VALUE IN LIGHT OF THE GIFT

8.0 Gift value

I have been mentioning another kind of implication of value that Marx and other economists have not considered: gift value, which is the implication of the value of the receiver for the giver, beginning with the value of the child for the motherer. This is the emotionally anchored value that is typically found in the 'private sphere'. It is transmitted by what Ruddick (1995) and many others would call 'caring labor'. Gift value received and internalized, becomes self-esteem, and enhances the capacity to creatively assimilate, to respond appropriately with gratitude, to give again and give value again to others. It is not the same as use value, which is understood simply as the utility of the need-satisfying good. The willing care of others, the 'investment' of the life force of the carer in satisfying their needs, gives value to the receivers by implication. Unfortunately the givers and the gift of care are burdened in our society both by malestream's taking and accumulation of their gifts and by the sentimentalization of giving, while exchange value is over valued and appears to be the most important quality in the 'real world'.[1] Gift value is usually transmitted as a side effect of (relevant) care and recognized only by individuals if at all. Like care, language is a service to others and to the world, and words are both its means and its by products. They have and they confer gift value.

Usually people who do not work for money, or who cannot find 'good' jobs, or any jobs, are de valued because all value is seen as coming from the market. Self-respect seems to come from deserving exchange value

---

1   The movement for the economics and ethics of care that has developed in the last decades as represented in the work of Nancy Folbre (2001), Joan Tronto (1993, 2013), Virginia Held (2007), Riane Eisler (2007) etc. is seeking with some success to counter this trend. However, these authors usually consider the care alternative within the exchange paradigm and patriarchal capitalist reality, not an alternative economic 'base' with caring values as its 'superstructure'.

(that is on having 'contributed' enough to receive money in exchange). Although the direct receivers of gifts and services sometimes are grateful and do freely acknowledge and give value to the givers, the importance given to exchange in our society makes receiving seem inferior so that when they accept gifts people sometimes do not feel respected. And in fact gifts are sometimes given to overpower others for the benefit of the 'giver'. Unilateral gift-giving and receiving in a context of exchange is almost always difficult and contradictory. Social mores and individual machinations regarding giving and receiving can be very complex power games. See for example the gift-giving in sixteenth-century France described by Natalie Zemon-Davis (2000).

Nevertheless, positive gift value continues to be transmitted to others through work, through care, through gifts and services. Community and solidarity are created when the gifts circulate and care givers themselves receive gifts and services from still others so that their value is also implied in the same way.

Instead, the market only rewards with a judgement of positive value those who accumulate gifts of profit consistently. At the same time it degrades those who do not succeed in doing so. Work is understood only as work for money, Marx's abstract(ed) labor, while gift work is ignored and devalued, often even by the people who want an alternative economy. In a gift economy the value of others is implied by gifts of labor, of time, of communication, of goods and of the imagination, gifts which are given and received in turn (not exchanged) among all the community members. There are also gifts coming from the past and gifts given towards the future, thereby including in the ongoing community and giving value to the people and the environment in both of those time frames. Still another kind of gift value occurs when someone gives something *for* another. This happens when we give for someone who is not herself able to give, when we are proxy givers. The motherer gives and receives for the child or s:he gives her children a present for the father who is too busy give it. We have invented a mythical figure, Santa Claus, for whom we give gifts, because he cannot actually give them himself. This is the way we give relevance to things by giving words to others for them (since the things cannot give those words themselves.) And motherers give the name of their child to others (thereby giving relevance to h:er) before the child can give h:er name to them h:erself.

Since linguistic gift-giving is only done by humans, it is human species-specific gift value that we transmit to others by giving to them linguistically. This value of the other is implied when we satisfy h:er communicative and cognitive needs with word-gifts. This gift value is always positive as far as the human relation is concerned, even though the linguistic gift which is 'benefactive' at the level of communicative and cognitive need-satisfying words (and syntax) can also be used negatively at the level of proposition, sentence or text, to lie, cheat, denigrate, hurt, condemn and even annihilate the receiver ('kill the wretch!'). Nevertheless, it is the benefactive aspect of word gifts, as we said above and their capacity to establish the species-specific[2] maternal human relations, that underlie communication, not the possibility of their use to harm.

Exchange value contradicts gift value except perhaps when the focus is on money as the material holophrastic 'word' added to itself. In this case, increasing quantities of money always give it more capacity to buy, making us believe that 'more is better'. Money can also appear positive when it is itself given without exchange as happens in charity. In this case however, the giver sometimes is given more value than the receiver and surreptitious exchanges and power plays ensue (as gift sceptics Derrida 1992, Bourdieu 1977, Baudrillard 2001[1988], Lyotard 2004 [1974], etc, saw).

Gift value may also be understood as the positive relevance or importance of world gifts as they are registered in word gifts, creating the linguistic value Saussure saw in the *langue*.[3] Here, where diachrony produces the gift values from which synchrony abstracts (as in any synchronic snapshot of prices on the market -and indeed prices are 'spoken,' made cash in the present), we see the totality of the *langue* as made of positive values, related negatively only in that each is not any of the others. The terms of *langue* are abstracted from gift value in that they have no (*parole*) receivers at the moment of the snapshot and no contemporary verbal co-gifts, givers and receivers in sentences. In this abstraction they are indeed similar to the exchange values of commodities on the market of which prices are the linguistic expression. A steady state economy where supply (expressed in price) meets effective demand (need expressed in money)[4] can provide the underlying metaphor for *langue* because both

---

2   We use them to identify ourselves as a species internally, not so much as against other species. However, we might have done that in prehistory as we distinguished ourselves from other hominids who did not speak. Now we try to include other species by speaking to them but they don't usually respond and we can't usually understand them when they do.

3   The is the system of linguistic signs as opposed to which is actual speech.

4   'Supply' can also be read as 'answer' and 'effective demand' as 'question', the need expressable in the money word, beyond mind-reading. No 'maternal thinking' is required or admitted!

abstract from gifts and from needs satisfied by gifts. Thus Saussure could base his concept of *langue* on the market as seen by Walras and the economic school of Lausanne (Piaget 1970: 77), which itself was based on the ideas of nineteenth-century physics (Mirowski 1989).

Finally, I would just like to suggest that if as I have been saying, the image schema of the gift can be extended to other schemas such as path to goal or even to virtualization, gift value can also be implied through the latter schemas. By moving or working towards a goal, we imply the value of the goal for us. Thus practical and moral values can also be seen as extensions of gift value. If the giving-for of virtualization also implies gift value, words can be seen as the receivers of the gift value given by the things they virtualize, whose names they are. They have a 'position' as values in the *langue* because they virtualize and are given for world gifts, and this process also gives them gift value. At the same time, spoken or written by those who take the initiative to satisfy the communicative and cognitive needs of others with them, they transmit gift value to their receivers.

8.1 Cognitive and communicative needs and gifts in the context of exchange

We use money to satisfy the combined cognitive and communicative need of others regarding the exchange value of the commodity (the gift of the not-gift). The cognitive need regards which money name the commodity has in the sequentially ordered quantitative *langue* of prices. The communicative need regards the 'giving' and 'receiving' of the specific material-virtual item, money, which functions as the means for changing human relations of private property regarding the commodity. The price satisfies the cognitive need and the money itself in the amount of the price satisfies the (contradictory) communicative community-forming need. The quantitative *langue* of prices is formed of virtualizations (namings) of an ordered sequence of quantities of the holophrastic material money-word-scream.

Market actors are able to understand and use exchange value by virtualizing the value of the commodity in the quantitative *langue* of price and re-materializing it as money. There is a general consensus about quantities of value related to each other in this way because everyone follows the same logic of implications of value. This common cognitive and communicative process, divided into the alternating roles of buyer and seller, constitutes the core of the interaction of exchange.

From this point of view, looking back at language, Saussure's *langue* is a non-hierarchical collection of mutually exclusive and delimiting (but relevant and mutually relevant) qualitatively different acoustic or written gifts, used in the virtualization of world-gifts. These word-gifts do not have exchange value, though their existence in the *langue* is evidence that what they stand for was at some time relevant enough to achieve semiotization/virtualization. Viewing language synchronically, in a kind of cross-section, allowed Saussure to think of words as what we could call 'value tokens' having value as position. Words do also have potential use value[5] and gift value since they are giveable to satisfy the cognitive and communicative needs of others, which arise regarding the material and cultural world. This giving creates relations to the world-gifts among the communicators as receivers and givers, who are also related to each other through their joint attention to the world-gifts. In a sense the speaker/giver creates her own relation to the world as an accompanied relation, by creating the relation of the other to it and to herself. This thread of mutual inclusion is looped back and twisted by the giving-back of an equivalent in exchange, where the exchanger is ego-oriented. That is because the exchangers mutually include each other specifically only regarding their mutual exclusion. From this competitive standpoint they attempt to leverage gifts from each other. The commonality and mutual inclusion that in language is benign and positive, in exchange becomes negative as a leverage point for exploitation.

Because of their similarity, we read language as exchange, leaving out the whole area of the gift. Admittedly the two are close together but that is because exchange is an offspring of language. The distinction needs to be made. For example, turntaking remains as a way of interacting that is not exchange. A reply is not an exchange but another unilateral linguistic gift, given by a present speaker on the basis of the previous linguistic gifts, given by the previous speaker.

Giving a word gift for something gives value to it also[6] as does taking care of it through housework, agriculture, 'husbandry' all the caring engagement of humans with the material and social world. The virtual giving of these world gifts to others, passes their value along to the others as well and there is thus a circulation of world and word gifts (and gift value) among humans, environment, creatures, ideas and behaviors now and in other times

---

5   Words are used as gifts to satisfy relational needs among people regarding things. They are used in a similar way to establish relations among words in syntax, and they imply gift value in both cases. This is a relational value and it is already social, not just individual as in the use value/exchange value distinction. It is also different from Wittgensteinian 'use'.

6   'for the roses had the look of flowers that are looked at', T. S. Eliot, 'Burnt Norton'.

and places that are named and discussed. Not a possible world as some linguists and philosophers surmise, but a possible commons, is created by giving and receiving both world-gifts and virtual gifts, word-gifts.

Giving something *for* someone or something also gives value or relevance to the one for whom it is given. Words, whether we look at them in the synchronic snapshot of a *langue* or not, come from the collective material and social elaboration of the kinds of things for which they are virtual gifts. When humans give those word gifts to each other they also give gift value to those things and kinds of things, revealing that they are relevant in some way, important, worth thinking about. Vice-versa they also give gift value to the words as gifts and to each other as receivers.[7] Thus language is an important element in the collective elaboration of the relevance of the world. We might think of it as bringing forward, specifying and making connections among the many detailed aspects of each community's evolutionary niche. Spiritual practices in which gifts are given to Nature make explicit the attribution of gift value to Nature, and they include H:er, our Niche, in the (altercentric) gifting community as a receiver as well as a giver.

These characterizations of language illustrate how linguistic value and exchange value can be understood as similar though they exist at different levels and are expressed in different 'mediums'. It is the addition of the idea of gift value that makes visible the underlying connections.

Making another terminological abduction, we can look at 'relevance' as a kind of value or vice-versa, value as a kind of relevance.[8] Although something can be relevant to ourselves alone, in the gift framework, relevance comes from our ability, not only to notice and attend to aspects of our surroundings but to relate these aspects to others as important[9] for them. That is, we place these aspects in a possible gift or path-to-goal (gift trajectory) schema, which we emphasize, with the element in the world as gift or giver, ourselves as proxy givers, givers of words *for* it, and the other person as receiver.

In order to do this we create a construction of word-gifts which are given

---

7   Doing this – or rather not doing it – regarding gift-giving has made it invisible, and I am trying to remedy this here by talking about it.

8   See Chiarcos et al eds. (2011) again Sperber and Wilson (1995) have explored relevance in the neoclassical cost/benefit economics framework, which as we shall see, brings with it very different consequences from the gift framework.

9   Relevance can have a direct positive gift value or an indirect gift value in that knowing about something problematic helps the listener/reader to avoid its negativity.

to other word-gifts sequentially, syntactically, while we give this gift product to the listener or reader. In writing we also give the words to the page or the computer, which receives them and gives us continuing evidence that it has received them, and that they are available as gifts to others who may happen to approach to receive them.

Summarizing: there are thus some five or six main gift transactions in language: (1) between the world (the perceptual or conceptual gifts) and the perceiver/speaker/writer, (2) between the world (the perceptual or conceptual gifts) and the perceiver/listener/reader, facilitated by the gift initiative of the speaker/writer who gives word gifts *for* the world gifts, (3) the construction of the linguistic gift by giving word-gifts to each other syntactically, (4) the speaker/writers' actual transmission – speaking or writing the verbal gift, which is given to the other to satisfy h:er communicative and cognitive needs. We add to this the fact that (5) language itself is given: word-gifts exist, already created by the linguistic community *for* perceptual or conceptual gifts that have been repeatedly relevant to others, that is, regarding which cognitive and communicative needs have repeatedly arisen and been satisfied in the past by giving and receiving linguistic gift constructions. Finally, (6) we live in a world that has been made relevant by the linguistic and material communication of others with others. Moreover the environment itself is a gift from past to future generations as we have recently been realizing. Our understanding has been jolted now that we see that collectively and individually we are destroying that gift of all gifts.

Value also accrues almost automatically to the giver as someone who has satisfied a need. This value of the giver can be appreciated or denied by the receiver who recognizes or refuses to recognize the source of h:er good. And the giver can modestly decline the spotlight or glory in it. Moreover, giving, actually succeeding in satisfying needs, usually feels good of itself. This does not imply that the giver does it in order to feel good, making it a kind of exchange or self-stimulation. Rather, the positive feeling is the emotional outcome of a process begun in infancy and continually exercised through language and in many other aspects of life.

Since gift-giving is not recognized as a fundamental aspect of human life, and continues to be exploited, gift value is not recognized as important either. Yet giving and receiving are emotionally invested and are almost as intensely felt by adults as they are by children, though usually less transparently. Many or most of the rhythms that make up our emotional lives are based on giving and receiving, beginning with breathing in and breathing out, and with the heart's pumping of the blood to the capillaries and returning it to the lungs to be oxygenated. Like preconscious selection, this physiological giving and receiving is Motherer Nature *in us*. The 'reading of the minds' of others and the satisfaction of their material needs and their relational needs through language (and other signs), our alignment with them and the relevance or gift value we attribute to them in this process, constitute the social regiving, renurturing, of the nurturing gifts of nature.

Greed is not just a character defect but it is a personal longing for gift value to be attributed to oneself and a contradictory attempt to *acquire* it through an accumulation of money, consumer goods and status symbols. Moreover, some gift value is actually transferred by implication through the gifts of profit that are forced towards those 'above' in the hierarchy from those 'below', who may not even realize they are giving gifts but only believe their own work is worthless. Giving importance to gift giving could change both of these perspectives. This can be done by recognizing it in areas where we have not seen it before, like language.

Neuroscientific investigation has revealed a preconscious engagement with the world that takes place in microseconds outside of our awareness.[10] This preconscious processing constitutes a kind of internalized maternal selection of what is 'important for us' from all the things in our surroundings that we could potentially attend to, not only as informed by our need for survival but by our stored memories and syntheses of previous experience. The interface between ourselves and the world is formed in part by our capacity to preconsciously explore our surroundings and find what is relevant before we know it. This ability constitutes part of our creative receptivity, which we also elaborate consciously. Our capacity to nurture others, to select some of the aspects of the surroundings as relevant to them and pass these 'chosen aspects' on to them repeats the selection process consciously and gives these aspects an extra charge of importance. They are relevant, they 'pop out' as 'salient'. We mother others by our selections but we also mother ourselves through our own physiological, neurological processes of preconscious selection.[11] Lan-

---

10 'Current evidence suggests that perception becomes conscious at a late-arising stage of focal-attentive processing concerned with information integration and dissemination' (Velmans 1999: 543). 'Consciousness of familiar stimuli, rather than *entering into* input analysis, appears to *follow it*, in human information processing. Information processing most closely *associated* with conscious awareness of input appears to *operate* unconsciously in the economy of mind'. (*ibid.*: 565), 'Is the Self the consciously experienced Self or the unconscious ground that supports it?...whether we think of ourselves as an agent, an entity or an organizing system, we are *both* the preconscious generating process and the conscious result' (Velmans 2014: 23).

11 We might think of proto conversation as a relevance game, each 'pops out' to the other in turn.

guage is thus a kind of social collaboration of our internalized motherers, taking care of each other and their children.

A selection of this sort is also performed in the market for us manipulatively by sellers who try to make their products come forward to our attention. And they bring them to the market through the chain of sale. Corporations and retail chains take over this ex maternal function and claim the respect we might once have given to the Great Mother. They bring forward endless products that they present as relevant to us and others and that we would buy if only we had the money to give for them, the wherewithal to materially 'speak' their quantitative holophrastic names. But *Caveat emptor!* Buyer beware!

8.2 Cognitive relevance theorists

Cognitive relevance theorists Sperber and Wilson (2004: 609) discuss linguistic relevance first as maximizing the positive cognitive effect – what we would call satisfying the cognitive need: 'a. Other things being equal, the greater the positive cognitive effects achieved by processing an input, the greater the relevance of the input to the individual at that time'. Secondl, they describe relevance as requiring least 'processing effort' which they see within an economic framework of cost/benefit to the listener: 'b. Other things being equal, the greater the processing effort expended, the lower the relevance of the input to the individual at that time'.

The idea of gift-giving circumvents the latter requirement because the speaker/writer/giver mind-reads the needs of the receiver as best s:he can and fashions h:er linguistic product as specifically and as appropriately as possible. Thus ease in processing for the listener is actually the result of a specific and appropriate gift – not just 'input'! – (as with so many other things, convenience for some is the product of unseen carework by others).[12] Mind-reading the needs of the other recognizes the needs and affirms the other h:erself as relevant and as a potential recipient of gifts and gift value. The appropriate word-gift is proof that this recognition has taken place and the gift value has been given. Moreover this communicative process is giving/receiving *in abundance*, since word gifts are almost infinitely reproduceable and recombinable, so cost/benefit is certainly altered, if not cancelled.

Sperber and Wilson think the receiver wants to use the least effort to

---

12   Thus the verbal product satisfies the communicative as well as the cognitive need.

receive the benefit of the communication. I believe the speaker/writer does h:er best to understand and satisfy the need of the receiver who benefits and receives gift value from this effort. The giver's effort is given freely while the receiver has to creatively receive what is given, but s:he has to do this anyway with all the gifts of her environment. The speaker/ writer has already done part of the creative reception for h:er by receiving the world gift, recognizing it as relevant and putting it in the gift schema in appropriate ways in order to pass it on to h:er.

But also s:he has to satisfy the 'need' of what she is talking about for proper expression, re-gifting, giving it value as well. When s:he does succeed, it is more clearly a gift to both the receiver and to the extralinguistic item or topic. S:he is altercentric towards what s:he is talking about as well as towards the person to whom s:he says it. And s:he does not 'count the cost'. The receiver is not passive but engages in understanding through the patterns created by the satisfaction of her cognitive and communicative needs by the speaker/writer's word-gifts. S:he does not usually 'count the cost' either, though she may give up if the interpretation is too difficult. That is, if the speaker/writer has not actually succeeded in mind reading and satisfying the listener/reader's communicative and cognitive needs. There is a radical difference in the view of relevance and the relation between speaker/write and listener/reader from the gift and from the cost/ benefit (exchange) perspective.

If the speaker/writer gives the 'wrong' or nonsense words, 'Twas brillig and the slithy tove...' or if s:he says 'dog' when she means 'cat' or 'exchange' when s:he means 'gift,' the listener/reader does not understand and may have to ask what the speaker/writer meant. If those distinctions are not made in the culture, neither may understand.

Although the listener/reader may expend effort in interpretation, this is qualitative gift effort for collaboration, not quantitatively calculated work for the kind of semiotization or virtualization that is exchange. Moreover, in a situation where there are abundant gifts for the giving, as there are in language and as there would be in a generalized maternal gift economy, cost/benefit is no longer the rule and the act or effort of giving and receiving (in the satisfaction of a cognitive or communicative need) is an act or effort of meaning, not of manipulation.

The kind of parsimony that philosophers call upon to explain success in communication is really mainly the accurate reading of the cognitive and communicative needs by the giver/speaker/writer and the appropriateness of the gift for the needs' satisfaction. However, the idea of parsimony, the limited budget, diverts attention away from the actual abundance that communication uses and can provide.[13] The idea of language as gift-giving raises our expectations. The production of value in the gift economy does not require scarcity.[14] In fact it is giving and receiving in abundance that permits the freedom of linguistic and symbolic creativity. The identification, satisfaction and elicitation of the cognitive and communicative needs of others arise not from parsimony but from the creative ability to use the abundance of language and experience.[15]

8. 3 Use value, gift value, exchange value

A use value, which is consumed by the person who makes it, is simply a use value. If it is given to another it implies the value of the receiver, and therefore it transmits or 'has' gift value (it 'has value to give'). If a product is exchanged on the market it becomes a commodity with exchange value, canceling gift value and implying the ego oriented value of the exchangers. The kind of value a product has depends on which process it is part of, and whether or not it performs an intersubjective mediation. Since nurturing by others is necessary in childhood and comes before exchange, the first use of products is as gifts and transmitters of gift value.[16] That is they are gifts even before they are simply use values.

Perhaps it is only because free work, especially reproductive work, has been ignored and exploited that gift value has not been taken into account, but this has left a lacuna in the theory of value. It has separated use from exchange and has made exchange value mysterious. Gift value is the relational alternative to exchange value and precedes it in the life of the individual and of the species. It is the value or importance of the receiver implied by satisfying h:er need. The good that satisfies a need is

---

13 See also the attempt by Kockelman (2006) to analyze the market using Peirce's semiotics and a neoclassical economic framework.

14 Gift value can also be given by sacrifice but sacrifice is only one special case of giving and is usually not necessary in abundance.

15 The creative use of linguistic abundance contradicts the problematic raised by Bataille's 'accursed share'. The use of abundance or 'excess' is a problem for the patriarchal market, not for maternal gifting.

16 This transmission of gift value brings with it the negative case of gifts denied, which imply a lack of value of the receiver for the giver. Advertising to children stimulates wants which parents are called upon to satisfy. The denial of those gifts by parents witholds gift value from the child, often causing desperation and even tantrums on the part of the child. It is not just the brightly colored fascinating object the child wants but the implication of her own value that comes with the gift.

a use value when it is seen only functionally, *outside* human relations, but when it is given it is also relevant as a gift and the vehicle of the implications of gift value.

In fact, taking the domestic sphere as an example, products, use values, are almost always embedded in the nurturing work of the housewife/carer and therefore carry or imply gift value. Moreover, the salary earned by work in the market, is used to buy the means of giving, and this also gives value to the family members. Even though the salary is procured through exchange and contributing it may be considered a duty, giving it creates a positive relation and implies the value of the family for the giver. This is part of the interface between the domestic sphere and the market. The worker who succeeds in 'providing' is recognized as a giver, because in the scarcity created by the market, there is no alternative to working for money. Because of the leveraging capacity of scarcity the salaried worker then seems more valuable than the giver who does not 'make' money.[17]

The patriarchal desire to be at the top, greed to be the one with the most are part of the market motivation to increase, its momentum towards 'growth', but many people are motivated by the need to provide. Each family is a kind of miniature gift community which is dependent on gifts coming from monetized labor, a gift community dependent on the gift-taking exchange economy. Thus the family functions as a kind of motor of needs that calls forth the monetized work of the providers. This fits together with a wider mechanism that is motivated by patriarchal aggrandizement, competition and greed, and which has as its moving parts individuals, groups and corporate entities that are striving towards perpetual increase.

For those who criticize Marx's idea of abstract labor value I can reply that utility for neoclassical economists is the need satisfying capacity of goods abstracted, hypostatized and made ready for quantification (placed in that frame). Relations are seen in terms of desire, preference and choice - what we choose to buy. 'Utility' is the renaming of use value, artificially generalizing and expanding it as a mass noun so that it can also be seen in terms of volume.

We discover the quantity of utility by 'mind-reading' the other (inside the area of the market or on the border between the domestic and the market spheres) and calculating her 'effective demand' perhaps with the help of psychological assessment techniques, in this case using our own other oriented gift sensitivity for exchange. That is, in order to calculate the quantity of products to be sold for the maximum price (or bought for

---

17   But women are also forced to do monetized labor in the home (Mies 1986).

the minimum) we are motivated to calculate the quantity of utility. How desperate is the other, the buyer, to have this product or the seller to have the money? What is the degree of h:er desperation, given the leverage of scarcity artificially created by the market i.e. by privatization, commodification and not-giving.

The consumer's wants can be compared quantitatively in terms of marginal utility of the products. Where does the commodity fit in h:er meager budget, h:er limited access to the material holophrastic word with its 'semantic field' that comprises everything for sale on the market?

In our society the scarcity, and thus the limitation of our budgets, as well as the specific (manipulated) character of the needs and desires, are created by the market itself (without scarcity there would be no need to exchange). Relevance in scarcity is different from relevance in abundance. Gift value can take place in abundance as well as scarcity but exchange value requires the leverage of scarcity. Moreover, in abundance there is no margin, all the needs can be satisfied. No either/or choice is necessary, it is all both/and. The gift process ends in the satisfaction of the needs not in the lack of the money word and the material 'silence' of the exchanger.

While it may seem that the exchangers confer exchange value upon commodities by their individual binary choices, this value depends upon (mostly artificial, market-created) scarcity, because without scarcity the choices would not be necessary. The buyer is required to juggle needs against each other, like a motherer required to decide which of h:er children to feed.

The marginalist approach uses the instrumentalization of gift processes without acknowledging it. It mistakenly identifies the (maternal) selection of goods and the choices constrained by scarcity in the market, as the origin of the exchange value of commodities. If anything, what the choices usually convey is not just utility of the products but their hypothetical relative gift value for others, quantified and renamed.

In the market, products vie for our attention, brought forward by the advertising that has invaded our preconscious selective function.[18] Nineteenth-century economists, who first thought of value as depending on subjective choices and marginal utility, could hardly have foreseen the immense capacity of the market and advertising to alter those choices. However, it is not the choices that transmit gift or exchange value but the relational use of the products and the relevance to others' needs (which the choices affirm).

That a commodity has exchange value is affirmed when it is exchanged.

---

18 The disciplines of semiotics and linguistics have made their 'contributions' to capitalism here.

Its price puts it in relation to other things of the same price within the market as a whole, in much the same way that the name of something puts it in relation to other things of the same kind. A commodity is one of a number of things that are exchangeable for money. Moreover it is one of a number of things having the same price or money name, exchangeable for the same quantity of money. The word-gift is related to all the world-gifts that are giveable virtually, creating human relations, by giving that word-gift. Products on the market also have in common their exchangeability.[19] Relevant world-gifts have in common their virtual giveability.

The choice to buy a consumer good expresses whether or not something has an 'affordance' (Gibson 1977) – whether it can be a potential need satisfying gift – for the individual or the family – and vice-versa whether they can 'afford' it. The choice acknowledges relative relevance or importance within the limited totality of family needs that are quantitatively and qualitatively determined by an artificially restricted budget. On the other hand money always has an affordance, the affordance of everything on the market (as well as the affordance of money as capital).

When we say that subjective choices determine value we are dangerously close to using gift value as the interpretative key without knowing it. The way gifts are given and the variety of gifts that are given to satisfy kinds of needs, inform the receiver about her culture and educate her needs. Marketing and advertising have invaded this aspect of life manipulating choices and subjectivities, tracking them on the internet, buying and selling them, occupying the territory of the gift, commodifying it again and again.

By looking at economic value in the context of other values as the (social) elaboration of relevance and bearing in mind the idea of monetized exchange as the externalized concept formation process, we can understand it more clearly. In fact we must ask: is there any individual preference, individual value, if the individual is a social product, a collective product? Individual preferences could be seen as an artificial construct coming from the elimination of the social (and the gift) from our idea of the development of the person. Consumerism is based on this elimination and the manipulation of the social production of the individual, that is on the manipulation of childhood and mothering (see, for example, Naomi Klein's *No Logo* (2009) and http: //mothersforahumanfuture.com/).

---

19   That is, they are exchangeable in general for money and in particular for a specific amount of money. This would correspond in language to world gifts being virtualizable by one general word-gift (*langue*), and the specific virtualization of world gifts in a context by that word-gift particularized by combination with others in a verbal construction (*parole*).

8.4 Locating economic value in a wider context

The recognition of the continuity between the kinds of value, which are found, attributed and received at different levels, can let us re-vision economic value by seeing it in a wider context. This contextualization allows us to see how, through our social interaction, we weave a continual re-elaboration of value, i.e. of the relational implications of gifts and services of innumerable kinds (even of the paradoxical gifts of not-gifts), for (socially created) individuals and for the community.

We can see ourselves as creatures who are elaborating implications of value or relevance from the beginning, in pre conscious filtering and selection of experience, in material giving and receiving, in altercentric infant-adult cooperative communication, pointing, joint attention and mind reading, in patterned interactions of emphasis, of scalar values, positive and negative, up and down, more and less. Like wasps we build ourselves a collective nest, a kind of niche of relevance and meanings registered in language.

The child first has the feeling 'I am relevant for others' coming from gift value. It is by knowing h:erself as relevant, valuable, that s:he can attribute relevance to other things. By knowing s:he is relevant 'for others' s:he can see other things as like h:er, relevant to others, others themselves as relevant, and others as relevant to still others. Sh: e projects h:er kinetic body map, generalizes, attributes similar feelings and perspectives to others. And sh:e emotionally recognizes h:er motherer as relevant to h:er. This is a 'like me' social feeling, an emotion coming from experience. And the motherer has it too.

Pointing, picking out and giving to the gaze of the other, some relevant object from a background of possible similars and dissimilars, is a pre-linguistic, so pre-virtual, affirmation of relevance or gift value. After language has been 'acquired' also, every phrase involves the individual and collective elaboration of the relevance of the world (to and through the other). Relevance develops into more or less permanent and collective values for the community, what we usually think of as cultural values. Exchange value interrupts this collective elaboration and puts the values of the market in the foreground.

When gift-canceling exchange comes into focus, we treat it linguistically as we would any other world-gift (though we use a mass noun for value as we would for a substance like water), not realizing that the process of exchange (and the quantification of value) is a wolf in sheep's clothing, a space alien in human disguise, a vampire made of our own gifting, reversed and alienated, and wreaking havoc on us and the planet. We need to recognize how economic exchange value (and its justification as individual preference) has recently occupied the whole field of relevance in our culture, making everything else secondary, threatening human social interaction and with it society itself.

Relevance is also experienced physiologically and emotionally. It can already be found in infancy in the rhythms and musicality of mother child interaction. Later it is the result of the preconscious level of maternal selection of perceptions (like Maxwell's demon the internalized mother selects what is relevant) which, together with a level of linguistically mediated, complex conscious selections, creates our common ground and the possibility of collaboration among us. This perceptual relevance is very different from the competitive (statistical)[20] relevance of so-called 'natural selection' of species based on the survival of the fittest.

In fact it is often remarked that the idea of the survival of the fittest is superstructural to the competitive capitalism of Darwin's day.[21] The hidden gifts of the many contributed to the success or failure of the capitalist enterprises and as has recently been explained, it is the gift giving and collaboration within our species that makes us better adapted for survival externally, among species (Sahtouris 2000). Not just the interspecies selection through competition but the intraspecies selection for cooperation makes us a success (gives us a competitive advantage!). Exchange wreaks havoc on intraspecies cooperation.

Throughout this book I have said very little about moral values. That is because I believe that the gift patterns are the human interactive need-satisfying ways that in an exchange based society, constitute what we call 'moral'. We train ourselves away from them in order to survive and thrive in the market, but this makes us party to all the negative aspects of exchange and patriarchy: violence, exploitation, war, lying, cheating, cruelty and degradation. Ethics as justice and the rule of law (balancing crime and punishment) are offshoots of exchange that mitigate some of its worst aspects, just enough to make behavior according to the market logic acceptable. They do this by applying derivatives of exchange like payment for crime to individual patriarchal exchange excesses. Ethics of care are the

---

20   There has been much discussion by the new infant researchers and others about the ability of young children to make an (unconscious) statistical analysis which allows them to connect words with their probable meanings. This circumvents any consideration of needs and gifts, and of preconscious 'maternal' selection according to relevance.

21   In itself this would not mean that survival of the fittest was mistaken, only that the emphasis that allowed it to be discovered came from the (motherless) economic structure (which also hid the importance of gift giving).

superstructure, the values that accompany the implementation of the gift logic. In a generalized gift economy what we now call ethical thinking and behavior would follow implicitly from the intersubjective base.

Aesthetic values have to do with the eliciting of new and unexpected needs that make our experience more general and our knowledge more accurate and satisfying. Our experience of them confers gift value upon us and we give them value, without exchange. They bring our responses forward in new ways.[22]

Linguistic value, gift value, exchange value and even moral and ethical value are all implications of patterns of social behavior coming ultimately from the schema of the gift and its perspectives. They are parts of the process of bringing forward aspects of the world as relevant to other people, as things to which they could or should attend. That is, they are products of maternal patterns. Because within the exchange paradigm they are not recognized as such though, they have not been seen as connected to the deep pattern of the hidden giver who comes forward on h:er own initiative to care, to give and to teach, to show by h:er own caring actions how and what is important.

Use value is actually the only 'value' that is not directed towards others. In fact, it is seen as the direct utility of the product as distinguished from, abstracted from its (albeit distorted) social role in exchange. When it is part of the gift interaction the use value can be seen as a gift and as a vehicle of gift value (the implication of the value of the receiver). On its own it is not gift value or exchange value but is only direct utility for the individual seen outside the social relation.

Gift value is everywhere socially and individually transmitted by giving gifts of all kinds, while linguistic value is the gift value of material and cultural gifts transformed into word-gifts by virtualization and passed on, given forward to others (that is, the world-gifts' general relevance 'for others'). Thus linguistic value is this givenness and givingness of words, which appears in Saussure's synchronic snapshot

---

22 A personal aside – in a museum in Lima, Peru, the guide who was showing us the (unmonetized) Inca gold artefacts, reminded us that gold and silver, like the stars, the sun and moon, are the only things that shine by themselves, i.e. they come forward to our attention on their own. Now commodities come forward from a background, brought by their sellers, while gold and silver, which shine by themselves, also come forward brought by the buyers. We need the things that come forward from others to satisfy our needs, and we need also the words that come forward from others, especially those words in songs or poetry that seem to shine by themselves, as well as all the gifts of the other arts.

langue as the result of the historical development of language, which he calls 'diachrony'.

In this light it is possible to see Marxian market exchange in a different way: exchange value as abstract labor value arises within a structural practice of an *altered* implication of gift value. It is the specific value of an individual item within a market, which is understood as a total social process of not-giving. Within the category of things that are affirmed by exchange as not-gifts, each item is related to all the others through the quantity of the common quality of economic relevance (exchange value), which it has within the whole, relative to other not-gifts, for the 'community' of mutually exclusive exchangers and hence for the individual as one of the many.

In the market, money re presents the product (the would have been or could have been gift) as an exchange value, and this very representation process forms the exchange which transforms the value of the product (now no longer overtly implying gift value) into exchange value. The product or labor time (which the producer cannot use h:erself) could have served as a gift and, being given, it would have given gift value directly to someone, value which also might have been passed on to still others by implication in the same or another form in a gifting community. However since the product or labor is exchanged for an equivalent, this implication of the value of the other is cancelled. The exchange implies instead only the ego-oriented character of the exchangers and the value-in-exchange of the commodity (the cancelled gift) in relation to all the other commodities of that kind on the market, as well as to the market as a whole. The value of each commodity is seen as a quota part of the value of the totality of commodities that are produced for exchange in that way at that time.

What would have been the product's gift value implication is deviated, split from its use value by exchange, and transformed into exchange value as the product is destined not for a particular other but abstractly and momentarily for all others. That is, the product (now a commodity) is a quota part of all similar products[23] destined for others in general who are exchanging in the society and it has a specific exchange value, expressed in a price. As such the commodity has a place in the synchronic snapshot of the market, which is the momentary *langue* of prices. The snapshots, registered by economists hoping to predict trends, are part of the market itself. The individual exchanges are their 'pixels' and they emerge from the diachronic development of the market, influenced by all the myriad cir-

---

23   It is a quota part of that branch of production, which is a quota part of the total production.

cumstances of production, exchange, accumulation, consumption, gifting and use that affect the relevance of the money-word. Both the market and language are collective enterprises and collective products, which makes them difficult for individuals to address. This is especially the case when the gifting aspects of both are denied.

In the market, the (gift) value-conferring capacity of the work and of the product (now commodity) has been displaced away from the individual and onto the societal level. The commodity is 'given' to market exchange and thus gives gift value to (confers value by implication upon) the market, of which it constitutes one small part. Meanwhile money re-presents and thus gives *back* to the product's (would have been) giver the gift value *transformed into* its exchange value. Even the unacknowledged gifts of profit continue to give gift value along with profit to the profit takers (and those who do not make profit do not receive gift value either – so their situation is doubly negative while that of the profit takers is doubly positive for them).

In language there are many moments and levels in which something can be apprehended newly as a gift. This happens when the world-gift is re-given at the level of the word-gift but also again at the level of the sentence or of the text. These can regard any relevant aspect or cluster of things in the perceptual or conceptual context. This new reception of the gift is very commonplace both in language and in our extra linguistic understanding of our surroundings; it also takes place in the identification of more and more general clusters or categories.

Money re-presents and gives back to the exchanger, the gift value of the commodity, transformed. This happens at the new level of the gift of the not-gift, the 'gift' of value-in-exchange when the product has been placed on the market. It allows us to calculate the relevance of that individual not-gift quantitatively with respect to all the other not-gifts.

In fact the product is given to the market (and to other buyers and sellers in general) for the purpose of being re-presented (re-given) in this contradictory way. The original gift value is cancelled and concealed by the exchange, and this is what makes it so hard to understand what exchange value is: i.e, a contradiction or rerouting of the implication of gift value. Although the product is physically transferred, it is not given (because it is exchanged), and therefore its relational implications are altered. We are not used to acknowledging the existence of gift value implications so we don't know we are doing this.[24]

---

24   At most we may be buying or selling the product in order to give it or give money to someone or to our families. The implication of gift value would thus resume once the product is bought or the money is given.

A unilateral gift coming from the other would give gift value to the receiver(s) (and an acknowledgment and 'co-muni-ty' connection to the giver as a participant in gift circulation). However, since the product is given in exchange, what the seller receives is only the money, the exchange value of the product, which does not imply the value of anyone else. When s:he becomes a giver again, by bringing h:er money home to the family, s:he enters into the gift value process again, and can be acknowledged as such.

In this process of the transformation of gift value into exchange value, there is also a change in perspective from the particular to the general and back, which is facilitated by shifts in perspectives similar to those between the one and the many in Marx's footnote (see p. 296 above) and similar to the shifts MacWhinney finds in language. And there is a parallel in the movement from Saussure's *parole* to *langue*, from the individual act of speech to the position of the word as a value in the langue.

The product achieves a kind of semiotization, in its virtualization and re presentation in money as an exchange value, like some particular aspect of the world becoming related to a sign, a sentence or text as its description or more generally to a word as its name. In the market it is as if we 'coin' a word for something – but then have to give it up, again and again, forgetting the holophrastic money-word every time we use it. In fact as I said above, language differs from exchange for money in that words 'accompany' the things they stand for, while money is binarily exclusive: either we have it or we have the commodity. The price accompanies the product (often physically attached as a price tag, which is removed after purchase) but what it re-gives, re-presents, is a moment in a binary exchange; either this amount or no transfer of the product.[25] In contrast, word gifts and perceivable world gifts are endlessly abundant and available to be given. Material commodities and money are scarce and only function as such in scarcity. The 'number words' of prices can of course also be almost infinitely said or given, while the amount of money expressed in the price is scarce, not readily available to all. It is this scarcity that facilitates the leverage point of monetized exchange.

---

25 Haggling is a kind of quantitative use of the competition model of language acquisition, for agreeing on a price.

8.5 Exchange value is gift value, transformed

Thus exchange value is gift value transformed, that is, the implication of the value of the receiver is negated and is given back to the 'giver' through the exchange value, the quantity of the money-word that names ('enunciates,' 'pronounces' the price) the commodity as one among many products of that kind on the market. The implication of the value of the commodity becomes a world-not-gift which is transmittable through the mediation of the money-word. In the exchange transaction, what remains of the product's (the would have been gift's) positive relation to others is just its impersonal similarity to all the other exchange values in the market. It is generalized and equated through money with all the other gift value that has been reversed, frozen in the product and turned back towards the individual material market-based communicative and cognitive needs of all the other ex-givers, all the other adversarial *homini economici*.[26] It is as the individual instrument of this general retroaction that the commodity has an exchange value, which is expressed in the relative non-sound 'volume' of the holophrastic money-word.

Exchange value is the relevance of the product for the other, who is h:erself no longer a simple receiver now but an exchanger. Because its value has been returned to the seller (the would-have-been giver) as money, the commodity is anyway not a transmitter of gift value, and like all the other products on the market, it has become an instrument of leverage. Without the transfer of its money equivalent, the product will not be transferred. Though the product is 'given in exchange', the value of the other as receiver is no longer implied. Instead it is given 'back' in its money-word form.

With language the relevance of things for others can be almost infinitely variable, qualitatively. In exchange there is only one kind of relevance of things for others and this relevance varies only quantitatively. In exchange we are always doing the definition, answering the question 'what is it?', not 'saying' anything else. The answer is always the same: x quantity of not-gift value, expressed in money.

In spite of the seeming ubiquity of money and exchange, gift-giving is the original and continuing independent source of relevance, and it doesn't depend on representation. It provides also movement, emphasis and rhythm, a focus and de-focus, increase and decrease. Relevance is also

---

26   The 'use value' of money is that it satisfies these rarified market-based cognitive and communicative needs.

both linguistic and non linguistic, and can provide a path-to-goal gift trajectory of something for others.[27]

Word-gifts are always benefactive as we mentioned above, because they
satisfy communicative and cognitive needs. However if what they are used
together to convey is negative or neutral, we can call this (virtualize it
as) 'relevance' rather than as 'gift' or 'value'. Knowing about the snake
in the grass is a gift but the presence of the snake is negative, so we say
that the knowledge is 'relevant'. When speaking of exchange and commodities, which are specifically not-gifts, we might expect to use the word
'relevance' but because money, like words, satisfies a cognitive and communicative need, it seems to have a similar benefactive aspect so we think
of it as positive and what it represents, the gift of the not-gift, as positive
also and we say money is valuable – even if it works like a scream.

Linguistic gift value is itself a result of implications of extra-verbal gift
value or relevance, which are transmitted to the speaker-to-be, who receives them, as perceptual and conceptual gifts that satisfy h:er perceptual
and cognitive needs and which gifts s:he takes the initiative to give again
by constructing verbal gifts that s:he passes on to others.

There are many different kinds of relevance and value, before, during,
after and alongside the use of language: maternal and other free gift and
care work continue to transmit gift value to others throughout life. The
relevance and resulting gift value for each of us of our perceived-received
natural and cultural surroundings (which we might describe as the perti-
nence or 'salience' of our ongoing cooperative 'niche construction') creates an emphasis, which we also pass on as a gift to others,[28] again giving
them value (giving value in both directions, towards others and towards
the world). There is the relevance of the giver and the gift value of the
receiver, as well as positive value and relevance of the gifts as satisfiers of
needs. Then there is pragmatic value, the relevance of practices, skills and
techniques; linguistic gift value and perhaps linguistic virtualization value,

---

27   Relevance is different from the purely positional value Saussure proposed. And,
      although exchange value does involve positionality, it maintains a positive charge,
      which comes from its being a transformation of gift value. The positionality in the
      quantitative scale depends on the relevance of these gifts to the needs of all as reg-
      istered and mediated by the market. Perhaps the 'value as position' of words in
      the langue just lacks the quantitative scale. The products are relevant to the needs
      of all not just to 'effective demand' and vice-versa these needs are relevant to the
      gifts. The needs call for or elicit the gifts as relevant to common humanity even if
      most of those who have the needs do not have the money to pay for the products.
28   Implying that those extra linguistic elements are valuable, relevant enough to pass
      on to others.

the positive value of giving-for (the relevance of the proxy), which can be found also in language-teaching and defining. Then there are the relevance and gift value of culture, of art, of husbandry and of some kinds of technology and science, and all the life enhancing production of past generations to which we have access. These are gifts, which are transmitted to us and which we can receive and pass on because we have the altercentric capacities that we developed in infancy through the processes of being mothered. Finally there is monetary exchange value, including money as means of exchange and deposit of value plus money of account and measure of value, deriving from the generalized gift of the not-gift.

Relevance is also implied by our preconscious choices, Mother Nature's (physiologically in us) selections of focuses of attention for our consciousnesses – the motherworld of meaning that keeps percolating up in spite of internalized barriers that would let pass only what is relevant to exchange. Lastly there are our conscious choices of what to give and what to keep, as we give value to others and to ourselves as well as to the gifts.[29] This is the area where so called 'free' will and marginal choices finally come into play.

Exchange value is gift value transformed into the abstract common quality of the materialized and externalized concept, which is the generalized process of exchange. Exchange value is not use value transformed because use value as such does not have the specific aspect 'for others' that gift value has. Labor for the market is abstract(ed) and altered gift labor, turned towards others (towards the many possible buyers) but only to be returned as money, as a not-gift. Gift labor value has energy and significance, a positive life affirming need-satisfying quality that in the market has been 'homogenized,' abstracted and diminished, virtualized in holophrastic money as exchange value while containing an unvirtualized gift residue that is extractable as profit when the product is sold.

It is the gift energy or impetus that provides the illusion of market equilibrium, where supply meets effective demand in a stable manner. This is an illusion because gifts and gift labor could satisfy all needs and keep pace with the diversification and specification of new needs, but neither overt gifting nor needs without the money to back them are admitted in the market category. Instead goods and needs are reconceived and renamed as 'supply and demand'. Understanding distribution in terms of supply and demand eliminates the other-oriented self-starting energy flow of the gift from the picture. It also eliminates or instrumentalizes the empathy and mind-reading

---

29   See Annette Weiner (1992) on the value of what is kept, not given or given in the
     family as inheritance.

of the giver and the trust and openness of the receiver, all of which go to make up the significance of giving-receiving as opposed to the adversarial abstraction, danger and lack of significance of virtualization-categorization considered on its own *without* the teleological altercentric gift component.

'Market equilibrium' as a state in which 'supply' meets 'demand' (a kind of translation of: in which 'gifts' meet 'needs'), was made into a kind of utopia, a Brigadoon of the market, but longed for and aspired to (and calculated into existence) by economists. Perhaps it is even an image coming from the happy and abundant household. But just the terms and concepts 'supply' and 'demand' suggest that we should try to find this equilibrium on the level of the market where it is being made impossible.

8.6 Marx's abstract labor is labor abstracted from gift-giving

> Man is in the most literal sense of the word a *zoon politikon*, not only a social animal but an animal which can develop into an individual only in society. Production by isolated individuals outside of society – something which might happen as an exception to a civilized man who by accident got into the wilderness and already dynamically already possessed within himself the forces of society – is as great an absurdity as the idea of the development of language without individuals living together and talking to one another. (Marx, 2009:268)

The process of material virtualization is accomplished through an equation of two extremely different kinds of things, money and commodities. Many millennia before monetized exchange arose in human history, it was preceded by the development of language, which is also the equation of two very different kinds of things: word-gifts and world-gifts, both of which are directed towards others. Though world-gifts and word-gifts are vastly different and enormously various, that other-direction (which is also specific to each case) is what they have in common. Commodities and money are directed towards others also but they are equated as not-gifts. They are gifts only at the rarefied contradictory level of negation. The others to whom they are directed are others in general, and only in a second moment, when they find their exchangers, are they destined for a particular other individual.

Words come from the linguistic community and exist for others in general at the same time that they are being combined and used to give to individual others. Word-gifts can be given again and again to many other people, creating human relations with them regarding the world gifts for which they are given. These remain as abstract but common human relations that take place even when the individual speaker and listener or writer and reader are not in personal contact.

In language, the 'altercentric' direction of the items, towards others, makes them more abstract and general than they would have been for an individual alone. It is their relevance to others, the fact that others have needs of various kinds that they may satisfy, that abstracts gifts from the immediate experience of the individual. Thus altercentrism, recognizing the relevance of things to others and their needs, is the beginning of abstraction and generalization. That is, it is the beginning of those ways of thinking.

Money and commodities are also given to others in exchange, creating common-uncommon relations with them and another way of thinking, the way that is usually identified as rational. Monetized exchange is abstract not because it moves transitively towards the other but because it leaves aside transitivity and moves toward an engagement in categorization.

There are innumerable one-to-many relations created in both language and exchange. However, the general equivalent character of money is probably the most important unconscious exosomatic model of the one-to-many relation in our society, where it also combines with other (pre existing and continually evolving) hierarchical one-to-many models of patriarchy. The exchange of commodities for money is this categorial abstraction process materialized, acted out on the physical plane, Sohn-Rethel's 'real abstraction'. Marx's abstract labor is thus gift labor that goes through through that process. It is abstract*ed* labor.

Marx's analysis allows us to see the weird character of the market, money and value, a strangeness, which has been denied and normalized by subsequent market apologists. These later economists have found ways of explaining exchange value in terms of 'market forces', supply and demand, utility and preferences that involve neither labor value nor the market actors' relations to others' unmonetized gifts and needs.

My approach asserts economic value to be neither intrinsic nor subjective. Rather value is a quality deriving from the social context, from the externalized concept, which continually plays out in the market as a kind of incarnated binary sorting process. Because products are inserted into that process, which makes their exchangeability – their virtualizability – relevant (their not-giveability giveable) the perspectives of the people who are engaged in the process change – they all become sorters – and the products are viewed as having a common quality that makes them sortable – exchangeable: economic value (as gifts of not-gifts) (but that quality is only relevant to that kind of process of sorting-exchange).

The one quality commodities have in common is that they are products of human labor, which is directed towards others' needs. This is gift labor that would imply the value of the product for the other – as means to the satisfaction of h:er need, (a stage in the gift process) – and hence it would imply also the value of the other – if it were not being contradicted through exchange.

That is, it is gift labor that in passing through this narrow door of exchange, is transformed into labor for exchange and now implies not the value of the other but only the exchange value of the product. This value of the product (of all the commodities on the market) is seen as all one quality, the substance to which the mass noun, the money scream corresponds. Abstract labor creates goods that others want/need but cannot have by gifting or by taking. Value is the relevance of the gifts of the world, of our need satisfying ecological and cultural niche, which we are adapted to receive, but which are denied us, though we can have them if we moan loud enough monetarily.

Money satisfies the (individual and) general *communitary cognitive need* (how much?) and the (individual and) general *communitary communicative need* – for a means of suspending and changing the property relation – of mutually exclusive exchangers to their commodities.[30] As such it is a moment of (socially imposed) virtualization, giving the virtual substitute in place of the world-gift. However the world gift is a not-gift and money is the holophrastic 'world-gift-word' that cannot be 'learned,' and will be given up again in another transaction. The work that travels down the twisted path of this process is abstract(ed) labor. It is co-muni-cation, giving (not-) gifts together, in a community of adversaries.

Although in exchange part of the transfer looks the same, in that the product and the money move alternately from the hands of one to the hands of the other, the implications of the transfer have shifted away from the logic of givers-receivers and communicators to that of exchangers. In exchange, it is not implied that the receiver is valuable for h:erself, because s:he is only a buyer, nor is the seller relevant as a giver: s:he is just giving to h:erself through the detour of exchanging h:er product for money. So gift value – relevance – is attributed to the product not to the people. The relevance of the product is expressed in a quantity of the material money.

Understanding labor as the source of value is also important because it is by recognizing labor in this way that anyone, capitalists themselves included, can realize how much of their own 'substance' comes from the gifts

---

30   Words also satisfy the communitary cognitive need but the individual communicative need is satisfied by their combination.

of others. The neoclassical school of economics interprets value as a matter of subjective choices and detaches those who 'make money' from the idea of the source of their good in others (Goux 2004). The patriarchal capitalist system and its ideology create greed as a motive for accumulation, but they also create the selective blindness that hides the sources of gifts and makes greed acceptable. Capitalists and corporations cover their own tracks too, so their part in the creation of their economic niche is invisible. Academic disciplines consciously or unconsciously often also serve this purpose by providing complex alternative explanations as decoys and cover-ups.

As I have been saying, the gift value transmitted to the other by implication is part of the relation to the other that is created by satisfying h:er need (which may be a material but also a communicative or cognitive need). The exchange value of the product is part of the relation *to others in general* that is created by exchanging the commodity for money, transforming it into a not-gift.

What would have been the gift value of labor or of the product (service or gift) given by one individual to another is altered, abstracted and transformed by its relation to all the other products on the market. In this situation the exchange value of the commodity, which is the relation of the product to others in general, is divided from its use value, which derives from its particular use and is suspended for the moment in the exchange process. Most of its gift value is cancelled by the exchange, though what remains of it is redirected towards the capitalist together with the hidden gift of profit.

With the recognition of labor value we can trace wealth back to its source, even in cases where it appears to come from the product itself, like the oil industry. Though exploration and refining are expensive, the labor of oil production is minimal. The oil itself is free, a gift of the Earth, but is paid for by the abstract labor of the many as expressed in their salaries, some part of which they spend in the purchase. And of course it has negative effects on the very many, by taking from them indirectly through pollution. This oil-energy gift is another way of leveraging the gifts of the many, distributing them to capitalists, corporations and shareholders. Like oil, nano technology and the printing of objects 'contain' very little human labor. There too the labor value comes from the salary of the buyers who have worked in some other branch of the economy to pay for them. All of this has much to do with the psychology of capitalists. They believe that value comes from their work, their knowledge, their clever trading, from luck, from the marketing of their products, from the conquest of new markets, even from satisfying needs. They do not usually realize it comes from taking the gifts of others. It is a bitter pill.

8.7 Exchange is the backwards image of gift-giving

Gift giving and receiving and the gift schema come before virtualization in early childhood. Looking at the process after language has already been 'acquired', one might think that both gift giving and exchange are embodiments of the schemas of language: the transitive gift schema or the intransitive virtualization schema, which are acted out externally as material gift or as material exchange.[31] The direction of influence certainly runs both ways but material gift-giving is primary and prelinguistic and continues throughout life, even if gift-giving is later *also* used virtually as the structure and medium of language. Virtualization arises with language and thus comes after material giving and receiving.

Material exchange is post-language-acquisition and only begins to be understood by the child around four to five years of age. Exchange is not a fundamental part of language but an offshoot of virtualization, a later development.

Gift value arises first through material giving and receiving; linguistic gift value arises through virtual-verbal giving and receiving and transitivity; exchange value arises materially through virtualization/substitution/exchange and the interruption and re-routing of giving and receiving transitivity.

Words are a means for aligning our cognitive and communicative relations with others'. In the beginning, in the altercentric mother-child relation, communication and cognition are one and the same thing with giving and receiving. Each knows the other and the many gifts and services involved through the experience of nurturing and being nurtured. The feelings of mutuality – as a communicative community of two – arise in the same process. Cognition and communication continue to be merged and aligned to some extent in giving and receiving language, though we have cognition also independently from communication – we don't have to talk about every thing we know all the time – and we have internalized at least some of our communicative processes.

In infant-motherer dyadic interaction and mutuality each participant has a relation to that part of the world, which is the other, which is similar to (and patterned on) the other's gifting relation[32] to the self. Exchange uses a kind of denatured and contradictory giving to reverse, suspend and reestablish the alignment of these early relations in a different way on the

---

31 To clarify: the gift schema as we have seen is already acted materially pre linguistically between mothers and children. Virtualization is linguistic. Monetized exchange is the acting out of the virtualization schema on the material plane.

32 Mediated by many specific gifts and services.

material plane. Because it contradicts early altercentrism, and is practiced obsessively by adults, exchange appears to be 'mature' while gift-giving appears 'immature'.

Gift-based alignment in mutuality is not part of the exchange process, or we might say that in the exchange process it has been transformed, rarefied, abstracted to address the single contradictory quality, exchange value. This is because the exchangers are communicatively and cognitively aligned primarily at a metalevel with regard to their adversarial mutual exclusion and not-giving. Even if one exchanger actually hands over the (need-satisfying) product and the other hands over the (communicative-cognitive need-satisfying) money, no other-oriented gift is intended. We find that we are similar in our mutually exclusive adversarial identities as property owners and exchangers and we each relate our property and money to that of the other through equations that abstract from and hide the gifts that actually have been and are still being given. Again, this seems to be adult behavior (to which children, especially masculated boys, are taught to aspire).

This effacement of the maternal gift economy is what Goux calls the 'effacement of a genesis from which fetishism is born' (in Roberts 2010). Since we ignore the development of exchange value from gift value, the altercentric gift interaction seems to have nothing to do with the rest of life. Here is the ancient but ever-present beginning of the split between the frames of gift and exchange. In each of the following areas and many others, the first is usually understood through the gift frame , the second through the exchange frame and looking at the one through the frame of the other requires a lengthy detour. The areas are for example, emotion and reason; body and mind; practical or corporeal cognition and abstract categorial cognition. This frame split is not originally a philosophical one but happens because we turn need-satisfying material gift reality (the ecological niche to which we are intricately adapted as receivers, givers and re-givers) in a contradictory interpersonal direction, a direction different from and indeed antithetical to maternal gifting in life and in language. Then we use both the gift schema and its frame and the exchange schema (derived from virtualization) and its frame as our interpretative keys.

Exchange for money is the backwards image of material and linguistic communication. By imposing an equivalent return for the transitive gift, exchange becomes *countertransitive*.We do not recognize exchange as such though, so it appears to be sui generis and ineluctable. This appearance of exchange as an independent process is part of the reason why, although we speak, read, write and engage in monetized exchange many times every day and although many tomes have been written about both linguistic communication and the market, not only academics but we, who are the daily users of these processes do not understand either one or their connections with each other very well.

If we bring forward gift-giving material communication and linguistic communication on the one hand and exchange as their distorted and partial reenactment on the other, we can construct a standpoint between the two, with a perspective that takes both into account. Thus we can see their frames from the outside as made up of the two opposing logics with their corresponding attitudes of personal altercentrism or objectively impersonal but interpersonally equivalent egocentrism.

A further step here is the use of exchange to accomplish gift-giving. For example we work for the market in order to acquire the means of giving to our families. We do this because the generalization and spread of the market does not allow any other sources of material gifts, even from nature.

Our explorations of exchange and language have to take place in language, a fact which conceals the external Archimedes point or vantage point that gift-giving and its various permutations, including exchange, actually provide. These permutations include: gift-giving as material communication; gift-giving in language; giving at different levels; the distorted material giving and distorted linguistic aspects of monetized exchange, pre- and post-market giving, profit as hidden gifts, etc. (and others like giving forward, obligatory social giving, giving for power-over; tracking of gifts among others and in nature).

Looking at each of these from the point of view of the others allows us to see the complexity of the whole market/gift conundrum. Investigating any of them without including the others makes our view necessarily partial. It is only by placing exchange in the wider context of the gift that we can see that exchange value/use value do not exhaust the field of economic value, and that both in the economy and in language there is gift value, which is transmitted by implication from giver to receiver (and which is often, though not necessarily, accompanied by the recognition and appreciation of the giver by the receiver). We should in fact call this a feminist maternalist standpoint (Hartsock 1983) not an Archimedes point. As feminists we often work in the market but retain gift values and gift practice as well, so we are between the worlds of gift economy and exchange.

From the maternal point of view of giving and language, we can see exchange as a distorted acting-out of the relation of virtualization between words and things on the material plane. That is what is happening when exchange functions to create a 'real abstraction',[33] that part of the exosomatic concept in which the immediate or present relevance of the materiality of the item is set outside of the gift relation in a hiatus (in the store), while it waits for a new gift-not-gift relation to be created between the persons regarding the money word-exemplar. And each exchanger's own private product-exemplar is successively relinquished while the common money-word-exemplar takes its place. One's work or product is sold and s:he arrives in the market place with the resulting money-word-exemplar in h:er pocket to shop for a commodity. S:he comes with the money-word-exemplar to give for the product and the seller is willing to take it. As the market expands and the exchange relation is generalized, the 'one' character of money becomes more evident in that it stands for and takes the place of every thing and every kind of thing. All the gifts are obliterated – nature, childhood, imagination, sex, internal organs, personal information. Money reigns.

The image of the successful 'one' ego grows up in the shadow of money. Not only the ego but the other one to many patriarchal structures have incarnated or reincarnated under its influence and in a second moment these hierarchies validate their 'parent' money by repetition.

This view can also help us understand exchange value as abstracted and distorted gift value. That is, the implication of the value (the relevance) of the other person, coming from the gift initiative, which is present in both material and in linguistic gifting has become homogeneous and self-contradictory in exchange, and regards only the abstract value of the individual commodity in relation to the totality of commodities on the market. The implication of the value of the other (and the secondary or metalevel emotional gift of the gift, including possible joy in giving and receiving) that would have been implied through concrete gift labor has been abstracted and transformed into a scalar quantitative value of the thing given in exchange and the labor producing that value has become relevant or as Marx says, it 'counts' only as abstract labor. The structure of the implications has changed.

Having understood this we can look back at language from exchange value and understand linguistic value as the qualitative relevance of the world-gifts that the words are given for[34] plus the value of the need-satisfying word-gifts as transmitters of this world-gift-value and of the implica-

---

33 There is a similarity here with the abstraction of the male child from the gift economy and his relation to the father as the exemplar of his gender identity.

34 A commodity is evaluated quantitatively with respect to all the others by identifying a quantity of money to be given for it. A world-gift is valued qualitatively with respect to all the others by giving a word gift of its 'own' for it. Words are quali-

tion of the value of the other/receiver/listener/reader. At the same time gift value is also given at the level of syntax by giving words to other words inside verbal 'packages' (sentences, discourses, etc).

Gift-giving has been hidden because it has not been distinguished from exchange and has not been accorded a primary ontological status of its own. By describing it here I am hoping to bring it into focus and also to make it visible as the ground against which the figure of exchange may at last be clearly seen and investigated anew.

Moreover, from the point of view which we are establishing *between* linguistic gift and exchange (between genuine linguistic abstraction and the distorted material 'real abstraction'), we can see both the similarity of the processes and the reversal of linguistic *and* extra linguistic gift-giving by exchange.

This perspective can help us understand the many permutations of value, and can also account for the very negative influence that, as a distortion of material and linguistic communicative gift giving, the externalized concept has had on our characters, consciousnesses, motivations and behaviors. This influence of monetized exchange has been invisible but it is driving us to disrespect, usurp and exploit mothering/gift-giving and thus to destroy motherers, their others and the Mother planet, a fact which appears to justify our attempting species and planetary suicide. This accelerating race to extinction is *not actually our fault*. We are being auto-piloted by the distorted cognitive/communicative mechanism of monetized exchange, which is also fueled by the competitive motivations of patriarchy.

Images of this mechanism proliferate throughout society. The one-to-many political, religious, military and academic institutions, embody the structure of judgement and permission, access and denial of entry that the sorting mechanism of money and the market provide. Like money, we 'buy' or discard our experience. Our much criticized binary reasoning is undergirded by the valueless/valueable, gift/exchange binary choices imposed by the market everyday. Even debt, guilt and punishment for crime, which we call upon to make ourselves and others 'take responsibility', are cognates of exchange. These cognates riddle our ideas of morality and law, reinfecting our gift initiatives with exchange logic and placing force above care as the means of changing behavior. Thus ideas of morality rarely gain enough traction to make change, especially in the individuals who are continually being stimulated towards success in the system.

Nevertheless, it is still in our power to access the gift mode in language

tatively various verbal monies. Money is a qualitatively homogeneous but quantitatively various material word.

and life and to take the initiatives and give the gifts that will satisfy the need for change. In order to do this we must understand how monetized exchange, language and gift-giving are linked together. This is where the standpoint between giving and exchange is actually the liberated, empowered and unclouded point of view of the conscious motherer. S:he can help us fix the brakes on the moving car we are riding in.

The standpoint between language and economics permits us to see how gift and exchange and their perspectives interact. In fact there is an abundant leakage of gifts around the social mechanism of gift-cancelling exchange. Unfortunately by serving the market through free labor, giving gifts of profit to it and through it, those who contribute to profit are giving gift value to the market and to capitalists and corporations by implication. In spite of themselves, through their gifts they are implying the value of those who take the profit, of the businesses and individuals who accumulate and plunder and of the rapacious system itself. In this way they unwittingly collude with their own oppression. Moreover, in scarcity, if there is no other way of having one's needs satisfied, even the not-gift of exchange is a 'gift', that is, it satisfies the (artificially created) need for some way of access to goods and we apprehend and appreciate it as a gift and a source of gifts at that paradoxical level.

Once we see that it is exchange that is embedded in a wider context of gift-giving, not primarily vice-versa, we can see that exchange value is a special case, a transformation and denial of gift value. Exchange value is the not-gift-relevance of the product to the collective cognitive and communicative externally embodied concept process, and which registers the relevance of this product relative to all the others as a quantity of its monetary exemplar-word.

8.8 Money and patriarchy: taking the place of the prototype of the mother

Our subjectivity, whatever its preferred 'natural' course of development might be, is presently artificially distorted by the existence of the social patterns or templates of private property and money. During the last centuries there have been historical challenges to some of these patterns, political revolutions and changes in property and family structures. However, they are still very powerful templates, and the more so because they are mostly invisible as such. Tracing their influences can be a step in liberating ourselves from them.

For the property template: my body (proprioception) is my property and my private property is an extension of my body, and both are mutually exclusive with everyone else's. In a relation that is like a graded category (or one of Vygotsky's complexes) but based on belonging rather than similarity, I am a kind of prototype of my property because there are many different items that belong to me, which are quite varied. Their only common relation is that of belonging to me. This 'complex' is superseded by the 'classical concept' exemplar-to-many money relation, where we alienate an item of property in exchange for money because all the items in exchange have the common social quality of exchange value.

A somewhat similar prototype-to-many mother-children 'complex' relation can be superseded by the father's patriarchal hegemonic 'property' of the mother, children and goods. Nevertheless, the father also functions as a general equivalent, because like a commodity, the boy child leaves the relation to his mother as prototype and relates himself to his father as the 'type of the genus homo' (see above Marx 1996|1867| note 19: 54). The gender binary recapitulates the binary of gift/exchange, of valuable/valueless, which spreads throughout the culture.

The little boy finds himself in a new category, with the valuable notgiving father as exemplar. In this way the male child is abstracted from the gift economy and must eventually struggle to become himself the exemplar of the human, creating a non nurturing 'like me' relation with his father, who has folllowed the same path before him. In patriarchy the one-to-many relation becomes the relation of male dominance. From the family to the nation, from the army to religion, the one dominates the many and the many give respect, obedience and nurturing to the one.

Slavery is the direct enactment of the property relation of humans over humans held in place by force. The general equivalent money is used to actually buy and sell people, it is not just a benign or neutral template of one-to-many.

The relation of items of property to each other – as mother to children and other chattel – is a prototype relation but she and they are also related to their husband/father/owner as many to one. An exemplar who speaks, he is different from them because of his authority, in the position of the word (he re-presents social power-over and high transitive hitting). The exemplar in relating to the maternal prototype gives rules and laws, naming and re naming, combining gift and virtualization schemas so that gifts are given vertically from the many to the one exemplar. The prototype gives way to the exemplar, becoming one of many to his one over many. Since this schema is repeated in the traditional Western family structure, it creates a pattern that organizes the multitude (Hardt and Negri 2004) from within in a pattern that repeats the top down hierarchical structure of patriarchal society in innumerable self-similar fractals. The money to many relation also confirms this human hierarchical structure in a horizontal register. The similarities make it difficult for the multitude to be a really alternative 'revolutionary subject' as Negri and Hardt propose. Although many people in 'advanced capitalism' are now moving out of hierarchical roles, they often become disconnected and adversarial individuals, due to the ego oriented exchange relation and many tend to assimilate the one-to-many structure internally in the construction of their own personalities. Moreover as some individuals in some societies become more egalitarian, the one-to-many relation is played out on a large scale among nations. The US has assumed the 'one' position after the fall of the Soviet Union and before any major challenge by China or the European Union or confederations of countries in the Middle East or Latin America.

The father as exemplar and the mother as (cancelled) prototype relate to each other like two poles of a magnet, like General Equivalent and relative commodity, forming the core of our problematic binary gender roles. In the patriarchal family the (female) mother is the prototype of property (and she takes care of the property and the children) relative to the father-owner-equivalent who is the family exemplar of property-owning 'man' (and if the knower is also an owner-equivalent, the father is also super knower as 'owner' of the mother – knower and known – prototype).

The father takes the mother's place in the same way that money takes the place of the commodity, but in a long term relationship in which further exchanges of the mother with other husbands-fathers are presumably forbidden. He is general equivalent and phallic exemplar of value (valor ?). He counts and is counted. The Freudian myth of the sons who murder the father is just the attempt of the sons to rise to their appointed places as exemplars. In contrast, the egalitarian transformation of patriarchy (and the economy) would indeed require an abdication of the 'one' position altogether and its replacement by the many in the family, in the wider society and in the economy.

For the general equivalent man in the patriarchal family, the woman is in the relative position, for the children she is the prototype. A child constructs h:er identity through h:er 'like me' bridge with h:er motherer, but then if s:he is a boy, finds that there is no longer and indeed there never was, a complete analogy between h:er male body and h:er female motherer's body. S:he then searches for a different model and finds it in the father, who, just because he has a male body, has the privileged, dominant exemplar-and-owner social position. This gender identification creates a long term psychological rebus for men in the West, which is sometimes never solved. In fact the relation to the father is abstract because the boy himself has been abstracted (and removed, suspended, extracted) from his mother-child identity construction. He is the alienable product whose value is mirrored in his relation to the exemplar father until he eventually takes the same place in a new family and establishes a similar 'ownership' relation to his own family and property while becoming that family's exemplar of mankind (as women have become equal to men they can also extract themselves from the nurturing identity and become 'masculated' exemplars).

This family configuration is similar to that of the market where exchange is meta categorization in that it socially recategorizes gifts as commodities and people as sellers and buyers, material communicators-virtualizers. It makes exchangers of all the private proprietors, each of whom is in a pro- totype to many, Vygotskyan complex relation to h:er possessions-things. In this recategorization, the (ego-centered) individual complex -prototype property relation is superseded by the collective exemplar – money-to- many concept relation.

The proprietors give way to the one-to-many concept form of money, suspending their property relation for the moment. The property transforms as it becomes relevant to other properties on the market and to potential buyers and sellers as commodity or as money, and the owners transform as they become exchangers, relevant to each other as owners of alienable commodities (many) or of money (one). Those who were givers/receiv- ers in their private lives become exchangers – of their property or of their labor time at least. They do virtual or metagiving, by giving (up) the mon- ey-word that refers to a commodity. They are repeating the original nam- ing (virtualizing) process again and again on the material level, bringing forward the world-gift to be named or giving up its appropriate money name. My money regards, is about, your property, meta to it. Yet my meta 'discourse' is limited to the judgment of value and its quantity. This mea- ger connection, which excludes gifts and givers, becomes the main social nexus among human beings.

In a society without property and commodity exchange all this would be different. The woman-mother would not be (like) property or (like) a commodity – and neither would the child. In this case the mother could be- come the prototypical model for both women and men. S:he would not be in the hierarchical one-to-many position because h:er model would not be backed up by an alignment with money, property ownership and exchange (but rather possibly an alignment with gift-giving distribution of goods to needs, with nurturing language and with h:er environmental niche).

In our present situation the existence of the money exemplar which excludes gift-giving and imposes exchange (and the equation of value) functions like a Vygotskian Zone of Proximal Development, an artificial 'scaffolding' for the (usually male) masculated identity that excludes (maternal) gift-giving.

The money-to-many externalized concept form, the one-to-many internal ('mental') concept form, and the masculated male identity all back each other up, creating a predominance of the 'classical concept' in philosophy while eliminating until recently the complex or graded prototype-based categorization, which was identified with so called 'primitive' peoples (Lakoff 1987). These were indigenous peoples free from markets and money, many or most of whom have eventually come under the heavy homogenizing rule of the General Equivalent. In Euroamerican capitalism children (and their supposedly 'childlike' 'good' mothers) also appear to be 'primitive' and 'pre' market.

Assimilation into the Patriarchal Capitalist market has now provided some women with the same status as men, as property owners and exchangers, subjects of legal rights, putting them in the prototype ownership position at least part time (but often also as sexual objects, who have only their bodies as property to give or to sell, and to sell-to-view or view-to-sell) and giving them access to becoming exemplars as 'breadwinners' and as divas, stars, CEOs and generals. Although many individual women have benefitted from the breaking of their centuries– old chains, the gift-plundering system itself has remained fundamentally unchanged. Indeed if anything it has gotten worse, causing the enrichment of a new elite few, the further impoverishment of ever-increasing multitudes and the devastation of Motherer Nature. Feminists who have gained a modicum of freedom by participating in the market, often do try to extend their privilege to other women. However, it is urgent that they/we use their presence in the system of privilege to radically change it. Although the increasing calls for women to 'wake up' and 'take their power' may appear to be only an exhortation towards individual improvement, actually they imply this need for women and especially mothers to lead the movement for radical change.They/we have to come forward as relevant, to make the gift relevant and generalize it.

8.9 The gift of profit

One problem with market economics is that it considers giving and receiving as destructive of economic value when instead it is its source. This happens because unpaid work such as housework and child care are not seen as economic. That is gifts are not recognized as part of the economy and the part (implication) of value that passes through gifts is ignored. People are sensitive to the implication of value. The child who is clean and well-nourished has been given value. We can see it. However, we don't consider it the result of an economy.

But there is an endless need for and validation of money. Making something out of 'nothing' – making profit (from the gifts of others), is the other sanitized side of getting something for nothing – sanitized free riding.

When labor is what is sold, the gift (of housework and surplus labor) is given by the laborer-seller to the capitalist. The housewife and/or salaried worker do not realize that their work gives gifts to the capitalist and thus implies h:er value. And the capitalist does not realize where h:er profit comes from, so s:he thinks s:he *makes* it and *deserves* (another cognate of exchange) the value implied to h:er (h:er 'high' – 'up is good' – social position – the perspectives from which s:he views and is viewed). Even though people in the society ignore the importance of gift-giving they configure their conscious respect around those to whom gifts and gift value are given by themselves or others. They unwittingly collude because of the systemic denial of giving and the lack of understanding of the implications of both giving and exchange.

When the commodity is bought, the buyer – the wholesaler, retailer or consumer – pays for the free portions coming from surplus labor and natural resources, unremedied pollution, and housework (as well as from differences in levels of life of the workers internationally and nationally so that the living wage they earn can be much lower in the producer than that in the consumer country). Then that extra portion of the money goes back along the chain of sale to the sellers as profit. After the exchange, the value of the commodity is taken by the sellers, as vehicled and expressed in the money-word, to exchange again, as s:he becomes a buyer in h:er turn. The value has been conserved and augmented. Exploitation is the forced extraction of gifts anywhere along the chain of production, purchase and sale, aided by scarcity and dependence on the capitalist.

Both the seller and the buyer are motivated by the desire to receive a gift: the seller to 'make' a profit and the buyer to receive more or better goods than s:he pays for. The quantity, the decibel level, of the money word increases for one of them due to gifts hidden by the 'equal' exchange. In a situation in which the cost of production is low, for example due to the reduced quality of material life in a country of the Global South, both exchangers in the North receive a gift, the seller in the low price of the labor, and the buyer because the product is less expensive than comparable goods would have been if produced in the North. In Marx's terms, it is as if an improvement in the means of production had changed the socially necessary labor time for that kind of product, so that producers of the same kind of product in the North have to work longer than those in the South to create the same amount of value. Instead it is the level of life that makes the difference.

The interaction of exchange transforms what would have been the implication of gift value (of the relevance or importance of the receivers and thus of the gifting community) into exchange value, a contradictory relevance of the product to money and thus to the not-gifting market at large. Concrete labor becomes abstract communicative labor, giving without giving, to others in general in order to receive from one of them a money token, a material word-exemplar. Through this token, taken as a quantity, a quota part of the whole, individual exchangers are related ideally to all others, and through the same token, taken as a material object, they are related practically to one or a few others by receiving it from or transferring it to them. The nurturing transmission and implication of gift value becomes indirect. Instead of enacting the gift schema together or taking turns, the exchangers materially enact complementary halves of the virtualization schema. One gives up the 'word' to the other and receives the thing, the other gives up the thing to the other and receives the 'word'.

In linguistic communication, speakers or writers sequentially virtualize many different aspects of experience as verbal gifts in order to give them again sequentially and syntactically, using the very versatile gift schema. In material exchange-communication on the other hand, they virtualize the many different need-satisfying goods as one inflexible thing only – money – which they give in order to exchange. The fact that words in language do not of themselves satisfy material needs sets a precedent for the money-word not-gift, which also does not directly satisfy needs, as communicative mediator of not-gift commodities. At the moment in which they are being exchanged, in the 'exchange abstraction', the not-gift commodities are the 'referents' of the money word. This process seems natural and obvious to us because we are doing something similar all the time when we use language.[35]

---

35   Another level of complication is created when products of language are what is bought and sold. They become the 'referents' of the money-word.

But the gift of profit is hidden inside the transaction. This gift continues to be transmitted even when it is not visible, not 'named' as such and instead is covered by economists with a term like 'externalities'. The gifts of Nature, housework and surplus value are not counted in the cost of production but eventually they are monetized and transferred to the capitalist in the price of the commodity when the buyer pays for it. From the point of view of the marginalists this price simply reflects the utility of the products for the buyer. The 'supply' (artificially scarce 'gift') meets the 'effective demand' (artificially delimited, monetized need).

The products that are made for the market are not considered gifts. If they have to be given as gifts (or wasted), not exchanged, because of 'lack of demand'[36] this is usually considered a dis-value, a business failure. Paradoxically it is the hidden gift portion of commodities that motivates all transactions, all the so called 'equal exchanges'. The gifts of profit , which the exchangers receive through the exchange process continue to give gift value to them, that is they continue to imply their relevance or importance (as did their mothers' free gifts), and this I believe, is one of the reasons for greed. That is, gifts imply the value of the receiver and unfortunately even of the taker, however s:he succeeds in getting them. Because of this, gift-giving unwittingly colludes with and rewards not only competition but also its own exploitation.[37] Making conscious the widespread presence of gift-giving and the implications of gift value can clarify the process, empower the workers-givers and debilitate the ego-building motivational aspects of profit 'making' or 'taking'. The aggrandizement of the capitalist comes not from h:er work, intelligence and expertise but from the gifts of the many that s:he has succeeded in capturing.

The social and natural gifts of our nurturing ecological niche are transformed into not-gifts by the market and their gift value is cancelled or transformed into exchange value, which can then serve as the 'objective' vehicle through which the hidden gift of profit is transported back to the capitalist. The end results of this transformation can be seen in the degradation of nature and of humanity through poverty, war, preventable disease and the diminishing of the bodies and souls of workers of all kinds and ages including the child and adult victims of commodification by prostitution and trafficking.

---

36   The creation of demand through advertising is now itself a commodity.
37   From this the zero sum game derives its significance. The winner receives all the gifts, which imply her value, and this implies her superiority over the ones who do not win. It would certainly be a factor in the prisoners' dilemma test.

Having followed the gift of profit into the hands of capitalists, we should not give up the trail. Profit is reinvested in profitable financial instruments, stocks and bonds whereby more gifts are extracted either through the use of the funds in industries and corporations or through risky financial speculation. The body of profit is diminished by dilution through inflation and fiat money as well as crooked financial instruments and 'bad' mortgages which take the gifts from the workers' future salaries. The accumulated gifts are volatilized (and our European settler ancestors criticized the 'waste' of potlatch!) or again profitably spent but wasted on war industries, paid for by the government, using the gifts of taxes. All this has as its product the rubble we see on TV, the infrastructure that will have to be rebuilt someday so it has a 'value'. Foreign corporations or those locals who serve them will make money on them. Exchange value is 'conserved'.

8.10 Is exchange value linguistic value transformed?

Again looking at exchange in the light of language, we see that in the market, in the place of the importance (relevance, value) of other people we put the importance of the commodity and of money. This is money as the means of the satisfaction not of the others' material need but of one's own communicative-cognitive need regarding the other's need, which turns out to be an infinitely expandable need for money itself. Money as a material holophrastic word is quantitatively hierarchically organized. We use it to name the commodity as a quantity of value and to create the common mutually exclusive human relations that allow the transfer of commodities and labor, goods and services among owner-exchangers. We also accumulate it against future needs and transactions, however, so that we can control the abundance of gifts coming to us and to others.

Because money is derived from language, the exchangers (in a common but mutually exclusive rather than inclusive way) give money for the commodity in much the same way that they give the word for the perceptual or conceptual gift.

We are able to compare money and language now because we have the idea of the importance of giving, without which we would not recognize the specific importance of the character of not-giving. Money, the material 'word', is qualitatively the same for all because it regards the strange but homogeneous and general gift of the not-gift, and it only varies quantitatively. Language on the other hand regards very many different perceptual and conceptual world-gifts while the word-gifts that are given for them vary qualitatively. Commodities as not-gifts are qualitatively the same and quantitatively comparable through the not-gift of money. Things we talk about are qualitatively similar as kinds of world gifts and again qualitatively comparable through word-gifts.

We said above that in linguistic virtualization (a linguistic equation of value), words are in the 'equivalent position' while things are in the 'relative position'. This allows us to see the lexicon as a collection of decontextualized verbal gifts, which are all in the equivalent position, on the virtual plane. In the *langue*, where words have 'value' as position but not relevance explicitly or gift value, they are all poised in their potential giveability (Saussure would say perhaps: their 'exchangeability' for an 'idea'). They only have a position in a kind of flattened hierarchy (like who can give to who, what to what, according to a sort of 'status' without the vertical scale). They have been de-motivated in a balanced field. As with market 'equilibrium of supply and effective demand', this is a characterization of the signifier and the signified that leaves the gift out. Words are assessed as values only according to relations (and categories) of similarities and differences, while any other relations are explained by rules of syntax. In this abstract way words as linguistic 'values' are made appropriate for being explained without mothering, without their gift connections, an explanation appropriate for the exchange paradigm.

I am using Saussure's idea of linguistic value because it allows us to discuss the aspects of linguistic abstraction in a way that is comparable to economic abstraction. I consider myself justified in this because Saussure took his idea from Walras' market in equilibrium (Ponzio 1974; Mirowski 2004). The psychological and philosophical meaning of the market seen in this way is that it seems to be a self regulating system without the intervention of any authority. Like language it functions on its own,[38] so it is a good analogy for language (even a genetically inherited linguistic capacity would function this way). Still, mothering/gift-giving is eliminated. Walras himself derived market equilibrium from the physics of the time according to Mirowski (1989). Neither mothering nor domestic labor was a prominent factor in either discipline.

In contrast consider the matriarchal Iroquois who named the members of the tribe according to their social functions. This 'grammar of social

---

38   Supply responds to effective demand in the market, and ignores the needs that are not expressed in money. And the needs of the prelinguistic child, not yet expressed in language? Who is satisfying them? The motherer, by mind-reading.

relations' is similar to value as position of words in the *langue*.[39] It names people in the community according to the gifts they give and services they perform. Their 'value as position' is 'motivated'. The proper name can change if the person's function changes. Then someone else can take the previous name along with the function (without private property all practice refers to the commons).

In Saussure's *langue* we see mainly the one-to-many 'naming' function with the word and the idea, which he also illustrates by a one-to-one exchange (of a five franc piece for a loaf of bread.) If we looked at *langue* in the light of the Iroquois we might see it as a metaphorical community with different roles for different parts of speech and different word-gifts as having the job of giving the world-gift of a certain perception or conception. Some words would have the capacities for being declined or conjugated, some the ability to connect other words in various ways. Thus value-as-position would be position as part of a collaborative community rather than value-as-position within a mutually exclusive group of private property owners. The 'members' would give value to other 'members' and to the community through their gift work.[40]

Words have gift value as giveable for some kind of world gift to satisfy human communicative and cognitive needs and they have a value as products of the collective material and linguistic communication of past generations. Words have 'social relations' with each other, egalitarian 'social positions', which actually depend on gift interactions, on who gives what to whom at the level of *parole* as happens in the 'grammar of social relations', in societies with common property and gift economies.

As we just said, there is a polarity in the *langue* between words and things, or words and 'ideas,' which is similar to that between money and commodities. Words in the *langue* are on the side of the equivalent in the equation of value and they are general. In fact they can be seen as a collection of general equivalents, as if they were a collection of monies with each standing for a different kind of 'commodity'.[41] This may be hard to

---

39 Our society with its one-to-many obsessions seems to be collectively exploring the function of the exemplar in concept formation.

40 'By Iroquois custom, each clan holds a set of personal names. When a child is born he or she is given a name "not in use". This "baby name" is usually later changed for an "adult name" that is not then "in use", that is, one belonging to someone now deceased or to someone whose name has been changed' (Tooker 1990: 112).

41 Like Schmandt Besserat's tokens but not one to one but one to many, kind by kind. One kind of money-token for tomatoes another for pears. Or more generally one for fruit and veg and another for livestock.

imagine given the differences in dimensions (words may seem very small and fleeting, while money may seem very large and permanent – or even vice versa), but the basic pattern is the same. The difference in such hypothetical 'monies' would be justified by the difference in the kinds of 'commodities'. That is, it would be 'motivated'. The reason for this similarity of words and money is not that exchange is primordial or that money is inevitable. Rather it is that money is a development of language, the rematerialization of linguistic virtualization.

8.11 Saussure's value

Saussure's *langue* is seen at a meta level in which the words are decontextualized 'values' in a system of differences. They are all equally abstract and pre selected by the community as valuable at a certain level of relevance. In our terms they have 'value' because their referents – their world-gifts – are relevant, and because the words can be given to others as gifts that satisfy their cognitive and communicative human needs which arise regarding those relevant parts of the world. They can confer gift value on the referent for which they are given, on the other words in the verbal gift construction and on the human receiver.

As a metalinguistic creation, the *langue* is composed of words suspended from their use, in the 'exchange abstraction' in the mental bank or warehouse. They are words abstracted from the act of linguistic giving and receiving. However, the same words are already there in others' minds also, like money which is already in the buyers' pockets in effective demand. The receiver already has them in her own mental bank account or storage room. S:he has a supply of verbal tokens that can be used to 'buy' images. The verbal exemplar 'tree' is 'exchanged' (Saussure's word) for the image of a tree (really a free non verbal exemplar-image, readily available). In effective demand also, we only give to others what they can pay for, that is, what they already have in a money form. What in language is united, in the market is divided. Words are shared while money is not. Then that division is projected back onto linguistic theory.

Words in Saussure's *langue* (and in most other linguists' and philosophers' understanding) are related to things by a kind of word-to-world path to goal, which starts from words with its supposed destination in 'reference', rather than by a path to goal that goes from world-to-word based on the activity of linguistic communicators satisfying needs and their consequent relations (or groups of relations). The word-to-world reference relation is symbolized by the word plus the image, for example: 'tree' plus the image tree. For Saussure it is the value as position of the word in the *langue* that lets us identify the image, what the speaker is talking about. The communicative and cognitive needs of the other seem to have nothing to do with it. No contingent or mediated world to word relation is taken into account.

Because the world-gift can even be absent or imagined, it seems that there is no relation. Nevertheless, there is a relation and it is provided by the relevance of that part of the real or imaginary world to others in the past, in the future and elsewhere. Others have attended to it and passed it on as relevant, a value. Although most of the things that are relevant to the community do exist, there are some that do not. The value or relevance of the world to humans is registered in the *langue*, not its existence (which has a relevance of its own). This difference allows room for play, fantasy and 'musement'. Value is an emphasis of relevance that we give and receive, long term and short term.

Langue and *parole* were the result of a previous distinction drawn by Saussure between the synchronic and the diachronic study of language.[42] The synchronic study is a kind of cross section of language as it is at any given moment, while by 'diachrony' he intended the longer historical view. However, if *langue* is a system of values, where do these values come from? They must come from diachrony, from *parole*, from the history of humans using language in the world. They arrive in the language as word gifts for relevant world gifts. Their relevance depends on the collective human experience of the world. People satisfied each others' cognitive, communicative and relational needs regarding relevant aspects of the world often enough and generally enough for a word regarding them to appear in the language and remain there. At a lesser degree of relevance those world gifts would have been talked about by using sentences made up of other words. A transitional example for a world gift that was new at the time might be 'horseless carriage', which was replaced by 'auto mobile' and finally 'car' (phonetically brief because intensely used – smoothed like a pebble in the rushing stream of language and life).

Saussure's *langue* is an abstraction from interpersonal use and relevance, gift value and world-to-word value, of words (while maintaining words' interverbal relations as syntax and their relevance or general gift character as value-as-position). Linguistic value is the by product of the relevance to many of the things that are talked about. It is collective relevance registered in individual verbal gifts.

---

42 Chomsky does not deal with diachrony so he does not see words as values.

Saussure also understands *langue* as consisting of exchange values as we mentioned (what can a signifier be exchanged for? A signified. This is a one to one relation which does not account for the generality of either side).[43] Signifiers are seen in their aspect of virtualization-exchange in the position of the money-word. On the other hand in our terms, *parole* consists of gifts and gift values. And the *langue* itself, which is a large but not unlimited field of word-gifts as relevance or value tokens, is the result of the collective virtualizing to give, which happens through the speech of the many, through *parole*.

Relevance is elaborated both through *parole* and through the non verbal life experience of many. It would follow that the world gifts that are usually perceived and received as relevant and whose relevance is passed on, spoken about by the community, are those for which a word-gift arises in the langue. So it is the things that are relevant to others, that receive the need satisfying (verbal) gifts as their names.

One can say that each time someone processes something as relevant and communicates it to others with 'parole', s:he adds a bit to the social 'volume' – the 'decibel level' of its relevance until this crosses a kind of threshold, becoming enough for that part of the world to achieve independent virtualization in the *langue*. Thus the most continuously socially relevant perceptions and conceptions would be given words as their names and they would be related for individuals to exemplars or prototypes of kinds as well as to other things in their areas of relevance[44] or semantic fields. When they have not reached this level, things, situations, events are spoken about in sentences, which convey what we can call their 'contingent relevance'.

Given the present bias towards quantification someone might want to quantify the amount of relevance that a world-gift would need for a word-gift to be 'coined' by the community. The precise quantity is probably unimportant – irrelevant – though. Language as *langue* + *parole* (and in its historical context) is mainly a qualitative project. Quantifying and computing its every move is like describing every move in riding a bicycle. It may be good for teaching computers to ride bikes but explained in this way it becomes much harder, even impossible for a person to understand. Nor does it tell us anything about what bicycle riding is for humans, what it means to ride a bicycle, or what the practical and historical significance of bicycle riding is. That is, what is the human cultural value of bike riding.

43   See Ponzio (1974) and Vaughan (1981).
44   Our sensitivity to such areas of relevance permits the statistical approach to word learning as proposed by Gopnik and others.

As far as Saussure's *langue* is concerned the abstract word-values are all seen at a very similar level of relevance and are related to each other only by their differences. Yet calling them 'values' is not wrong, because they coexist at a level of abstraction that leaves aside *parole*. That is, that leaves aside their use in the satisfaction of human (communicative, cognitive and relational) needs, in the same way that the exchange value of commodities abstracts from gift giving and use in the satisfaction of material needs. In fact the *langue* is very similar to the market where the product is virtualized in a money name, its price, because it is related to others in general.

Leaving aside the satisfaction of needs leaves aside both use value and gift value. And it is mainly in their function as use values in satisfying others' communicative and cognitive needs and thus as relational gift value transmitters that words are relevant. But in the *langue*, linguistic value is an abstraction from gift value and use value. In the market, exchange value is also an abstraction from gift value and use value. Money is the materialized one-holophrastic-word language and broadcasts exchange value back onto its verbal look-alike kinfolks.

Phillip Mirowski has shown that the neoclassical economists took their idea of equilibrium in a field from the physics of the time.[45] Thus, if we take into account Piaget's comment that Saussure derived his ideas from neoclassical Walras, the inheritance of this influence passed from grandfather physics to father economics, to son linguistics and, then from Saussure, it branched out into the Structuralism of Levi-Strauss and Lacan. Saussure's idea of *langue* was thus also based on the concept of the market energy-field equilibrium as a field of linguistic (exchange) value, which was distinguished from practical linguistic use value: *parole*. Moreover, as we mentioned, the idea of supply and demand had already displaced that of gift and need, establishing a point of view that took exchange for granted.

Langue and linguistic values in the system of differences, are purely abstract. Language is unmotivated according to Saussure. Thus it seems detached from any but structural relevance. However, as we have been saying words have gift value or relevance: for each other in syntax (interverbally), as vehicles with which speakers/writers give value to listeners/readers (interpersonally) and as gift relay-items for human creatures of the Earth to pass on to each other the perceptual and conceptual gifts of the world. Since people talk to each other about what is relevant, the words that remain in

---

45 'The progenitors of neoclassical economic theory boldly copied the reigning physical theories in the 1870s...they copied their models term for term and symbol for symbol, and said so' (Mirowski 1989: 3).

the *langue* regard things, perceptions, conceptions, events and ideas that are relevant to the community. The *langue* is made up of word-gifts, which can be given for specific, qualitatively different, relevant parts of the world. By considering words in the *langue* only as a system of differences Saussure abstracted them, taking them away from that human-mediated relevance to our interconnectedness in the world. Then he looked at words as values in a system of similarities and differences, not as use values or as gift values.

There is another hidden source of metaphor for Saussure's *langue* (passed down through the neoclassical economists and the nineteenth century physicists) and evident also in the economy itself. That is, mutually exclusive private property. Each proprietor is in a relation of mutual exclusion with all the others, just as each term in the *langue* is in a relation of mutual exclusion with all the others. Although linguistic terms and human proprietors do seem to be apples and oranges, the patterns set up by material life do influence our thinking, and vice-versa, as we have been saying.

We can look at the relation of private property as an 'incarnation' and distortion of the prototype-to-many graded category, where the prototype-owners are mutually exclusive. Here the relation of the many to the prototype does not depend on similarity but on ownership and control while the prototype of maternal nurturing is reversed in that the many items of property nurture and serve the one owner. Moreover the proprietors in Saussure's (and Walras') time were all male and their property and their propertyless wives (whose 'having to give' they controlled) as well as their children belonged to and gave to them.

Into this collection of mutually exclusive 'family name' complexes (proprietor-property graded categories) steps money as general equivalent, an abstract and streamlined classical concept form, mediating the transfer of alienable items and reflecting all of them as having a quality in common: value-in-exchange. The exosomatic concept process makes holophrastic money, the gift-not-gift exemplar-word the 'one' to which are related the 'many' of this huge but exclusionary semantic field, and value comes forward as their relevant common quality.

8.12 Mirowski on the gift economy

Unfortunately, in his chapter on the gift economy like so many others who write about the gift economy, Mirowski (2004: 376-400) does not begin at the ontogenetic beginning of life but approaches gift-giving when the market is already established for the individual and for society. The same can be said for the anthropologists who study gift *exchange* in non-Western societies. One might remark that the implications of free housework in our patriarchal capitalist society have not yet fully dawned upon them.

Gift work provides the context in which children's altercentric sociality can flower and their 'like me' bridges can establish a common embodied knowledge of giving and receiving (and of gifts). A unilateral gift economy outside the market does exist in every child's and in every motherer's life. It also exists in those many aspects of exchangers' lives in which they are doing gift-giving – including language. The contemporary research foregrounding infant sociality and altercentrism provides the perspective necessary for recognizing the existence of the fundamental area of giving beyond the market. It is this perspective that, together with the recognition of gift-giving as an alternative economy, gives us a new piece of the mosaic that rearranges the whole picture. Once the infant is no longer seen as egotistical and solipsistic, everything changes. The challenge then becomes how *not* to socialize the already altercentric child into the 'adult' egotistical and solipsistic exchange paradigm.

The gift economy does not disappear even when it is submerged by the market because it continues in language and in many aspects of life from acts of kindness to perception to breathing. In fact we all know a lot about it. We are experts in gifting without studying it, but we disbelieve it and are usually even more expert in the self interested logic of exchange in which we do believe. Cynicism even seems to be an aspect of masculine superiority while credulity is 'feminine'. So says our expertise.

In discussing the many attempts to use the gift economy as 'an alternative to neoclassical understandings of exchange' Mirowski (2004: 395) comments 'the crux of the problem, perhaps unrecognized by all these parties, resides in the specification of the quality and the character of the invariants which are presumed to govern the actions and interpretations of the participants'. He continues a little farther on saying that the neoclassical economists have a retort to the skeptics who say that value theory is futile. 'Value invariance, they insist, exists in the mental recesses of individuals; their orderings, while idiosyncratic and personal, are inviolate' (*Ibid.*: 396) The neoclassicals find self-interest in the mental recesses of individuals, while here we are finding altercentrism and the image schema of the gift anchored in the motherer-child relation in even deeper mental recesses, beneath and beyond the market-based self-interested orderings.

However Mirowski only mentions the neoclassical project in order to try to refute it from another direction. He says: 'putative psychological regularities of the transactors play no essential role in the structure. "Value" here simply refers to the outcomes of a system of exchange' organized into what he calls 'bottom up and top down forces' (*Ibid.*)

However, as we have been saying throughout this book, the gift cannot be explained on the basis of the market. It is the market that must be explained on the basis of the gift. And the same goes for value, at least if it is the case that exchange value is gift value transformed. That is, the outcome of the system of exchange is that the implications of the would-have-been gifts are transformed. From the quality of gift value implied of the receiver (and of the gift as means and of the giver as source) the implications transform through the exchange process to result not in the gift value of the other but the exchange value of the product.

Value in the gift economy is gift value, the value of the other (the receiver) that is implied by the unilateral gift. It is also the value or relevance of the giver for the receiver, as source of the gift, whether recognized as such or not, and it is the value of the gift as means of satisfaction of the need and therefore also as means of the creation of positive relations. The implications of this kind of relevance are part of the construction of the relations of mutuality and trust among givers and receivers. Though based in common schemas these relations vary qualitatively according to the variety of the gifts and services given and received, a variety that is registered by the many and the ones among the many, emotionally, kinetically and also linguistically and culturally.

In the market economy, exchange value is an implication as well.[46] It is an invariant implication because the human interaction from which it emerges is an invariant interaction of mutual adversarial leverage (although it seems to grow or diminish: actually it accumulates or loses gifts).

Exchange value is the importance of the product for the other as an instrument of leverage – not the importance of the other as a receiver for the giver. This is a displacement of the implication of gift value away from the other and onto the commodity, the product-in-exchange. Since in the market everyone is doing this, and the buyer can presumably buy from any seller (and vice-versa the seller can sell to any buyer) the exchange value of the product is related to that of all similar products in terms of the quantity of money that will 'pop out' for it in exchange. It is the implication of the importance of the other for the give/producer, denied by the process of exchange and transferred to the product.

---

46   Marx (1996: 51-2) insists on the social character of value: 'exchange value is a definite social manner of expressing the amount of labour bestowed upon an object' and 'So far no chemist has ever discovered exchange value either in a pearl or a diamond'. This social character is an implication of relevance that everyone accepts and it is validated by practice.

Value seen as the 'object permanence' of substance is qualitatively invariant because it is an implication of relevance that is maintained throughout the exchange processes, even though the object in which the value is embodied changes. That is because products on the market are seen by everyone as generally relevant to and substitutable by the money word. And the money-word has a 'linguistic' value because it satisfies a cognitive and communicative need. It expresses a qualitative invariance as a general equivalent, which by taking its place, allows the embodiment of any quantity of value. Money provides the standard and the means for calculating quantitative variance and invariance. It tells us 'how much' and it is given for, substituted for, the product in a linguistic way, creating a kind of common human relation of agreement towards it (satisfying the communicative, community-making need towards it) even though the interaction is one of mutual exclusion. The product is abstracted and then reconcretized. It is first particular, then made general in exchange for money and then becomes particular again as private property. In spite of the exchange mechanism, quantitative invariance is difficult to obtain because the hidden gifting that makes up profit is not calculable in a precise way. For example how is it possible to calculate the monetary value of products, the production of which is influenced by the amount of free housework each one contains, as manifested in the well being of the worker and thus of the labor time and efficiency necessary for the work? This well being could also be influenced by the free housework and childcare given by the workers' mothers and grandmothers. The gifts of nature, of surplus labor, the gifts seized from the people and the planet of the future by pollution are anything but invariant.

In fact, exchange value does not exist on its own and would not exist as such if gift-giving were not happening and gift value were not being implied all around it. The gift giving in language and in cognitive relation to perceptions, experiences and ideas,the innumerable gifts in daily life, the gifting-gifted mesh of our 'co-created' environmental niche constructions, the use of the gift structure on the material plane in the labor process (e.g. the giving of the blows of the hammer to the nail; the giving of the nail to the wall; the giving of the support of the wall to the roof) but also the taking up again of the bought use value into gift processes in the domestic sphere: all the variety of life that is not centered in the market, necessarily continues to function according to gift-giving and to variously imply gift value and relevance. The market cannot exist without it, without the gifts of the altercentric interaction of the many.

8.13 The budget

Because the material money-word is quantitatively divided while remaining holophrastic, each market actor can potentially access some quantity of it, while it continues to 'mean' the economic value of everything[47] (the one *implies* the many). In the context of scarcity created by the market, the amount we have or can 'make' determines how much of everything we will get, how much of the money-word's 'referents' we can acquire and possess, i.e. bring in to our property-container, to make up part of our available 'energy'. This energy can be seen as an individual and personal foreshadowing of Mirowski's concept of energy in physics and economics. The budget can be seen as the individual's bounded energy field, her portion of the semantic field of the money-word.

We internalize (and privatize) the semantic field of the money word as our budget, the amount we have to cover the 'affordances' related to our needs, or the family's needs, providing for our and their personal energy now and in the future. Or we consider what we would spend if we bought everything we want, or what others spend, or what the country spends on wars or education.

If our needs were already met in an abundant gift economy, budgets would figure much less significantly in our mental spaces. However at present they legislate and limit our imaginations as to what we can personally do, exchange or give. The bounded capacity of each individual to access goods can be seen as a kind of individual container of energy, of the gift initiative. It is a personal monetary energy field, of what we have to or can give. Our priorities in satisfying needs receive a quantitative expression. The gift value of the receiver seems to be determined proportionately by the amount she receives in competition with the others rather than directly by the gift initiative and care of the giver, and the appropriateness of the gift. Marginal choice is influenced by the internalized holophrastic word-budget-field. We also translate it into the assessment of our own energy levels. What we have to 'spend'. We 'weigh' our own desire, our needs, our altruism comparatively. So we create competition internally as well as between our own and others' needs because of scarcity. We calculate time also in this way, holophrastically conceived and quantitatively divided. In fact, 'time is money'. Physicists talked about energy and the economists wanted to imitate stochastic physical equilibrium

---

47   Is this 'word' then really 'ubuntu'?, the connection of all with all, made quantitative and conditional upon exchange? (Marx, 'Money is the alienated essence of mankind').

in an energy field, but both disciplines left out the energy of the gift that moves toward higher organization, repeatedly contradicting the second law of thermodynamics by attention to the needs of the other (instead, individualistic competition does not bring about a stable higher order). It is not the (mythological) invisible hand but as economist Nancy Folbre (2001) says it is the (real) invisible heart that brings the higher order to pass.

8.14 Transfer metaphors

In the discussion of the conduit metaphor for communication by Reddy, Lakoff, Johnson and many others, the idea of communication as a transfer was heavily criticized. This made it unavailable as a parallel for physics and economics where transfers of force and goods do take place.

In the conduit metaphor, one is reminded of the flow of water through a tube or electricity through a wire, which reference the concept of energy (or the circulation of blood used as metaphor by nineteenth-century economists). Lakoff's example of the communicative 'link' metaphor is the umbilical cord.[48] However he sees it only as a cord that ties items together. This is particularly telling because it is precisely the transmission of nurture to the unborn child through the umbilical cord that is the basic function of this tie. That is, the umbilical cord is not just a string but a conduit if ever there was one. It is the carrier of the earliest dynamic 'material communication' between mother and child.

It is not that I would like to repeat the gesture of the neoclassical school of economics which assimilated physics into economics (Mirowski) nor would I assimilate economics into the study of language as did Saussure nor would I restore the conduit metaphor to cognitive linguistics. Rather I would see the transfers of the gift economy as containing the germinal form of all three *in nuce*. The transfers of cause and effect and agent and patient are understandable as watered-down or altered transfers of gifts between persons. The transfers in conduits or outside of them – am I getting the idea across? – are closer to our childhood frame of giving/receiving than are the more objective physical forces.

The gift in 'Jane baked the cake' both refers to and is a transfer of 'energy', an accomplishment of intention, an act of nurture on three levels:

---

48 'Our first link is the umbilical cord. Throughout infancy and early childhood, we hold onto our parents and other things, either to secure our location or theirs. To secure the location of two things relative to one another, we use such things as string, rope, or other means of connection' (1990: 274).

the level of semantics, of syntax and of language transmission. It is a gift from speaker to listener or from writer (yours truly) to reader (yourself) – though now I am just giving it to you as an example because I guess you need one. It functions because it is structured like the original core or prototypical interaction that has become the schema of the gift: A gives x to B, B receives x from A. B can repeat the other's action, give in turn, passing it on. Motherer feeds (cares for) child, and child receives food (care) from motherer, and imitates, gives in turn or passes it on.

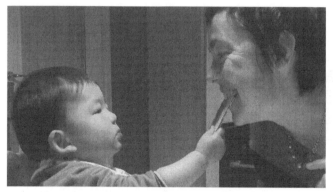

Figure 23. Child feeding mother, Milo and Emma 2015.

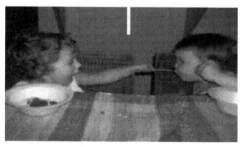

Figure 24. And passes the gift on to others.

Undergirding language and projected as a self-and-other interface onto the world,[49] the giving/receiving interaction is the foundation for the understanding of all the other human and non human, physical 'inter' actions and goings-between. The implications that come from and through gift-giving are common to all and are understood by everyone because they are laid down in childhood and continue to function in life and in language, even if unconsciously. They can also be extended by analogy to relations among things making them meaningful even in terms of our own kinetic mapping. These extensions regard actions, which we can understand as cause and effect for example, by momentarily leaving aside the benefactive aspect of the gift frame. Thus they would not transmit gift value (the child can push the ball just to see what it does without thinking of benefitting it or anyone or giving it a goal). Sometimes the steps to provide a gift require several or many of these kinds of actions with the gift suspended or left aside. When the gift is finally given, the previously neutral actions can be seen as transmitting part of the gift value also.

The point of giving is not to conserve and augment value but to satisfy needs. In this light the consumption of the good is not a disutility but the culmination of the value and bestowal of gift value onto the 'other,' which also permits or encourages the other to give in turn. The gift 'energy' is 'conserved' because it is 'reborn' in the receiver's life energy and also in h:er new gift initiatives, eventually called forth by the needs of someone else again.[50] Moreover the material gift is transferrable onto the virtual plane by giving word gifts for it.

Human needs are not just a pretext for the formation of exchange value and the accumulation of capital, they are the foundation of relevance (of which economic value and linguistic value are specific moments) and of transitivity. It is just because humans use their bodies to actively satisfy other human's bodies' needs (and they register the implications of that) that they develop a frame in which non human body-motion-value (Mirowski 1989) makes sense. Not acknowledging the importance of this frame of care for epistemology allows us to develop a physics that produces nuclear bombs, a biology that modifies life haphazardly for profit, a botany that develops terminator seeds that cause the suicides of poor farmers, a chemistry

---

49   Once again the blind spot that covers this important aspect of the process of knowlege is due to a division of labor in which the men who are usually the scientists and who are doing the investigations do not do the care of infants. They have not been and are not supposed to ever be the adult half of the mother-child altercentric, nurturing dyad.

50   This would be consonant with the idea of of human death and rebirth often found in matriarchal societies.

that poisons and dominates agriculture and exterminates bees, a technology that has become a destroyer of worlds, an economics that drives all of the above and a narrative about all this that justifies it.

Our actions are contrary to what constitutes us as human, not in accordance with it. But this does not justify our species' suicide. We have just lost the way because we have disrespected the mother and mothering.

8.15 Another word about Chomsky

For Chomsky's genetically inherited Universal Grammar and all those who have (socially) inherited that approach from him, the gift patterns are given not by society or by mothering but by the genes and they are seen as hierarchical rules or laws, or sui generis abilities like MERGE not as egalitarian relational constructions and implications (they are genetically patriarchal rather than matriarchal).

Saying that Universal Grammar is not genetically inherited is not denying there are physiological processes involved. Human brains are indeed prepared for language and for gifting social interaction. However, human language and social interaction are also prepared for brains and these brains are in bodies that depend for their existence on care given by others in community. In ontogeny language derives first from the schemas of this necessary care but it is also a product of a culture in which this derivation has happened repeatedly and the language used by adults has been embraced by children over and over again.

Infant researchers Bråten, Trevarthen, Meltzoff and their collaborators have a much more general genetic approach than that of Chomsky. They tell us that humans are innately social beings. Infants are capable almost immediately of engaging in social communicative relations, which they do with others materially and by using multi modal signs and, as they grow older, eventually, words. Emotions are an integral part of this sociality and babies experience them in tempos and intensities, in attunement with their caregivers, regarding many things in their surroundings. I have been saying also that the schema can be turned outward towards the world-as-motherer (and recognized on the external by tracking third-party gift schemas).

The schemas of the gift and of virtualization (which, as a projection, may also be a gift derivative) create meaning and communication at many different levels. Rewriting them with grammatical notation, like NP and VP, frames them as rules at a level of abstraction which would presumably be unavailable to very young language learners. Since children do learn to speak, the only explanation seems to be that the abstract rules are genetically inherited. The abstract rules are thus seen as independent from emotions, from intersubjectivity and sociality, from nurturing and being nurtured, giving and receiving. On the other hand if what Chomsky describes as Universal Grammar is actually the schematization, replay and elaboration of the interpersonal giving and receiving that infants have been doing from birth with their mothers (and even in the womb), the patterns of behavior are constitutive not normative. They are not rules but schemas of the way human interactions work. The abstraction from the context of real life is minimal. What is inherited is the (enjoyable) sociality that elicits the care that ensures survival. The patterns of language derive from this necessary interaction.

CHAPTER IX

MATERNAL GIFT SEMANTICS

9.0 Meaning as the extension of gifting subjectivity

Philosophers of language have found the concept of meaning to be problematic, so much so that they often avoid the term, in the same way that economists avoid the word and the concept 'value'. Both disciplines have been caught in the logic of exchange and categorization – so here again, restoring the mother, I want to show what emerges with the gift in mind and propose an idea of meaning based on maternal gift-giving, communication and community.[1]

Because of the exosomatic concept form and the over-use and reciprocal validation of the schemas of virtualization and exchange, the perspective of the giving and receiving subject has been eliminated from language and linguistics just as it has from the economy and economics. In the study of language, gift-giving is hidden behind the schema of virtualization, and in economics it is hidden behind the schema of exchange. In each case there seems to be no giver, just a speaker/writer or an exchanger, a worker, a consumer, a neutral ungiving linguistic or economic operator.[2] Nevertheless gift-giving and receiving is the creative maternal source. I will try to show that it is the source of subjectivity as well as of communication and of meaning in language and in life. In the market it is the source of profit, as I have been saying.

Doing gift-giving with words, sentences and texts throughout our lives,

---

1   Wittgenstein (in PI: 43) tells us to look for the use of words. 'For a large class of cases – though not for all – in which we employ the word "meaning" it can be defined thus: the meaning of a word is its use in the language'. However in exploring the use of words, like so many other male philosophers, he also left out gifts and gift value of words, their maternal relational aspects

2   Philosophers of language look for the speaker's 'intention' (Searle 1995) but do not consider this a gift-giving, need-satisfying intention, as we have described above. A partial exception might be H. P. Grice's 'cooperative principle' (1989) but I believe gift-giving is prior to cooperation and its prerequisite.

we continue to construct our altercentric subjectivity even as adults. This gives us a chance to practice what we might call 'abstract care' on a daily basis and perhaps could educate us towards more other oriented behavior if we realized we were doing it.[3]

If meaning in life derives from satisfying needs, we can take it as a clue for where to look for meaning in language. Vice-versa understanding meaning in language as the satisfaction of communicative and cognitive needs can help us understand meaning in life. The figure of virtualization/exchange blocks this kind of investigation because it appears to provide meaning by neutral 'categorization' or 'representation', both of which which seem to take place without other orientation or satisfying needs. By grounding giving/receiving in mothering/being mothered and meaning in giving/receiving, we can understand the origin not only of the process but of the dynamic 'charge' and the emotional tones of meaning. Subsequent gifts, even the intangible gifts of language, carry much of the emotional charge that is part of that original relation on which children's survival depends. With language there is always a detour through the other, with all that this implies.

The interactive bridge of the gift establishes the roles of child and motherer and confirms the significance of each for the other long before epistemological questions and solipsistic doubts can arise. In fact if either motherer or child were a solipsist, the survival of the child would be compromised. Need-satisfying gifts at all levels continue to have the potential for creating a bridge of solidarity that maintains the significance and joy of the survival and well being of the self and of the other even in maturity. Giving/receiving confirms oneself both as provider and as valuable to a provider. The co constructed 'like me' bridge of nurture is the basic foundational structure of life and language. The existence of each player in the gifting-gifted roles implies that of the others. Perhaps it is just because the gift is so fundamental that it can be used in so many different ways: projected onto the world, abstracted in language, but also contradicted in exchange, used for dominance and submission, for manipulation and leverage 'I will give you this only if you...' or 'because I have given you this you must...'.

The many different kinds of gifts imply gift value as do the many different kinds of givers. Nurturing with milk ensures early survival while nurturing with solid food comes with the relevance of a certain age and

---

3   But we also construct abstract discourse for power over – creating privileged jargons and elitist 'common' topics.

capacity of the child; similarly throughout the stages of life in childhood, adolescence and maturity, different gifts, given and received, bring about new needs and different conditions, which are relevant in different ways. Each different kind of gift brings with it somewhat different consequences and connections.

Following Mauss (1990 [1923]), much has been written about the kind of gift-exchange that causes debt and obligation. Many think that our basic human bonds are created by debt and that without debt the relationship would cease (Graber 2011). However we are saying that the maternal gift is unilateral and that the child responds unilaterally in the 'like me' bridge way, entering by mimesis into a scansion of unilateral gift initiatives directed towards and coming from the motherer, which result in coordinated interaction and protoconversation. Each desires the other's response but there is not a *quid pro quo* exchange. They both enjoy being similar, taking turns, fulfilling each others' expectations.The cry or the laugh or gesture of the child is received by the motherer as a gift that satisfies h:er communicative need. It 'means something', is relevant, to h:er, satisfying h:er need to know what the child needs. Similarly for the child the motherer's actions and expressions satisfy h:er need to know as s:he experiences them through kinetic mapping and mirror neurons. Like giving, mimesis as voluntary imitation comes before exchange with its imposed equivalences and manipulative nurturing. Mimesis creates a qualitative likeness that is not an equation and a responsivity and a relatedness that are not based on debt.

Linguistic communication is modeled on the unilateral gift and voluntary mimesis, not on exchange. Language is learned during the period of intense unilateral mothering. It is a multi level construction made of a variety of unilateral gift initiatives, trajectories, receptions and re givings. As the child learns to take the points of view of the roles of giver, gift and receiver in turn, to recognize the motherer's role and compare it to or distinguish it from h:er own, and to imitate it, s:he begins to be able to give communicatively like the motherer does, expecting the motherer's response. The motherer participates and imitates the child. These roles and points of view are thus available later for the child's linguistic constructions. Moreover, they are already in common use in the linguistic constructions of adults and older children.

When a physical gift such as food or a toy is given, it is a third element that mediates between giver and receiver as the object of their attention (and I mentioned that the child can be handed from person to person as well, so s:he has that experience). Pointing at something outside the dyad to create joint attention puts motherer and child in the same role as receivers of the same perceptual gift. Thus they are related to each other as 'like me' receivers (on the same side of the bridge). By saying the same word as the adult, the child is 'like h:er' as a verbal giver and vice-versa the adult is like the child as verbal receiver.

9.1 Joint attention and mind-reading

Although 'give' usually figures among childrens' early words, it is not always among the very first. This is probably because like adults, children don't know they are giving and receiving experientially and verbally. They are immersed in the experience. If they say 'cookie' to request a cookie it is because they have been engaging in giving and receiving with their mother-ers and they name the world-gift they want to receive. Although babies do 'giving' inevitably in expelling body products like feces and urine and al-though they play at giving food, and objects, and do giving also in commu-nicative behaviors, they are usually on the receiving end of most nurturing interactions. In naming what they want, they satisfy the motherer's need to know, her cognitive need. Unfortunately the motherer sometimes does not give the desired gift so the child repeats the word, and cries, increasing the decibels, making her own perceived need very relevant to the giver.

Young children name objects and actions as requests and imperatives: like 'juice!' or 'down!' (for 'put me down') but they also increasingly use declaratives, naming what they see and sharing perception in joint attention with their caregivers. The recognition and reception of perceptual and ex-periential gifts as sharable gestalts 'coming forward' from a background is the basis of declarative naming, often accompanied by pointing: 'doggy'. The pointing finger is an icon both of salient 'popping out' and of the one to many relation. Moreover, as I said, it singles out one item from a back-ground (see 6.14b) and traces a path for the gaze of the other.

Various aspects of nurturing can be relevant both for gifting and for other activities. For example 'milk all gone' may describe the end of the gift in consumption. 'All messy' a need to clean up.

I believe most kinds of 'doing' are attenuated or watered down kinds of giving and receiving gifts and services;[4] at least a very many of them are, a core of important ones. They can also be steps along the trajectory of the

---

4   I continue to find curious the fact that 'do' is first person singular for 'give' in
     Italian and that it seems to have been neutralized into 'do' in English (and like-
     wise in 'don't').

gift, considered independently. For example, warming the milk can be seen on its own without taking into account its destination in nurturing the child. Of course words can be gifts even if their lexical meanings are not in any way a permutation of the word 'gift'.

Joint attention is joint reception of perceptual and conceptual gifts. The attending is part of the creative – not passive – receiving. Pointing is an instrument for receiving together. It shows others what we think it is relevant for them to receive. Usually we think of cognition as 'grasping,' even 'penetration' (with all the phallic resonances associated with that word). However it is by understanding cognition as creative receiving (with vaginal resonances perhaps?) that we can understand the gift character of the world.

The alignment of their cognition with others through joint attention allows communicators to ascertain that they are receiving the same perceptions that others are receiving and thus that the contents of their consciousnesses are similar at the moment. This permits better 'mind-reading' later in the same interaction and in other interactions as well, in the sense that in the presence of such a perception one knows that the other could probably perceive it also, given the right circumstances. Pointing and naming, giving a perceptual and a verbal exemplar, create a window onto the contents of the mind of the other, providing a perceptual commons that can be recalled and an aligned relation to the world-gift. The initial lack of this alignment of attention, perceived by the pointer who sees that the other's gaze is directed elsewhere, can be understood by the pointer as a need of the other for a means to that alignment.

Mind-reading the other involves attending to what s:he is potentially perceiving from h:er point of view. The ability to point provides the additional possibility of giving to the other a means to a joint attentional relation to something to which s:he may not be attending at the moment. H:er disattention is for a speaker the form of h:er cognitive need, which s:he satisfies by giving h:er a word gift. The satisfaction of this cognitive need of the other creates the human communicative gift-or-service relation at this level. Thus the cognitive need is also the occasion of a communicative need in that the speaker/writer satisfies both the alignment of attention and the creation of a common human relation by h:er word gifts. Communication in this case is a means to joint cognition and vice-versa (information is only transmitted through an altercentric human relation!).

We can be very creative about identifying the other's cognitive needs in relation to the knowable world. She may not be thinking about neutrinos or cats or sonnets but we realize she needs to know something about them, something we know, which is relevant to her or both of us in some way. By

satisfying her need with a word-gift we put her in relation to us and to them
– word and thing – as if we were perceiving that part of the world together.
And we usually do more than name the world-gifts, we say something
about them, giving h:er a bit of a new perspective.

Children change perspectives by moving, and adults change the children's perspectives from being on the ground to being carried, where many
different things are visible. A child needs to be lifted to see certain things
as the adult sees them. One person gives the other a perception (giving
h:er a point of view). The capacity to create joint attention is the basis of
understanding 'mind-reading' as the identification of cognitive and communicative needs of others.

'Mind-reading' is complicated for the writer and the reader by the fact
that it depends even more heavily on educated guesses about what readers
will need in order to understand and on giving and receiving various kinds
of cues in the written text (and context). When we speak to the public in
general or write a book, we have to mind-read and satisfy the communicative needs that anyone, or perhaps specific kinds of listeners or readers,
would have regarding the relevant aspects, the gifts and gift configurations
of the world that we are trying to pass on to them. Not recognizing the
gifting character of communication, we usually see this as our own need
to express ourselves or 'transmit information'. The speaker/writer understands by empathetic, altercentric mind-reading that others need to know
something and she realizes that she can make it a gift for them by taking the
initiative to enact verbal gift schemas regarding it at the moment, giving
the perception or conception to them with word gifts.

In writing s:he mind reads others in general. What anyone would need to
form this relation with others, is the objective meaning of the word, its dictionary entry. If we can say that needs can be known by what we use to satisfy them – for example the need to drink is satisfied by water or the need
to eat is satisfied by food (including all the variations of food and drink,
likes and dislikes, connected with memories of daily life and and special
occasions) the need to breathe by inhaling and exhaling air, etc. perhaps we
can say that the dictionary entries for word-gifts are the descriptions of the
needs the words satisfy, a sort of impersonal mind reading of the possible
cognitive and communicative needs of the public mind. On the other hand
the encyclopedia entry would satisfy the cognitive needs that might arise in
the public mind regarding a world-gift including the kinds of material and
social needs it might satisfy.

9.2 How the process works

Because language is not usually considered on the basis of giving and receiving, I want to describe briefly and in a simple – if laborious – way how I think the process works, recapitulating some of what I have already said: The construction of gifts in the sentence or text conveys – gives – a shared or shareable social relation to a configuration of (usually) extra linguistic gifts. Our cat is on our mat for our joint attention. S:he is ours-together perceptually at least and for the linguistic community in general s:he would be perceptually 'ours' as 'the cat'. But since 'our' in the perceptual sense is not distinguished from 'others'' as private property (but is shared), we use 'the' or 'a'. The cat is only giveable linguistically by the human community and so s:he is only a cat or the cat or my cat as our cat. Only after s:he is our cat in this shared sense can she become your property or mine (or even close companion as one of a kind).

'Cat' has a need for a specifier or determiner (this is really our need for 'cat' to be specified) so we give it the definite article 'the' or the indefinite article 'a'. A need to distinguish which cat we want to talk about may arise from the non verbal context. Otherwise the listener might be confused. That is, the listener needs the speaker to distinguish that cat from others. The speaker already knows this. So we say 'the gray cat'. If we want to talk about the color of the cat, we need to give 'gray' to 'cat'. That is, the word 'cat' cannot express that color without the word 'gray' so it needs it in that sense. The listener or reader's need, the speaker or writer's need, and the word 'cat's need coincide. Even the cat on the reality plane may be said to have a need for us to mention her color as in 'feed the gray cat but not the white one'. This is expressed by linguists when they say 'cat' has a 'slot' for color adjectives like 'gray' and 'white'.

In the gift schema, the speaker is the giver, 'gray' is the gift and 'cat' is the receiver, making the combination 'gray cat'. The speaker is again the giver of the gift of 'the gray cat' to the listener as receiver. S:he gives the whole sentence to h:er as well: 'the gray cat licked h:er fur'. In this sentence 'the gray cat' is in the role of giver, 'licked' is in the role of gift or service and 'h:er fur' is in the role of the receiver.

If we say 'the cat is gray' we verbally virtualize h:er color at this moment and we do so because we think it is relevant that s:he has that (m) otherworld property, the perceptually giveable gift of that color, on the reality plane. The linguistic gift can be seen as a meta gift, the gift of a gift and a gift about a gift. When we construct a sentence gift we are making it and giving it now[5] and this creates gift value at the moment for the other who receives it, but also value is given to the gift for which it is meta – for which it is the virtual gift – and to the other words in the sentence and to the things in the world that are placed by the interlocutors in the image schema of the gift.[6] Recognition is also at least potentially given to the speaker-giver and the sentence-subject-giver (as well as to the listener-receiver and the grammatical 'object'-receiver of the verb or of the preposition). We make the word-gift for the listener but we also make it for the world-gifts we are talking about, giving them a second kind of presence among us, making clear their importance and sometimes even honoring them, by describing them poetically. The 'point' is what the linguistic gift is meta to, what it is that we are pointing at linguistically. Where is our attention to be directed in order to become joint, in order for us to receive the perceptual or conceptual gift together with the speaker or writer?

'Gray' has a linguistic gift value for the color gray, because it can be given for it, and a linguistic gift value for 'cat' because it can be given to 'cat,' and 'cat' has a linguistic gift value for 'gray' because it can receive that word-gift. Together they have a gift value for the cat (and for us) as the gray cat's relation-creating virtual gift-substitutes. Each of these kinds of value is somewhat different,[7] and we would need to distinguish among them.

Projecting giving and receiving onto the reality plane: grayness has a kind of gift value as given to the cat, and the cat has a value as the receiver of grayness and this value, which we characterize more generally as relevance, is confirmed or brought forward as linguistic gift value when we say 'gray cat'. 'Gray' has a value also as given to other words, 'skies', 'hair', 'ashes', 'dress'. Grayness – the relation among gray things to a gray exemplar which is substituted by the (exemplar) word-gift 'gray' – thus has a general qualitative value or relevance, which is expressed by giving the word-gift 'gray'.

The object of the joint attention elicited by verbal giving, is itself a gift

---

5   We could say with Ferruccio Rossi-Landi that this value is created by linguistic labor (gift labor) but actually gift value is given even when the gift is effortless. R-L might reply that this appearance of effortlessness is due to the fact that we are dealing with previously accumulated linguistic capital. Still it is the act of giving something appropriate *gratis* to satisfy the needs of the other that gives value to the other. This giving can be work or not, effortful or not. It's the thought that counts.

6   It is implied that they are vauable because they have been given. In the economy, where abundance is not usually the case, the implication may be the opposite: they are valueless because they have been given.

7   'Gray' has a (metagift) value for the color gray, and a gift value for 'cat' because it can be given to it. 'Cat' has a value as a receiver for 'gray' because 'gray' can be given to it.

and is given value because it has been relevant enough to talk about, giving value to the listener in the process. Someone has given word gifts for it (they have 'paid' their attention 'forward' using their words). This is also important for the speaker because as s:he speaks, s:he creates a parallel and aligned gift relation for h:erself with others.

The weaving of gifts inside, between and among sentences creates a text that carries or directs joint attention to possible or actual gift configurations in the world, in the immagination (or in language itself as we are doing now). We attend to the word-gifts' possible areas of reference, semantic fields, in order to receive perceptual/conceptual gifts from them together. The particular sentence (or phrase) gift, located in the context of other sentence-gifts provides the instructions for identifying the gifts that give rise to them, on the perceptual or conceptual plane. At the same time there are many (verbal and nonverbal gestural) accents of relevance or value that incite us to feel in various ways about it, or at least tell us how the other feels. They provide 'intensity', 'volume' and 'hue'.

The linguistic gift configurations are then accessible to memory, much as those of direct experience would have been. However, they have the second presence and second relevance of having been given to us by others through language. For the listener/reader the meaning of a word, phrase or sentence might answer the question 'why is s:he giving me this virtual gift now?' part of the answer to which is given in the surrounding words, phrases and sentences. 'S:he said "cat" because s:he wanted to tell me it is hungry': those world-gifts are given to each other.[8] S:he wanted to make it relevant to me as it was to her. We might implicitly ask 'what does s:he think I don't know here? What don't I have a relation to? What need of mine is s:he satisfying? What gift is s:he giving me?'. Such questions are easier to answer because we have a lot of practice. We take the same kinds of gift initiatives towards others ourselves, 'reading their minds' in other moments, identifying and satisfying their communicative needs, creating joint attention. I believe this is a development of mothering also in the sense that mothers do mind read their children's material, communicative and cognitive needs from the beginning because the children cannot tell them what they need. Linguistically, we mother each other.

---

8   While this may seem to be similar to the communication of the speaker's intention as many philosophers of language (for example Searle 1995) might say, here the receiver's needs are taken into account in the production of the gifts, and the function of the linguistic process itself, which is always beneficial, is to satisfy those needs. On the other hand the speaker's intention in putting that process into practice, may also be harmful.

9.3 Meaning in life

A dedicated doctor or other provider of special services, may have what is called a meaningful life, satisfying others' needs. However, practicing medicine mainly for profit usually alters or deviates the giving and the meaning. Little gift value is given to the other and the gift schema is cancelled.

The accumulation of wealth appears to be meaningful perhaps because it shows that the wealthy person has a lot to give (what anthropologists call 'costly signaling'). However if a person doesn't actually give gifts at some level, enacting the schema and passing the gift on, s:he does not create community-making (communicative) meaning. That is, s:he is engaged in continuously repeated virtualization of gifts into money, which s:he accumulates as capital.

Typically capitalists reinvest profits endlessly in order to re virtualize them in money and make more profit. However they sometimes derive personal meaning by giving away portions of the wealth they have accumulated to good works or to their children. By these gifts of philanthropy and legacy, they extend their gifting subjectivity (and the meaning of their actions and lives) 'horizontally' through space and 'vertically' through time. They are able to practice gift-giving on a large scale with money. Thus ironically at the top of the exploitative system, they return to the logic of the behavior of the nurturing source. In doing this they find 'meaning' in their lives. 'Wealth is not to feed our egos, but to feed the hungry and to help people help themselves'. — Andrew Carnegie (1835–1919). They do not usually realize that their ability to give comes from their successful participation in a system which encourages them to take the hidden and forced gifts of innumerable others.

On the other hand, there is also the perpetration of violence, which unfortunately also creates a kind of meaning for the perpetrator. This 'giving' of violence makes the violent subject 'superior' and allows h:er to dominate others including the givers of gifts. Giving violence s:he also punishes the givers, making them 'pay,' bringing the gift into the mode of exchange again.

The processes of exchange and profit 'making' provide only the value of the schema of virtualization/exchange, not gift value coming from the gift schema. They are not themselves meaningful because the money and commodities are not shared and meaning in life as in language is interpersonal, other-oriented (altercentric) and based on giving to satisfy needs. Just the fact that we can use the same word, 'meaning' in both areas is a clue to the similarity of the processes. Indeed if meaning in language is based on gifting, communicating linguistically continually exercises our capacities in that direction even if we don't recognize it and if we believe that meaning comes from virtualization/categorization.

Since the gift schema is versatile, it integrates into the market, reappearing at many different levels. Thus there is a kind of meaning within the capitalist system in that the capitalist can 'give' the gifts of jobs and perhaps commodities of social benefit (Bill Gates, Steve Jobs, Warren Buffett). However s:he only does this by participating in a system that is taking gifts from women, from workers, from consumers, and from nature locally and globally. In fact, capitalist philanthropists are not original givers, maternal sources of economic gifts, but at most they are passing on some of the gifts that they have leveraged. Nevertheless entrepreneurs sometimes dedicate themselves passionately to their work in order to achieve a kind of meaning at this level. Teachers give the gifts of their knowledge and attempt to satisfy their students' needs to succeed in the capitalist system. Researchers try to find answers to the many questions that plague market-based society. Scientists try to find beneficial knowledge. Medical researchers try to find cures for diseases. Doctors and therapists try to heal. Politicians and activists try to solve social problems. All of these gifts and potential gifts are or can become commodities however.

Patriarchy also achieves a kind of contradictory semblance of meaning through the transformation of giving into 'high transitive' hitting, resulting in the individual's or the nation's power over others. Giving way to others, allowing oneself to be dominated also seems to give them a kind of gift value so victims unwittingly give value to perpetrators by implication (and the perpetrators want it).

Power is a *do ut des* social mechanism in which verbal command-gifts are given 'downwards' in a hierarchy, and gifts and services of obedience are given 'upwards'. The power of the one at the top is achieved through the control and redistribution upwards of the gifts of those below, often forced by high transitive constraint, though the appearance may be very different.[9] Thus in power hierarchies the gift schema and the virtualization schema are combined to the detriment of the many below and the dominance of the ones above. This happens at many levels from the family to the nation.[10]

---

9   See Marx footnote (1995: 54 note 22) again, one is king because others are related to him as his subjects ... they imagine that they are subjects because he is king.

10   The expansion of the (one-to-many dominant) (exosomatic concept-based rather than giving-in-the-sentence-based) subjectivity of the one who gives commands is perhaps complemented by the diminution of the (one to many) subjectivity of those who obey (as gift agents?). Yet they do give to him – their gifts and services and their will – and gift value.

Together, patriarchy and capitalism (Capitalist Patriarchy, Patriarchal Capitalism) create a complex system of domination based on the taking and redistribution of gifts and thus on the deformation of meaning in life. Nevertheless, though distorted by the market and patriarchy and elusive in a culture based upon exchange, the meaning that has its source in the mother-based gift economy continues to be available. In our epoch, speaking truth to power has become one of the greatest gifts that can be given, because of the lies that governments, corporations and media use – in the mode of exchange – to manipulate the attention of the public and thus to alter the perceptual and conceptual commons. Democracy can only have its source in a gifted and shareable commons and it is therefore precluded by the lies. The truth tellers are made to pay for their gifts in much the same way that battered wives are punished for gifting. Exchange reigns supreme even in the motivation of 'justice'.

The hardship in which most people are forced to live constrains their gifts to a micro level, focussing them among the family and neighbors. Ironically those who do the most giving often have the least material goods to give and they are forced inside of traditional patterns of domination. Givers are socially denigrated as victims, as if the market system itself could not stand the competition of the successful giving model.

People doing gifting inside the system as volunteerism and social activism do sometimes achieve meaningful lives but they are also often disappointed by the systemic character of the problems they face. Politicians and activists cannot solve the deep systemic problems because, without recognizing the importance of the maternal gift economy, their analysis is incomplete and they cannot create an appropriate strategy for change or envision a really different economic and social system. They often continue to accept acritically the logic of exchange and to believe that the market is the solution to the problems the market itself is creating.[11] The abstract and anti nurturing discipline of economics has much of the responsibility for validating the market, but the other Patriarchal Capitalist academic disciplines also give their 'contribution'.

As systemic entities, nations make war on each other rather than giving to each other to satisfy needs.[12] They derive (and validate) negative meaning[13] from violence rather than positive maternal meaning. Even if the

---

11   One particularly important contemporary example of this is microcredit.
12   Commerce is said to do this but it easily becomes a means of leveraging more profit and dominating foreign economies.
13   Perhaps this negative meaning is neutralized to high transitivity by those not personally involved.

soldier 'gives' h:er life – or death – to and for others, war is an exchange. As in a zero sum game, the ones who 'give' more lives lose. The sacrifice of one's life is thus usually meaningless or pernicious in spite of government fanfare and lavish funeral ceremonies. War serves the double purpose of eliminating excess young men and making their lives 'meaningful' or 'valuable' by giving them (up) 'for' something.[14]

Because we do not recognize that the source of meaning is maternal gift-giving, we believe meaning comes from virtualization/categorization and we strive to be in the 'right' category of gender, race, class, religion, nation, profession, group or gang (with phallic symbols from monuments to missiles, scepters to guns and sticks). The exemplar is hypostatized, and becomes a position of domination, available on many different levels for those who cannot find gift meaning. Then those below give their gifts and the implication of gift value upwards to h:er or it.

The linguistic elaboration of relevance has the potential for directing the communicators themselves towards gift-based meaning but it is usually denatured by their focus on exchange and the relevance they attribute to the market.

9.4 Meaning in language

Communicative meaning (both on the linguistic and the material level) is an extension of maternal gifting (nurturing) subjectivity. The initiatives of the human speaking/writing subject and the (projected)similar initiatives of the corresponding grammatical subject extend through the sentence. Similarly, the gifting initiative extends through the gifts and services that an individual agent is giving in life. Words come to the speaker/writer from h:er abundant lexical repository and s:he gives them to each other together in gift constructions, which s:he gives to other people. H:er linguistic process intention is to satisfy communicative and cognitive needs and in doing so, s:he creates gift relations and new initiatives, trajectories, arguments and implications in and through h:er sentences and texts, choosing relevant words and bringing forward topics to be shared. Leaving aside the differences in size or scope, we can see that s:he is doing much the same thing in language that s:he does with gifts in life in interpersonal care and provisioning.

---

14 Remember Cindy Sheehan's question 'What noble cause?' did her son die for in Iraq, http: //edition.cnn.com/2005/POLITICS/08/07/mom.protest/. See also Carolyn Marvin and David Ingle, *Blood Sacrifice and the Nation*.

The speaker/writer may have to do a number of other things (gesticulating, raising h:er voice, writing h:er book) to satisfy the communicative and cognitive needs of others but s:he maintains the gift focus or initiative throughout the various stages of h:er phrases, h:er sentences and h:er discourse. That gift initiative also regards the world as relevant giver, whose gifts the speaker passes on to the listener/reader, as I said[15] above.

The subject of the sentence (the virtual giver) is qualitatively and quantitatively elaborated through the gifts of the 'modifiers' (e.g. adjectives, adverbs, prepositional phrases) it receives and the gifts it gives (e.g. verbs, articles, pronouns) to a sentential receiver (e.g. noun), or combination[16] of receivers (e.g. noun phrase) which can also be elaborated, and, shifting perspectives, the gift of the receiver's reception is also given to the giver: 'the girl hit the ball' ('the boy kissed the girl who hit the ball').

Meanwhile the human giver is giving this and other sentence gifts to other human receivers, developing her own subjectivity in this way, while they develop theirs as receivers for the moment, regarding the many kinds of gifts they can creatively receive and the many ways they can receive and use them and then also give them again, becoming verbal givers in their turns. Putting the gift schema into practice in language enhances the gift subjectivity of the speaker/writer by allowing her to do verbal gifting in many different ways regarding many different things, even when she is not doing material gifting. The human speaking/writing gifting subject aligns with the spoken/written gifting grammatical subject and the human listening/reading receiver aligns with the spoken/written receiving grammatical object. The verbal product is a gift and as such it aligns with the syntactic gifts to gifts that are internal to it.

For the human giver, the perception and knowledge of the receiver's reception is the end of the trajectory of the gift, its present completion, though s:he can always give again and s:he knows the receiver can do so as well. The receiver responds with cognition and perhaps also recognition, creating a communicatively aligned relation with the giver (the speaker is after all a part of the world external to the listener that has 'come forward').

The reception or 'answering comprehension' of the linguistic receiver is a positive response containing gratitude or something like it, perhaps 'altercentric recognition', and a disposition that rises to use the gift,

---

15   Symbolic gift exchange is a kind of replay and exploration of meaning in language and it would be illuminating to study it in that light.

16   The combination is also acheived by giving-receiving. 'Into the barn' is made of three words given to each other, the article to the noun and the preposition also, while the whole prepositional phrase is given to 'the horse ran'.

which has been given. Also, mimetically it follows the model of the giver, possibly to reply, to give in turn, as the receiver learned to do already in childhood protoconversation.[17]

Word meaning has to do with the specific cognitive and communicative needs a word satisfies and thus it depends to a large extent on the kinds of things for which the word is the substitute exemplar, ie. for which it can be a gift. It is also influenced by the syntactic relations of giving and receiving into which it can enter with other words in the specific language and these are influenced by the kind of thing the referent is as a world gift. Is the world gift an entity? then in English the word gift must be a noun. Is it an action, a service? then a verb. A quality? An adjective or adverb. One role has a 'slot' – a need – for the others. Phrase, sentence or text meaning is the extension of gifting through a variety of verbal gifts, a passing on of the givers' initiative or energy through the gift concatenations.

9.5 Gift subjectivity and linguistic meaning

We usually ignore and leave aside the gift subjectivity of the speaker even when s:he is speaking in first person (unless what s:he says specifically regards giving). Even the speaker h:erself thinks s:he is only performing a sui generis (speech) act (Austin, Virno check), or that she is an 'agent' naming or talking or writing or signing (or singing), not giving, and that the listener/reader/receiver is a 'patient' only, receiving a neutral (non-benefactive) transfer, perhaps just allowing h:erself to be acted upon, influenced or manipulated.[18] Or she thinks she is 'picking up' or 'grasping' the speaker's intention, or making or receiving and interpreting a construction of form – meaning correspondences – not a focussed gift construction made of fine tuned other-oriented (maternal, altercentric) relation-creating, gift-transmit-

---

17 Knowledge-cognition may be considered as a kind of neutralized gratitude (see Vaughan 1997).

18 According to Searle the receiver 'picks up' the 'intention' of the speaker, enacting a kind of tolerated scrounge. For Arbib the receiver "grasps it" (2005). According to *vox populi* s:he receives a transmission through a conduit (Reddy's conduit metaphor), for information theorists, bits of information through binary choices, for Grice (1989) the speaker puts into practice the cooperative principle based on maxims, for the Sperbers (1995) s:he receives a cost effective enhancement of knowledge, for Goldberg (1995), s:he follows rules for semantic interpretation of 'form and function pairings', etc.

ting need-satisfying gifts.[19] Why does it matter that we dont know what we are doing? We misassign our gratitude so our knowledge is faulty.

In our terms, speech/writing is an act of satisfying needs: gifting verbally, and it is therefore not a separate autonomous capacity but is located within a context of many other important kinds of material, perceptual and conceptual ways of giving and receiving. Thinking is mainly hypothetical giving/receiving whether the thinker is using language mentally or not.

Words are *gifts of the gifts* of the motherworld and of aspects of the collective linguistic and conceptual or cultural commons, created by those before us in their life processes. We learn words and thus have access to them to use whenever we want to give them to other people in gift constructions. The speaking/writing subject is thus a giver not just an 'agent,' while the listener/reader is a creative receiver, not just a 'patient'; s:he finds h:er needs have been satisfied by the speaker and responds with knowledge-gratitude. S:he is not just passive, acted upon, but s:he is also not an exchange-agent. H:er ability to speak/write in h:er turn liberates h:er from any inferiority or subjugation she might have regarding the others' capacity to satisfy h:er communicative and cognitive needs unilaterally. (But she must be given - or take -a *turn*. See the question "Can the subaltern speak?" Spivak 1988).

Caught as we are inside the exchange paradigm, where the idea of the gift, of the motherworld or the commons hardly occurs to us, we try to understand language by placing the receiver, the giver, the verbal products and the interactions among them in the schema of virtualization-naming (which resonates with its incarnation in the exosomatic concept of monetized exchange), redefining, renaming and rewriting them with grammatical or logical notation. Even the speaker/writer does not realize that when s:he is making sentences and texts s:he is also and primarily satisfying others' cognitive and communicative needs, placing h:er verbal products in the gift schema (and knowing that the listener/reader will do likewise).

---

19   Perhaps the teaching of sign language to primates has been influenced by our concept of language lacking the gift schema. Although the primates are dependent on their trainers for food, it is used more as a bribe than as a gift, which would make it consistent for them to use sign language to beg. If they are only able to sign names without putting them in grammatical phrases, it seems clear they are doing virtualization rather than giving. Wouldn't this seem to make the virtualization schema simpler that the gift schema? The challenge would be to study how the primates do mothering, imitate it and transition it to human mothering of the baby chimp or gorilla in order to teach the gift schema. The interesting film by James Marsh on Nim Chimpsky (*Project Nim* 2011) shows how little his relationships with his chimpanzee mother and his human mother figures were respected or considered pertinent to his language learning.

Gift value is invisible too, though by communicating verbally speakers and writers continue to give it.

Describing the speaker as the source of gifts reveals that her agency as giver/speaker/writer is important in the creation of her subjectivity, and demonstrates the relevance of the self to others and to herself. The self is relevant as the motherworld is relevant, as having to give, as giver but also as the source of the immediate initiatives that she can identify as her 'own'. Part of what s:he has to give to the other can be information on her own needs, e.g. the child says 'want cookie', the adult says 'Give me a kiss to build a dream on!" or "Give me liberty or give me death'). Moreover s:he also gives to herself, imagining, thinking, planning, and providing. S:he is a receiver of h:er own gifts as well as of the gifts of others. So the self is positioned in between the roles of giver and receiver – of the gifts of others, of the world and of the gifts of the internal giver, gifts that can also be given to the other or to the self as other. S:he is a kind of relay station elaborating relevance in the realm of the gift. However, when s:he gives in exchange s:he contradicts h:er own internal gifting which is based on use and use value not on exchange.

All this has as a consequence that the speaking and (usually) the writing subject is constituted as a giver like the grammatical subject, and as a receiver like the grammatical object. Though many other grammatical positions are possible, as in the passive construction or the object in the prepositional phrase.[20] The verb too as the gift is animated by the giver and anticipates its reception by the receiver, paralleling the movement of the voice of one to the ears of the other (disguised a bit in writing and reading where the word gifts do have to be 'picked up' from the page by the eyes of the reader).[21]

In conversation many non verbal and verbal cues communicate the specifics of the gift initiatives of the speaker and of the reception and understanding of the message by the listener.

It is the combination – the giving together – of gifts at different levels that makes it possible for the speaker/writer to give articulated verbal products that s:he believes the listener/reader will be able to receive. That is, the listener/reader will be able to (almost automatically) place them in h:er

---

20   Look at Chomsky's (1956: 118) famous early example of ambiguity 'They are flying planes' where the subject, 'they' is either the giver of 'flying' to 'planes' or the phrase is a definition (virtualization) formed with a pronoun 'they' which is substituted by a noun phrase using the copula.

21   The unconscious can also be understood as a maternal giver because it takes gift initiatives.

own preexisting image schema of the gift (which s:he also learned by being mothered/nurtured in infancy), causing in h:er own mind implications of relevance and of gift value and attention to the transmission of gifts on the world plane, which are the same or similar to those recognized and intended by the speaker/writer.

These implications and understandings create the new momentary synthesis, the 'epiphenomenal' gift of (phrase, sentence, and discourse) meaning (specific relevance, qualitative value) regarding gifts to gifts in the world. Each new 'package' of given words also gives a newly integrated dynamic gift of aspects of relevant world-gifts, brought forward and passed on to the listener/reader by the speaker/writer as the focus of the joint attention of both. The epiphenomenal gift has its own logical and relational implications due to its salience, the focus upon it, its 'popping out' and the alignment of different kinds of gifts inside and outside the verbal product at different levels (of interlocutors, of world-gifts, word gifts and syntax, of sentences and relations among sentences and among the world gifts they re-present, i.e. regive). Thus the epiphenomenal gift itself creates a new level of gifts, the topic of the actual communication, conversation, locution, text. The many different kinds of gift combinations in the world can have specific new or refreshed meanings and implications too, and the speaker/writer attempts to pass these gifts on. Linguistic creativity is thus not only creativity directed towards the communicative and cognitive needs of the other, satisfying them with word-gifts but on this basis, it can also reveal new world-gifts that have not been seen and shared before. Others receive these new gifts (everyone has a need to know the new) because they too are well-practiced in detecting, receiving and passing-on the gifts of their experience and their surroundings, of which in the moment, the verbal product of the other is an especially relevant one.

The speaker also understands the meaning of the linguistic gift s:he gives and s:he receives – hears – it as s:he speaks it (or sees it as s:he writes it). That is, her own linguistic gift becomes a perceptual gift, which she too receives/perceives. S:he knows what s:he has said with all its gifts directed towards the other.[22] H:er own relations to the world-gifts (now seen as the topic) become relations that are aligned with those of the others, to whom s:he has given the word-gifts in the moment and vice-versa the receivers' relations to the word-gifts and the world-gifts

---

22   This is the case even if s:he only imagines saying something. Otherwise how could writing function with what is often a long interval between production and reading?

are aligned with h:ers. Their[23] perspectives are similar cognitively even if they may be different in other ways. The judge and the prisoner are aligned cognitively to the word gifts and to the world gifts: 'hang h:er at dawn!' even if their perspectives and relations to the events are very different (and their ability to give the command as well).

Both when s:he imagines saying something and when s:he actually says it the speaker/writer mind-reads the real or imagined, particular or general listener/reader in order to understand what words are needed and what this linguistic communication will mean or has meant to h:er/them. S:he has a lot of practice in doing this, and s:he can even speak or write for others in general as does a TV announcer. S:he can altercentrically take the other's perspective, following the implications and even feeling some of the emotions the listener/reader might feel in understanding what is said. If the listener seems puzzled, the speaker may realize that h:er cognitive/communicative needs were not satisfied. Then s:he can rephrase what s:he said, creating a new (more appropriately fashioned) verbal gift.

On the other hand, while the speaker/writer has something s:he wants to say/give by satisfying the listeners'/readers' communicative needs, which s:he mind reads, s:he does not usually know the complete relevance of what s:he is talking about nor can s:he know all of the experience, life synthesis and preconscious selectivity of the receiver, so the communicative gift s:he gives is only h:er best guess, and may satisfy more or less or other needs that s:he does not know about. The listener/reader collaborates; s:he also mind-reads the speaker/writer in order to understand what needs of h:ers the speaker believes s:he satisfying and with them, what schemas, implications, references and relevances the verbal construction 'conveys'. That is, what gift or virtualization schemas the listener/reader should recreate in h:er own mind or recognize among gifts in the world according to the speaker's gift, schematic 'mould' or 'blueprint'.

The result of our gift-based communication is that we co-construct and re-emphasize topics and points of relevance in common. We have co constructed an environmental niche that is relevant, that gives to us, responds to us maternally but we have to mediate its gifts by giving and receiving verbally *and* materially to each other (because if not we freeze the gift process). The listener understands the speaker's intention to give and to imply, i.e. to create specific implications by giving.

---

23   They are aligned as members of a species that does this vocal gifting, vocal nurturing. Humans assert and construct our species relation all the time verbally even though we may be acting inhumanely.

The speaker gives gift value to the listener by satisfying h:er needs, and to the words as need-satisfying gifts to other words, which thus receive gift value and to what s:he has said, i.e. for which s:he has given those word-gifts gifts together. Value is also given to the speaker by the listener, with a kind of gratitude. That is, s:he is recognized as relevant. S:he has come forward.

9.6 The 'hau' as meaning

9.6a In speech

I have discussed word meaning throughout the book and in 6.13. In gift terms 'speaker's meaning' (Grice 1989) is the extension of the maternal gifting (nurturing) initiative. The subject's gifting spirit, what we can describe as the individual speaker's own '*hau*' extends though h:er sentences with h:er breath. Like the spirit of the gift that passes from person to person in a gifting circle along with the gifts, the spirit of the gift and of the giver passes from word to word in the sentence, and that 'spirit' is real. It is the breath, the voice.

I feel justified in using the idea of the '*hau*', taking it from anthropology, beginning with Malinowski's and Mauss' work on gifting among the Trobriand Islanders, to explain meaning, in the same way that I have been tryng to use money to explain virtualization and virtualization to explain money. Again it is the anatomy of 'man' that gives the clues to the anatomy of the 'ape'. The nature of the 'parent' (language) is seen in the 'progeny' (here money or symbolic gift exchange). Perhaps these social forms of material communication – the market or symbolic gift exchange – can even be seen as collective cultural explorations of what language is, collective philosophy on the material plane. We are not alone as individual thinkers, wondering what we are doing when we speak, think and act. Whole cultures do it too and give their answers.

Looking at symbolic gift exchange like the Trobriand Kula in this light we can see it not as exchange but as material conversation. On the other hand we can look at the *hau* at the level of sentences and texts as the spirit of the gift that passes from word to word, phrase to phrase. For this, we only need a certain amount of dexterity in changing scale, an ability to shift focus from the macro level of the culture as a whole to the micro level of the combination of words and phrases.

The spirit of the gift calls for the gift to return to its original giver. This characteristic of the *hau* has been interpreted as the principle of reciprocity, often seen by Westerners as a kind of proto-exchange. Instead we should look at it as the conversational reelaboration of the process of mimesis, first seen in the relation between the child and the motherer. Imitating the giving of the motherer, the child gives in turn, and this not only in bodily actions and 'body mapping' but also vocally and eventually verbally. The reply in conversation is a repetition of unilateral giving, of taking the initiative, of giving in turn, of giving forward. It is not so much that the verbal gift requires reciprocity, a counter gift or exchange, but that it invites a reply, perhaps the continuation of a rhythm. Thus in language the spirit of the gift returns to the original giver from others as a repetition of the unilateral model, as coming forward, as relevant continuation, turn taking, not as exchange. (Ears and mouth are assymetrical! We can't speak and listen, give to the other and receive from the other simultaneously like we do in material exchange.) The listener, becoming a speaker in h:er turn, gives h:er own verbal gifts and gift schemas to the previous speaker. The speaker can count on the listener's disposition to reply, to give in turn, without the interaction's becoming an exchange.[24]

On the material plane[25] the individual's spirit or intention also extends throughout the many gift trajectories in her life and in others' lives. Sentence meaning is a limited version of this in that the transitive gift schema channels the '*hau*', the spirit of the gift, from the grammatical subject, through the verb: gift or service, to the receiver: object (and similarly with other word orders) with the corresponding perspectives and implications intact. The grammatical subject altercentrically gives the verb to the object which altercentrically receives it. Replaying and recognizing this in the sentence is not difficult because in the original interactive dyad, the child takes the motherer's complementary and opposite perspective as well as h:er own (though autism is an exception as I mentioned, and see Bråten 2013). Like the gift schema as a whole, the individual giver-gift-receiver perspectives are available to be projected into grammar and onto the world from the beginning of life. Even the kinetic sense of giving (movement) between bodies and within the body can sometimes be felt in the meaning of sentences. Moreover, the front of the mouth receives food and gives it

---

24 But there are some verbal exchanges, for example teacher's interrogations and students' answers, or even just questions and answers generally.

25 Mauss (1990 [1923]) saw the *hau*, the spirit of the gift, as the evidence of necessary reciprocity, but as we have been saying it is the unilateral satisfaction of communicative needs that is the basis of communication, not exchange. In early childhood this is experienced as altercentric turn taking and surely each person is conscious of the spirit of the gift of the other. See also Lewis Hyde on the increase of the gift and the creation of community through its circulation (2007: 32ff).

to the back, which swallows. Air comes in through the nose or the mouth, while in speech air comes from the back of the mouth and out through the lips: we receive breath and give breath again. And we form our breath into words. From the point of view of the gift paradigm, we are always receiving (breathing in) and giving again (breathing out).

Both the speaker and the listener can take the perspectives of the different gift roles in speech. They take the perspective of the object (receiver) in the sentence as well as that of the subject(giver); their speech is itself the gift in motion. So in 'Jane baked the cake' the speaker, aligned with the subject-giver also takes the perspective of receiver, 'the cake' (a perspective that s:he has developed since childhood by being a receiver as well as a giver), and s:he has a sense of its 'response' called forth by the verb-gift of the 'baking', and of the reality plane cake's 'response' to being baked. To these correspond the perspectives of the speaker as giver, the word-construction-in-process as gift, and the listener as receiver, who also responds with comprehension if not always with another verbal gift in reply. Because of h:er own life-long experience with giving and receiving, the receiver can take the perspective of the speaker and also of the subject-giver in the sentence, of verbs as gifts and of other parts of speech as givers/receivers (fillers and slots),[26] of gifts to gifts and of the grammatical object/receiver as her own perspective. These are all altercentric relations within the sentence itself.

In the elaborate gifting circle of the Kula, gifts go around slowly from island to island and the *hau*, the spirit of the gift maintains identities and relationships of the givers and receivers over long periods of time (perhaps in this way they gain 'substance', 'object permanence'). The histories of all the givers and receivers of the gifts are remembered. Similarly for language we can recognize the *hau* as the spirit of the giver-speaker, the breath that forms the sequences of verbal gifts in schemas and passes through them, from gift to gift, connecting them in a construction that satisfies the listener's cognitive and communicative needs and at the same time repeats the patterns of the interaction itself (the positions of unilateral giving and receiving are the positions of speaking and listening, of subject and object). The 'return' of the gift can be seen in the creative receptivity of the listener, h:er comprehension but also h:er initiative in response, h:er own new unilateral gift construction, which often creates a joint or common elaboration of the relevance of the topic. H:er verbal gift constructions also carry and

---

26   These are adverbs and adjectives that are given to nouns and verbs, prepositions that implement different kinds of giving of phrases to phrases.

are carried by h:er breath anɑ h:er *hau*. Each also gives gift value to the other and to the common ground in and through h:er gift constructions. This is not exchange but turn taking in unilateral giving.

The speaker/writer is a receiver of perceptions and conceptions from the world directly and/or through the communications of others; s:he becomes a giver, gives a virtual giver-gift-receiver sequence as a transitive sentence gift. For example s:he gives a virtualization schema 'x is y' or a combination of both schemas 'this is the cat that chased the rat'.

9.6b In writing

We are called upon to turn our attention towards the speaker/writer to receive her verbal gifts. Although we do not have to reciprocate to understand (and particularly in reading and in other media we do not) the speaker's initiative calls us to converse, to add our gifts and to pass h:ers on. This does not happen through the logic of exchange, but through the adult elaboration of unilateral giving. Our own gift initiatives reach back to what the previous speaker received from the (perceptual or conceptual) world as we pass them on, adding more gifts of our own experience, creating common ground. The meaning becomes a topic: 'it's a pretty day' says one. 'Yesterday's rain cleared the air' says another. 'Let's take a walk' says a third.

As I said above, intransitive sentences implement or replay the virtualization schema. They constitute a more foreshortened, abbreviated version of the gift schema, using the copula as a meta gift-attributor so that the speaker can give the words to each other and the perceptual or conceptual gifts to the listener with her words. Because the *hau* changes level for a moment in this meta gift of the copula, we give a lot of importance to 'being'. In fact the copula is the verbal cognate of money.

The gift interaction is not displayed in the main structure of the intransitive sentence as it is in the transitive sentence but only takes place more locally among parts of speech like determiners, adjectives and nouns or morphologically by the application (giving) of prefixes and suffixes to 'roots', and of course, interpersonally between the speaker/writer and listener/reader. With the transitive sentence, the gift schema is present both inside the sentence and outside (among interlocutors) and on the reality plane as well, creating chains of gifts that form new short term gifts. Inside the intransitive sentence, the schema of virtualization, not the schema of the gift, is the main structure, while outside (among interlocutors) and on the reality plane, the gift schema remains. There are also mixtures between the two types of schemas (gift and virtualization) as provided by gifts of determiners, modifiers, phrases, clauses and other 'attributions'.

If writing developed as Schmandt-Besserat says, from the tokens in Mesopotamia, first the exosomatic token and then the graphic drawing of the token, then more complex cuneiform signs, virtualized the world-gifts – the concepts of wheat or wine or sheep – that were relevant to the accountants of the epoch. Later, with alphabetic writing, a way was found not to virtualize the world-gift directly but to virtualize the linguistic sound, which was itself already a virtual verbal gift for the world-gift. That is, the letter of the alphabet is the written exemplar, the 'one' for the many spoken sound-gifts of a kind that together with others constitute a specific word gift. In other words, the same process that takes place in establishing word meaning (which we saw in section 6.13, Sounds of language), is repeated in writing. The sound is virtualized upon the page (or the papyrus or the slab) and the writer and reader are able to give it sequentially to the other re-virtualized sounds that are there, creating the one-to-many written exemplar of a spoken word. Thus the reader receives the verbal gift of the writer, which can satisfy almost any competent reader's cognitive and communicative need even at a great distance or many centuries later. It is possible as speed-reading experts teach us, to skip the vocal image of the word and go directly to the non verbal exemplar or concept. That is, the written word can stand as the one to many substitute exemplar for the items in the concept in relation to each other. However many people do sound out the words at least mentally as they are reading them.

To those who say that language derives from gestures, I would reply that giving and receiving are the first and most significant gestures. Moreover, even giving a mark to a surface is giving-to-view, giving something that others can receive visually. Since gifts can be material as well as verbal, they can also be carriers of the *hau*, as symbolic gift exchange shows us. Thus the schema of the gift can be transferred back to the material plane from the verbal plane. Like money, the concept exemplar that becomes a material word, the virtual gift schema can be devirtualized. Thus we can follow the gift schemas and their variations and elaborations when they are given to us in writing, while the *hau* of the writer continues to animate them even at a distance of space and time, satisfying the readers' communicative and cognitive needs sequentially.

These gift constructions provide joint attention, a common focus, shared to a large extent by both speaker/writer and listener/reader. Thus it is possible to create a relevant perceptual and conceptual commons, a common ground (*topos*, topic), as a group of meanings , which are connected among themselves, 'merged' through gift relations.

The meaning that we Patriarchal Capitalist Westerners would have found in the material giving, which contains and transmits the spirit of the gift in the same way that the '*hau*' is transmitted in speech, is trapped at the meta level in the material-virtual money-word. We reenact the process of virtualization over and over materially but this cannot provide the transitive altercentric meaning that comes from the schema of the gift, which we are still unconsciously enacting linguistically all the time.

Much communication through the media is done for exchange so it does not give value to the other like personal communication does, even though the words that are used do satisfy those communicative needs of everyone. The market creates a situation in which language is no longer in alignment with its human and humanizing gift origins and capacities. In the exchange mode we use our linguistic gift constructions not to satisfy the needs of others, which would include an accurate understanding of a shared reality, but in order to receive the satisfaction of our own needs, using the other's understanding as means. Thus the verbal gift capacity is used to lie, and the source of perceptual and linguistic gifts, the motherworld, to cheat. Elections, issues and politicians are bought and sold.

Although we talk about the 'circulation' of goods and money in the market, exchange actually interrupts gift circulation every time it happens. Then we strive to create meaning by 'making' and having more money as if we could increase the significance of the holophrastic money-word, making it louder, accumulating and spending more. Think of the screaming decibels of the wars in the Middle East and Afghanistan.

In Patriarchal Capitalism, we are stuck in virtualization on the material plane, repeating the one holophrastic word. We have lost the good spirit of the gift, the *hau*, and we are not finding it in language or in life. We are making life meaningless and we are spreading our market disease, everywhere. This disease is made more virulent, more 'communicable' because everyone who speaks has the capacity for virtualization that is extrinsicated in the money-word and thus also the capacity to engage with the exosomatic concept form.

But everyone also still has the capacity for meaning, for creating and giving the gift using the *hau*, the spirit of the gift. We take gift initiatives with every word we speak or write and every word-construction we make. We receive gifts with every word and word-construction we hear or read and understand.

Perhaps finding the gift of meaning in language can help dissolve the paralysis of the heart created by exchange and liberate gifts at all levels to be given to satisfy needs. This is how we will create a society of co-munication. This is how. This is the *Hau*.

CHAPTER X

GENERALIZING THE GIFT

10.0 The model of the motherer

The gift schema is part of the world as giving and having-to-give. It is not a substitute. It is embedded in the world. People do it, the world does it, a lot. However we don't have in the foreground the cultural model (the prototype or exemplar) of the motherer around whose image we could consciously generalize the gift schema. The schema of exchange for money cancels the gift while the schema of virtualization (parent of exchange) cohabits with it. Things are not generalized by being virtualized but by being given, over and over again, and in different contexts. Societies that have the prototype of the mother, or Mother Earth, women-centered and matriarchal societies and gift economies, do recognize the schema of the gift and generalize it in various ways, implementing it in the provisioning distribution of gifts, in gift 'exchange', in festivals, in story telling, transmission of knowledge, rituals etc., and even in 'having to give'. If we can recognize the structural importance of gift-giving and receiving in language, perhaps we too can begin to recognize and generalize the model of the motherer for our understanding of the human.

Figure 25. Perhaps Willendorf was the prehistoric human Ideal Cognitive Model.

Word-gifts, given to each other sequentially provide the links of short signifying chains, sentences, the 'horizontal axis' on which the virtual interaction of giving and receiving takes place (with its ever-present reality-plane motivation and vehicle, the speaker's/writer's initiative to give verbal gifts to hearer/readers), and the 'vertical axis' of virtualization, where the (gift character of the) extra linguistic or perceptual or conceptual gift is shifted/gifted/'lifted' (breathed in and breathed out), moved from one plane to another.

The fact that specific given words are being placed together now in an internally related and organized gift configuration to satisfy someone's communicative need regarding something, implies or brings to the fore the give-ability (and potential relevance) to each other of the (kinds of) things related to each word and to the word-combinations in the sentence. It also implies their giveability for still other people when they want to talk about them (that is, their giveability is implied by the existence in the language of the verbal gifts to which they are most often related as many to one, their names).

Understanding language as gifting thus allows humans to turn towards the world as motherer. It restores to us our continuity with the mother-care we experienced as young children. Giving verbal gifts for nonverbal world-gifts brings (back) our attention to the non verbal gifts in our surroundings and experience. The merging and gift schema role-playing of the verbal gifts implies the merging or gift schema role-playing of the non verbal gifts. The fact that words are being related to each other in the sentence and given to the listener/reader implies that the world gifts (perceptions and conceptions) are related by being or having been given to each other on the non verbal plane and perceptually to the person who has received/perceived them and who is passing them on in the schema to us. This also comes from the givenness and relevance of perceptions and ideas, their popping out at us as gifts to satisfy our needs (due to our own maternal preconscious selective perceptual activity). We are receivers of gifts from all our surroundings and we pass them on verbally. We turn altercentrically towards our cultural and environmental niche, *co-creating with it* rather than dominating it. Our perceptual world is the motherworld.

10.1 Exchange-virtualization cancels gift meaning – cancels the hau

In the market, profit consists of the (unseen and misnamed) gift aspects of the exchange interaction, which go to the benefit of one, not both, of the exchangers. There is (given gift) profit for one and (taken gift) loss for the other, addition and subtraction (the zero sum game), though this is usually covered over by an assertion of equality of value. In fact there is an emotional and often a physical disconnection between profit taker and worker, buyer or seller (and both seller and buyer in the North get gifts by exploiting the global South).

The chain of exchangers mind-read each other in manipulative ways in order to profit from the exchanges as much as possible. The business of marketing takes a lot of the guess work out of the mind-reading. Because of the scarcity created by exchange and private property, i.e. by not giving and having not-to-give, the ego-centric motivations of 'making a living' or 'making profit' or 'consuming' are already understood as real and necessary by everyone. The middleman who brings the product forward to the market or the clerk at the store counter serve a disconnective as well as a connective purpose.The exploiter is shielded from the effects of h:er gift-taking and even sees h:erself as economically 'independent' and part of a system that benefits everybody. The exploited person also believes that s:he is economically independent when s:he is earning a salary and buying consumer goods and often does not recognize the hidden gifts s:he is giving to the capitalist individuals or corporations and to the system itself. Naming – and framing – these gifts as 'profit' as we all do, is an important factor in maintaining their invisibility and hijacking them.

Once made, profit can be used for giving again, by the profit-taker to support others in a family or elsewhere. It can also be used for buying status objects and for giving oneself lavishly to the view of others (making oneself into a sign – of superiority). In this case it does 'have meaning' coming from the giving, even if the meaning is made for the purpose of bringing the individual forward into focus and giving h:er a position in a top down hierarchy of relevance. It does not recognize the source of h:er gifts as the gifts of others whose loss is harmful for them. Rather it seems s:he deserves them, as if s:he had contributed more, like the 'big man' who has given the most gifts (Sahlins 1965) and who as biggest giver may seem to be a big mother (though his wives may be the ones actually providing the goods).

The reinvestment of accumulated capital is directed towards the future, towards making more profit and acquiring more goods, security and status. This becomes an illusion of endless 'path to goal'[1] positive accumulation and positive status as if the person's not-gift value or relevance increased on a vertical axis along with the amount of money and goods

---

1   The denatured gift trajectory provides a look-alike of gift-based meaning.

s:he possesses. Again, in a situation of scarcity and private property, the virtualization schema defines the person by the money s:he has or 'makes'(the gifts of profit she has received), putting her in an inferior or a superior category, as if the money were h:er personal value equivalent. This model for identity does not function because naming with money does not on its own provide meaning. It is only virtualization, outside the gift schema. The '*hau*' of communication and community is lost in the holophrastic money-word. Similarly with the kind of identity through categorization that the money model provides (see ch. 13 above on Fetishism and the 'like me' bridge). Thus the 'identity crisis' of so many and the attempt to create an identity by categorizing oneself through clothes, tatoos, consumer objects and relating oneself to a 'one'.

10.2 Quantification

Using money to count value and to mediate exchange leaves needs and gifts aside also because quantification itself leaves needs and gifts aside, or perhaps we should say, it schematizes them in a new way.

Counting seems to be a sui generis process, a giftless listing of numbers. Instead, plus one can be seen as giving one more to a collection. Minus one is giving from a collection. The perspectives change. In the process of addition,the collection is the receiver of the items and in subtraction, it is the source from which they are given. The counter is a giver of number words by which s:he tracks (virtualizes) the accumulation or diminishing of collections of world-gifts. S:he gives the next number when s:he adds one but h:er giving is not seen as such. Rather it is virtualized with a new name, 'counting'. In fact, counting is the recitation of a list of number names taught originally to children by adults, which appears to be relevant on its own, other than, and even superior to, giving and receiving. The list of numbers is at first a kind of trick, a sequence of word-gifts that children are supposed to imitate even though they do not understand the quantitative assessment of world-gifts for which they are given. They may be able to remember the number words and hold up fingers, but they often say them in the wrong order.

Counting discounts giving because it creates a sequence of word-gifts that seems to be outside the gift schema. The giver, even if oneself (the speaker) is discounted as giver, because when one counts, one counts oneself (more) as a counter than as a giver. Counting is giving apparently giftlessly. We rename giving in the language of the number series and discount it. Gift relevance is altered and abstracted form.

Quantification is a kind of undergeneralization, where we count only gifts without qualities, only the giving itself, the plus one, which leaves aside the giving that is directed towards the need of the other, and simply give something, anything, the same thing, to add on, to count and to be counted.

One who counts recites a list of number names each of which means one more thing has been given, one more act of giving-to has taken place, without specifications (without counting it as giving as such). Thus we have e-quality, beyond or leaving aside quality. Subtraction is giving *from* a sum (3 is 5 'take away' 2, say children. Why not 'give away 2'?). Addition seems to be from the giver perspective, subtraction from that of the taker.

Understanding giving and receiving as the basis of counting might allow us to avoid the interpretation of arithmetic as 'rule following' and therefore to avoid the 'rule following paradox'. In fact 'plus' can be seen as the revirtualized command 'give!' and therefore if gift-giving is so fundamental for meaning in life and language, 'plus' is a very special case. It is the virtualization of giving to and from collections in this peculiar quantificatory way, that leaves aside qualities, renaming the collections formed in that way according to the sequential number names.

The nature of quantification has been a philosophical quandary with which many philosophers have struggled. A recent example is Saul Kripke's discussion of the invented word 'quus' in place of 'plus'. 'Quus' does not mean 'give!' as does 'plus' (because it has been given not socially but privately by Kripke; it has not been publically 'coined'). 'Plus' should be analyzed as a command to give to collections (leaving aside qualities), not as a rule. A command puts the other person in the place of the giver. 'Run!' : the speaker exhorts the listener to be giver of that action. 'Add one': the speaker exhorts the listener to be giver of one to the previous collection or s:he is simply saying that one has been given: 5 = 4 plus 1.

But as far as the gift of the word 2 itself is concerned, or 3, it is still one-to-many. 2 is related to all 2s, 3 to all 3s so they have the common quality of being that number (of gifts or givens) but without other qualities and without saying what needs they satisfy if any. Probably these are just cognitive or communicative needs for identifying and virtualizing quantities.

The narrative of quantification leaves out qualities but recounts another story, the secret narrative - that even arithmetic is based on giving.Leaving aside quality leaves aside gifts and needs. You don't need 5 but 5 of something. But you do need 5 (or 3 and 2 or 4 and 1) to give to 5 to make 10. So the needs are abstracted too.

The focus on money and the maximization of profit hides the gifts, which are not counted, that is, which are not collectively virtualized as such. Thus what has a price becomes over visible while what does not becomes undervisible or invisible. Price is the linguistic virtualization of quantities of money, in their collective relevance and giveability.

In speech and writing the name of something is given to (merged with) other word-gifts and given together with them to satisfy the listeners'/readers' communicative and cognitive needs arising from the ongoing topic or context. Different money-word denominations can be combined by producing number names appropriate to their merged quantities. These are 'operations' not made with the breath – monetary quantification is taking and giving without the hau.

Monetary quantities are merged without qualities in a sum, which will satisfy the seller's communicative and cognitive needs in the particular case, regarding the product as prefigured(linguistically named) in the price. The world-gift of the particular commodity not-gift has become relevant in a special way, to a special kind of name, the price, which is also the name of a quantity of money, which can be exchanged for it. The price of the hat is $20.

Money forms a vertical quantitative hierarchy (making change, the possibility of analysis, remains in the background). It virtualizes the values of all products as it takes their places, when it is 'given' as a not-gift horizontally in exchange.[2]

In the early childhood gift economy, relevance is intimately connected to the emotions and to the interactive, interpersonal body. Exchange among adults allows or imposes emotional detachment. Instead, exchange value itself forms an abstract hierarchy of emphasis or relevance, where the most is the strongest or biggest. The emotion is not felt but it is distanced and displaced onto the quantitative scale of exchange value as expressed in money. It is that cry of infinite decibels for which we have no ears, but we weigh its volume kinetically (with gold or silver or coins).

10.3 Philosophers and scientists vs motherers

Marx's analysis of capitalism was, as he put it, an application of Hegel's Idealism, 'turning it on its head', peeling off the 'shell' and finding its real

---

2   We can just mention telling or recounting as a parallel to counting. Here our speech satisfies the needs of the story much as it does the needs of the listener. We add plus one to spin a yarn, a thread. Story-telling is a kind of abstraction from the context like counting is. Bank employees are tellers who stand behind counters to give the clients their money and receive it from them. They count it for them.

life 'kernel'. By adding mothering-gift-giving as an ontogenetically and phylogenetically (psychologically and historically) earlier economy that contrasts with monetized exchange, we can give the issue still another twist and speculate that what Hegel was describing as the Notion or the Idea Becoming History, 'Spirit emptied out into Time', was actually a characteristic of European thinking under the influence of monetization. That is, under the influence of the extrasomatic concept process that I have been trying to show monetized market exchange to be.

Ever since the cognition/categorization process, extended beyond the mind into the world, exchange for money has fed back into our thinking as a powerful but semiconscious and unrecognized template and model.[3] This model denies the importance of maternal gift-giving and thus has colluded with the patriarchies of the centuries. The general equivalent (word/exemplar) money has combined with other patriarchal 'one' positions (the father, the military leader, the king, the hero, the phallus), validating them and replacing the prototype of the mother. This concept model was projected philosophically into the Platonic ideals but has also appeared prominently in the monotheistic patriarchal deities who repeat the word/exemplar-to-many pattern.

The very complex network of these embodied patterns and their continual restimulation and reconfirmation on a daily basis by exchange for money, create a distorted and illusory picture of the way we know, which it has been hard for philosophers to clarify. Various philosophical systems understand money and the denial and exploitation of mothering/giving 'through a glass darkly'. Through a mirror imperfectly (as Bible interpreters say), and in a mirror we can only 'mind-read' ourselves.

The kind of approach now possible in cognitive psychology and neuroscience, which treats concepts as mental processes that can be tested, allows us to demystify them and to recognize their embodiments. Similarly the detachment of money from the gold standard, the coexistence of national currencies, the cruelty and failure of the markets, manipulative finance and banking, inflation, and the computerized revirtualization of the money-word have shaken our blind faith in money and allowed us to critique it, to recognize its weird, uncanny character and its biopathic function. Alternative currencies have further eroded the monolithic character of the One.

In the vein of Sohn-Rethel, my own contention is that the philosophical inventions of centuries of Western civilization are actually attempts to

---

3   It is unrecognized as virtualization also because it is 'horizontal' rather than 'vertical'. Horizontal is temporally different too.

interpret commonplace cognitive processes that have been and are being continually influenced and altered by the models of patriarchy and of monetized exchange (which are fused in the exosomatic concept). Philosophy does not carry high flown spiritual mystery, but registers, reproduces and tries to make sense of the altered processes that 'infect' us and foment our greed for power and accumulation, driving us automatically by a wrong idea of who we are and should be.

The market has left aside the mother and gift-giving and has thus created two levels of intentions and transfers. At one level the purpose of 'equal' exchange for money is precisely not-giving, while at the same time at another level its purpose is precisely 'profit making': leveraging gifts. The gifts of profit are hidden behind the screen of equal exchange, like gifts of meaning moving through our virtual word-gifts with our breath, and they are perhaps what was projected by Hegel as the Spirit moving through History.

Women have not been philosoph:ers mostly because we have not had the time. We were doing much of the gift-giving that the market and philosophy captured, exploited and denied and we were not in the 'one' positions. The problems of the exosomatic concept form have plagued women not just philosophically but in reality. We have been 'manies' with respect to our husbands and fathers, kings and bosses as 'ones' (signifieds to their signifiers); we have been private property, owned as slaves (along with many of our brothers and our children), subjugated carers of our owner-prototypes and authoritarian exemplars; we have been placed in the role of commodities and traded as Irigaray (1985) described. We have been the unrecognized world-gifts to their word-gifts, and the irrelevant sources of relevance. It has sometimes seemed to us that the way out of our oppression was marrying or electing or worshipping the 'ones'. Instead we needed then and need now to instate and generalize the inclusive prototype, the ideal cognitive model of the motherer.

For now the prototype of the motherer is unclear because it has been overlaid, painted out, over written not only by the patriarchal exemplar but by money and the property relation which require mutual exclusion of each owner-prototype and h:er properties from every other.

10.4 Neutral neuroscience

Scientific discourse also takes place through abstraction from mothering. We saw above with Mirowski that modeling economics on physics involved leaving mothering out of both disciplines.[4] And we discussed Saussure's division between synchrony and diachrony, *langue* and *parole*, as a legacy passed down from grandfather physics to father economics to son, linguistics. This chain of inheritance left out mothering in three seemingly independent fields that are unified in their patriarchal solidarity and in denial of the explanatory capacity of maternal gift-giving. All of them were/are of course also functioning in the market context.

Recently neuroscience has made great strides in explaining language and cognition, including that of young children, without making mothering itself central. The bias towards giftless descriptions has influenced the otherwise fascinating work of child development researchers like Mandler, Gopnik, Kuhl, and mirror neuron discoverers Arbib, Gallese, Rizzolati while even Bråten, Trevarthen, Meltzoff, Tomasello, have concentrated more on the child than on the mother(er). Nurturing and the body are usually not in focus except for that particular material part of the individual body that is the brain, together with the differently located 'actions' inside it, the many paths-to-goal impulses that make up brain activity, and at another level, consciousness, and thinking. These scientific explanations may indeed be 'true' but they leave out the maternal gift frame that is the basis and method of meaning.

Mirror neurons rather than gifting, care and altercentrism are used to explain sociality. We can understand neurons without considering the mode of distribution of goods in the society in which the people who have them are living. Yet the people would not be living without those goods, just as children who are perceiving, focussing or not focussing on toys in experiments would not be living without their motherers' material gifts and services. By concentrating on the brain as an area in which social-material nurturing can be ignored and taken for granted as a given, neuroscience once again leaves out the gift economy and the motherer. It starts from language or even from perception rather than from the satisfaction of material life needs.

Above we gave the example also of Gallese and Lakoff's (2005) study of mirror neurons and grasping, which is not seen as part of the wider process of creatively receiving something that has been given by another

4   Karen Wendy Gilbert (2007: 79-83) proposes to 'give up the metaphor of the body as a thermodynamic machine' created by the capitalism of the industrial age. She wants to use instead the gift economy as model for the 'turbulent body' according to Serres' interpretation of the gift as a *'ferret'*, a 'hot potato' passed from hand to hand (which also confers identity by 'its possession or location'). Unfortunately here again provisioning transmission for need-satisfaction is left out and there is circulation without mothering.

person or by the child's surroundings. The hand that is grasping is visible, the complementary hand that is giving is not.

Leaving aside material communication and the economy of the motherer allows the material interactions of neurons in the brain to be taken as the whole or the main explanatory key. Innatism has a similar function of avoiding and abstracting into matter and away from mothering/ meaning. The maternal gift *economy* is the basis of meaning; explanations of the brain leave aside the economy. All the detailed scientific explorations of child cognition now being done create this abstraction from mothering because they abstract from the economy of material care and/or take it as a given.

In mothering, whatever the physical neuronal processes are, the early social process of giving and receiving materially and later giving and receiving linguistically, take over as the epistemological framework that is the basis of meaning, through which we read everything, even the physical processes. It is this framework, which is social, interpersonal and has gift value implications, that explains language in a meaningful way, not the neuronal underpinnings. Of course the neuronal processes are necessary for language. Necessary but not sufficient.

So the maternal interaction and economy overlie inherited capacities and make them meaningful. Without meaning we would not have science. Nor would we have evolved as (maternally) human. Language, together with the material nurturing which is its structural model, continually repropose this maternal meaning frame for us even in adulthood.

The distortion of language and mothering by monetized exchange gives us a second superimposed frame through which to view everything as neutral, not nurturing, and not social but 'inherited' and physiological. The brain is asocial (nonmaternal) matter taken as the basis of the social.This neutrality seems to be apolitical. If social interaction and meaning are the basis of the political – denying them is political too; it has meaning as general relevance to others. The asocial apolitical brain like other apolitical scientific objects, is wide open to prospecting by the market, full of lucrative mineable gifts. It is open to plunder and privatization. The new frontier.

10.5 Language and the self

Gift-giving in language continually exercises and elaborates a kind of human identity based on gift processes even though we are not usually conscious of it. This is the secret gift in the heart of language and is perhaps what has attracted so many researchers to the study of language during the last centuries of increasing domination by the market and its values of separation, domination and egocentric accumulation. In spite of the marginalization of the gift economy and the discrediting of nurturing, we remain *homo donans* because we continue to practice altercentric gift-giving at many levels in language. We remain linguistic givers and receivers, altercentric selves. Not only do we have a sense of agency, but of agency as *givers* and *creative receivers* as we speak. Even[5] as very young children we are already like our motherers in this.

As we grow up the spans of innumerable possible but similar transactions beyond our own constitute the basis of our linguistic competence. We know what will mean what for others 'objectively' and we can give many of these gifts appropriately ourselves. We also have communicative and cognitive needs that can be satisfied by others' linguistic gifts and so we have a subjective creative receiving capacity that recognizes word constructions as gifts for relevant world-gifts and is able to establish a relation (of cognitive alignment) with the givers in that regard. With language, speakers and listeners (or writers and readers) all access a collective resource, a linguistic commons, the collection of word-gifts that is 'ours together' and that we use to make verbal gift constructions to give to each other, recreating our human relations over and over as we pass on the gifts of the commons of our shared motherworld.

If we understand language in this way, we will see that even as adults, the mother-child relation is still with us. Nurturing continues to teach us to be human through the way we communicate, if only we recognize it... But even if we don't recognize it, we are still doing it and it is still teaching us.

Children who are inadequately mothered often have retardation in their language skills. However most of them do learn language eventually. Perhaps that is because language as a collective product, is the result of the altercentric interactions of many generations. It teaches itself and at least some gift-giving as it is learned. Speakers are mothering listeners and listeners are being mothered verbally without knowing it.

The market rewards detachment, competition, deceit, domination, ego-oriented and patriarchal behavior. In our cynical times there may seem to be no reason for acting otherwise. Language provides a reason.

---

5   This is the reason computational linguistics is misleading. The subject becomes the mere operator of programs, of computations, even without actually knowing what s: he is doing and how. Even in the crib, s:he seems to follow the model of the scientist, not of the motherer (see Gopnik, Kuhl and Meltzoff 1999).

By looking at the market in comparison with language , we understand how exchange has alienated us from gift-giving, which is its 'other' and also its source. In exchange, where each person gives contingently upon the other's giving, objects enter into the more abstract 'linguistic' schema of virtualization rather than into the schema of the gift. The exchangers participate in money-naming.There is a 'name': money, and a 'referent': a commodity; in order to complete the process both of these have to be relinquished, not given as in material nurturing, nor given as in language from the endless abundance constituted by each one's perception, cognition and ready collection of verbal gifts. Money is an unlearnable language made of one material word-exemplar without the *hau* of the breath: a holophrastic material scream of fear and desire that can never be permanently learned.[6]

Our participation in the exosomatic concept and the material schema of virtualization that constitute monetized exchange, creates within us a different and specific structure of subjectivity, an identity based on the assertion of the exemplar-ego, and categorization, similarity and difference. Our giving and receiving subjectivity persists, carried along and continually recreated by the hidden gift-giving in language and life, but the exchange-based identity structure discredits and overrides it. Our own interpretation of who we are and what we do, passes through a filter of categorization that is consonant with money, exchange and the equation of value, making us believe that similarity and difference are more important than giving and receiving and that similarity to money, the exemplar of value, is the most important similarity.

The linguistic aspect of exchange goes no farther than 'naming', causing momentary cognitive alignment but creating a communicative dead end! One person gives up the name, the other gives up the 'referent', the gift-not-gift, the commodity. Verbal syntactical giving and receiving is transformed into quantification: addition (giving to) and subtraction (giving from) quantities of the money name.

It is paradoxically the exchangers' relation of mutual exclusion regarding the product and money, that is relevant and 'shared' when a commodity is virtualized in money and exchanged for it.[7] The exchangers 'share' the relation of exclusion, and a consequently 'privatized', 'possessive individualist' identity (MacPherson 2011 [1962]), but not the products. They

---

6   When we are little our parents have it and we don't, so it seems to be a mark of maturity, a non-nurturing language that we are too little to use.

7   We know that is its money name because the other accepts it as such, in just the same way we know that a word is the virtual gift for some particular kind of thing.

enact the linguistic virtualization schema on the material reality plane. As linguistic givers and receivers, they are in internal contradiction with their mutually exclusive identities as private owners and exchangers. Patriarchal identities of individuals as 'high transitivity' hitters and dominators align with owning and exchanging identities. They act out mutual opposition internally and externally, protecting their own[8]. That is, protection from other similarly configured individuals or groups, becomes their social function, the artificial need they satisfy, the gift they give as economically created mutually exclusive entities.

Once a product is virtualized, once its money name is given up for it and the exchange is complete, the product can again become a use value or can even be used as a gift with which to nurture another. In contrast, the market provides no genuine gift schema to put the money in. Money can only be added to or subtracted from repeatedly and used in another exchange-virtualization process. Within these limitations capitalism has found its way to amass huge wealth for the few and create widespread poverty for the many. It uses virtualization/exchange to add (give) money to itself, reinvesting the gifts of profit in order to accumulate ever more capital and inventing ever new ways of using privatization-categorization and virtualization to do so. Witness the commodification of water, seeds and fertilizer, the patenting of genes and of previously free plant and animal products, the copyrighting of knowledge, and the surveillance-based privatization and sale of individuals' preferences through the internet, etc.

Gift selves develop through altercentric childhood, linguistic giving/receiving, acts of care and kindness, common relations to others and to the motherworld commons. They are displaced and 'submerged' because, through the logic of exchange, we are engaged in practical relations of mutual opposition and indifference so that we usually only find our connection with each other through categorization and abstract identity. This can be expressed in money – what someone is 'worth': the exchange value of their work or how much money they own, or kinds of possessions or appearance, that is, class or race, religion, nationality etc.

Our exchange-based identities are standardized now like our commodities. We are subjects of virtualization, nameable, classifiable and (even for ourselves) quantifiable with a numerical IQ, a weight, a grade average, a salary, rather than consciously finding and constructing our selves through giving and receiving a great variety of things in many ways with many people in a community. The exosomatic concept's common qual-

---

8   And see the high transitive chain reactions we have created in nuclear bombs.

ity or essence, which is the exchange value of commodities, expressed in the money-word, maps onto the stereotypical common qualities of people divided into categories: genders, races, religions and classes, also organized as to their 'essences' and what they are 'worth'. Exchange value itself becomes the general source area from which are metaphorically projected the 'necessary and sufficient common qualities' that are mapped into the structure of abstract classical concepts. These common qualities can be many: masculinity, femininity, intelligence, patriotism, self-righteousness, perhaps even the feeling of belonging itself. Thus, as I have been saying the graded prototype-to-many relation is taken over, 'occupied' by the mutually exclusive property relation, which is mediated by one-to-many (the exemplar-of-value-to-many) monetized exchange.

We find our human identities relative to each other according to who we are equated with, which category-container we are in, inside which gender, which race, which religion, which national boundaries, which field, which block, which apartment or house, which room (or which refugee camp and tent). Our identities depend on which patronymic family name designates us, which father or husband (or rock star or king or president or national hero) we relate to as our 'exemplar' and how much money s:he 'makes' or owns. We are similar to the others in our category because we are all related to the same human (or divine) exemplar 'ones' but also because we are all related in the same way to property, money and exchange. In fact, the one-to-many General Equivalent is now the main source or template of the way we categorize and the way we understand categorization, of the way we judge and categorize ourselves and other people: it determines the way we think.

Although we unwittingly continue to develop our selves through gift-giving interaction, in this society we focus a great deal on categorization just as we focus on exchange (and of course we talk about them both). Our own relevance or value seems to come from 'having' and 'belonging' (being had) not from giving and receiving. But this is not really the case. Even the categories to which we belong are mainly important to us because they determine what kinds of gifts we give/receive, to whom and how (our participation in the 'grammar of social relations'). Our senses of self and belonging, our emotional relations and fulfillment still come to us mostly from the verbal and non verbal gift-giving and receiving that we engage in everyday beyond exchange.

10.6 Positive Homo loquens-donans

If gifting and receiving gifts has an important place in subjectivity, where does that leave the 'self' of homo economicus? Language is always automatically elaborating the self. Though s:he doesn't realize it, the speaker/writer is the giver and receiver of word gifts, which are always positive and unilateral as words received from the community and given again to others to satisfy their human communicative and cognitive needs regarding the world. Even though what the speaker is talking about may be negative or s:he may speak to deceive, to hurt or even to destroy, the words s:he uses are positive in that they satisfy specific communicative and cognitive needs of the receiver.

The speaker/writer gives words unilaterally and the listener/reader creatively receives and understands what the speaker/writer says – without an exchange – though of course s:he may reply. The communicative gift of each speaker is unilateral even if s:he and the listener do take turns. The listener knows more about the speaker's further needs because s:he understands what s:he has said and uses this information as the basis for further mind-reading, by which s:he knows what words to give the receiver regarding the topic which has been 'brought up'. The writer is in an even more clearly unilateral giving position than the speaker, and s:he has to use h:er own previous verbal constructions in the text as a basis on which to assess the reader's communicative and cognitive needs. S:he has to try to mind read h:er audience of others-in-general for their needs, so as to know what word-gifts to give.

The consequence of the function of unilateral verbal gift-giving is that whatever the situation may be, however negative or depleted, degraded or cruel, the speaker/writer remains a positive need-satisfying gift-giver at a very basic structural level. Moreover, the projected gifts inside the sentence – the 'giving' of verbs to their objects by the words that constitute the subject of the sentence, or the 'giving' of adjectives to nouns, of prepositional phrases to noun phrases, or of prefixes and suffixes to roots, etc. – create an alignment with the giving and receiving done by the speaker/writer or listener/reader at the interpersonal level. Perceptual gifts come to us from outside and complex conceptual gifts come from thinking, imagination, and our internal and external experience. We pass them on to others virtually, so the speaker/writer is not only a giver but a (previous) receiver as well as a passer-on of gifts (and other speakers/writers are like h:er in this – we are all anyway in the same category of self-constructing gifting communicators). On the other hand what the speaker or writer says by combining word gifts, giving them to each other, may be negative. It may be highly transitive, as verbal violence or it may be simply information about unwelcome topics – or even false information. The word-gifts themselves remain positive throughout, however in that they freely satisfy communicative and cognitive needs. All of this gives us a positive character for each other as humans even if in our society we behave as *homo economicus* and even if we have superimposed a one-to-many identity in the image of the externalized concept on top of our internal gifting/receiving self-constructions. It may be that knowing about this artificial one-to-many ego could allow us to liberate ourselves from it nonviolently.

10.7 Homo sapiens sapiens *in denial*

Looking at consciousness from the perspective of the gift paradigm, it seems likely that it plays the roles of the gift schema virtually internally, mostly without words, while also internally 'scanning' the roles, perceptions, experiences and memories that arise. We preconsciously maternally select and consciously receive experience from the internalized motherer. Consciousness 'contains' the virtual leftovers from virtual and real experience. Many of our ideas and thoughts seem to arise out of nowhere from an inner giver. Or they may first be present to us as feelings, nudging us towards some thought or course of action. We receive them in our mind-containers[9] and store them or make them ready for use or for giving again. We give possible solutions to each problem (again, solutions to problems may also be seen as gifts, satisfactions of needs). We use our imaginations to prefigure aspects of what will happen and how we and others will behave. We also 'mind-read' ourselves at this or future moments, depending on what our situation will be, so we are conscious of our own needs and the possibilities we have for filling them(see the subsection above on inner speech).We can also begin to verbally virtualize our inner and outer experience to ourselves without finishing. Our inner speech only sketches needs and gifts we actually have. We don't need to think of a word for something if we are already in relation to it or if no relation to it is needed. For example, I do not need to say 'chair' to myself to think of the chair in which I am sitting, but just feel myself sitting in it. Suppose someone is coming to see me and I want to move the chair from the next room into this one, I can think of the chair without saying anything to myself, feeling it and perhaps visualizing part of it (metonymic visualization) and can partially feel myself going into the other room, carrying it, etc.

---

9   Our 'mental spaces', as Fauconnier and Turner (2002) say.

Usually we think of consciousness in terms of self-reflection – an idea which I believe comes from the equation of value in exchange, which itself comes from the schema of virtualization. Looking in the value 'mirror' of exchange, one 'mind-reads' primarily ones own needs and the other's only instrumentally.

A non-metaphorical mirror does not provide another human gaze but only one's own perspective in the place where another's would have been. The mirror image lacks the (gift) initiative of the other, and all the variations in tempos and activities that are not one's own, as well as the other's variable states of attention towards oneself and one's needs, to which one might respond. Like exchange itself, the mirror image is ego-oriented and abstract.[10] It only allows us to see ourselves when we are seeing ourselves, not when we are doing something else. We can see in the mirror something of what our faces look like when others mind read us, but perhaps more of what we look like when we mind-read others.[11]

In Lacan's mirror stage (2002 [1966]: 75-82), the boy child looks at himself in the mirror, unable to integrate his body parts, while the mother looks on. Indeed, he is separated from h:er gift-giving gaze and h:er mind-reading care (including his image in h:er mind) by which his body-consciousness would remain integral and his 'like me' kinetic mapping confirmed. In contrast, money is a 'mirror' of exchange value, which is already giftlessly social, and the most important relation of the commodity, which in the moment of exchange is an exchange value, is its relation through money to all the other products on the market.

Money as exemplar and general equivalent is a mirror because it gives back to the seller the quantitative social 'image' of the value of the commodity and both the commodity and its image abstract from gifts. Even the material mirror precludes gift-giving because we cannot give to or receive from that reflected 'other'. This character of money encourages us to abstract from gift-giving and need satisfaction as well.

The imitation of another is quite different from looking at one's own reflection in a mirror. Imitation brings in new information from the initiatives, actions and reactions of others as well as from one's own. Self-reflection requires remembering one's actions, thoughts and motivations as well as those of others, as much as possible, and it is easily infected by money-based categorization and judgement. In fact the basis of the mirror is the

---

10   In Lacan's mirror stage the mother is only the onlooker.
11   It would be interesting to know how our mirror neurons react to our own image in the mirror.

equation between the viewer and her image, which is likely to be overlain by the equation of value: x quantity of commodity y = z quantity of money. This equation has to do with qualitative and quantitative assessment as do our self-conscious self-assessments. The mirror contrasts problematically with the 'like me' bridge. The image in the mirror is 'like me', but there is no one else there. In exchange also there is actually no one there for us because the money only reflects the value of the commodity, not the other's value or our own. And the other exchanger is like me only in that, like the face on the coin, s:he is /we are both looking elsewhere.

In the gift framework we would consider ourselves internally as valuable in terms of having-to-give: the motherworld within – and as having received: gifts and gift value from others, perhaps experiencing a kind of transparency towards ourselves and others. In the exchange framework we are caught in self-reflection, comparing ourselves to an exemplar (for example an idealized concept model of our gender). We judge ourselves, like money and in terms of money, feeling jealousy and guilt and longing for revenge. We[12] may consider our bodies and our selves in terms of private property, which we have to identify as our own, care for and defend against those who would take or destroy them. And, in fact, in Patriarchal Capitalism, without community relations based on gift-giving, it often happens that no one else cares for us and there is a great deal of violence and predatory behavior from which to defend our property, our bodies and our selves. Scarcity and lack of community require that we exchange, that we reason according to cost-benefit, that we not give without being sure that we will get, that we defend ourselves and even that we take revenge.[13] In societies without private property and markets, the internal human configuration, even if it were self-reflecting, would not have that exosomatic corroboration of the equation of value in exchange. Even slight differences in structure might make the quality of consciousness in a gift economy quite different from our own. Similarly perhaps with the relations between at least some motherers and children and their consciousnesses even in our own exchange based society.

Many American indigenous people on their first encounters with Europeans could not understand what the settlers were thinking and why. On the other hand the Europeans themselves explained the difference by saying the indigenous people had not 'progressed' to the 'advanced' European

---

12   See the book *Pay Back - The Case for Revenge* (Rosenbaum 2013).
13   The film 'The Interrupters' on Chicago gangs brings this home.
http: //interrupters.kartemquin.com/

stage of development. They were thought to be 'childlike' or 'primitive' gift-givers in contrast to the Europeans' patriarchal and exchange-based 'maturity'. These differences may be attributed to different kinds of subjectivities and consciousnesses in societies based on exchange and patriarchy in contrast to those in more functional societies based on the gift economy and its maternal values.

In the exchange mode, inside ourselves we are each in h:er own private consciousness, which is the consciousness of the legal owner (or of the legally dispossessed).We are blind to the giving and receiving configurations of our own consciousnesses. We are expected to be autonomous and self sufficient, neither giving nor receiving unilaterally but earning, trading, manipulating or forcing gifts from others, self-made by work, rather than self-and-other-making by giving/receiving, 'deserving' rather than nurtured. We are categorized, judged and defined, our capacities and achievements evaluated quantitatively with regard to others', sometimes in status 'points' but often and most importantly in money. We give in order to receive, even from ourselves, a positive judgment in terms of a comparison with some exemplar like money, or some gender or social or religious ideal. Perhaps this desire, even craving, for a positive judgement is what Derrida, 1992, was thinking about when he was insisting on the impossibility of the pure gift.

Our self-mirroring consciousness appears to be an achievement but perhaps in its present configuration, it is only the result of practicing ego-oriented exchange and the equation of exchange value instead of other-oriented gift giving and the transmission of gift value. I said before that we should be calling ourselves *homo donans* instead of *homo sapiens*. I would also like to challenge the designation *homo sapiens sapiens*. Isn't our self-consciousness, this knowing that we know, deeply influenced by gift canceling exchange? but we don't know it? And of course the designation '*homo*' hides women. We should at least write *h:omo*. But before we do that, we should tell *homo* that what s:he doesn't know that s:he doesn't know is that s:he is a maternally giving being who is trapped within the addictive exchange paradigm and s:he is in denial.

Sometimes we see our selves in terms of virtualization and judgment, almost as if *we were* money, taking the one to many point of view of money, excluding gifts and deciding what is valuable and what is not. Often we do not even notice our own gift initiatives in communication, our gift subjectivity, which we are practicing all the time (though they may feel good). We misinterpret what we are doing. When we do give a gift consciously, we are impressed with ourselves. We get an ego reward as Derrida surmised. But we are not actually separate from the world of which we speak. In language we do give something to others for something else but not in either/or binary opposition to it as when we give money to another for a commodity. And we do it all the time.

On the other hand when the transitive gift schema of language is turned around, reversed, superseded, made bilateral and virtual in exchange, the role of the receiver is superimposed over the role of the giver. We primarily mind read ourselves to discover our own needs. Self-interest takes the place of other orientation, but this bending back and distortion of the trajectory of attention is not so much a personal defect as it is an artifact of the exchange process.

Subjective theories of value make much of individual choice as the source of value. But what and who are the individuals who make the choices? As market actors they are already divided internally, their gift patterns overlaid by patterns of virtualization/exchange. Then advertising and propaganda alter their choices even further by insinuating lies into what remains for them of the perceptual and conceptual commons.

In spite of, or perhaps because of this, most people are starving for gifts and gift value to be given to them, and this motivates their pathological taking, status seeking and consumerism while increasing their greed for money.[14]

10.8 The essence and the commons

The problem is that nurturing-gifting *is not seen* at a meta level because virtualization *is seen* and indeed is conspicuously foregrounded because naming in money is itself another level of virtualization; it is virtualization on the material plane. In exchange the commodity, the not-gift, is confirmed at a metalevel by its virtualization first in a price and then in an embodied quantitative money name, while the gift is not.

One might think that prototype theory could be considered more maternal than classical concept theory, in that at least for 'base level'[15] graded categories, many different kinds of associations and similarities to the prototype are taken into account. If this has a developmental aspect as Vygotsky believed, thinking according to prototypes or what he called 'com-

---

14   At the same time there may be others who are at least unconsciously longing to give. And there are many who are sick because they do not give.
15   Base level categories are inclusive categories at a mid level of generality. used in 'folk taxonomy'.

plexes' in childhood, comes before classical concept thinking. It would therefore be more common in the early mother-child relation. Similarly, indigenous societies without markets and money often use graded categories with prototypes.[16] In Euroamerican capitalism children (and their supposedly 'childlike' 'good' mothers) also appear to be 'primitive' and 'pre-' market. Instead, we should say that their reasoning has not (yet) been infected by the one-to-many form of the externalized concept, money.

The gift-giving mother-in-relation to the child is the prototype for the child's concept or 'complex' of the human, which is therefore more inclusive than the classical concept exemplar against which the many are compared as to their possession of a common quality. However, if the 'classical' concept has been influenced by money, the exemplar of exchange value in the exosomatic concept, as we have been saying, and the mother is the prototype of gift-giving, a deep contradiction arises between the two kinds of structures. They become identified with gender so that women are seen as prototypes of gift-giving (and users of 'less rational' prototype thinking) while men are identified as not-giving exemplars of 'mankind' (and as philosophers and logicians using classical concepts) and who therefore have a more abstract and universal character more similar to money. Perhaps this was the reason why men in the European Middle Ages were seen as having abstract and universal souls while women were thought to be without them. It also gives men the authority to make binary decisions about relevant and irrelevant 'properties', so-called 'rational' decisions regarding self-interest and other-interest, like and unlike, good and bad and even life and death as they exercise their power.

In the graded category with the prototype in the center, many different members can be included. The category that has the robin as its prototype can include penguins and ostriches. Similarly the category of the human that has the mother as its prototype can include babies, brothers and sisters, fathers, the next door neighbor and even foreigners and slaves (who are forced to give). In contrast, the classical category of the human with the male as the exemplar, excludes the gift-giving mother, the infant, the daughter, the aunt, the neighbor. Nevertheless, the father/exemplar can include the foreigner by activating gift patterns, giving to him, like the mother does, in hospitality. As the exemplar, he includes and is included in the category of kings, generals, CEOs, fire chiefs, divas and rocket scientists,[17] all of whom are 'ones'.

---

16   See Lakoff's discussion of graded categories (1987: Part 1).

17   We could look at it as a metacategory of which the 'one' exemplar element of concept formation is the common 'property'.

When the boy child realizes that in some important ways he is not like his female motherer who, in patriarchy and capitalism is usually the only one doing the nurturing, he is put in a position not only of having to change categories but of having to use a different kind of categorization. Parental expectations and the use of the word 'boy' or 'male' as the name of his gender identity in opposition to that of the motherer as 'female,' places him in an abstract relation to his father, who becomes for him the exemplar of a classical one-to-many gender category. At the same time he is placed in binary opposition to his mother who is the concrete altercentric other with whom he has been developing his gift-giving and receiving identity, and who is the prototype of an inclusive graded category.

In patriarchy, the 'necessary and sufficient' common quality or property for the classical concept of man appears to be the possession of the penis (also the Lacanian 'phallus'). As an exemplar of the category of property it belongs to the meta category of 'ones'. Thus money as the exemplar of the externalized concept form influences patriarchy by validating an internal (classical) concept form in which the penis appears to be the necessary and sufficient characteristic for the exemplar of the human.[18] In patriarchy, men are the exemplars of the human, because they all possess this property, while women do not. In children's reasoning perhaps the penis seems to have been given to them as a gift by their mothers (who would therefore have lost theirs) but having it seems to contradictorily exclude the men's capacity to *be* gift-giving mothers (and to have nurturing breasts). If mothers have given away their penises to their boy children, they seem to have given them the power and capacity to be 'ones' – exemplars of the human – while giving up their own, thus implying the males' (gift) value over and above themselves. [19] This is an example of one of the ways the externalized concept form of money and the exchange of private property validates false ways of reasoning.

As adults then males seem to have to own their mothers, sisters, wives and daughters as their property, maintaining a mutually exclusive relation, of constant equation and differentiation, a kind of phallic ownership, with

---

18   Is this form strong enough that the positions of penis and money can be reversed, so that a woman with money can also be in the 'one' position?

19   Talking about the absence of gender in their native Syilx language, Jeanette Armstrong (2007 ch: 1) asked her aunt, "'How come we don't have that idea?''. And my aunt looked at me and she said, "Well, it has to do with being a person". I asked, "What does it have to do with being a person?" She replied, "If you were to say 'he' or 'she' in our language, you would have to point to their genitals, you would have to point to what's between the legs, and why would you talk about a person and point between their legs?". She said, "It doesn't make any sense."' (2007).

other men, as members of the meta category of ones, where each one has one penis and is one-to-many regarding his family and his property. Perhaps they do this because the 'like me' and prototype-to-many identity relation with the mother is no longer possible, since she does not have a penis. There is also something like a word-gift (male) to world gift (female) relation in the marriage structure, which is similar to the money-commodity relation of exchange.[20] Moreover it puts men in competition with each other to be the exemplar of exemplars, understood as the 'one' at the top, the one 'one'.[21] Now some women, wives and mothers who used to nurture 'their men' in this competitive configuration, are playing out the same strange syndrome, competing to become 'ones' themselves as CEOs and divas (with a lot of phallic money). Others are ones as single mothers, barely making it at the bottom of the pyramid.

Until very recently with the rise of feminism and then with the LGBT movement in the West, most women and mothers, men and fathers believed in the binary distinction of male and female gender and so taught it to boys and girls in various ways, 'for their own good'. But, if we are all *homo donans*, this is false and alienating categorization. Moreover, women are placed in a role which is the binary opposite of the male who has given up mothering and in which they are expected to give (not to not-give) preferentially to men who not only do not-give but dominate (and all too often practice violence, 'high transitivity') instead. This strange illogical configuration discredits the mother as the gift-giving human prototype even further and discredits women who are not mothers as well (perhaps because they are not *even* prototypes). And it discredits indigenous societies' gifting.

Following upon these false distinctions, some ways of giving are also provided for males. These are mostly roles justified by the market and patriarchy such as being the 'breadwinner', protecting one's family from violence and plunder by other men or giving one's life for one's country in wars against other nations. More importantly, being the 'one' at the top of any hierarchy gives one authority, allowing h:er to categorize others below her, and to impose the categorization through laws and by force. This creates a situation of constant, potentially destructive leverage, usually accepted by all as 'just the way things are'. Those who do not succeed in taking or maintaining the One position often try to impose their exemplarity through the transformed and denatured 'gifting' of violence. If they do not succeed they are humiliated, 'brought low'.

---

20   See again (Irigaray 1985) on exchange of women.
21   See (Vaughan 1997) for a more extended discussion of this issue.

I think that to find out how our concepts might 'really' be formed without the influences of money and gender, we would need to investigate them
empirically,early in child development keeping these kinds of hypotheses
in mind. If I may be allowed to speculate, I believe that as there is probably
an unconscious comparison among perceptions at a very early age.[22] Non
human animals that recognize things they have encountered before also
seem to engage in similar cognitive processes. The prototype or the exemplar-to-many form would be later social elaborations of early rudimentary
physiological-mental process.

Language learning influences the formation of concepts first in the graded prototype one-to-many sense and later in a classical exemplar-to-many
conceptual sense. That is, unless the classical concept is really only an artifact of the exosomatic concept, a philosophical reflection of money and the
Phallus. Even if it is only that, we continually act it out as adults, caught in
the practice and the ideology of the market and patriarchy.

The classical concept is constructed around common qualities, which
are also understood as 'essences'. The 'essence' shared by money and
commodities is exchange value, while the 'essences' shared by the child
and adult possessors of the penis-phallus is masculinity. Both of these are
social common qualities that seem natural. That is, they are 'fetishized'
in Marx's terms. The female 'essences' is then abstracted and understood
as the opposite of the male 'essences', so it is also 'fetishized'.[23] It is not
a binary originally opposed to masculinity as the norm, however. It is a
third step, an antithesis of the antithesis,[24] where the original thesis is the
'like me' giving and receiving identity created between child and motherer,
prior to the boy's understanding of his gender categorization as different.
It is with regard to that socially imposed male gender differentiation that
the girl later finds her gender category in binary opposition. Since the category 'male' does not include mothering, 'female' appears to include only
or mainly mothering as its essence. Categorization and virtualization (and

---

22 Retaining some phonetic prototypes while losing those not in one's own language
    is a development of this (see Patricia Kuhl's Native Language Magnet theory
    1991), already separating the relevant from the irrelevant. Jean Mandler (2004)
    theorizes an automatic perceptual identification process accompanied by develop-
    ing conceptual processes. The automatic process 'perceptual meaning analysis'
    would probably be active in Kuhl's Native Language Magnet.

23 Moreover women's and children's – both boys' and girls' – all those who are not
    'ones' – bodies are analogously located and trafficked as commodities in relation
    to the money-Phallus.

24 This dialectic never arrives at a proper synthesis but perpetuates itself into the
    next generations.

private property and exchange) take over from giving and receiving and transitivity as the basic principles of life.

The binary reasoning that is so strongly criticized by postmodernists and postmodern feminists, is more consonant with classical than with graded categories. Like exchange, which opposes valuable to valueless, and commodities to gifts, binary reasoning functions to select relevant and exclude irrelevant characteristics and to find common qualities for our categories. Of course, it is not so easy to find the binary opposite of a graded category that includes many different kinds of members. In fact, binary reasoning functions much better with classical categories having necessary and sufficient characteristics and a unified common essence to which other classical categories with other characteristics and common essences can be opposed. The supposed maternal or feminine 'essence' of women depends on the kind of classical categorization – influenced by money – that is used both in the construction of gender and in thinking about gender. Classical categorization for centuries has cancelled the relevance of the graded category for thinking about thinking. With feminism and multicultural studies it is beginning to re emerge.

Statistical analysis and dichotomous and polytomous logic developed for computers detour away from the consideration of essences but they also function in denial of the mother. In this vein see Claudia von Werlhof's (2011) view of technology as the destruction of the mother and her replacement by male alchemical technological inventions.

Anti essentialist feminists should struggle not primarily against the idea of a feminine essence itself but against the social forms, influenced by money, that lie behind classical categorization and invisibly determine it to the detriment of women, children and even of the patriarchal men who are using the motherless logic and creating the mother-substituting technologies.

At present the social forms of gender (+ or - the phallus) and the exosomatic concept feed back especially into our classical concepts of concepts as well as into the concepts themselves, creating the new forms of exemplars, we have mentioned, like divas, rock stars, sport stars and film stars, imitated and even loved by the many, rewarded by large amounts of the holophrastic money-word. There are also phallic (and monetarily endowed) CEOs (Trump, Branson), presidents (Bushes, Clinton) and prime ministers (Berlusconi) some of whom seem to need to dominate sexually as well as politically. Does this mean that we democratically though unconsciously elect phallic representatives who want, or who we would want, to dominate our gene pool?

While it might appear to be a good thing that everyone can become an exemplar, have their day in the sun or fifteen minutes of fame on TV, being the 'one' is actually an improbable illusion for most of the 7.5 billion people on Earth who comprise the many, most of whom are economically mute, deprived of any significant amount of the phallic, holophrastic word-exemplar. And the payoff to the ego of the person who does succeed in taking the 'one' position is often not actually very satisfactory anyway (so s:he always thinks s:he needs more). We need to understand better the effects these phallogo-chremato-centric concept processes have on us and liberate ourselves from them at last.

The phallus, the classical concept and monetary exosomatic categorization fit together in the categorization of people according to how much money they have. They appear to have or not have the common quality of a quantity of exchange value. They can both have that value as potential payment for their labor capacity or they can own it in the form of capital, which will give them access to the labor power of others. If they have the right quantity of money they can 'make' more and then buy the right things so that they can belong to the upper 'class' and get better education and jobs. If not they are located in the lower 'class' where much of their work is discredited because it is done free or for little money, that is, because it is mostly a gift. The effects of scarcity are such that people who have little money sometimes believe in its power even more strongly than those who have it , so they risk internalizing its judgement upon them.

Racism in Capitalist Patriarchy also follows the money-based logic of the classical concept with the white male exemplar of the human and the binary distinction white/not white. There are many oppressive intersectionalities here as discussed by Kimberlé Crenshaw (1993), Patricia Hill Collins (2008) and others. I propose that underlying the intersectionalities is a cluster of one to many (power invested) general equivalent forms surrounding the externalized concept form, which are used to deny, manipulate and appropriate the gifts of the many, especially those of women, of people of color and of people of the Global South. The negative influence of patriarchy, money and the market makes white people more racist, but also our racism allows us to be more deeply influenced by patriarchy, money and the market.

Though it is preserved in language, adult altercentrism is invisible to us because it is not recognized or generalized in Capitalist Patriarchy. It is appropriate in a society of community and the commons, but disadaptive in a society of private property, accumulating and not giving. Thus it looks like a special quality of women and especially of mothers (and mothers of color). Mothering is necessary but seems exceptional, a moment of care in a cruel world.

In capitalism social nurturing has been painted into the corner of mothering. A common essence of women as nurturing is contradictory because it is not only the process of women, it is the commons, the common process of everything. That is, of what we know and how we know it, of words and world, of gift and exchange, of women, men and children, creatures and environmental niches. It is the common process , the principle of the commons (and of 'commoning'). The issue is only that gifting is contradicted by exchange and all the constructions built upon it, which indeed privatize, divide and hide the commons and make the community difficult.

In patriarchal capitalism the sharing of the commons is reduced to its essence, its core, in the altercentric mother-child (motherer-child) relation, like a lake that has dried up except for some small pools around the springs that were its source. This relation is 'essential' in the sense that it is necessary for the survival and the development of the social child. It is also 'essential' because the core process of the adult human, of communication, and community. And the commons is maternal, altercentric nurturing, gift-giving and receiving, so everybody is actually already doing it (in language and life, in physiological processes like breathing, drinking and eating and in giving signs of all kinds to others and receiving them) without recognizing it. Welfare, the helping professions, volunteering, teaching, movements for social change, aspects of religions, philanthropy, are all informed by gift-giving to some extent. Now the 'sharing economy' though still mostly framed as exchange, is spreading like beneficent wildfire.

Saying that women have the common property or essence of mothering is an under generalization. Nurturing is the functional process (not common quality or essence) of human beings and of language and of nature (in the co creative interface between organism and environmental and social niche). Exchange is only the same process turned back upon itself, and even the market is not-nurturing by nurturing, using the filling of needs to leverage and extract profit. Moreover, throughout life and language, we continue to give and receive, elaborating the social relevance of everything by gift value implication.

10.9 The mind under the influence of money

The deep similarities between money and language, influence us surreptitiously, beyond our knowledge. In fact, the market and money seem normal, natural and inevitable because they are the external incarnation and therefore look-alike of conceptual processes, which then feed back into our thinking about language, life, gender, economics, science – everything! For example, Platonic ideals can be seen as general equivalents, exemplars of one to many categorization processes. They are early projections of the general equivalent concept-exemplar, under the influence of the newly instated use of coined money (600 BCE). In ancient Greece, Plato only had to take an individual exemplar of a category, generalize it, perfect it and place it in the empyrean, to create the ideals, which he understood as the best, the most valuable exemplars of each kind. From our perspective what he was looking at was really the way we form concepts, seen for the first time in his epoch through the lens of money, the extended mind one-to-many form embodied now in material objects on the market and not in patriarchal human relations only. Ever since Plato (and Aristotle after him), the 'classical concept' has dominated Western philosophy although we have not usually imagined the influence of money upon it.

A similar relation already existed in other one-to-many patriarchal structures: kings and subjects, generals and their armies, and the Phallus and other body parts (Goux 1990) as well as one's own phallus and other phallusses.

However the externalized concept form is more basic than any of these. Each of them might be seen as a different extra-individual exosomatic incarnation of the concept form, confirmed by and in turn confirming it. Indeed, the fact that there is such a proliferation of these general equivalent one-to-many figures in our society might actually be taken as confirmation of the existence in our minds of the classical concept form (reinforced as it is by money). The collective consciousness seems to be trying to communicate with us, expressing the problem over and over, acting it out in these (mostly harmful) one to many configurations.

Now after more than two millenia the participation by young people in the fans-of-the-rock-star phenomenon, is an enactment of the same process, whereby they find a category of human identity to belong to, relating themselves to each other as similar through their common relation to the star as exemplar and in the many-to-one ruler hierarchy configurations, including the military, the law, academia and the democratic representative government variations, with elected officials as the increasingly general exemplars from the local to the national level. The same process is evident now in consumerism, which has given a new impetus to status symbolism, making the car, the house, the jewelry, even the university degree, the necessary (phallic) possession that will allow us to be one to many, belonging to an uber-meta class of ones.

I believe we can also understand the phenomenon of rampage shooters in this way. Most of them are ineffectual young men who are under pressure to become 'ones' but find no socially approved way of doing so. They take on the 'one' exemplar position by high transitivity, hitting many with bullets, killing – giving death – with phallic guns. As a solution, controlling guns (which are also one-to-many like phallusses) may restrict potential shooters' ability to carry out the pattern somewhat, but it is the pattern itself, which is the main foundational structure in capitalist patriarchy, that is the problem. This is a pattern that has the capacity to repeat itself at many levels from the individual to the collective so that young men in wars shoot as ones-killing-manies so that their nation can prevail as one over many.

There are also huge high-transitive nuclear bombs that can wipe out many not only in the moment but in the long term of millenia.

Males seem to have a position of ones in front of all females as many, while racist white people singly or in groups consider themselves ones to many people of color. Religions too, with their monotheistic gods, vie with one another to be the 'one' religion.

The motherer continues to be excluded both as the prototype and as the model of the altercentric gift-giver (and intersubjective co creator) and matricide is sometimes a corollary of the one-to-many syndrome. This was the case with the killer of twenty children in the elementary school of Newtown, Connecticut, who killed his mother before going to the school. The media also contributes to the status of the shooter (almost always a white male) as a 'one', publicizing his image after the fact.

There is now also the membership in the economic 1%, which satifies the stratosphereically rich that their lives are meaningful by placing them far above the many according to what they (phallically) have, how loud they can holophrastically scream.

Although prototype theory may be only a partial alternative to classical concept theory, it provides a demystifying distance from which to see the classical concept (and money) as limited and partial. That is, it is not the only way of thinking about concepts. Nor is exchange the only way of distributing goods to needs. From this perspective we can see the money-exemplar as only an anomaly, a singular streamlined giftless prototype, tied to and occasioned by the paradoxical kind of 'distribution' we have at present.

Money denies gifts and affirms the 'common quality' of commodities, their exchange value. The philosophers' classical concept functions in the same way, according to the exclusion of irrelevant and affirmation of relevant, necessary and sufficient 'common qualities' in the category. The Platonic ideal is also the permanent empyrean exemplar of the relevant common quality, for example, the Good, which can be perceived embodied in the world of appearances.

Jerry Fodor (1972) once wrote a scathing criticism of Vygotsky's experiment on concept formation in which he accused Vygotsky of doing not experimental psychology but experimental philosophy (and not doing it well).[25] However, the origin of philosophy is actually the origin of psychology. Plato was describing how concepts are formed psychologically under the influence of money. His experience of this part of the collective materially extended concept, made him (and many others after him) think he was looking through the veil of illusions at how the universe works and instead he was just seeing how some aspects of human cognition work.

Plato's ideas also have the character of prototype, in the sense of the original model from which instances are copied. While as I mentioned above, contemporary 'prototype theory' does not overtly embrace this aspect of the term 'prototype,' I believe it is still there in a hidden way and that it influences the popularity of the term. In fact there is a sense of origin of an idea in the first example or exemplar, against which we compare other things, to see if they are of that kind. Plato hypostasizes the exemplar (the streamlined prototype), making it the *cause* of the qualities as we experience them. This character of origin might even be considered appropriate in the case of money, where it is the use of money in market exchange that is the necessary but not sufficient cause of the existence of the quality of exchange value and thus of the pattern of the exosomatic concept which was influencing the birth of philosophy. Aristotle's idea of the unmoved mover also harks back to the 'ones' in a number of different spheres, and he concludes the Metaphysics Book 12: 'The rule of many is not good; one ruler let there be'.[26] At present

---

25   Recent experiments in cognitive psychology are also experimental philosophy.

26   In spite of whatever influence the exosomatic concept may have had on Aristotle unconsciously, he already understood that we also often judge our experience and our own behavior according to whether it will help us make money or not (Meikle 1997). That is, gifts of all kinds become relevant to exchange and money- making rather than to satisfying needs directly, a circumstance, which alters the content of our consciousnesses as well as our points of view. We become 'chrematocentric'. While many of us lament this state of affairs we usually naturalize it and have no cognizance that things could indeed be different.

we might think of the influence of the dominant dollar or euro, but also of the movement for a one world currency.

What we are really looking for in philosophy, what is actually lacking, is not the monetary exemplar but the prototype of the abundant mother, the origin not of exchange and patriarchy but of a society of the gift-giving human. 'Matriarchy' according to Goettner-Abendroth (2012) means mothers-in-the-beginning, matri-arké. Matriarchal, mother-centered, *egalitarian* societies have existed since the beginning of time although in the last 5000 years they have been increasingly taken over by patriarchies, which in the last 500 to 1500 years, have also merged ever more fully with the market. Maternal prototype images come to us from prehistory through the work of Marija Gimbutas and the Institute of Archaeomythology and from 'suppressed history' in the work of Max Dashu and others in the feminist movement who are trying to bring to light the women and mothers who have been ignored for the last millennia. They also come from the goddess movement, made up of (mostly) women worshipping the 'divine feminine'[27] as it is revealed in a multiplicity of beings – human and non-human – as opposed to the monotheistic 'one to many' dominant figures of patriarchal religions.

10.10 Some consequences for feminism

I believe that when feminists discuss patriarchy we have to take into account the peculiar gift denying aspects of money, its consonance with other one-to-many social structures and its influence on them and on our thinking as an extrasomatic embodiment of the concept in its function as the exemplar of (exchange) value. Perhaps we should say all the one-to-many structures are 'phallically invested'. However, they are at least as much invested by money as the main socially hypostasized infinitely expandable exemplar as they are by the phallus.

It is unlikely that we can radically change capitalist patriarchy without

---

27   I don't agree with this terminology because it has given rise to its complement 'divine masculine'. As the reader will understand, I believe that as long as masculinity is constructed in opposition to the mother, it will be distorted and pernicious. The positive chateracteristics that are supposed to be masculine like strength, energy and creativity can also be feminine. The negative social characteristics of dominance, competition and being the 'one' that I have been describing are not divine at all and in fact are destroying the planet. We need to begin to think of the divine human, *homo donans*, s:he.

addressing all of the one-to-many structures together. In fact, feminists have rejected phallocentrism but have often embraced the centrality of money (chrematocentrism) and thus have become reintegrated into the gift plundering system.

By this I do not mean to say that women should not work in the system at all. For many it is necessary for survival. However some women and men are choosing to start alternative communities and perhaps they will succeed in 'walking away' (as Barbara Mann suggests). I believe we need to walk away in consciousness first. We need to understand what is happening and look critically at the patriarchal capitalist economy and culture, and whenever we can, we need to stop giving our gifts and gift value to it. First we need to stop believing in it.

If we want a world based on a liberated and generalized maternal gift economy we can call on mothering and on matriarchal and non matriarchal gift economies to guide us but we can also call on language itself. Language as virtual giving and receiving in abundance gives us a way of seeing what could happen if everyone were living and giving in an abundant economy of material gifts. Exchange makes us plunder and deny the motherworld that language and living in gift-based community mediate and would help us to create. Even in the domestic sphere in patriarchal capitalist market life we can get a sense of gift community. Exchange leads us into a labyrinth, a (Mauss) trap. It is not the way out.

In the light – or shadow – of exchange we have developed social and 'hard' sciences which investigate the world in a gift denying way. Although these ways of knowing are producing important practical and commercial results and new descriptions of what it is to think and to be a human being, they do not help us solve the socio-economic problems that are undermining human and non-human life on Earth.

They investigate language in terms of brain functions or computationally where gifts as such are not relevant.They leave aside the meaning of the gift of language itself and they see it primarily in physiological terms as 'inherited' (gift word). The meaning of maternal gift-giving and receiving is also unseen, though there is now the new field of 'generosity studies', which also seeks physiological, sociobiological, neurological exchange-based explanations, like 'payoffs' for altruism in terms hormones like dopamin, endorphins, and especially oxytocin. Unfortunately by not giving importance to the gift schema, to human mothering/being mothered and to the projection of mothering onto culture and Nature, we remain out of contact with the rest of the Earth and beyond her, with the rest of the Universe. Only by reinstating mothering/being mothered, gift-giving and receiving, and the gift paradigm as a major part of our human worldview will we be able to return home from our centuries of alienation, nurture future generations and pass on mothering to them, sharing the commons with them instead of stealing the gifts of Earth from them. As of now, while we concentrate on the physiological explanations of our humanity, we are not passing the gifts of Earth and culture on to the children of the future but passing them into the garbage dump.

It has become popular among New Agers to think they are evolving beyond the planet to some higher consciousness, leaving the Earth behind. To me this seems to be the arrogance of alienation, a symptom of the gift destroying disease, still another way of arriving at the 'One' position.

Philosophy, religion, science and morality do not have enough traction in us to lead us out of the trap created by patriarchy and monetized exchange. They are riddled by the externalized concept pattern. The material and linguistic gift economy could help us find the way, if only we could see where they already exist socially, inside and outside ourselves. The immediate challenge is to recognize the maternal patterns even in male-initiated gift economy theories and experiments, to establish their link to mothering/being mothered and to point out the dangers of money and patriarchal processes.

Mothering/being mothered is the fundamental human experience at the beginning of meaning. It is replayed at the verbal level, and in knowing and interacting with a meaningful gifted and gifting world. This experience evolved over time into different kinds of gift economies in the societies of indigenous and matriarchal peoples but in present patriarchal market culture, the gift economy has been travestied and many of the gifts of nature and culture have been squandered and destroyed. The ignorance of the gift economy and of its basis in mothering and language has created a situation in which we cling to the externalized concept form as the central element of life and find our survival in the ability to succeed in ithe market and manipulate others by means of money. Ignoring the value of what is free we are free to destroy it. But this can never be.

The 1% have to stop taking the gifts and find a way to restore what they have taken, free. The 99% have to find a way of receiving the gifts in a good way without harm, passing them on to others and to nature. This has to be done with dignity and without humiliation (Lindner 2010).

Mothering and other free gift labor have been discredited and burdened by the market, which contradicts the nurturing process while capturing and redirecting its gifts into profit. If mothering is the basis of language and cognition, denying the mothering economy and substituting it with its artificial determined opposite, exchange, is an abstraction from mothering, *and* from language *and* from cognition. This abstraction is one reason the denial of nurturing is so pervasive. That is, the market almost automatically denies - does not see- the gift economy and this denial extends to its 'superstructure,' the various domains of giftless thought. The sexism that pervades society is functional to this denial, making it male privilege to receive and to not-give or even, paradoxically, to appear to give the most, while remaining within the exchange frame. Racism works in much the same way: while EuroAmerican corporations and individuals appear to be the biggest givers as philanthropists, non white peoples of many nations have been forced to give their resources and the substance of their lives to create the wealth of the Anglo 1%. Nevertheless many of them had and some continue to have gift cultures and traditions. For example the philosophy and practice of *ubuntu* in Africa, gift traditions of native peoples of North and South America, Polynesia and Asia and gifting among matriarchal peoples wherever they survive worldwide. To this must be added the many popular traditions of mutual help and solidarity among non-Europeans and among Europeans who still have traditions beyond capitalism within capitalism itself. The foundation is still there.

White privilege is the privilege not to give but to take in a disguised way – a way, which appears to be the opposite. That is, racist white people seem – at least to themselves – to deserve to receive and to take because they are white. One result of all this is that Western philosophy and many other academic disciplines have focussed on just the areas from which explanations based on mothering have been removed because it was necessary to find or invent some other explanations for the logical structure that was rightly felt to be there but invisible. The willing satisfaction of others' needs and the creative reception of gifts is this missing underlying transitive logical and psychological structure. The logic of categorization and identity/difference has been used in place of the gift to bring about transfers using virtualization/exchange in the context of private property. In addition, as we have been saying, cause/effect and agent/patient have been seen as underlying patterns which, given the denial of mothering, to some extent take the place of the transitive gift structure. This is possible because they are already its extensions or dilutions. Giving/receiving provides a structure of knowing, while cause/effect and agent/patient seem to be structures of reality without the gift, and perhaps part of the structure of knowing also. But we could not have known cause and effect, agent and patient as such without the psychological (epistemological) structure of the gift.

The elimination of mothering as an explanatory key has created a realm of discourse from which mothers themselves have been excluded, and this has had the effect of taking from them a way of understanding their own practice as socially relevant. Male psychologist Daniel Stern says that he often hears mothers say, regarding what he calls the 'motherhood mindset', 'You have described my experience exactly, but I did not know what it was until I heard it. I've never been able to put it into words' (1998: 26). How is it that a male academic has to be the one who gives the words to female motherers to speak their own maternal experiences?[28]

An area in addition to epistemology from which the mothering explanatory key has been excluded, is normative ethics. The motherer-child dyadic altercentric interaction sets the stage for later communication and community and in abundance it can also be pleasant and fun for the child and for the motherer. The provisioning interaction of the dyad is social but biologically necessary for the child's survival. When altercentrism is maintained in adult life through a gift economy, care can develop and generalize into a common mindset of social altruism. Here ethics as we know it would no longer apply because nurturing would already be the social norm. Altercentrism is not originally a moral choice but the pragmatic experiential basis of our formation of our subjectivities, our personalities as communicating human beings. Gifting is powerful and rational because it is structural[29] but it is now interrupted and cancelled, overwritten by the market and patriarchy, the creation of scarcity and the values of the exosomatic concept process. Altercentrism is no longer available as the structure of the main model of behavior. Mutual other orientation is replaced at best by mutual non interference, which is legislated and imposed by hierarchical structures and aided by categorization. Even more negatively, mutual other orientation is replaced by dominance and submission (agent and patient), facilitated by violence – 'high transitivity' – as in the transposed 'gift' of hitting.

10.11 Conclusion

In the West, the liberation of the gift model requires an end to the market and to patriarchy. This is necessary in order to create an egalitarian society that will function according to maternal values. Gifting within the model of competition, domination and power-over is a contradiction in terms and it cannot ever bring a peaceful society. Nor will gift-giving for power-over ever create peace.

---

28   Miranda Fricker's 'epistemic injustice' is relevant here, but so is the whole economic and ideological situation I have been describing.

29   And there are even endorphins that reward us for this pro-social behavior: it feels good.

Thanks to feminism, the LGBT movement and the men's movement, many people are already questioning the gender stereotypes under which we are now living. However, unless we recognize the important economic aspects of gender –- and the gendered aspects of economics – we will not solve the problems. Conscious economists need to recognize the gendered and patriarchal aspects of capitalism so as to begin to envision something else. Neither eliminating capitalism while maintaining patriarchy, nor eliminating patriarchy while maintaining capitalism will bring a solution. This needs to be taken as a guiding factor for the cultural turns away from capitalism and patriarchy, money and markets that have already begun.

If we realize that language is based on the gift schema perhaps those women and men who earn their livings by using/manipulating/buying and selling language will also be able to respect their own maternal origins and throw off the parasite of the exchange economy. We all use language to some extent, so this is actually a possibility for everyone.

Whenever we are awake we are also in receivership of endless perceptual gifts. Our eyes are continually exploring our environment even if we don't realize it, finding the gifts, the 'affordances'. We breathe in gifts of air and breathe out carbon dioxide which is a gift for plants. Our hearts pump oxygenated blood out to nurture our cells, and back to be replenished. Sounds, images, smells, chemical stimuli, pheromones, come to us from all directions, sometimes, if they are too many, changing from giving to hitting (from 'low' to 'high' transitivity) as we are 'bombarded' by them. We also unconsciously give off signs and signals to others and we receive them from them.

Our market economy is composed of private property owners or would-be owners and exchangers in the midst of a sea of gifts we do not recognize as such. At least we do not recognize them until we find ways of turning the gifts into commodities, as our corporations have done recently with water, seeds, genes and language itself, which has been commodified even before we knew it was a gift made of gifts.

The virtual abundance that there is now online is like the virtual abundance in language and is conducive to gift-giving and to the positive human relations carried by the gift economy. Egalitarian projects like free software, Wikipedia, peer-to-peer networking, freecycling, Time Banking, the movement against copyrights, the promotion of free information and even hybrids with exchange as in the shareable economy and crowdsourcing, demonstrate the viability of the gift economy (see Appendix). Unfortunately this opening has also left the users of the internet vulnerable to commodification of their private information through data mining and surveillance.

There is a mistaken idea among the powerful that 'the masses'[30] need to be controlled, that otherwise they could not live peacefully together in abundance. This idea is used to justify the creation of scarcity, the seizure of the gifts and the surveillance of the many by the few who dominate and control them (see the documentary by Adam Curtis, *The Century of the Self*, 2002). Instead it is the birthright of everyone to live in abundance in a nurturing gift economy in an atmosphere of trust.

We have distorted our concepts of who we are and what we should do by superimposing an alienated economy of exchange on a human communicative economy of the gift. Recognizing this is the first step in making the change towards an economy based on free material and linguistic communication and the elaboration of the altercentric mother-child relation.

If we conceive altercentric mothering/being-mothered as gift-giving and receiving, if we recognize the very positive maternal gift character of indigenous matriarchal gift economies, of the ancient virtual invention of language itself and of social incarnations of linguistic giving in symbolic gift exchange, and most recently in the maternal and linguistic aspects of the modern internet wiki economy, of volunteering, of social experiments in gifting communities, of ecological initiatives like permaculture, we will find the way to a positive material economy of abundance and a culture of peace.

10.12 A parting gift

> ... the immediate biological task is not to teach the infant to recognize the mother but to teach the mother to recognize, acknowledge and care for the infant.
> (M. C. Bateson 1979: 69)

The prosocial infant elicits learning by the prospective motherer. The motherer – female or male, sibling or aunt – is not however a blank slate. Language, by repeating mothering at another level, maintains the altercentric giving/receiving capacity for those children who will become motherers so they are able to do altercentric interactivity again as adults! That is, would even adult or adolescent birth mothers (some fifteen years after their own infancy) on their own without language devote themselves to the needs of their children in such a detailed way and for such a long time period? By reenacting the maternal model in language, people's unilateral

---

30   This is the multitude seen as a collection of one-to-many patriarchal proprietors and propertyless proprietors.

gift capacity is maintained after childhood, ready to be used in their own practice of mothering. Thus language would have a selective advantage in that more of the children of speaking mothers would survive, grow up and have children who would survive. Language functions as a kind of refrigerator, storing the altercentric nurturing capacity in the child as s:he becomes an adult, keeping it fresh for later use.Thus contrary to the commonplace ideas of the maternal instinct and the 'language instinct' (Pinker 1995), verbal giving as a social transposition of mothering, would function to offset the *lack* of maternal instinct, especially after the initial hormonal drives of the birth mother are terminated.

This capacity of language can expand and generalize. It functions also when we use it for nurturing each other individually and collectively and when we care for Mother Nature. Even though our society is going mad we maintain our capacity for altercentrism intact through language.

Both gift-giving and language bridge the gap between the human community and its environmental niche while maintaining and elaborating the border between them. In exchange, where the principle is mutual exclusion, nothing new can develop. Instead in a community where relations are created through gift-giving in life and in language, gifts, givers and receivers can multiply exponentially qualitatively, co creating and making relevant all the aspects of the environment and the culture. Doing this will allow us to respect, love and protect the creatures and the elements that together create life on the planet. It is on this basis that we can give a better world forward to the human and other species of the future.

10.13 What to do?

Walk away
Do many small projects
Raise consciousness, grapple with exchange vs gift
Recognize gifting where it already exists.
Do theory with unilateral gifting in mind.
Raise boys and girls with the maternal model
Communities of motherers
Gift Economy studies
Matriarchal studies
Alternative communities with the gift as final goal
Unite the movements on a gift basis

I believe that problem-solving is a kind of gift-giving, the satisfaction of a need. This lets me include as gifts all the innumerable initiatives for social change that people as *homo donans* do to solve the problems created by the patriarchal capitalist system. Below are some already existing gift interactions inside the system. I have included some of their transformations into exchange:

mothering and being mothered
housework
food sharing
baby sitting mothers' groups
extended family care ... salaried domestic work
neighborliness
free services, for example:
many kinds of volunteering and helping:
volunteer fire department,
neighborhood watch
love making ... prostitution ... sex trafficking
ride sharing ... public transportation
hitch hiking ... taxis, uber cars
yellow bikes
couch surfing ... air B and B
blood and organ donation ... commerce in blood and organs
twelve-step programs ... commercial therapies
charity ... moneymaking NGOs
philanthropy
social change philanthropy
social change activism
social change solidarity
solar and wind energy ... privatization of solar, wind etc.
welfare ... welfare bureaucracy
government subsidies ...
legal aid ... legal profession
healing ... medical industry
indigenous remedies ... Big Pharma
gardening ... Agribusiness
manure ... chemical fertilizer
seeds handed down ... terminator seeds
choices from life experience ... choices from advertising

Political volunteering ... election commerce
True news, indie media ... Manipulated commercial news
Landless workers movement
(*Movimento dos Trabalhadores Sem Terra*)
Zapatismo
Political attempts like Bolivarism,
The Law of Mother Earth
Remittances by immigrants to home countries
Rainbow gatherings
Burning man gatherings
Michigan Women's Music Festival
Nipun Mehta's Service Space
Pay it forward restaurants
Gift circles movement (Alpha Lo)
Shikshantar, the learning city
Schumacher College

People living without money
Heide Marie Schwermer, Mark Boyle and others

Transition towns ... Gated communities
localism ... corporate imperialism
gift communities
Tameera
Findhorn

permaculture
urban gardens
guerrilla gardening

Internet gift economy ... surveillance and data mining
facebook, twitter ... surveillance and data mining
Free software ... commercial software (planned obsolescence)
Wikipedia
Search engines
Firefox
Free online education programs ... indoctrination
copyleft, creative commons

Hybrids between gift and exchange

alternative currencies
crowdsourcing
shareable economy

There has been much research done on altruism and generosity recently.
One among many is Science of Generosity
www.generosityresearch@nd.edu
Another is The Center for Building a Culture of Empathy
www.progressivespirit.com/empathy. Still another is the Stanford
Center for Compassion and Altruism www.ccare.stanford.edu.

The End ... that is, The Beginning.

APPENDIX

Here are some shifts in perspective that I have encouraged throughout the book and that can help to think about the gift economy in all its manifestations.

Exchange paradigm	Gift paradigm
1. Mothering is aneconomic	1. Mothering is economic
2. Mothering is not an economic 'base'	2. Mothering is an economic 'base' and has a superstructure
3. Market creates abundance	3. Market creates scarcity
4. Communication is exchange	4. Communication is turntaking unilateral gift-giving
5. Gift exchange	5. Turntaking gifting, not exchange
6. Active giver-passive receiver	6. Active giver-active receiver
7. Solipsistic infants	7. Socially interactive altercentric infants (new infant research)
8. Equal exchange debt and obligation produce positive human relations	8. Giving/receiving produces positive human relations
9. Perception is a sui generis activity	9. Perception is a (maternal) selection and reception of perceptual gifts
10. Language is self-expression	10. Language is satisfaction of communicative and cognitive needs[1]

---

1   Words do not signify independently but by satisfying and eliciting interpersonal communicative and cognitive needs. Thus, they are gifts and create positive human relations. We have not understood this so our analysis is off and our understanding of alternatives is inaccurate and limited

11. Language is based on inherited Universal Grammar	11. Language is based on the image schema of the gift and its extensions
12. Language is rule-governed	12. Language enacts gift schema constructions
13. Communication is exchange	13. Communication is turn taking unilateral gift-giving
14. Language is based on questions and answers	14. Language is based on mind reading
15. Syntax as rule following	15. Syntax as gifts to gifts
16. Subjectivity is agency	16. Subjectivity is gift agency as modeled on material giving and language gift construction, but identity also includes creative receptivity
17. Supply and effective demand	17. Gifts and needs
18. Problem is capitalism, the stock market, the knowledge economy	18. Problem is exchange itself and the elimination of the model of gift-giving
19. Social contract	19. Shared structures of implications
20. Narrow idea of need satisfaction as utilitarian ...	20. An expanded idea of needs including psychological, cognitive, communicative, spiritual needs, etc.
21. To use value and exchange value	21. Add gift value
22. Epistemology based on categorization	22. Epistemology based on gifting
23. Language as exchange	23. Language as gift-giving ... exchange as altered language
24. Money as a convention or a symbol of value	24. Money as an embodied word/exemplar
25. The market as a normal and unavoidable fact of life	25. The market as a piece of extended mind, the exosomatic conceptualization process of the alienated human community
26. We can create a better market	26. We can only solve our problems beyond the market
27. Feminists should succeed in the market	27. Feminists should dismantle the market and start over on the basis of gift-giving/mothering

BIBLIOGRAPHY

Abrahams, Yvette, 'The Khoekhoe Free Economy: A Model for the Gift' in G. Vaughan ed., *Women and the Gift Economy, A Radically Different Worldview is Possible* (Toronto: Inanna Press, 2007).

Abram, David, *The Spell of the Sensuous; Perception and Language in a More-Than-Human World* (New York: Random House, 1996).

Alaimo, Stacey, and Heckman, Susan eds, *Material Feminisms* (Bloomington: Indiana University Press, 2008).

Anderson, Danica, Blood and Honey Icons: *Biosemiotics and Bioculinary* (Olympia WA: Kolo Collaboration, 2012).

Anzaldùa, Gloria, *Borderlands/La Frontera: the New Mestiza* (San Francisco: AuntLute Books 2012 [1987]).

Arbib, Michael, 'Interweaving Protosign and Protospeech, Further Developments Beyond the Mirror', in Interaction Studies 6.2, 2005, pp. 145-71.

Armstrong, Jeanette, 'Land Speaking' in Simon Ortiz, ed. *Speaking for the Generations* (Tucson: University of Arizona Press, 1997), pp. 174-95.

Armstrong, Jeanette, 'Indigenous Knowledge and Gift Giving: Living In Community', in G. Vaughan, ed. *Women and the Gift Economy* (Toronto: Inanna Press, 2007).

Armstrong, Sharon Lee, Gleitman, Lili R. and Gleitman, Henry, 'What some concepts might not be', in *Cognition*, 13, 1983, pp. 263-308.

Austin, John, *How to Do Things with Words: The William James Lectures delivered at Harvard University in 1955*, J. O. Urmson and Marina Sbisà eds (Oxford: Clarendon Press 1962).

Barthes, Roland, *The Fashion System* (Berkeley: University of California Press 1967).

Bates, E., and MacWhinney, B., 'Functionalism and the Competition Model,' in B. MacWhinney and E. Bates eds, *The Crosslinguistic Study of Sentence Processing* (New York: Cambridge University Press, 1989), pp. 3-73.

Bateson, Mary Catherine, 'The Epigenesis of Conversational Interaction: A Personal Account of Research Development' in *Before Speech: The Beginning of Human Communication*. M. Bullowa, ed. (London: Cambridge University Press, 1979).

Bataille, Georges, *The Accursed Share, Vol 1, Consumption*, trans. R. Hurley (New York: Zone Books, 1991).

Baudrillard, Jean, *Selected Writings*, Mark Poster, ed. (Cambridge: Polity Press, 2001 [1988]).

Bennholdt-Thomsen, Veronika, 'Women's Dignity is the Wealth of Juchitán,' *Anthropology of Work Review*, 10, 1, (1989), pp. 3-10.

Berteau, Marie-Cécile, Miguel Goncalves and Peter Raggat, eds, *Dialogic Forma-
    tions: Investigations into the Origins and Development of the Dialogical Self*
    (Charlotte, N.C.: Information Age Publishing, 2013).
Berti, Anna Emilia and Bombi, Anna Silvia, *The Child's Construction of Econom-
    ics*, European Monographs in Social Psychology. Duveen, Gerard trans. (New
    York, NY: Cambridge University Press, 1988).
Bickerton, D., 'Mothering Plus Vocalization Doesn't Equal Language', in *Behav-
    ioral and Brain Sciences*, 27 (2004), pp. 504-5.
Bird-David, Nurit, 'The Giving Environment: Another Perspective on the Eco-
    nomic System of Gatherer-Hunters', in *Current Anthropology*, 4-1 (1990).
Blurton Jones, N.G. (1987). Tolerated Theft. Suggestions about the Ecology and
    Evolution of Sharing, Hoarding, and Scrounging. *Social Science Information*,
    26 (1987), pp. 31-54.
Bourdieu, Pierre, *Outline of a Theory of Practice* (Cambridge: Cambridge Univer-
    sity Press, 1977).
Bowlby, John, *Attachment. Attachment and Loss*, vol. 1 (New York: Basic Books,
    1969 repr. 1999).
Boyle, Mark, *www.Themoneylessmanifesto.org* (accessed 2014).
Bråten, Stein, 'Born with the Other in Mind: Child Development and Cognitive
    Science implications or: Infant's Minds and Social Feelings: Dialogue, Devel-
    opment and Collapse of Concern' (www.SteinBråten.com 1991), ch.1.
Bråten, Stein, ed., *Intersubjective Communication and Emotion in Early Ontogeny*
    (Cambridge: Cambridge University Press, 1998).
Bråten, Stein, 'Altercentric Infants and Adults' in S. Bråten ed., *On Being Moved, from
    Mirror Neurons to Empathy* (Amsterdam: John Benjamins, 2007), pp. 111-36.
Bråten, Stein, 'Altercentric Perception by Infants and Adults in Dialogue: Ego's
    Virtual Participation in Alter's Complementary Act' in Maxim Stamenov and
    Vittorio Gallese, eds, *Mirror Neurons and the Evolution of Brain and Language*
    (Amsterdam: John Benjamins, 2002), pp. 273-94.
Bråten, Stein, *Roots and Collapse of Empathy* (Amsterdam: John Benjamins,
    2013).
Bruni, Luigino, *The Genesis and Ethos of the Market* (New York: Palgrave Mac-
    Millan, 2012).
Bundgaard, P. and Stjernfelt, F., 'René Thom's Semiotics and its Sources', in
    Wildgen, W. and Brandt, P. A. (eds), *Semiosis and Catastrophes* (Bern: Peter
    Lang, 2010).
Butler, Judith, *Gender Trouble Feminism and the Subversion of Identity* (New
    York: Routledge, 1990).
Caillè, Alain and Jacques Godbout, *The World of the Gift* (Montreal: McGill
    Queens University Press, 2001).
Carey, Susan, *The Origin of Concepts* (Oxford: Oxford University Press, 2009).
Carey, Susan, 'The Origin of Concepts: A Precis' in *Behavior and Brain Science*,
    34 (3) (2011), pp. 113-62.
Chiarcos, Christian, Claus, Berry and Grabski, Michael, eds, *Salience: Multi-
    disciplinary Perspectives on its Function in Discourse* (Berlin/New York: De
    Gruyter, 2011).

Chodorow, Nancy, *The Reproduction of Mothering* (Berkeley and Los Angeles: The University of California Press, 1978).

Chomsky, Noam, 'Three Models for the Description of Language,' *IRE Transactions on Information Theory*, 2 (1956), pp. 113-24.

Chomsky, Noam, 'Introduction', in A. Schaff, *Language and Cognition* (New York: McGraw-Hill. 1973).

Chomsky, Noam, *Rules and Representations* (New York, Columbia University Press, 1980).

Chu, Judy Y., *When Boys Becomes Boys* (New York: NYU Press, 2014).

Cixous, Helene 'Sorties: Out and Out: Attacks/Ways Out/Forays,' in Alan Schrift, ed., *The Logic of the Gift* (New York: Routledge, 1975, repr. 1997).

Clark, Andy and Chalmers, David, 'The Extended Mind' (ANALYSIS 1998), pp. 7-19.

Curtis, Adam, *The Century of the Self* (BBC documentary film series 2002).

Damasio, Antonio, *Descaters' Error, Emotion, Reason and the Human Brain* (New York: Harper Collins, 1994).

Damasio, Antonio, *The Feeling of What Happens, Body, Emotion and the Making of Consciousness* (London: Vintage Books, 1999).

Damasio, Antonio, *Self Comes to Mind* (New York: Random House, 2010).

Day, Rachel, L. Laland, Kevin Laland and John Odling-Smee, 'Rethinking Adaptation: the Niche Construction Perspective', in *Perspectives in Biology and Medicine*, 2003, pp. 80-95.

Derrida, Jacques, *Writing and Difference*, trans. A. Bass (Chicago: University of Chicago Press, 1980).

Derrida, Jacques, *Given Time, 1, Counterfeit Money* (Chicago: University of Chicago Press, 1992).

de Saussure, Ferdinand, *Course in General Linguistics*, C. Bally and A. Sechehaye, eds (Chicago, Open Court Publishing: 1915, repr. 1998).

Diprose, Rosalyn, *Corporeal Generosity: On Giving with Nietzsche, Merleau-Ponty, and Levinas* (Albany State: University of New York Press, 2002).

Divjak, D. & A. Arppe, 'Extracting prototypes from exemplars. What can corpus data Tell us about Concept Representation?', in *Cognitive Linguistics*, 24, 2013, pp. 221-74.

Douglas, Mary, 'Foreword' in Mauss M., *The Gift: The Form and Reason for Exchange in Archaic Societies* (New York: Norton 1990).

Du, Shanshan, *Chopsticks Only Work in Pairs* (New York, Columbia University Press, 2003).

Ducat, Stephen, *The Wimp Factor: Gender Gaps, Holy Wars and the Politics of Anxious Masculinity* (Boston: Beacon Press, 2004).

Dunbar, Robin, Grooming, *Gossip and the Origin of Language* (Cambridge: Mass. Harvard University Press, 1996).

Dunbar, Robin, 'Theory of Mind and the Evolution of Language', in J. Hurford and M. Studdart-Kennedy, eds, *Approaches to the Evolution of Language* (Cambridge: Cambridge University Press, 1998), pp. 92-111.

Eco, Umberto, *From the Tree to the Labyrinth*, Anthony Oldcorn, trans. (Cambridge, MA: Harvard University Press, 2014).

Eisenstein, Charles, *Sacred Economics, Money, Gift and Society in the Age of Transition* (Berkeley: Evolver Editions, 2011).

Eisler, Riane, *The Chalice and the Blade* (New York: Harper Collins, 1988).

Eisler, Riane, *The Real Wealth of Nations: Creating a Caring Economics* (San Francisco: Berrett-Koehler 2007).

Falk, D., *Finding Our Tongues: Mothers, Infants and the Origin of Language* (New York: Basic Books, 2009).

Fauconnier, Gilles, *Mental Spaces: Aspects of Meaning Construction in Natural Language* (New York: Cambridge University Press, 1994).

Fauconnier, Gilles and Turner, Mark, *The Way We Think. Conceptual Blending and the Mind's Hidden Complexities* (New York: Basic Books, 2002).

Fine, Cordelia, *Delusions of Gender: How Our Minds, Society, and Neurosexism Create Difference* (New York: W. W. Norton, 2010).

Fodor, Jerry, 'Some Reflections on L. V. Vygotsky's Thought and Language' in *Cognition*, 1 (1) (1972), pp. 83-95.

Folbre, Nancy, *The Invisible Heart: Economics and Family Values* (New York: New Press 2001).

Food and Agriculture Organization, 'Women in Agriculture: Closing the Gender Gap' http://www.fao.org/docrep/013/i2050e/i2050e02.pdf (accessed February 2015).

Foreman, Grant, *Sequoyah* (Norman: University of Oklahoma Press, 1938).

Fox Keller, Evelyn, *The Mirage of a Space between Nature and Nurture* (Durham and London: Duke University Press, 2010).

Frege, Gottlob, *The Frege Reader*, M. Beaney, ed. (Oxford: Blackwell, 1997).

Freud, Sigmund, 'On transformations of Instinct as Exemplified in Anal Eroticism' in *Freud and Women, a Reader*, E. Young-Bruehl ed. (New York: W. W. Norton, 1990), pp. 196-204.

Freud, Sigmund, *From the History of an Infantile Neurosis* (Read Books – digital-2013).

Fricker, Miranda, *Epistemic Injustice: Power and the Ethics of Knowing* (Oxford: Oxford University Press, 2009).

Furnham, Adrian and Michael Argyle, *The Psychology of Money* (Abingdon, Oxford: Psychology Press, 1998).

Gallese, Vittorio and Lakoff, George, 'The Brain's Concepts: The Role of the Sensory-Motor System in Conceptual Knowledge', in *Cognitive Neuropsychology*, 22: 3 (2005), pp. 455-79.

Gallese, Vittorio, Morris N., Eagle and Mingone, Paolo, 'Intentional Attunement: Mirror Neurons and the Neural Underpinnings of Interpersonal Attachment', in *Journal of the American Psychoanalytic Association*, 55 (2007), pp. 131-76.

Gibson, Eleanor J. and Pick, Anne, D., *An ecological approach to Perceptual Learning and Development* (New York: Oxford University Press, 2000).

Gibson, J. J., 'The Theory of Affordances,' in R. Shaw, Robert and J. Bransford, John, eds, *Perceiving, Acting and Knowing: Toward an Ecological Psychology* (Hillsdale, NJ: Lawrence Erlbaum Associates, 1977), pp. 67-82.

Gibson, J. J., *The Ecological Approach to Visual Perception* (Boston: Houghton Mifflin, 1979).

Gibson, Martha, *From Naming to Saying: The Unity of the Proposition* (Oxford: Blackwell Publishing, 2004).

Gilbert, Karen, Wendy, *The Affective Turn: Theorizing the Social*, Patricia Clough, ed. (Durham, NC: Duke University Press, 2007).

Gilligan, Carol, *In a Different Voice* (Cambridge: Harvard University Press, 1982).

Gilligan, Carol and Richards, David A., *The Deepening Darkness* (Cambridge: Cambridge University Press, 2009).

Gillmore, David, *Manhood in the Making: Cultural Concepts of Masculinity* (New Haven & London: Yale University Press, 1990).

Gimbutas, Marija, *The Language of the Goddess* (San Francisco: Harper and Row, 1989).

Godbout, Jacques with Alain Caillé, *The World of the Gift*, trans. by D. Winkler (Montreal: McGill/Queen's University Press, 1998).

Goettner-Abendroth, Heide, *Matriarchal Societies: Studies on Indigenous Cultures across the Globe*, trans. Karen Smith (New York: Peter Lang, 2012).

Goldberg, Adele, *Constructions: A Construction Grammar Approach to Argument Structure* (Chicago: Chicago University Press, 1995).

Goodluck, Helen, *Language Acquisition: A Linguistic Introduction* (Hoboken, NJ: Wiley, 1991).

Gopnik, Allison, *Amazing Babies*, Interview: www.edge.org (accessed 2009).

Gopnik, Allison, *The Philosophical Baby: What Children's Minds Tell Us About Truth, Love, and the Meaning of Life* (New York, Farrar: Straus and Giroux, 2010).

Gopnik, Allison, Andrew Meltzoff and Patricia Kuhl, *The Scientist in the Crib* (New York: Harper Collins, 1999).

Goux, Jean-Joseph, *Symbolic Economies: After Marx and Freud*, trans. J. C. Gage (Cornell: Cornell University Press 1990 [1978]).

Goux, Jean-Joseph, 'Marx et Walras: Un Déplacement Ethique' in Marcel Drach, ed., in *L'Argent* (Paris: La Découverte, 2004), pp. 131-8.

Graeber, David, *Debt: The First 5000 years* (Brooklyn, NY: Melville House, 2011).

Grandin, Temple, *Thinking in Pictures* (New York: Vintage Books, 2008).

Grandin, Temple and Catherine Johnson, *Animals in Translation: Using the Mysteries of Autism to Decode Animal Behavior* (New York: Scribner, 2005).

Gratier, Maya and Colwyn Trevarthen, 'Voice, Vitality and Meaning: On the Shaping of the Infant's Utterances in Willing Engagement with Culture. Comment on Bertau's 'On the Notion of Voice', in *International Journal for Dialogical Science*, 2, 1 (2007), pp. 169-81.

Grice, H. P., *Studies in the Ways of Words* (Cambridge: Harvard University Press, 1989).

Gurevich, Andrew, 'The Sacred Marriage of Visible Logos and Epigenetic Consciousness: A Paradigm for a New Humanity,' www.RealitySandwich.com (accessed 2012).

Gurven, M., Allen-Arave, W., Hill, K., and Hurtado, M., 'It's a Wonderful Life: Signaling Generosity Among the Ache of Paraguay,' in *Evolution and Human Behavior*, 21 (2000), pp. 263-82.

Gurven, M. et al, 'From the Womb to the Tomb: The Role of Transfers in Shaping the Evolved Human Life History', in *Experimental Gerontology*, 47-10, (2012), pp. 807-13.

Haarmann, Harald, *Early civilization and literacy in Europe: an inquiry into Cultural Continuity in the Mediterranean World* (Berlin: Mouton de Gruyter, 1995).

Hampe, Beate (ed.), *From Perception to Meaning: Image Schemas in Cognitive Linguistics* (Berlin: Mouton De Gruyter, 2005).

Hardt, Michael and Negri, Antonio, *Empire* (Cambridge, MA: Harvard University Press, 2000).

Hartsock, Nancy, *Money, Sex and Power* (Boston: North Eastern University Press, 1983).

Harvard University, Center on the Developing Child (2009), 'Working Paper 1. Young Children Develop in an Environment of Relationships' *www.developingchild.harvard.edu* (accessed April 10, 2015).

Held, Virginia, *The Ethics of Care: Personal, Political and Global* (Oxford: Oxford University Press, 2007).

Hoeller, Hildegaard, *From Gift to Commodity: Capitalism and Sacrifice in Nineteenth-Century American Fiction* (Lebanon: N.H. University of New Hampshire Press, 2012).

Hopper, P. J., and Thompson, S. A., 'Transitivity in grammar and Discourse', in Language, 56, 2 (1980), pp. 251-99.

Horner, Robyn, *Rethinking God as Gift: Marion, Derrida and the Limits of Phenomenology* (New York: Fordham University Press, 2001).

Hardy, Sarah, *Mothers and Others: The Evolutionary Origins of Mutual Understanding* (Cambridge, MA: Belknap Press of Harvard University Press, 2013).

Hyde, Lewis, *The Gift, Creativity and the Artist in the Modern World* (New York: Vintage Books, 2007).

Irigaray, Luce, *Speculum of the Other Woman*, trans. G. Gill (Cornell: Cornell University Press, 1985 [1974]).

Irigaray, Luce, *This Sex Which Is Not One*, trans. G. Gill (Cornell: Cornell University Press, 1985[1977]).

Irigaray, Luce, *Elemental Passions,* trans. J. Collie and J. Still (London: The Athalone Press, 1992[1982]).

Ironmonger, Duncan and Faye Soupourmas, 'Output-Based Estimates of the Gross Household Product of the United States 2003–2010: And some Interactions of GHP with Gross Market Product during the Great Financial Crisis (2008–2009)', 32nd General Conference of the International Association for Research in Income and Wealth (Boston, MA: 2012).

Isla, Ana, 'The Tragedy of the Enclosures: An Eco-Feminist Perspective on Selling Oxygen and Prostitution in Costa Rica', in G. Vaughan, ed., *Women and the Gift Economy: A Radically Different Worldview is Possible* (Toronto: Inanna Press, 2007).

Jackendorf, Ray 'Precis of Foundations of Language', in *Behavioral and Brain Sciences* (2003), pp. 651-707.

Johnson, Mark, *The Body in the Mind: the Bodily Basis of Meaning, Imagination, and Reason* (Chicago: The University of Chicago Press, 1987).

Johnson, Mark, *Moral Imagination: Implications of Cognitive Science for Ethics* (Chicago: University of Chicago Press, 1993).

Johnson, Mark and Lakoff, George "Why cognitive linguistics requires embodied realism' in *Cognitive Linguistics*, 13-3 (2002) pp. 245-263.

Keil, Frank, *Concepts, Kinds and Cognitive Development* (Cambridge, MA: M.I.T. Press, 1992).

Klein, Naomi, *No Logo* (New York: Picador, 2000).

Kockelman, Paul, 'The Semiotic Ontology of the Commodity', in *Journal of Linguistic Anthropology*, 1,16 (2002), pp. 76–102.

Kristeva, Julia, *Desire in Language: A Semiotic Approach to Literature and Art*, trans. L. Roudiez (Oxford: Blackwell, 1980 [1969]).

Kristeva, Julia, *The Kristeva Reader*, Toril Moi ed. (Oxford: Blackwell Publishers, 1986).

Kuhl, P. K. 'Human Adults and Human Infants Show a 'Perceptual Magnet Effect' For the Prototypes of Speech Categories, Monkeys Do Not', in *Perception & Psychophysics*, (1991), pp. 93-107.

Kuokkanen, Rauna, *Reshaping the University: Responsibility, Indigenous Epistemes and the Logic of the Gift* (Vancouver: UBC Press, 2007).

Lacan, Jacques *Ecrits, a selection*, trans. Bruce Fink (New York: W. W. Norton and Co., 2002 [1966]).

Lakoff, George, *Women, Fire and Dangerous Things, What Categories Reveal About the Mind* (Chicago: University of Chicago Press, 1990).

Lakoff, George, 'Cognitive Models and Prototype Theory', in U. Neisser, ed., *Concepts and Conceptual Development: Ecological and Intellectual Factors in Categorization* (Cambridge: Cambridge University Press 1987,b).

Lakoff, George and Mark Johnson, *Metaphors We Live By* (Chicago: University of Chicago Press, 1980).

Langton, Rae, 'Review of Epistemic Injustice: Power and the Ethics of Knowing by Miranda Fricker', (*Hypatia* 2010).

Lindner, Evelin, *Gender, Humiliation, and Global Security: Dignifying Relationships from Love, Sex, and Parenthood to World Affairs* (Santa Barbara, CA: Praeger Publishing, 2010).

Lugones, Maria, *Pilgrimages, Pelegrinajes: Theorizing Coalition against Multiple Oppressions* (Lanham, Maryland: Rowman and Littlefield, 2003).

Lyotard, Jean-Francois, *Libidinal Economy* (London: Continuum, 2004 [1974]).

Lyra, Maria, 'Self and Symbol Emerging from Dialogical Dynamics,' in M-C, Bertau, M. M. Goncalves, and T. F. Raggat, eds, *Dialogic Formations: Investigations Into the Origins and Development of the Dialogical Self*, (Charlotte, NC: Information Age Publishing, 2012).

MacPherson, C. B., *The Political Theory of Possessive Individualism* (Oxford: Oxford University Press, 1962; repr. 2011).

MacWhinney, Brian, 'The Emergence of Grammar From Perspective,' in D. Pecher and R. Zwann, eds, *Grounding Cognition, The Role of Perception and Action in Memory, Language and Thinking* (Cambridge: Cambridge University Press, 2005), pp. 198-224.

'Malikam' (Malika Grasshoff), *The Magical Life of Berber Women in Kabylia* (New York: Peter Lang, 2007 [1996]).

Mandler, J. M., *The Foundations of Mind: The Origins of Conceptual Thought* (New York: Oxford University Press, 2004).

Mann, Barbara Alice, *Iroquois Women: the Gantowisas* (New York: Peter Lang, 2000).

Margulis, L. *Symbiosis in Cell Evolution* (San Francisco: Freeman, 1981)

Marvin, Carolyn and David Ingle, *Blood Sacrifice and the Nation*, Totem Rituals and the American Flag (Cambridge: Cambridge University Press, 1999).

Marx, Karl, *Grundrisse: Foundations of the Critique of Political Economy*, trans. M. Nicolaus (London: Penguin Books, 1993 [1857]).

Marx, Karl, *A Contribution to the Critique of Political Economy*, trans. N. I. Stone (Cornell University Library, 2009 [1859]).

Marx, Karl, Capital, *A Critique of Political Economy, Volume One*, trans. Samuel Moore and Edward Aveling (Moscow: Progress Publishers, 1996 [1867]).

Marx, Karl and Frederich Engels, *The German Ideology* (Moscow: Progress Publishers, 1964 [1932]).

Mauss, Marcel, The Gift: *The Form and Reason for Exchange in Archaic Societies*, trans. W. D. Halls, fwd Mary Douglas (New York: Norton 1990 [1923]).

Meikle, Scott *Aristotle's Economic Thought* (Oxford, Clarendon Press 1997).

Melis, Alicia P., Hare, Brian and Tomasello, Michael, 'Do Chimpanzees Reciprocate Favours?', in *Animal Behaviour*, 76 (2008), pp. 951-62.

Meltzoff, A. N., 'Social Cognition and the Origins of Imitation, Empathy, and Theory of Mind' in U. Goswami, ed., *The Wiley-Blackwell Handbook of Childhood Cognitive Development*, Malden, MA: Wiley-Blackwell, 2013)

Meltzoff, A.N. ans Moore, M. K. 'Imitation of Facial and Manual Gestures by Human Neonates', in *Science*, 1977, pp. 75-8.

Meltzoff, A. N., and Prinz, W., *The Imitative Mind: Development, Evolution, and Brain Bases* (Cambridge, England: Cambridge University Press, 2002).

Meltzoff, Andrew and Brooks, Rachele, 'Intersubjectivity before Language: Three Windows on Pre-Verbal Sharing', in Stein Bråten (ed.), *On Being Moved: From Mirror Neurons to Empathy* (Amsterdam/Philadelphia: John Benjamins Publishing Company, 2007), pp. 149-74.

Meltzoff, A. N., Kuhl, P. K., Movellan, J. & Sejnowski, T. J. 'Foundations for a new science of learning' (*Science*, 2009), pp. 284-288

Merchant, Carolyn, *The Death of Nature, Women, Ecology and the Scientific Revolution* (San Francisco: Harper, 1979 repr. 1990).

Messinger, Daniel, 'Give and Take: The Development of Conventional Infant Gestures', in *Merrill-Palmer Quarterly*, 1998, p 444 pp 566-590.

Mies, Maria, *Patriarchy and Accumulation on a World Scale* (London: Zed Books, 1986).

Miller, Jean Baker, *Towards a New Psychology of Women* (Boston: Beacon Press, 1979 repr. 1987).

Mirowski, Phillip, *More Heat than Light: Economics as Social Physics, Physics as Nature's Economics* (Cambridge, Cambridge University Press, 1989).

Mirowski, Phillip, *The Effortless Economy of Science* (Durham: Duke University Press, 2004).

Morgan, Robin, *Sisterhood is Global* (New York: The Feminist Press, 1984).

Muraro, Luisa, *L'Ordine Simbolico della Madre* (Rome: Editori Riuniti, 1991).

Murphy, Gregory, *The Big Book of Concepts* (Cambridge, MA: MIT Press 2004).

Narvaez, Darcia, Valentino, Kristin, Fuentes, Augustin, McKenna, James, Gray, Peter, eds, *Ancestral Landscapes in Human Evolution, Culture, Childrearing and Social Wellbeing* (Oxford: Oxford University Press, 2012).

Narvaez, Darcia, 'Mothers, Dialogues, and Support: Commentary on Garvey & Fogel and on Duarte & Gonçalves', in M. C. Bertau and M. M. Goncalves, T. F. Raggat, eds, *Dialogic Formations: Investigations Into the Origins and Development of the Dialogical Self* (Charlotte, NC: Information Age Publishing, 2012), pp. 197-202.

National Scientific Council on the Developing Child. (2004). *Young Children Develop in an Environment of Relationships.* Working Paper No. 1. Retrieved from http: //www.developingchild.net

Nelson, Anitra, *Marx's Concept of Money: The God of Commodities* (London: Routledge, 1999).

Nelson, Julie, 'Getting past 'Rational Man/Emotional Woman' Comments on Research Programs on happiness economics and Interpersonal Relations', in *International Review of Economics*, 57 (2010), pp. 233-53.

Newman, John, *Give, A Cognitive Linguistic Study* (New York: Mouton-De Gruyter, 1996).

Newman, John, ed., *The Linguistics of Giving*, Studies in Typological Linguistics, 36 (Amsterdam: John Benjamins, 1998).

Ninio, Anat, 'Model Learning in Syntactic Development: Intransitive Verbs,' *International Journal of Bilingualism*, Sept. 1999, pp. 111-31.

Noddings, Nel, Caring: *A Feminine Approach to Ethics and Moral Education* (Berkeley: University of California Press, 1984).

Odling-Smee, John, Laland, Kevin and Feldman, Marcus, *Niche Construction, The Neglected Process in Evolution* (Princeton: Princeton University Press, 2003).

Odling-Smee, John and Laland, Kevin, 'Cultural Niche Construction: Evolution's Cradle of Language', in R. Botha and C. Knight, eds, *The Prehistory of Language* (Oxford: Oxford University Press, 2009).

Orwell, George, 'Politics and the English Language', in *A Collection of Essays* (London: Harcourt, 1946).

Pashukanis Evgeny, *The General Theory of Law and Marxism*, ed. D. Milanovic, trans. Barbara Einhorn (New Brunswisk, NJ: Transaction Publishers, 2001).

Peirce, Charles Sanders, *Collected Writings*, 8 vols, Charles Hartshorne, Paul Weiss and Arthur W. Burks, eds. (Cambridge, MA: Harvard University Press 1932-58).

Petrilli, Susan, *Signifying and Understanding: Reading the Works of Victoria Welby and the Signific Movement (Semiotics, Communication and Cognition)*, (Berlin and New York: Mouton de Gruyter, 2009).

Pinker, Stephen, *The Language Instinct* (New York: Harper Collins, 1995).

Pollack, William, *Real Boys: Rescuing Our Sons from the Myths of Boyhood* (New York: Henry Holt, 1998).

Ponzio, Augusto, 'Linguistica Saussuriana e Economia Politica', in *Filosofia* XXV, 3 (1974), pp. 253-63.

Ponzio, Augusto and Petrilli, Susan, *Semiotics Unbounded* (Toronto: University of Toronto Press, 2005).

Quine, Willard Van Orman, *Word and Object* (Cambridge, MA: MIT Press, 1960, repr. 2015).

Reddy, Michael J., 'The Conduit Metaphor: A Case of Frame Conflict in our Language about Language,' in Andrew Ortony ed., *Metaphor and Thought* (Cambridge: Cambridge University Press, 1979, repr. 1993).

Rizzolati, Giacomo and Arbib, Michael, 'Language Within Our Grasp,' *Trends in Neurosciences*, 21, 5 (1998), pp. 188-94.

Roberts, Ben 'The Gold Standard and Literature: Money and Language in the Work of Jean-Joseph Goux', in *Culture, Capital and Representation*, Robert Balfour ed. (London: Palgrave Macmillan, 2010), pp. 132-47.

Rodriguez-Pereyra, Gonzalo, 'Paradigms and Russell's Resemblance Regress' in *Australasian Journal of Philosophy*, 2004, 82 (4) 2004, pp. 644-51.

Romberg, Alexa R. and Jenny Saffran, 'Statistical Learning and Language Acquisition', in *Wiley Interdisciplinary Review of Cognitive Science*, (2010) pp. 906-14.

Rosch, Eleanor, 'Principles of Categorization' in E. Rosch and B. Lloyd eds, *Cognition and Categorization* (Hillsdale, NJ: Lawrence Erlbaum, 1978), pp. 27–48.

Rosenbaum, Thane, *Payback: The Case for Revenge* (Chicago: University of Chicago Press, 2013).

Rossi-Landi, Ferruccio, 'Signs and Bodies', in *Between Signs and Non Signs*, S. Petrilli, ed. (Amsterdam: John Benjamins, 1992), pp. 271-76.

Ruddick, Sara, *Maternal Thinking, Towards a Politics of Peace* (Boston: Beacon Press, 1995).

Rymer, Russ, *Genie: A Scientific Tragedy* (New York: Harper Collins, 1993).

Sahlins, Marshall, 'Poor Man, Rich Man, Big Man, Chief; Political Types in Melanesia and Polynesia', in *Comparative Studies in Society and History*, 5 1963), pp. 285-303.

Sanday, Peggy Reeves, *Women at the Center: Life in a Modern Matriarchy* (Cornell: Cornell University Press, 2002).

Sahtouris, Elizabet, *Earthdance* (Westport, CT: Praeger, 2000).

Schmandt-Besserat, Denise, *Before Writing: Volume 1: From Counting to Cuneiform* (Austin: University of Texas Press, 1992).

Schmandt-Besserat, Denise, *Tokens: The Cognitive Significance*, M. Budja, ed. (Documenta Praehistorica: 1999), pp. 21-7.

Schlain, Leonard, *The Alphabet versus the Goddess, The Conflict Between Word and Image* (New York: Viking Press, 1988).

Schwermer, Heidemarie, *www.Livingwithoutmoney.org*, (accessed 2014).

Seaford, Richard, *Money and the Early Greek Mind: Homer, Philosophy, Tragedy* (Cambridge: Cambridge University Press, 2004).

Seyfarth, R. M. et al, 'Monkey Responses to Three Different Alarm Calls: Evidence of Predator Classification and Semantic Communication', in *Science*, 1980, pp. 801-3.

Searle, John, *The Construction of Social Reality* (New York: The Free Press, 1995).

Shaw, Rhonda, 'Theorizing Breastfeeding: Body Ethics, Maternal Generosity and the Gift Relation' *Body and Society*, 9–2 (2003), pp. 55-73.

Slobin, Dan, 'Cross-linguistic, Evidence for the Language Making Capacity' in D. Slobin, ed., *The Cross-Linguistic Study of Language Acquisition* (London: Psychology Press, 1985 repr. 2013).

Sohn-Rethel, Alfred, *Intellectual and Manual Labour* (London: MacMillan, 1978).

Sperber, Dan and Deidre Wilson, *Relevance: Communication and Cognition* (Oxford: Blackwell, 1995).

Sperber, Dan and Wilson, Deirdre, 'Relevance Theory' in L. Horn and G. Ward, eds, *Handbook of Pragmatics* (Oxford: Blackwell, 2004), pp. 607-32.

Spivak, Gayatri, 'Can the Subaltern Speak?', in C. Nelson and L. Grossberg, eds, *Marxism and the Interpretation of Culture* (Bassingstoke: Macmillan Education, 1988), pp. 271-313.

Stephens, Julie, *Confronting Post Maternal Thinking, Feminism, Memory and Care* (New York: Columbia University Press, 2012).

Stern, D. N., 'Vitality Contours: The Temporal Contour of Feelings as a Basic Unit for Constructing the Infant's Social Experience', in P. Rochat, ed., *Early Social Cognition: Understanding Others in the First Months of Life* (Mahwah, NJ: Erlbaum, 1999), pp. 67-80.

Stern, D. N., *The Interpersonal World of the Infant: A View from Psychoanalysis and Development Psychology* (New York: Basic Books, 2000).

Stern, D.N. and Nadia Bruschweiler-Stern, *The Birth of a Mother: How The Motherhood Experience Changes You Forever* (New York: Basic Books, 1998).

Still, Judith, Feminine, *Economies: Thinking Against the Market in the Enlightenment and the Late Twentieth Century* (Manchester: Manchester University Press, 1997).

Susi, Tarja and Ziemke, Tom, 'On the Subject of Objects: Four Views on Object Perception and Tool Use', in *Triple C: Cognition, Communication, Co-operation*, 3, 2, (2005), pp. 6-19.

Talmy, Leonard, *Towards a Cognitive Semantics*, 1 (Cambridge: MIT Press, 2000).

Talmy, Leonard, 'The Fundamental System of Spatial Schemas in Language' in Beate Hampe ed., *From Perception to Meaning: Image Schemas in Cognitive Linguistics* (Berlin: Mouton de Gruyter 2005).

Tazi-Preuve, Mariam, *Mothering in Patriarchy* (Berlin and Toronto: Barbara Budrich Publishers, 2013).

Thom, René, *Semio Physics* (Boston: Addison-Wesley, 1990).

Thompson, John, N., *Interaction and Coevolution*, (Chicago: University of Chicago Press, 1982).

Thomson, George, *The First Philosophers: Studies in Ancient Greek Society* (London: Lawrence & Wishart, 1955 repr. 1972).

Tomasello, Michael, 'One Child's Early Talk About Possession' in J. Newman ed., *The Linguistics of Giving* (Amsterdam & Philadelphia: John Benjamins, 1998), pp. 349-75.

Tomasello, Michael, 'Joint Attention as Social Cognition' in C. Moore and P. Dunham, eds, *Joint Attention its Origins and Role in Development* (New York: Psychology Press, 1995 repr. 2014).

Tomasello, Michael, *Origins of Human Communication* (Cambridge, MA: MIT Press, 2008).

Tomatis, Alfred, *The Ear and the Voice*, trans. Roberta Prada (Lanham, MD: Scarecrow Press, 2004).

Tooker, Elizabeth, 'Women in Iroquois Society' in *Iroquois Women: an Anthology*, ed. W. G. Spittal (Oshwegan, Ontario: Iroqrafts 1990).

Trevarthen, Colwyn, 'Musicality and the Intrinsic Motive Pulse: Evidence from Human Psychobiology and Infant Communication', in *Rhythms, Musical Narrative, and the Origins of Human Communication*, Musicae Scientiae, special issue (1999), pp. 157-213.

Trevarthen, Colwyn, 'Communication and Cooperation in Early Infancy' in M. Bullowa, ed., *Before Speech: The Beginning of Human Communication* (Cambridge: Cambridge University Press, 1979).

Trevarthen, Colwyn, 'Stepping Away from the Mirror: Pride and Shame in Adventures of Companionship,' in C. S. Carter, L. Ahnert, K. E. Grossman, S. B. Hardy, M. E. Lamb, S. W. Porges, and N. Sachser, eds, *Attachment and Bonding: A New Synthesis, Dahlem Workshop Report 92* (Cambridge, MA: The MIT Press 2005), pp. 55-84.

Trevarthen, Colwyn, 'What Is It Like To Be a Person Who Knows Nothing? Defining the Active Intersubjective Mind of a Newborn Human Being', in *Infant and Child Development. Special Issue: The Intersubjective Newborn*, 2010, pp. 119-35.

Tronto, Joan, *Moral Boundaries: A Political Argument for an Ethics of Care* (New York: Routledge, 1993).

Tronto, Joan, *Caring Democracy, Markets, Equality and Justice* (New York: New York University Press, 2013).

Turner, Mark, *The Literary Mind*, New York (Oxford University Press, 1996).

Vazquez-Rozas, Victoria, 'A Usage Based Approach to Prototypical Transitivity', in N. Delbeque and B. Cornillie, eds, *On Interpreting Construction Schemas: From action and Motion to Transitivity and Causality* (Berlin: Mouton de Gryuter, 2007), pp. 17-39.

Vaughan, Genevieve, 'Communication and Exchange', in *Semiotica*, 29–1/2 (1980).

Vaughan, Genevieve, 'Saussure and Vygotsky via Marx', in *Ars semiotica* (1981), pp. 57-83.

Vaughan, Genevieve, *For-Giving, A Feminist Criticism of Exchange* (Austin: PlainView and Anomaly Press. 1997).

Velmans, Max, 'When Perception Becomes Conscious', *British Journal of Psychology,* 90(4), (1999), pp. 543-66.

Velmans, Max, 'Conscious Agency and the Preconscious/Unconscious Self', in S. Menon, A. Sinha and B. V. Sreekanton, eds, *Consciousness and Self: Interdisciplinary Perspectives* (New York: Springer, 2014), pp.11-25.

Virno, Paolo, *A Grammar of the Multitude: For an Analysis of Contemporary Forms of Life* (New York: Semiotext[e], 2004).

Volosinov, V. N., *Marxism and the Philosophy of Language*. Translated and with an introduction by L. Matejka and I. R. Titunik (New York: Seminar Press. 1973. [1930]).

von Uexkull, Jakob, *Foray into the Worlds of Animals and Humans: With A Theory of Meaning*, trans. J. D. O'Neil (Minneapolis, University of Minnesota Press, 2010 [1934]).

von Werlhoff, Claudia, *The Failure of Modern Civilization and the Struggle for a 'Deep' Alternative: On Critical Theory of Patriarchy as a New Paradigm* (New York: Peter Lang Publishing, 2011).

von Werlhoff, Claudia, 'Foreword', in Mariam Tazi-Preuve, *Mothering in Patriarchy* (Opladen, Berlin and Toronto: Barbara Budrich Publishers, 2013).

Voorspoels, Wouter, Vanpaemel, Wolf and Storms, Gert 'A Formal Ideal-Based Account of Typicality', *Psychonomic Bulletin Review,* 18, (2011), pp.1006–14.

Vygotsky, Lev S., *Thought and Language*, trans. and ed. by E. Hanfmann and G. Vakar (Cambridge, MA: MIT Press, 1962).

Walker, Alice, "Democratic Motherism" in *The world will follow joy: turning madness into flowers (new poems)* (New York: The New Press, 2013) p.180-183.

Waring, Marilyn, *If Women Counted: A New Feminist Economics* (San Francisco: Harper & Row, 1988).

Warneken, Felix and Tomasello, Michael, 'Altruistic Helping in Humans and Young Chimpanzees', in *Science*, 311, 5765 (2006), pp. 1301-3.

Warneken, Felix and Tomasello, Michael, 'Helping and Cooperation at 14 Months of age', in *Infancy*, 11-3, (2007), pp. 271-94.

Watson-Franke, Maria-Barbara, 'A World in Which Women Move Freely without Fear of Men: An Anthropological Perspective on Rape', in *Women's Studies International Forum* (2002), pp. 599-606.

Webley, Paul, 'Playing the Market: The Autonomous Economic World of Children', in *Economic Socialization: The Economic Beliefs and Behaviors Of Young People*, P. Lunt and A. Furnham, eds (Brookfield, Vermont: Edward Elgar Publishing, 1996).

Webley, Paul, 'Children's Understanding Of Economics', in *Children's Understanding of Society*, Martyn Barrett and Eithne Buchanan-Iarrow, eds (New York: Psychology Press, 2005).

Weiner, Annette, *Inalienable Possessions: the Paradox of Keeping-while-Giving* (Berkeley: University of California Press, 1992).

Wetzel, Linda, *Types and Tokens: On Abstract Objects* (Cambridge, MA: MIT Press, 2009).

Winnicott, Donald, *The Maturational Processes and the Facilitating Environment: Studies in the Theory of Emotional Development* (London: Karnac, 1990).

Wittgenstein, Ludwig, *The Blue and Brown Books* (London: Basil Blackwell, 1958).

Wittgenstein, Ludwig, *Philosophical Investigations*, P. M. S. Hacker and J. Schulte, eds and trans. (Oxford: Wiley-Blackwell, 2009 [1953]).

Wolff, Richard, *Capitalism Hits the Fan: The Global Economic Meltdown and What To Do about It* (Northampton, MA: Interlink Publishing, 2013).

Wood, David, Jerome Bruner and Gail Ross, 'The Role of Tutoring in Problem Solving', in *Journal of Child Psychology and Psychiatry*, 17 (1976), pp. 89–100. New York, Psychology Press 2005), pp. 43-64.

Wrangham, Richard, *Catching Fire: How Cooking Made Us Human* (New York: Basic Books, 2009).

Wray, Allison Wray, 'Protolanguage as a Holistic System for Social Interaction', in *Language & Communication*, 1998, pp. 47-67.

Yan, Yungxian, *The Flow of Gifts: Reciprocity and Social Networks in a Chinese Village* (Palo Alto: Stanford University Press, 1996).

Yarbus, Alfred, *Eye Movements and Vision*, trans. by B. Haigh (New York: Plenum Press, 1967).

Zemon-Davis, Nathalie, *The Gift in Sixteenth-Century France* (Madison: University of Wisconsin Press).

NAME AND SUBJECT INDEX

480 The Gift in the Heart of Language

MIMESIS GROUP

www.mimesis-group.com

MIMESIS INTERNATIONAL

www.mimesisinternational.com

info@mimesisinternational.com

MIMESIS EDIZIONI

www.mimesisedizioni.it

mimesis@mimesisedizioni.it

ÉDITIONS MIMÉSIS

www.editionsmimesis.fr

info@editionsmimesis.fr

MIMESIS AFRICA

www.mimesisafrica.com

info@mimesisafrica.com

MIMESIS COMMUNICATION

www.mim-c.net

MIMESIS EU

www.mim-eu.com

Printed by Digital Team

Fano (PU) in March 2015